Financing the British Film Industry

For John Charmley

Financing the British Film Industry

Capital, Cash and Quota, 1896–1945

James Chapman

EDINBURGH
University Press

Edinburgh University Press is one of the leading university presses in the UK. We publish academic books and journals in our selected subject areas across the humanities and social sciences, combining cutting-edge scholarship with high editorial and production values to produce academic works of lasting importance. For more information visit our website: edinburghuniversitypress.com

© James Chapman, 2025

Edinburgh University Press Ltd
13 Infirmary Street
Edinburgh EH1 1LT

Typeset in Garamond MT Pro
by Manila Typesetting Company

A CIP record for this book is available from the British Library

ISBN 978 1 3995 4020 9 (hardback)
ISBN 978 1 3995 4022 3 (webready PDF)
ISBN 978 1 3995 4023 0 (epub)

The right of James Chapman to be identified as the author of this work has been asserted in accordance with the Copyright, Designs and Patents Act 1988, and the Copyright and Related Rights Regulations 2003 (SI No. 2498).

Contents

List of Tables	vi
List of Abbreviations	vii
Acknowledgements	viii
Introduction	1
1 Growing Pains	8
2 Challenges of War	24
3 The Road to Protection	36
4 Capitalisation and Consolidation	52
5 Quota Production in the Early 1930s	71
6 Korda and the City	86
7 Boom and Bust	104
8 The Bank of England and the Film Industry	124
9 Renewing the Quota	140
10 Recovery and Revival	157
11 The Film Bank	171
12 Remittances and Quotas	188
13 The Rank Empire	203
Conclusion	221
Appendix I: Statutory Costs of British Quota Films, 1 April 1932– 31 March 1933	225
Appendix II: Schedule of Bank Loans to Film Producers and Repayments	231
Appendix III: Statutory Costs of British 'Long' Quota Films, 1 April 1938– 30 November 1939	239
Bibliography	246
Index	252

Tables

1.1	New cinema exhibition companies registered in the United Kingdom and their total registered capital, 1908–14. Source: *The Cinema: Its Present Position and Future Possibilities*, p. 2.	14
5.1	Quota liabilities and total quota footage registered by major British and American renters in the quota year 1 April 1933–31 March 1934. Source: Simon Rowson, 'A Statistical Survey of the Cinema Industry in Great Britain in 1934'.	72
5.2	Cost range of British quota films registered in the quota year 1 April 1932–31 March 1933. Source: The National Archives BT 64/97: Particulars of British Films Acquired by Renters during the Quota Year 1932–3.	76
6.1	Production costs and distributors' receipts of feature films produced by London Film Productions, 1933–6. Source: Prudential Group Archive Box 2357: London Film Productions: Cost of production and receipts to 24 April 1937.	91
7.1	Estimated budgets and final production costs of feature films produced by the Capitol group, 1936–7. Source: Aviva Group Archive CU 540/1: Schedule of Films Produced by the Capitol Group, 28 June 1937.	112
7.2	Total liabilities of insurance companies holding guarantee policies for film loans, 1937. Source: Aviva Group Archive CU 550/5: Insurers Statement of Total Liabilities.	117
8.1	Loans and charges registered by producers, and their trustees, in the two years to 30 June 1936. Source: Bank of England Archive SMT 2/39: Statement of the Charges Registered during the two years ending 30 June 1936.	132
10.1	Cost range and quota status of British quota films registered between 1 April 1938 and 30 November 1939. Source: Bank of England Archive SMT 2/42: British Features from 01.04.1938 to 30.11.1939.	159

Abbreviations

ABPC	Associated British Picture Corporation
ATP	Associated Talking Pictures
BBFC	British Board of Film Censors
BEA	Bank of England Archive
BFPA	British Film Producers' Association
BIP	British International Pictures
CEA	Cinematograph Exhibitors' Association
FBI	Federation of British Industries
GBPC	Gaumont-British Picture Corporation
GCFC	General Cinema Finance Corporation
GFD	General Film Distributors
KRS	Kinematograph Renters' Society
LFP	London Film Productions
MGM	Metro-Goldwyn-Mayer
SMT	Securities Management Trust
TNA	The National Archives
UA	United Artists

Acknowledgements

This book is what in film industry terms would be described as a 'prequel' to *The Money Behind the Screen: A History of British Film Finance, 1945–1985*: it comes after publication of the former book but covers the preceding period. When I began researching the history of British film finance a decade ago, I envisaged it as just the one monograph. As the research progressed, however, it became apparent that there was sufficient archive material for another book covering the period before 1945. A third volume – *Capital, Commerce and Culture in the British Film Industry Since 1985* – will complete a trilogy on the fiscal politics of the film production industry in Britain. To this extent the project somewhat resembles the production of the *Star Wars* films insofar as the 'middle' part came first, followed by the 'beginning', and will be followed in due course by the last part bringing the narrative up to the present.

Like its predecessor, *Financing the British Film Industry* is based predominantly upon archival research. All historians are dependent upon the knowledge and expertise of professional archivists who rarely receive the recognition and credit they deserve. My sincere thanks therefore to: Thomas Barnes and the Aviva Group Archive (Norwich); James Darby and Barclays Group Archive (Manchester); Joseph Hettrick and the Bank of England Archive (London); Sarah Law and the Special Collections Unit of the British Film Institute (Berkhamstead); John Porter and the Prudential Group Archive (London); and the staff of the National Archives at Kew. You are all members of the behind-the-scenes production unit of this film.

Many colleagues in the British cinema history community have contributed to this book – often without knowing it – in sharing their knowledge, sources and references: my thanks to all, but especially to Dr Llewella Chapman, Professor Mark Glancy, Dr Lawrence Napper, Professor Jeffrey Richards, Professor Justin Smith and Professor Sarah Street.

Again I am grateful to Gillian Leslie, Kelly O'Brien and their colleagues at Edinburgh University Press for their highly positive response to the proposal and to EUP's readers for their exceedingly generous and supportive comments on the outline.

The total amount of funding I have received for this book is £300 from the School of Arts, Media and Communication at the University of Leicester, which supported one of my research visits to the National Archives.

An earlier version of Chapter 5 was published as 'British Quota Production and Film Costs in the Early 1930s', *Journal of British Cinema and Television*, 21: 2 (2024), pp. 153–92.

Llewella has once again gone beyond the call of duty in offering constructive criticism, sharing research materials, providing IT support (pivot tables, yay!) and mixing the daily gin and tonic at 6 p.m. It might be a cliché to say that I could not have completed this book without her love and support, but like many clichés it happens to be true.

It is a pleasure to dedicate this book to Professor John Charmley. At the University of East Anglia, John was an inspiring lecturer (no script, no notes, no PowerPoint) and is one of the pre-eminent historians of modern Britain. My undergraduate dissertation on Winston Churchill and the British film industry set me on course to becoming a film historian. I will always be grateful to John for encouraging me to undertake postgraduate work and for his collegiality, warmth and generosity of spirit.

Introduction

> The film is primarily an article of commerce. From the day, now over 40 years ago, when the public was first permitted to view the startling novelty of 'pictures in motion', commercial consideration alone has been responsible for the continuous progress, the steady expansion and the extraordinary development to which the industry bears ample witness to-day.
>
> Simon Rowson[1]

Simon Rowson (1877–1950) was the leading academic expert on the film business in Britain in the early twentieth century. A Fellow of the Royal Statistical Society, Rowson specialised in tax reform before getting interested in the film industry as managing director of Ideal Films in the early 1920s. He was elected President of the Kinematograph Renters' Society in 1926, served as a member of the Cinematograph Films Advisory Committee between 1927 and 1933, and was President of the British Kinematograph Society between 1933 and 193X. His paper 'A Statistical Survey of the Cinema Industry in Great Britain in 1934' was the first comprehensive account of the economic structure of the industry.[2] Rowson was a consultant for the Board of Trade in its review of the Cinematograph Films Act in the mid-1930s and for the Bank of England when it was tasked with exploring the possibility of establishing an official film bank in 1937. And as a temporary civil servant during the Second World War, he played a significant role in advising the Board of Trade both in respect of support for film producers during the war and planning for the post-war structure of the industry.

Rowson's insistence that 'film is primarily an article of commerce' and that 'commercial consideration alone' had driven its progress exemplifies what Robert C. Allen and Douglas Gomery, in their influential study of film historiography, *Film History: Theory and Practice*, describe as economic film history: the recognition that film is a business and that its history has been shaped more by commercial imperatives than by artistic aspirations or consideration of its social import.[3] As I noted in the introduction to *The Money Behind the Screen: A History of British Film Finance, 1945–1985*, most histories of British cinema have focused on films and film-makers rather than on the industry. Rachael Low's multi-volume *History of the British Film* – published between 1948 and 1985 and covering the period between 1896 and 1939 – is a notable exception, including details on the raising of finance gleaned from the trade press, while Margaret Dickinson and Sarah Street's *Cinema and State* remains the authoritative history of the film policy of the British government between the Cinematograph Films Act of 1927 and the winding down of state protection for the industry in the 1980s. Beyond those indispensable works, however, Jon Burrows' *The British Cinema Boom, 1909–1914*, which explores the rapid expansion of the exhibition side of the industry before the First World War, stands alone as the only study focusing solely on finance for the early period, while other works, including John Sedgwick's *Popular Filmgoing in 1930s Britain* and Steve Chibnall's *Quota Quickies: The Birth of the British 'B' Film*, include some valuable detail on the market for British films in the 1930s.

The major critical project of British film historiography for several decades now has been to claim British cinema as a site of artistic interest and cultural value in response to a traditional view – famously expressed by the likes of François Truffaut and Satyajit Ray – that British films were inferior to both the popular cinema of Hollywood and the European art cinema tradition.[4] This helps to explain why so much attention has been afforded to British film genres and directors. It is also, perhaps, a legacy of film culture in Britain, which has prioritised film (albeit not necessarily British film) as an expressive art form rather than as a commercial enterprise. Indeed, the relationship between the creative and business sides of the industry has often been presented as a site of tension. The terms of the debate are familiar: culture versus commerce, art versus the box office, the creative ambition of the film-maker versus the philistine world of finance. This tension is evident, for example, in Paul Rotha's *The Film Till Now*, published in 1930:

> When considering the commercialism which surrounds the producing and exhibiting of any one film, the unscrupulous dealings and double-crossing which occur when a production is launched, it is surprising to discover how far the cinema has really advanced as a medium of dramatic expression . . . Moreover, and it must be stressed, the primary aim of film producers is to make the maximum of financial return in the shortest possible time, a method hardly congenial to so intricate an art as the cinema.[5]

John Grierson, acknowledged as the intellectual driving force behind the British documentary film movement of the 1930s and one of the most articulate advocates of the social utility and educational value of cinema, saw the creative film-maker as existing 'in a closed circle from which he can only by a rare failure of the system escape. The financier-producer will prevent him going deep lest he becomes either difficult or dangerous . . . Commercial cinema, being the monstrous undisciplined force it is, has done a great deal of harm.'[6]

While not all commentators were quite as outright hostile towards financiers as Rotha and Grierson, there was nevertheless a sense that commercial demands were an impediment to the development of the medium even though capital was a necessary precondition for film production. Anthony Asquith, one of Britain's most critically acclaimed directors, but also no stranger to popular success with films including *Pygmalion, Fanny by Gaslight* and *The Way to the Stars*, attempted to reconcile the competing demands of art and commerce in an article for the first issue of the *Penguin Film Review* in 1946:

> Companies aim at profits for their shareholders, so they cannot be blamed for playing safe – underrating the taste and intelligence of their public. Economically this may be excusable: aesthetically it must be deplorable; and yet is this not the reason why the film is the only example of popular art – art where the unbridgeable chasm between art with a capital A and mere popular entertainment has not been irrevocably dug – where some artists create for the intelligent few while a mass of artisans cater for the unintelligent, undiscriminating many?[7]

Ernest Lindgren, the first curator of the National Film Library, saw the creative film-maker as subordinate to finance-capital in his book *The Art of the Film* in 1948:

> [A] nascent Bernard Shaw of the screen, however convinced he may be of his own ability, will have no chance of making a film unless he can command large capital resources. If he has none of his own, he must either work in some subordinate capacity for those who have, and help to put *their* ideas on the screen, or else he must borrow, and this he will only be able to do if he can provide convincing assurance, not only that the money will not be lost, but that it will yield handsome dividends proportionate to the heavy risks the lenders will be incurring; that is to say, he must convince his backers that the film will be well distributed and that it will have the widest possible appeal.[8]

And Roger Manvell, whose Penguin paperback entitled simply *Film* did much to promote film appreciation in Britain in the 1940s, summed it up this way: 'The film industry shows the clash between economic and artistic issues in one of the most openly-contested struggles of the commercial world ... Films are like meals: occasionally you get a good one; but you must go on eating regularly just the same.'[9]

These examples – and many more could be cited – all present finance as a necessary evil. The fact that investors are interested more in the commercial than the artistic value of films no doubt led to their being cast as philistine capitalists. E. W. and M. M. Robson seem to have been the only contemporary critics to have dissented from the consensus:

> Film producers or cinema proprietors, either as individuals or grouped in trusts, are neither good nor bad, neither benevolent nor greedy, neither cruel nor kind. It is childish to elevate them as gods or denounce them as demons ... You cannot blame or praise people for being born into a competitive world at a moment in time when the development of the cinema like an 'ill wind' became a veritable tornado which left some floating in comfortable boats, others on shaky rafts half in and half out of the water, others clinging to spars, and others, countless others, to disappear below the waves without a trace.[10]

The Robsons – whose published film criticism suggests that they leaned towards the political right – were staunch advocates of the cinema's potential as a medium of national projection and dissemination of ideas; to this extent they shared common ground with John Grierson, who sat on the other side of the political spectrum. What made the Robsons unusual in this instance, however, and where they differed from Grierson, Rotha and others, was their refusal to accept that producers and exhibitors were philistines just because they were led by market conditions. Only in a classical Marxist world-view is capitalism imbued with moral value: the film industry is more capital-intensive than other creative industries such as book publishing, theatre and music, and therefore more open to a political economy critique.

For those working in the industry, the relationship between art and commerce was understood differently. Michael Balcon, regarded as one of the more socially progressive British producers and a leading proponent of British cinema as a national cinema, accepted that box-office success was necessary to sustain the film industry:

> [As] a source of employment, the film industry is a national asset, and the greater its success, the greater its national value. It can only achieve that success by turning out films that will not only repay the money spent on their production, but will also show sufficiently large profits to enable the producer to embark on more ambitious and therefore larger staffed undertakings.[11]

Many producers and directors had reason to be thankful to J. Arthur Rank, who emerged as the leading finance-magnate in the British film industry in the early 1940s and by the end of the Second World War was supporting films such as *Henry V*, *Caesar and Cleopatra* and *A Matter of Life and Death* that were the very antithesis of economic or cultural conservatism. Even Michael Powell, whose memoir attests to his belief in the art of film with a capital A, explained that he and his long-term collaborator Emeric Pressburger were willing to put up with the managerialism of the Rank Organisation because Rank offered financial stability: 'We accepted all this in return for being fully financed. Continuity of production is the hope and aim of every producer worth his salt. We always had one film in production, one film being edited and one film in preparation.'[12]

Financing the British Film Industry explores the provision of finance for filmmaking in Britain from the origin of the industry to the end of the Second World War. It maps the transition of the cinema industry from a novelty attraction to a mature business enterprise; it documents the growth of capital investment in the production sector and the vicissitudes of an industry that was prone to periods of boom and bust; and it explores the various initiatives – some realised, some not carried through – to provide financial support for the domestic production sector. Like *The Money Behind the Screen*, to which this book is a prequel, *Financing the British Film Industry* explores three interrelated themes: the economic and institutional structure of the industry, focusing particularly on the ups and downs of film production, and documenting how both the major combines and independent producers raised their capital; the sources of film finance, including both domestic and foreign (predominantly American) interests that invested in the British production sector; and the role of government in supporting British film production through the introduction of a mandatory 'quota' for British films in the Cinematograph Films Acts of 1927 and 1938.

Like its predecessor, *Financing the British Film Industry* is based mostly on archive and primary source research. The archival sources for this period turned out to be much more extensive than I had originally thought. The Board of Trade records at the National Archives provide evidence relating to film costs and film finance as well as the inter-governmental and trade correspondence over the Cinematograph Films Acts and support for the industry during the Second World War; the Bank of England Archive includes records of the Securities Management Trust, relating to the initiatives to set up an official film bank in 1937, and again in 1940, and the Exchange Control Commission, which was involved in the implementation and monitoring of US dollar remittances during the Second World War; the Prudential Group Archive includes details of the financing of Alexander Korda's London Film Productions, and the Aviva Group Archive holds documents relating to the film insurance scandals of the 1930s; and the Special Collections Unit of the British Film Institute holds the personal papers of Michael Balcon, head of production for the Gaumont-British Picture Corporation and later Ealing Studios, and other collections including various financial records. British archives are supplemented by some American sources: the online Media History Digital Library includes the corporate records of United Artists, which invested in British production in the 1930s.

Archives do not necessarily reveal the whole story: paper trails are often incomplete and rarely answer all the researcher's questions. However, they do provide a valuable source of hard evidence. For example, the Aviva Archive, which includes the records of the Commercial Union and its subsidiary the British General Insurance Company, holds ledgers detailing bank loans, insurance policies and ultimate losses that shed significant new light on the failure of Max Schach's Capitol Group and other independent producers in the 1930s. The Michael and Aileen Balcon Collection at the British Film Institute yielded production costs and receipts for the films of Gainsborough Pictures that I have not seen published elsewhere. Archive materials also provide a corrective to some received wisdoms. For instance, Alfred Hitchcock's last film for British International Pictures, *Number Seventeen* (1932), has often been described as a low-cost film and even as one of the 'quota quickies' that were the curse of British cinema in the 1930s. However, a Board of Trade ledger itemising the statutory costs of all British quota films in 1932–3 reveals that *Number Seventeen* cost significantly above the average: in fact it was British International's second highest-cost film of the year and in the top twenty most expensive films overall.[13]

I have supplemented unpublished archival materials with published primary sources, including trade year books and directories, and the trade and business press. *The Economist* and *The Financial Times* reported on capital issues and liquidations of film companies from an early date, and as the industry grew they regularly reported on the state of film finance. The film trade press, represented by *Kinematograph Weekly*, *The Bioscope* and *The Cinema*, includes news and commentary relating to industry, legislative and financial matters.[14] The trade press during this period often demonstrated a patriotic hyperbole towards British films: however, it also provides an invaluable source for trade debates around matters affecting the industry including the quota and the provision of finance. There is also a wealth of memoirs and autobiographies by major film producers and directors: these include Michael Balcon's *A Lifetime of Films*, Sydney Box's *The Lion That Lost Its Way*, Adrian Brunel's *Nice Work*, Cecil Hepworth's *Came the Dawn*, Walter Mycroft's *The Time of My Life*, Michael Powell's *A Life in Movies* and Herbert Wilcox's *Twenty-Five Thousand Sunsets*. Memoirs need to be treated with caution of course: they are often rich in anecdote but are not necessarily reliable on points of detail. There is also sometimes a revisionist tendency at play. For example, Walter Mycroft, the head of production at British International Pictures, a company known for its budgetary parsimony and aversion to financial risk, retrospectively sought to associate himself with the progressive impulse that had emerged in British cinema during the Second World War: 'Personally I believe that films are a communal service . . . [Profits] should not be the only consideration in film-making. The men who grow rich by catering to the film masses also have a duty to them, and whether they like it or not, one result of the war will be that they are going to be forced to recognise that duty.'[15]

Financing the British Film Industry therefore aims to offer a new 'take' on the history of British cinema in the early twentieth century that places the economic and fiscal contexts of film-making at its centre. The early chapters chart the capitalisation of the industry during its early years, while later chapters consider the costs of film production, the introduction and renewal of the quota, the strategies of different producers including high-end 'quality' producers and low-cost quota specialists, and the initiatives (ultimately abortive) to establish an official film bank in order to provide greater stability for the domestic production sector. The picture that emerges is that the history of British film finance during this period is more complex than has hitherto been assumed – for example the industry's problems cannot all be attributed to the lack of available capital, although this was undoubtedly a significant factor – and that the formative years of British cinema cannot be properly understood without some appreciation of its commercial contexts.

Notes

1. Board of Trade, *Minutes of Evidence Taken Before the Departmental Committee on Cinematograph Films together with Appendices and Index* (London: His Majesty's Stationery Office, 1936), p. 109 (2).
2. Simon Rowson, 'A Statistical Survey of the Cinema Industry in Great Britain in 1934', *Journal of the Royal Statistical Society*, 99: 1 (1936), pp. 67–119.

3. Robert C. Allen and Douglas Gomery, *Film History: Theory and Practice* (New York: McGraw-Hill, 1985), pp. 135–52.
4. See, for example, Charles Barr, 'Introduction: Amnesia and Schizophrenia', in Charles Barr (ed.), *All Our Yesterdays: 90 Years of British Cinema* (London: British Film Institute, 1986), pp. 1–30, and Alan Burton and Julian Petley, 'Introduction', *Journal of Popular British Cinema*, 1 (1998), pp. 2–5.
5. Paul Rotha, with Richard Griffith, *The Film Till Now: A Survey of World Cinema* (London: Spring Books, 1967 [1930]), p. 87.
6. John Grierson, 'Summary and Survey: 1935', in Forsyth Hardy (ed.), *Grierson on the Movies* (London: Collins, 1946), pp. 104, 106.
7. Anthony Asquith, 'The Tenth Muse Climbs Parnassus', *The Penguin Film Review*, 1 (August 1946), p. 18.
8. Ernest Lindgren, *The Art of the Film: An Introduction to Film Appreciation* (London: George Allen & Unwin, 1948), p. 16.
9. Roger Manvell, *Film* (Harmondsworth: Penguin, 1946 [1944]), pp. 15–18.
10. E. W. and M. M. Robson, *The Film Answers Back: An Historical Appreciation of the Cinema* (London: John Lane/The Bodley Head, 1939), p. 33.
11. Michael Balcon, 'The Function of the Producer: 1. The Studio Producer', *Cinema Quarterly*, 2: 1 (autumn 1933), p. 6.
12. Michael Powell, *A Life in Movies: An Autobiography* (London: William Heinemann, 1986), pp. 660–1.
13. James Chapman, 'Hitchcock's *Number Seventeen* (1932) and the British Film Quota', *Historical Journal of Film, Radio and Television*, 43: 4 (2003), pp. 1183–91.
14. *Kinematograph Weekly* was a continuation of *Optical Magic Lantern and Photographic Enlarger* which had begun publication in the 1880s: it became the *Kinematograph and Lantern Weekly* in 1907 and *Kinematograph Weekly* from 1919. *The Bioscope* was published between 1908 and 1932. *The Cinema* (full title *The Cinema News and Property Gazette*) followed in 1913.
15. Walter Mycroft, *The Time of My Life: The Memoirs of a British Film Producer*, ed. Vincent Porter (Lanham, MD: Scarecrow Press, 2006), p. 111.

CHAPTER 1

Growing Pains

While Britain did not invent motion pictures, a process that film historians now understand as an international process of parallel discoveries, it did nevertheless play an important role in the origin and early history of the medium. The claim that William Friese-Greene developed a functional moving-picture camera before Thomas Edison in the United States – a myth perpetuated in the Festival of Britain film *The Magic Box* (1951) – has long been debunked, but British pioneers Robert Paul and Birt Acres had certainly done so by 1895, and they presented the first public exhibitions of cinematograph films in Britain early in 1896.[1] Early British cinematographers made important contributions to the development of film form and technique in the decade between 1896 and 1906: other pioneers included William Haggar, Cecil Hepworth, G. A Smith and James Williamson. By the early 1910s, however, Britain had been overtaken by other film-producing nations, especially France and the United States. British films were being squeezed out of their home market by imports, and British film-makers were slow to respond to new developments in form and style, especially the rise of the longer 'feature' film. A narrative had taken shape by the First World War that the underlying problem for the British cinematograph industry was that it was under-capitalised from the start. As the trade paper *The Bioscope* remarked in 1915:

> The industry was a financial weakling at its birth. It was not ushered in as a great invention, world-wide in its scope, but as an item of amusement to play its part and disappear as similar items had before it. No man of finance stood as its sponsor, and the English financial world looked on the cinematograph as a new toy, likely to hold the public favour for a time, and then be forgotten.[2]

The standard histories of early cinema in Britain present it as a narrative of enterprising but short-sighted pioneers and missed opportunities. The familiar narrative is that the cinematograph remained a cottage industry: the early pioneers saw it as a short-lived novelty attraction and their failure to adjust their business practices when it proved its durability meant that they lost out to foreign competitors. The historiographical orthodoxy is best exemplified by the early volumes of Rachael Low's *The History of the British Film* (the first was co-authored with Roger Manvell), which characterises the first decade of British cinema as a 'burst of undiscriminating enterprise' driven by a small group of pioneers:

> The dozen or so companies which produced films in this period show a typical pattern of development which is in most cases the story of one man of exceptional versatility and initiative ... Almost every firm was dominated by one man, who devised his own equipment and methods; wrote, produced, and as often as not acted (with members of his family) in his own films; and marketed and sometimes exhibited them himself. In most cases he also sold cinematograph equipment, as well as carrying on an extensive export business.[3]

Low contends that the development of film form and technique was a process of accidental discovery rather than foresight: the pioneers 'stumbled inevitably on the devices proper to the telling of a story or an idea by means of a celluloid film, almost all misunderstood and misused their discoveries, and exploited as tricks and theatrical effects what should in fact have been integral elements of a new medium'.[4] And the British cinematograph industry is berated for its parochialism: Low avers that 'in the first ten years of the British film industry talent tended to flow into the small production companies rather than into the purely commercial branches and by 1906 so little further progress had been made in market practice that Britain appeared backward in comparison with some other countries'.[5] Most of the first generation of pioneer British film-makers had left the industry before 1914. Low attributes their demise to their failure to adapt: 'Film producers in America, Italy and France, chasing the future with all the zest the British had previously shown, put this country to shame, and by 1911 British production was oppressed by a feeling of inferiority which subsequent efforts had not succeeded in removing when they were interrupted by the war.'[6]

Other accounts of the early years of the cinema in Britain have largely echoed Low's foundational work. Charles Oakley averred that early British film-makers 'failed to make the transition from amateurism to professionalism' and saw the collapse of the US Motion Picture Patents Company – an attempt by Thomas Edison to establish a monopoly in the supply of film-making equipment – as the point when the US industry moved ahead of Britain: 'The American industry celebrated its new freedom by leaping forward with furious activity. The British industry, bereft of leadership and inspiration, virtually collapsed (for the first but by no means the last time).'[7] Ernest Betts similarly laid the blame for the eclipse of the British cinema industry on 'British producers [who] were painfully slow to learn what films were about and showed a deplorable provincialism of outlook compared with Europe and Hollywood'.[8] And John Barnes – whose detailed accounts of each year between 1896 and 1901 provide a 'deep dive' into the history of the Victorian cinematograph – felt that British film-makers were too slow to respond to the rise of the fiction film in preference to actuality non-fiction subjects: 'There can be little doubt that the success of the Jubilee films [in 1897] was one reason why film makers in England continued to favour the production of actuality films when producers in France were already concentrating on the production of "made-up" films and thereby gaining a dominant position in the world film markets which was to last for well over a decade.'[9]

Other scholars have emphasised the economic conditions in which cinema developed rather than the narratives of patents and pioneers. Roy Armes, for example, points out that cinema 'was a product of late nineteenth century capitalism' and that it 'evolved in a free competitive market situation, without preconceptions or state interference'.[10] This context was different from the origin of later mass media radio and television that emerged during an era of state regulation and bureaucratic control. Michael Chanan similarly contends that 'the absence of a commercial tradition or of any trade bodies to regulate it, necessarily contributed to chaos' and that 'the industry was plunged into a variety of price wars and trade combinations characteristic of capitalist competition in a pre-monopoly stage'.[11] The popularity of narrative films such as Cecil Hepworth's *Rescued by Rover* (1905) and William Haggar's *The Life of Charles Peace* (1905) marked the point at which 'the novelty of film as a phenomenon gave way to the novelty of individual films'.[12] Chanan suggests that the instability of the industry 'delayed the entry of finance capital into the cinema in Britain, in complete contrast to the policies adopted by finance capital in the United States – another reason for the exposure of British cinema to North American penetration'.[13]

However, the narrative that early cinematographers were pioneers first and foremost and businessmen last and least has been challenged by the emergence of a revisionist historiography that presents the period before the First World War as one characterised by a spirit of entrepreneurship tempered by no small degree of commercial acumen. Several historical studies published since 1999 – including Ian Christie's *Robert Paul and the Origins of British Cinema*, Frank Gray's *The Brighton School and the Birth of British Film*, Richard Brown and Barry Anthony's *A Victorian Film Enterprise: The History of the British Mutoscope and Biograph Company*, Simon Brown's *Cecil Hepworth and the Rise of the British Film Industry* and Luke McKernan's *Charles Urban: Pioneering the Non-Fiction Film in Britain and America* – have questioned the 'pioneer myth' and have suggested a more complex and nuanced history of early film-making. All of these studies reconsider the efforts of early cinematographers in relation to other contexts, including scientific and commercial as well as aesthetic and formal contexts. This revisionist scholarship has shed new light on the commercial as well as creative contexts of early cinema and has prompted a reconsideration of the standard version narrative. As Brown and Anthony observe, understanding film-making as a commercial activity provides 'an invaluable indication of the contemporary perception held by those working in the business, and they indicate why considerable attention ought to be given by film historians to commercial aspects, with the films produced and the technical advances made being assigned an important, but not necessarily leading, part in events'.[14]

In fact the first decade of cinema was neither the parochial cottage industry suggested by Low nor the chaotic free-for-all described by Chanan. The Board of Trade records at the National Archives hold the certificates of incorporation and registers of shareholders of joint stock companies registered at Companies House: these suggest a greater deal of foresight and planning than has often been allowed. While some film-makers preferred to rely on their own or borrowed capital – for example Cecil Hepworth's memoirs attest that he set up in the film manufacturing business with £200 raised from his cousin – the most common route into the industry was through the formation of a joint stock company with a nominal capital of around £10,000 (not all the capital would necessarily be issued).[15] This was the easiest means of raising capital as, like most new industries, the cinematograph was regarded with suspicion by traditional sources of finance: banks were generally disinclined to lend to film companies due to the large number of bankruptcies in the fledgling industry, and the bank interest rate (4.25 per cent in 1899) was prohibitively high for most small companies. The memorandum of association for the Cinematograph Company – incorporated in May 1898 with a nominal capital of £5,000 – exemplifies the broad terms of reference of early film companies: 'To establish and carry on the business of manufacturers and dealers in photographic apparatus and materials, projecting lanterns, apparatus for taking and projecting animated photographs or cinematographs, including photographic films and transparencies, and for accepting engagements to procure and exhibit animated photographs, and for obtaining animated phoographs of any subject to order.'[16]

There were many failed share issues in the early years. Brown and Anthony analyse a sample of twelve joint stock companies formed in 1896 and 1897: all bar one had been dissolved by 1901.[17] Many of the early company formations involved inventors seeking to exploit patents on new cinematograph processes. In 1897, for example, Robert Paul sought to raise £60,000 for Paul's Animatographe: the prospectus declared that 'the undertaking bears conclusive evidence of security; whilst with ample capital to be provided by this issue, the possibilities are enormous, without involving more than ordinary commercial risk'.[18] However, the share issue was under-subscribed and the offer had to be withdrawn. An editorial in *The Financial Times* in May 1899 suggests that the novelty value of new variants of the cinematograph was already wearing off:

> The ingenious idea of exhibiting a series of photographs in such rapid succession as to produce a faithful, if jerky, representation of, say, a street scene, a skirt dance or a stretch of scenery can no longer claim the charm of novelty. We have had the biograph and the cinematograph, and similar adaptations of the same principle under other names in the leading variety halls. We have had the mutoscope for several months installed in odd shops over the metropolis and elsewhere . . . This is obviously a serious consideration for the people who are trying to convince the public that money sunk in the Artoscope Syndicate, Limited, will be in hundred per cent dividends, or even more satisfactory results.[19]

'In a way', the article went on, 'the concern is modest: its capital is only £10,000; and as the purchase price is a mere £2,000, four-fifths of the sum will remain as a working fund.' But it detected more than a whiff of hubris in the promotion: 'The prospectus contains extravagant forecasts, the degree of excess being denoted by black letters, small capitals and large capitals, and it is underlined like a woman's diary.'

An embryonic film production industry emerged in Britain between 1897 and 1903: the major players were the British Mutoscope and Biograph Company (incorporated in 1897), Mitchell and Kenyon (1898), the Gaumont Company (1898), the Warwick Trading Company (1898), the Hepworth Manufacturing Company (1900), the Sheffield Photo Company (1900), the Charles Urban Film Company (1903) and the Pathé Cinematograph Company (1903).[20] The best capitalised of these early production companies by some distance was the British Mutoscope and Biograph Company. Brown and Anthony's *A Victorian Film Enterprise* demonstrates that the early British cinematograph industry was far from being the parochial undertaking that has so often been portrayed. This company – an offshoot of the American Mutoscope and Biograph Company of New York – was registered in London in 1897. It had nominal capital of £250,000 with fourteen regional Mutoscope companies (the Mutoscope was a peep-show machine similar to Thomas Edison's Kinetoscope) worth another £382,000.[21] The British Mutoscope and Biograph Company produced 650 films between 1897 and 1907: they included topical news items (W. K. L. Dickson shot a series of scenes of the South African War) and short fiction films (including Herbert Beerbohm Tree's staging of *King John* at Her Majesty's Theatre in 1899, believed to be the first Shakespearean performance on film). British Mutoscope and Biograph recorded profits of £28,451 in 1899 and £34,300 in 1900: the chairman's report in 1901 noted 'the large profits which they had made from the sale of positive films of war pictures to other companies'.[22]

Sources regarding the economics and finance of the early cinematograph industry are fragmentary and, as what survives tend to be from successful companies rather than those that failed, may not be representative. Nevertheless, there is evidence to suggest that there were substantial profits to be made in the early years of the industry for those who were first out of the blocks. John Barnes unearthed G. A. Smith's cashbook for 1897: this shows annual turnover of £334 9s. 2d. arising mostly from sales of films but also including equipment sales and printing services. Smith's most famous films from this year are short comedy sketches such as *The Miller and the Sweep* and *Hanging Out the Clothes*, but his cashbook reveals that his most remunerative subjects were films of local football matches.[23] Luke McKernan's study of the American-born Charles Urban – whose career again demonstrates that early British cinema was not at all the parochial affair that some accounts suggest – includes monthly sales in films and equipment for the Warwick Trading Company between 1898 and 1901: its total annual sales increased from £15,448 in 1898 to £45,528 in 1901 and the height of its success came in February 1901 when its film of Queen Victoria's funeral brought monthly sales of £5,593.[24]

Even from the fragmentary sources, it seems that the costs of film-making in the early years were relatively modest. The main costs involved were cameras and raw film stock. In January 1897 G. A. Smith bought a cine camera from Alfred Darling for £16 and throughout the year spent a total of £46 3s. 7d. on film rolls supplied by the Blair Camera Company: otherwise, his main expenses were developing chemicals and travel.[25] Stephen Bottomore's analysis of advertisements published in *The Era* in the early 1900s suggests that a firm specialising in local subject matter such as the Lancashire-based Mitchell and Kenyon could produce and print a 100-foot film for as little as £4.[26] In the early 1900s the Warwick Trading Company was selling films at £2 10s. per 50 feet for what it called its 'Class A' subjects and £1 10s. per 50 feet for 'Class B'.[27] In 1902 it was reported that Warwick's film of the coronation of King Edward VII involved a 'very great outlay' of £1,200 on a replica set and props for the interiors of the film (the cameras could not film inside Westminster Abbey: the procession to and from the abbey was actuality footage).[28] The 350-foot 'Special Coronation Film' sold for £17 cash.[29] However, this was exceptional. *Rescued by Rover* – regarded as one of the most successful films from this period and one of the few for which cost and sales records exist – cost only £7 13s. 9d.: it is reported to have sold 400 copies, which at the catalogue price of £10 12s. 6d. would have returned some £4,250.[30]

Charles Barr has argued that *Rescued by Rover* represents a turning point for the early cinematograph industry: '*Rescued by Rover* may point the way to the future but it also belongs firmly to the primitive years . . . The "cottage industry" which produced *Rescued by Rover* could not survive the new developments in the international film market.'[31] *Rescued by Rover* was very much a family affair: the actors include Hepworth himself, his wife and daughter. 'Rover' was the family's pet dog. However, the years following 1905 would see major changes in film production and distribution practices. The main shift was from direct sales to offering films for rental: this reduced the costs of printing hundreds of copies of each film. It was also the start of the separation of the business into different sectors rather than individuals acting as film-makers, salesmen and exhibitors. In fact, Hepworth had started renting his films through the Gaumont Company from 1900 and for some years operated a dual system of both direct sales and rental. Simon Brown's study of Hepworth challenges the view that his career peaked with *Rescued by Rover* and that thereafter he struggled to adapt to a changing industry. Brown shows how Hepworth used the profits of *Rescued by Rover* to invest in a purpose-built studio facility in order to streamline production. He contends 'that Hepworth did attempt to adjust to the changing market in order to boost sales through the manner in which he produced and packaged his films, an approach that would ultimately prove unsuccessful owing to the unpredictability of the distribution and exhibition sectors'.[32] The conditions that brought about Hepworth's downfall were largely not of his own making: he had been successful in selling his films to the United States, but this market was severely curtailed following the formation of the US Motion Picture Patents Company in 1908. Brown concludes that 'it was both the fact of the small size of the British film industry, and the manner in which its structure developed – specifically the birth of the new distribution sector and the resulting loss of control over film sales – that caused economic uncertainty and crisis for Hepworth and other British producers'.[33]

From a commercial perspective, the years between 1906 and 1914 were very far from being a period of stagnation and decline. In fact, this period saw a significant increase in capital investment in the cinematograph industry. There were several reasons for this. One was that, after a decade, it seemed clear that the cinematograph was here to stay. As *The Financial Times* recognised in 1908: 'In the world of entertainment the cinematograph has already conquered for itself a prominent position . . . It would appear also that it has reached little more than the starting point of its career.'[34] As the cinematograph became a permanent feature of the leisure and entertainment economy, so the nature of film exhibition changed. Hitherto the exhibition of films had been a peripatetic business: it was largely the preserve of travelling showmen who would present films in music halls and fairgrounds where they were one of numerous 'attractions'. From 1906–7, however, the emergence of permanent fixed-site cinemas transformed the nature of film exhibition. The Daily Bioscope in Bishopsgate, City of London, which opened in May 1906, is reckoned to have been the first fixed-site cinema in Britain. According to a contemporary report: 'It is simply a scheme of cheap cinematograph shows – "news in pictures" . . . The management told our representative that it was the intention of the syndicate presently to run their "Daily Bioscope" on similar lines all over London – on the principle of the ABC shops with an almost continuous service of performances from noon until nine o'clock in the evening.'[35]

It was the growth of the exhibition sector that occasioned the first major investment boom in the cinematograph industry. The number of fixed-site cinemas in Britain increased exponentially from a few dozen in 1908 to around 3,500 by 1914.[36] The report of the Cinema Commission of Enquiry on behalf of the National Council of Public Morals, published in 1917 as *The Cinema: Its Present Position and Future Possibilities* – concerned primarily with the social effects of cinema on juveniles but also a valuable source of statistical data on the industry – calculated that £11.3 million had been invested in 'picture palaces' between 1908 and 1914 (this figure refers to public companies: it estimated that a further £2 million of private capital was invested). Table 1.1 highlights the growth of the exhibition sector in terms of both the number of new companies registered per year but also the total registered capital (not necessarily all issued) of those companies.

According to statistics published by the Inland Revenue, some 1,833 public companies with an interest in cinema exhibition had been registered by the end of 1914: these companies held combined capital of £11,304,500 and included both

Table 1.1 New cinema exhibition companies registered in the United Kingdom and their total registered capital, 1908–14

YEAR	NEW COMPANIES	TOTAL CAPITAL
1908	12	£167,000
1909	78	£708,000
1910	231	£2,183,700
1911	254	£1,214,400
1912	400	£1,627,400
1913	544	£2,954,700
1914	314	£2,449,300

Source: *The Cinema: Its Present Position and Future Possibilities*, p. 2.

single-venue enterprises and companies that owned numerous sites. However, the 271 liquidations – representing a total capital value of £2,347,700 – during the same period indicate the volatility of the business.[37]

Jon Burrows contends that '[the] way in which investment capital was mobilised to fuel such rapid and comparatively extravagant expansion of the film exhibition sector was quite unprecedented in the field of spectatorial entertainment'.[38] Burrows suggests that the only comparable investment booms in recent times had been railway construction (1844–5) and the mining industry (1895–6): these have been characterised as 'manias' or 'fevers' and they shared with the cinema investment boom an influx of apparently easy capital into a rapidly expanding industry fuelled by highly speculative prospectuses and often unscrupulous promoters promising spectacular returns on investment. There were several contexts for the investment boom. One was the Companies Act of 1907, which liberalised the regulation of the business sector: specifically it created a distinction between public joint stock companies, which were able to raise capital by inviting investment from the general public in return for the publication of annual balance sheets, and a new category of private joint stock companies, which could solicit up to fifty private investors without a public share issue and without being required to publish their accounts. This was of benefit to small cinema entrepreneurs who 'could now secure the protection of limited liability status without having to make sensitive data about their assets, trading expenses and annual turnover accessible to competitors'.[39] Another factor was the Cinematograph Act of 1909 – the first legislative intervention in the new industry – which empowered municipal authorities to licence cinemas: this was in response to concerns over safety following several cinema fires caused by highly flammable nitrate film. This had the effect of aligning cinema exhibition with the property development business: Burrows calculates that 38 per cent of the cinema companies registered between 1908 and 1914 had at least one director involved in the property business.[40]

The cinema trade press was concerned about what it saw as excessive speculation. In November 1909 *The Bioscope* reported: 'In "the City" . . . they are simply falling over each other in trying to get in at the start. Scarcely a week goes by without the promotion of half-a-dozen new companies, the objects of which are either to deal with apparatus, films or new theatres, being recorded in our columns.' But it sounded a cautionary note:

> There is plenty of money still to be made in pictures, and there is plenty of room for many more shows than at present exist. But there is another danger which should be guarded against, and it is one which is ever present – over-capitalisation. That is the rock upon which many a public company has come to grief. A small company with a reasonable capital, meaning one or two small shows which pay, is far preferable to a gigantic concern with a capital extending into hundreds of thousands of pounds, and running a number of shows, out of which only a few show any return on the capital outlay.[41]

Kinematograph & Lantern Weekly shared this concern and also pointed a finger at the role of promoters who had no knowledge or experience of the industry:

> No one who has the welfare of the trade at heart can be altogether pleased at the prominence which the company promoter has obtained of late. Until a year or two ago he was unknown in connection with the industry in this country, manufacturers, renters and exhibitors being content to conduct their business with their own capital . . . Now, however, we have all manner of schemes, some of them sound, some of them very much the reverse, presented to the public with an appeal for capital . . . We do not argue against appealing to the public to finance a *bona fide* scheme; – merely to sound a note of warning to those who may be led by specious 'anticipation of profits' to put their money in companies which cannot by their constitution ever be successful. Many are hopelessly over-capitalised at the start, the purchase many paid to some mysterious 'vendor' being an incubus sufficient to doom them.[42]

The lack of trade experience was a recurring theme: 'Every Tom, Dick and Harry, whether he be grocer, tailor or candlestick maker, thinks he is capable of running a show. Companies are being formed in all directions, whose directors know nothing whatever about the trade.'[43]

The size and capital issues of these companies varied enormously, but it was the large companies created to manage several cinemas that inevitably attracted most attention. The biggest company was Provincial Cinematograph Theatres (PCT). This company – backed by the brewer and racehorse owner Sir William Bass – was founded in November 1909: its aim was to build new cinemas in major cities and its prospectus anticipated a profit of £64,000 from ten sites. *The Financial Times* was sceptical of the offer: 'It is not often that as blindly speculative an undertaking is presented in the industrial market. In effect, however, the public are asked to put up £75,000 out of a total capital of £100,000 and leave the entire disposition of the money unrestrained and without knowledge of how it is to be applied to directors who are not even named in the abridged prospectus.'[44] However, PCT's business model – based on large, purpose-built and well-appointed cinemas in major cities including London, Belfast, Birmingham, Dublin, Edinburgh, Glasgow, Leeds, Leicester, Liverpool and Manchester – proved successful. It paid dividends of 10 per cent in 1910 and 1911 and 20 per cent from 1912. In 1912 its managing director R. T. Jupp noted 'the very satisfactory growth which has taken place in their receipts' and announced a profit for the year of £35,168.[45] It raised further capital through a £50,000 debenture issue in July 1912, which was over-subscribed.[46] In 1913 the company's share capital was increased to £400,000: *Kinematograph & Lantern Weekly* could declare that PCT 'is the largest, as it undoubtedly is the most prosperous, company at present engaged in the kinematograph theatre business'.[47]

However, Provincial Cinematograph Theatres was unrepresentative both in its success and the extent of its capitalisation. Only four other cinema companies had registered capital of £100,000 or more – Associated Provincial Picture Houses (£500,000), Amalgamated Cinematograph Theatres (£150,000), Electric Theatres

(1908) (£100,000) and United Electric Theatres (£100,000) – and many companies were much smaller. Burrows calculates that the average capital issue of new exhibition concerns between 1908 and 1914 was only £2,088: it needs to be borne in mind that the large majority of these were single-venue companies.[48] And public share issues accounted for only a quarter of the total capital invested during these years. *The Financial Times* put total investment between 1908 and the first four months of 1914 at £10,350,800, but noted that:

> The striking feature about this relatively huge volume of capital assigned to the kinema industry is the very small proportion that has been offered with a public prospectus. This is due to two reasons. The first is that 75 per cent of the companies are private, and the second is that promoters have found it easier to carry on propaganda by post than to court the criticism of public advertisements. As already pointed out, the average company is a small one. An enterprise of this nature is easily started, it runs up as flimsy a building as the law allows, it gets its films from a supply organisation, and on the strength of early reception and monthly or quarterly dividends the promoters are able to place many of their shows among greedy and gullible investors.[49]

There were certainly many casualties. *The Financial Times* – whose editorial position was consistently critical of the cinema investment boom – reported in 1913 on 'the extent to which dry rot has set in mainly amongst the smaller cases of kinematograph establishments'. It reported that between the beginning of 1912 and mid-1913, there had been twenty-eight voluntary liquidations of cinema companies, another nine companies in receivership, and that a further eleven had been removed from the register of companies at Somerset House as they had filed no accounts. An estimated £1 million of invested capital 'has already vanished'. There was a common cause for many of the liquidations:

> In only a very small number of cases do we get anything like detailed reports of the numerous liquidations that have taken place, but these are of so uniform a character, that they may fairly be taken as a reliable guide to all the rest. Where excessive competition is not the reason of collapse it is invariably injudicious investment in kindred enterprises of a subsidiary, and in not a few instances heavy promotion expenses have been a formidable handicap, and have proved a primary factor in dragging the undertaking down.[50]

The article concluded: 'It is little wonder that kinematograph enterprises carried on on these lines failed to succeed.'

The biggest casualty – and whose demise stands as a counterpoint to the success of Provincial Cinematograph Theatres – was the Cinematograph Finance Corporation. This was the first all-purpose cinema investment company: its share prospectus declared that 'large and increasing profits are still being made by private individuals and incorporated Companies owning Cinematograph Theatres and similar ventures' and declared that 'the Cinematograph Finance Corporation will be the first Joint Stock Company of its kind to take full advantage of the situation by timely acquisition of Shares in the best among those Companies both for temporary as well as permanent investment'.[51] It was floated in November 1910 with a capital issue of £100,000: however, only £13,791 of the share issue was subscribed.[52] The major shareholders were its own directors W. J. Watson, George Edwards, Reginald Moreton and Philip Yorke: the lacklustre response to the share issue was attributed to it being made in the run-up to a general election the following month. Managing director Philip Yorke explained that in view of the under-subscribed capital, it was felt that 'the best policy was to temporarily abstain from actual investments, and employ the capital available in making advances to the companies owning kinematograph theatres on security approved'.[53] The Cinematograph Finance Corporation lent £9,515 to the London and General Electric Theatres Company for the leasing and equipping of cinemas: all but £900 of the loan was lost when London and General Electric went into liquidation in the summer of 1911. An extraordinary meeting in January 1912 was reported to have been 'not a pleasant one for the shareholders and such of them as were present took little trouble to disguise their feelings in the matter'.[54] The company was liquidated in March 1912, owing £13,596 to shareholders. *The Financial Times* presented it as a cautionary tale:

> The public enquiry into the promotion and collapse of the Cinematograph Finance Corporation, Ltd . . . is an instructive lesson as to the dangers run by investors who dabble in such ephemeral concerns without full knowledge of the details of management . . . In the case of the Cinematograph Finance Corporation there seems really to have been hardly any genuine business transacted, the shareholders' subscriptions, apart from what was needed for preliminary and other expenses, being loaned to the London and General Electric Theatres Ltd, which was actually the promoting syndicate, and went into liquidation last autumn. The latter concern seems to have squandered a great deal of the money in extravagant motor tours and other lavish expenses, and it is not surprising that it came to an inglorious end.[55]

However, the growth of capital investment in the exhibition sector was not matched in the field of film production. Burrows calculates that the total capital invested in sixteen British film production concerns in 1910–11 – including several survivors of the earliest years such as the Warwick Trading Company, Hepworth Manufacturing Company and Charles Urban Trading Company, as well as newcomers such as W. Butcher & Sons (established 1907) and the British and Colonial Kinematograph Company (1908) – amounted to only £228,100.[56] Unlike exhibitors, producers usually did not make public share issues, and so were dependent upon their own resources and debenture loans. James Williamson, one of the pioneers who had already left the industry, observed that 'the British capitalist does not believe in picture production as a profitable investment'.[57] Cecil Hepworth affirmed this view in his evidence to the Cinema Commission of Enquiry: 'English picture makers have always been short of capital. For some reason, the English investor has regarded this industry as far too precarious to command his serious attention, and opportunity after opportunity has slipped by and fallen to the credit of our rivals.'⁵⁸ Following a failed share issue by the Warwick Trading Company in 1913, when it looked to raise £27,000 of new capital, *Kinematograph & Lantern Weekly* observed: 'When any of the established firms, or a new company, inaugurated by men of standing and knowledge, whose business is to be film manufacture, appeals to the investing public for capital and fails to get an adequate response, there will be some reason for an outcry as to lack of enterprise in this country, in the manner of the provision of capital for film manufacture.'⁵⁹

The need for expanding capital in the production sector was because film-making had become a significantly more expensive business than it had been a decade earlier. Films were becoming longer and more elaborate, and the ascendancy of the story-film over the actuality subjects that had proliferated in the first decade involved expenditure on actors, sets and costumes. In 1910 a 'cinematograph operator' was reported in a syndicated newspaper article that '1000 feet of the highest form of stage representations known as art films cost £800 to produce'.⁶⁰ An early film-making manual published in 1912 suggested that a 'conventional modern comedy' might cost £500 but that 'a gorgeous [sic] production runs well into £6,000'.⁶¹ Will Barker's attempt to imbue his films with a higher degree of cultural prestige by recruiting renowned stage actors saw him pay Sir Herbert Beebohm Tree £1,000 for *Henry VIII* (1911) and nearly £8,000 on artistes' salaries for *Sixty Years a Queen* (1913).⁶² The *Kinematograph Year Book Diary and Directory* reported that the British and Colonial Kinematograph Company's *The Battle of Waterloo* (1913) was sold for £5,000 and that 'something like £10,000' was spent on *Hamlet* (1913), produced by Cecil Hepworth for the Gaumont Company and starring Sir Johnstone Forbes-Robertson.⁶³

From 1912 there were two developments in film production that would have a major influence on the future development of the industry. One was the emergence of the 'feature' film – understood as being six reels (approximately 6,000 feet) or more – and the other was the practice of selling important films on an exclusive basis by auction rather than through the open market. This period saw the emergence of historical spectaculars from the United States and Europe. The Selig Polyscope Company's *The Coming of Christopher Columbus* – reported to have cost £6,000 – was released in Britain in 1912.⁶⁴ And 1913 saw a veritable flood of historical and costume epics from France and Italy including *Quo Vadis?*, *The Last Days of Pompeii*, *The Three Musketeers* and *Antony and Cleopatra*: the last of those was reported to have cost £40,000.⁶⁵ These films were offered as exclusives. The £7,000 paid at auction by the owner of the Kinema, West Ealing, for exclusive UK rights to *Quo Vadis?* was reported as 'a record price for a cinematograph film'.⁶⁶

British producers were slow to respond to the rise of the feature film. There were both economic and cultural reasons for their reticence. On one level the increased costs of feature production made them a riskier proposition than short films as recuperation was less certain, especially given the increasing competition from imported films. And there is some evidence that audiences (or at least exhibitors) were resistant. The distributor William Jury of Imperial Pictures told the Selig Company in December 1914 that he was having difficulty in booking its film

The Spoilers on account of its length: 'Long films are practically done in this country for some time and I do not say this without knowing. I have just had to cut a 9000 ft film to 4000 ft . . . There was no other way of getting it on the market and I can get just as much money for a four-reel production as I can get for a twelve.'[67] However, Cecil Hepworth later suggested that he was not necessarily resistant to the feature film:

> Although I have admitted by innuendo that my company was slow to take up the challenge of the specially expensive feature film made from copyright books and plays, it must not be assumed that we were still playing about with unimportant open market pictures mainly. On the contrary we had for some time been making lengthy and important pictures and had won great success with most of them. But I had always had the feeling that picture making was an art in itself and should depend upon its own original writers for material. It was while I was waiting for those original writers to show up that I agreed to the making of such films from books as those quite successful Dickens films and the plays I have mentioned.[68]

Hepworth's production strategy in the early 1910s shifted towards what would subsequently be described as 'heritage' subjects – including adaptations of Shakespeare (*Hamlet*, 1913) and Dickens (*David Copperfield*, 1913) – but this has typically been seen by film historians as evidence of his retreat into a culturally and aesthetically conservative mode.[69]

By the eve of the First World War the British cinematograph industry had assumed an industrial and economic structure built around three sectors – production, distribution and exhibition – that would persist until the Cinematograph Films Act of 1927 acted as a catalyst for reorganisation and the emergence of vertical integration. Each sector had its own trade body – the Kinematograph Manufacturers Association (formed in 1906), the Cinematograph Exhibitors' Association (1912) and the Kinematograph Renters' Society (1914) – but the industry was highly fragmented insofar as it was comprised of a large number of small companies and no single firm was dominant in any sector. The first *Kinematograph Year Book Diary and Directory*, published in 1914, stated that 'no precise figures are available as to the capital invested in the kinematograph industry, picture theatres, film manufacturers, etc, etc. It has been estimated at thirteen millions, and whether it be approximately that sum, or much more, or a little less, it is, undoubtedly, very considerable.'[70] However, most of that investment was in the exhibition sector rather than in production. And there was already evidence that British films were losing ground in their home market: this trend would become even more acute following the outbreak of the First World War in 1914.

Notes

1. Acres presented a series of films at the Royal Photographic Society on 14 January 1896, Paul at Finsbury Park College on 20 February 1896 – the same day that the Lumière brothers of France exhibited their Cinematographe at the Regent Street Polytechnic.

See Ian Christie, *Robert Paul and the Origins of British Cinema* (Chicago: University of Chicago Press, 2019), pp. 26–33.
2. 'Want of Finance', *The Bioscope*, 25 November 1915, p. 878.
3. Rachael Low and Roger Manvell, *The History of the British Film 1896–1906* (London: George Allen & Unwin, 1948), pp. 13–14.
4. Ibid., p. 43.
5. Rachael Low, *The History of the British Film 1906–1914* (London: George Allen & Unwin, 1949), p. 41.
6. Ibid., pp. 92–3.
7. C. A. Oakley, *Where We Came In: Seventy Years of the British Film Industry* (London: George Allen & Unwin, 1964), p. 53.
8. Ernest Betts, *The Film Business: A History of British Cinema 1896–1972* (London: George Allen & Unwin, 1973), p. 34.
9. John Barnes, *Pioneers of the British Film* (London: Bishopsgate Press, 1983), p. 8.
10. Roy Armes, *A Critical History of the British Cinema* (London: Secker & Warburg, 1978), p. 17.
11. Michael Chanan, *The Dream That Kicks: The Prehistory and Early Years of Cinema in Britain* (London: Routledge & Kegan Paul, 1980), p. 237.
12. Ibid., p. 248.
13. Ibid., pp. 259–60.
14. Richard Brown and Barry Anthony, *A Victorian Film Enterprise: The History of the British Mutoscope and Biograph Company, 1897–1915* (Trowbridge: Flicks Books, 1999), p. 3.
15. Cecil Hepworth, *Came the Dawn: Memories of a Film Pioneer* (London: Pheonix House, 1951), p. 41.
16. The National Archives (TNA) BT 31/7995/57468: Memorandum of Association of the Cinematograph Company Ltd, 23 May 1898.
17. Brown and Anthony, *A Victorian Film Enterprise*, p. 28.
18. Quoted in Christie, *Robert Paul and the Origins of British Cinema*, p. 270.
19. 'The Latest Peep-Show', *The Financial Times*, 4 May 1899, p. 2.
20. TNA BT 31/10401/78346: The Pathé Cinematograph Company was successor to Pathé Frères (London), a subsidiary of Societé Pathé Frères of Paris. Pathé Frères (London) Ltd to Registrar of Joint Stock Companies, 17 August 1903.
21. Brown and Anthony, *A Victorian Film Enterprise*, p. 77.
22. 'British Mutoscope and Biograph Company, Limited', *The Economist*, 14 July 1900, p. 18; 'British Mutoscope and Biograph Company, Limited', *The Economist*, 6 July 1901, p. 17.
23. John Barnes, *The Rise of the Cinema in Great Britain: The Beginnings of the Cinema in England 1894–1901. Volume 2: Jubilee Year 1897* (London: Bishopsgate Press, 1983), pp. 200–11.
24. Luke McKernan, *Charles Urban: Pioneering the Non-fiction Film in Britain and America, 1897–1925* (Exeter: University of Exeter Press, 2013), p. 24.
25. Barnes, *The Rise of the Cinema in Great Britain. Volume 2*, pp. 200–11.
26. Stephen Bottomore, 'From the Factory Gate to "Home Talent" Drama: An International Overview of Local Films in the Silent Era', in Vanessa Toulmin, Simon Popple and Patrick Russell (eds), *The Lost World of Mitchell and Kenyon: Edwardian Britain on Film* (London: British Film Institute, 2004), p. 36.
27. 'Warwick Film Subjects', *The Era*, 7 September 1901, p. 28.
28. 'The Coronation', *The Daily Telegraph*, 20 June 1902, p. 9.

29. 'Special Coronation Film', *The Era*, 2 August 1902, p. 29.
30. Simon Brown, *Cecil Hepworth and the Rise of the British Film Industry 1899–1911* (Exeter: University of Exeter Press, 2016), p. 114.
31. Charles Barr, 'Before *Blackmail*: Silent British Cinema', in Robert Murphy (ed.), *The British Cinema Book* (London: British Film Institute, 1997), p. 9.
32. Brown, *Cecil Hepworth and the Rise of the British Film Industry 1899–1911*, p. 83.
33. Ibid., p. 141.
34. 'The Cinematograph', *The Financial Times*, 29 December 1908, p. 6.
35. 'Daily Bioscope', *The Morning Leader*, 24 May 1906, p. 5.
36. Low, *The History of the British Film 1906–1914*, p. 22.
37. *The Cinema: Its Present Position and Future Possibilities. Being the Report of and Chief Evidence taken by the Cinema Commission of Enquiry instituted by the National Council of Public Morals* (London: Williams and Norgate, 1917), pp. 2–3.
38. Jon Burrows, *The British Cinema Boom, 1909–1914: A Commercial History* (London: Palgrave Macmillan, 2017), p. 3.
39. Ibid., p. 12.
40. Ibid., p. 22.
41. 'Finance and Films', *The Bioscope*, 25 November 1909, p. 3.
42. 'The Company Promoter', *The Kinematograph & Lantern Weekly*, 10 June 1909, p. 199.
43. 'The Picture Trade and the Public', *The Kinematograph & Lantern Weekly*, 23 December 1909, p. 361.
44. 'Provincial Cinematograph Theatres', *The Financial Times*, 20 November 1909, p. 4.
45. 'Provincial Cinematograph Theatres', *The Financial Times*, 1 March 1912, p. 4.
46. 'Provincial Cinematograph Theatres Ltd', *The Manchester Courier*, 31 January 1912, p. 4.
47. 'Kinematograph Finance', *The Kinematograph & Lantern Weekly*, 14 August 1913, p. 15.
48. Burrows, *The British Cinema Boom*, p. 25.
49. 'Kinematograph Registrations and Liquidations', *The Financial Times*, 11 June 1914, p. 6.
50. 'Kinema Liquidations', *The Financial Times*, 9 June 1913, p. 4.
51. TNA BT 31/19732/112756: The Cinematograph Finance Corporation Limited, share prospectus.
52. Ibid.: Return of Allotments of the Cinematograph Finance Corporation from 28 November 1910 to 14 December 1910.
53. 'Cinematograph Finance', *The Financial Times*, 2 March 1911, p. 3.
54. 'A Finance Company', *The Kinematograph & Lantern Weekly*, 4 January 1912, p. 525.
55. 'Kinematograph Finance', *The Financial Times*, 13 July 1912, p. 6.
56. Burrows, *The British Cinema Boom*, pp. 173–4.
57. 'Men of the Moment in the Cinematogaph World', *The Cinema News and Property Gazette*, May 1912, p. 10.
58. *The Cinema: Its Present Position and Future Possibilities*, p. 48.
59. 'Financiers and Film Manufacture', *The Kinematograph & Lantern Weekly*, 24 April 1913, p. 10.
60. 'The Cinematograph: What Pictures Cost', *Stonehaven Journal*, 19 May 1910, p. 4.
61. Frederick A. Talbot, *Motion Pictures: How They Are Made and Worked* (London: William Heinemann, 1912), p. 114.
62. Low, *The History of the British Film 1906–1914*, p. 119.
63. *Kinematograph Year Book Diary and Directory 1914* (London: Kinematograph & Lantern Weekly, 1914), p. 31.

64. '"Christopher Columbus" at the Opera House', *The Derry Journal*, 1 May 1912, p. 8.
65. 'The Cinematograph', *Hornsey Journal*, 27 February 1914, p. 10.
66. '"Quo Vadis" at the Kinema', *The Middlesex County Times*, 12 July 1913, p. 7.
67. Quoted in Burrows, *The British Cinema Boom*, p. 206.
68. Hepworth, *Came the Dawn*, p. 148.
69. Barr, 'Before *Blackmail*', p. 15.
70. *Kinematograph Year Book Diary and Directory 1914*, p. 17.

CHAPTER 2

Challenges of War

It has often been maintained that it was the First World War that dealt a fatal blow to the British cinematograph industry insofar as it brought about the conditions whereby American films came to dominate the British market. Looking back from 1922, *The Times* averred that 'the war came as a shattering blow to the hopes of British producers. It came at the moment when the British industry saw a chance of establishing itself on a firm basis which would make it a serious competitor, if not an equal, with that of the United States.'[1] This was also the view of government. According to Sir Philip Cunliffe-Lister, the President of the Board of Trade, in moving the Cinematograph Films Bill in 1927: 'It was during the four long years of War when the whole effort of this country was concentrated on winning the War, that our competitors in the film industry in America forged ahead, very often by using British talent in production in their acting, writing and technical skill.'[2] With the domestic production sector depressed and the supply of films from continental Europe disrupted by the war, American renters were able to secure a strong foothold in Britain. However, Rachael Low contests the narrative of wartime disruption, arguing that the impact of the war merely exposed existing structural weaknesses of the industry: she argues that 'the shortage of capital for British film production, its fundamental weakness, dated from before the war. There is no reason whatever to suppose that, had there been no war, British production would have been able to withstand the irresistible growth of the American output.'[3]

The war played an important role in establishing the position of the cinema industry in the national life of Britain. Hitherto political elites had tended to regard cinema as a low-brow and somewhat disreputable form of amusement: now there was increasing recognition of its value as a powerful vehicle for reflecting and influencing public opinion. The cinema reached a wide audience: in 1917 the Cinema Commission of Enquiry conducted by the National Council of Public Morals estimated that there were approximately 4,500 cinemas in the British Isles and around 3,375,000 cinema attendances per day. It reckoned that 'half the entire population, men, women and children, visit a cinematograph theatre once each week'.[4] The Ministry of Information, set up belatedly in 1918 to co-ordinate the propaganda activities of various different official agencies, evidently recognised the potential of cinema for national publicity:

> When War broke out the Cinema was almost universally regarded as an instrument for the amusement of the masses: the educated classes thought of 'the pictures' as

responsible for turning romantic shopboys into juvenile highwaymen, as a sort of moving edition of the 'penny dreadful'. Here and there its vast potentialities were beginning to be recognised before the War, but it is only now that its value and importance as an agent for good or for evil is being slowly appreciated both by the public and by the Government. For this the War is responsible. In the early days of the War the military authorities would have none of the cinematograph operator, but now he occupies a recognised position on all Fronts.[5]

The memorandum added: 'It is not, perhaps, too much to claim that the motion picture is the most powerful agent for publicity now in existence.' And it suggested that the industry was now being managed on more capable lines than in its early days: 'Of late years the Cinema Industry has attracted a very much better type of business man than was associated with it in its infancy. Some of the disrepute which attached to it in the beginning still clings to it in the public mind, but with the growing recognition of its importance this must rapidly disappear.' Cecil Hepworth affirmed this view in his evidence to the Cinema Commission: 'The cinematograph is undoubtedly destined to exert a tremendously powerful influence upon thought and understanding in every phase of life . . . It is intensely important, from a national point of view, that good and worthy pictures of home production should be exhibited in the cinema theatres of the Homeland.'[6]

However, the war presented major challenges for the growing industry. Most obviously the war marked an interruption to normal business conditions that made it difficult to raise capital for new ventures. The availability of adequate manpower due to war service and the disruption to the export trade both created uncertainty that made investors more wary. H. B. Montgomery, finance correspondent of *Kinematograph and Lantern Weekly*, noted this in September 1914:

> No serious attempt had been made to obtain additional capital in the best manner possible, viz., by appealing to the public for it and emphasising the potentialities of the British film business. If the public had been satisfied on this head, the necessary capital would, of a certainty, have been forthcoming. Of course, in existing circumstances it is hopeless to appeal for this capital now to develop the film business in this country, and apparently it is hoped that sentiment money may be trusted to do duty instead.[7]

At the same time, Montgomery argued, the war also presented an opportunity for British producers to regain a dominant share of their home market:

> Owing to the war the film manufacturers of this country have now an opportunity not likely to recur. A good deal of the competition which hitherto obtained has been removed from their path, while they are provided with a topic which interests every man, woman and child in the country, and will draw them to the picture theatres if it be properly treated. What the British film-makers should do, in my opinion, is to abjure mere appeals to sentiment about all-British programmes and to determine a vigorous enterprise in the evolution of the British film industry.[8]

On this point, however, Montgomery was mistaken: while the supply of films from continental Europe declined, the gap would be filled by American films. In 1913, American films accounted for 50 per cent of all the films released in Britain: by 1915 this had risen to 56.8 per cent, by 1916 to 69.8 per cent and by 1917 to 77.2 per cent.[9]

There are more sources of statistical and financial data for the 1910s than for the years before the First World War: the first *Kinematograph Year Book Diary and Directory* was published in 1914, and in 1917 the Cinema Commission of Enquiry published its report *The Cinema: Its Present Position and Future Possibilities*. The *Kine Year Book* put the number of cinemas in 1916 at 6,000 (a higher figure than the 4,500 suggested by the Cinema Commission), estimated that £30 million of 'British money' had been invested in the cinema industry in the United Kingdom, and calculated that the industry's aggregate capital (including both public and private companies) at the end of 1915 was £11,739,000.[10] It listed sixteen large public joint stock companies with a total capital worth £1,822,000: four of the five largest concerns with capital of £100,000 or more – Associated Provincial Picture Houses (£500,000), Provincial Cinematograph Theatres (£400,000), United Electric Theatres (£150,000) and Electric Theatres (1908) (£100,000) – were in the exhibition sector of the industry. The London Film Company (£93,000), in which Provincial Cinematograph Theatres held a large shareholding, was the best capitalised production concern.[11] Further, the *Kine Year Book* reported that 212 mortgages and charges had been registered by companies connected with the industry: 148 of these were under £2,000 but there were twenty of £10,000 or more, of which most again were in the exhibition sector.[12]

To put these figures in context, contemporary sources estimated there were between 15,000 and 20,000 cinemas in the United States and between 10–15 million admissions per day: the US domestic market was therefore between four and five times that of the United Kingdom. In 1916 the *Los Angeles Times* put the total capital invested in film production at US$100 million (around £22 million) and reported that the American public spent US$297 million a year on motion pictures.[13] The size of the domestic market in the United States gave its industry two significant advantages: it could afford to spend more on its films – hence American movies came to be seen as having superior production values – and it could reasonably expect to recover production costs and even return a profit from the home market alone. It was during the 1910s that Los Angeles emerged as 'the film capital of the world', with modern purpose-built studio plants clustered around the suburb of Hollywood: Universal City, which opened with much fanfare in 1915, was reported to have a weekly payroll of US$45,000 for its 2,000 employees. The US film industry was already on the road to structural and economic consolidation that would lead to vertical integration: the Fox Film Corporation (founded 1915) and the Famous Players-Lasky Corporation (1916), later Paramount Pictures, were the first companies to combine interests across all three sectors of the industry – production, distribution and exhibition.[14]

In comparison to the United States, the British film industry was highly fragmented. The *Kine Year Book* for 1917 lists sixty-two registered 'picture play producers', 215 companies under the heading of 'film brands, film manufacturers, importers and film agents' (some companies such as Gaumont and Fox were listed more than once as their regional offices were counted as individual companies), and 483 renters (142 in London and 341 in the provinces, Scotland, Wales and Ireland).[15] A total of 235 new companies were registered during the year, mostly in exhibition: of twenty-three companies with authorised capital of £10,000 or more only three – Renaissance Films (£10,000), Premier Productions (£11,000) and the Film Company of Great Britain (£25,000) – were listed as producers rather than as exhibitors or 'dealers'. Approximately 69 per cent of the new capital made available for the industry in 1916 was in the exhibition sector with only 10 per cent invested in production: the balance was made up of equipment manufacturers and dealers.[16]

The trade statistics further highlight a marked contrast between a flourishing exhibition business and a weak domestic production sector. Some 3,145 films were released on the open market in 1916: the total volume of films offered had decreased during the war (this figure was down from 4,790 in 1915 and 6,648 in 1914) although the number of films offered as exclusives had increased from 400 to 823 over the same period.[17] To some extent the decreasing number of films was illusory as it also reflected the growing prominence of the longer feature film. However, the popularity of films – especially the demand for topical war subjects – was such that British producers were unable to meet demand. In September 1915 *The Bioscope* remarked that '[the] supply of British films is at present so inadequate that exhibitors would still be forced to rely largely upon American films for which they would have to pay much more'.[18]

Film imports came under intense scrutiny during the first eighteen months of the war. A leading article in *The Times* early in 1916 saw film imports as an unaffordable luxury:

> We are buying American films to the extent of £2,000,000 a year at a time when there are only two legitimate objects on which English money should be spent. One of those objects is the production of victory in the field; the other, which is closely allied, is the promotion of a sound national spirit in the people at home. The importation of American films, so far from promoting either of these objects, is a direct obstacle to both.[19]

In fact statistics issued by the Board of Trade indicated that in 1914 Britain spent a total £1,215,000 on imported films, of which 91 per cent (£1,113,000) was spent on American films: even so this was still a significant amount.[20] In September 1915 a duty was imposed on imported film stock by Chancellor of the Exchequer Reginald McKenna: the duty – part of a package of new tariffs on luxury items also including motor cars and watches known as the McKenna Duties – was set at eight pence per foot on negative film, a penny per foot on positive film and a halfpenny per foot on unexposed film.[21] These levels were subsequently reduced slightly following lobbying by the trade associations. However, the duty seems to have had little impact on the supply of foreign films. *The Bioscope* reported that 528 foreign films were released in Britain in January 1916 compared to only 53 British films.[22] Kristin Thompson, in her book *Exporting Entertainment*, finds 'little evidence of adverse reaction to the tariff from American firms . . . The American position in Britain was simply too lucrative for the tariff to affect it to any great extent.'[23]

Another government action did have an important long-term effect on the film industry. Until early 1916 London was the centre of the re-export trade for films: American renters would send most of their films to London for re-export to other markets. In March 1916, however, the British government mandated that exports from the United Kingdom would need to obtain an export licence: the purpose was to prevent firms from trading with the enemy through neutral countries (for example it had been found that some films sent to Denmark subsequently found their way to Germany) but an unintended outcome as far as the film business was concerned is that renters began to channel their films through New York rather than London. In March 1915 the total value of film exports from London was £22,000, of which re-exports accounted for £6,000; a year later the total value of film exports had fallen to only £6,500, of which re-exports were £4,000.[24] In April 1917 *The Bioscope* warned: 'Until a short time ago London was the acknowledged and undisputed centre of the film world – the international exchange through which practically all dealings in film were conducted. To-day this supremacy is threatened. We are faced with a danger of the world's film export trade leaving Great Britain for America.'[25]

The eclipse of London as the exchange capital of the international film trade and the shift to New York reflected the growing economic hegemony of the US film industry. Furthermore, it was during the war that the American film established its technical and cultural supremacy over other film-producing nations. As Thompson observes: 'American films were longer and had popular stars, lavish *mise en scène* and skilful cinematography; during the war these changes in the Hollywood film gained for it a definite following and other national industries would have difficulty in creating films as attractive.'[26] The mid-1910s saw the production of American epics such as D. W. Griffith's *The Birth of a Nation* (1915) and *Intolerance* (1916) and Fox's *A Daughter of the Gods* (1916): these super productions set a standard for narrative and visual spectacle that could not be matched by any other film-producing industry. Michael Hammond has documented the extraordinary impact that *The Birth of a Nation* had on British audiences in the middle years of the war.[27] British producers could not match the scale of films such as these, but even the more routine American films were more expensively and sumptuously produced than their British equivalents. Low avers that '£4,000 seems to be an average production cost throughout the war', although costs of up to £20,000 were reported for the London Film Company's *The Manxman* (1916) and the Ideal Film Company's *The Second Mrs Tanqueray* (1916), but adds that 'by the end of the war anything from £15,000 to £30,000 or even £50,000 was said to be normal for an American film'.[28] According to a contemporary press report, Lawrence Cowan's film *It is for England* (1917) – a ten-reeler that reportedly set out to a 'British *Birth of a Nation*' – 'represents an outlay of over £40,000'.[29]

British producers were operating at an economic disadvantage in two key respects: on the one hand, the British market was too small for them to match the costs of American films (even if they had the capital resources to do so); on the other hand, they were competing in their home market against imported American films that were produced on a more expensive scale. An article in the *Pall Mall Gazette* explained how British producers faced an uneven playing field:

> We in England are used to many forms of unfair foreign competition and there have been few forms of competition from abroad more invidious than those of the film trade. A very important point, of which the uninitiated are scarcely aware, but which can be set forth very simply, is the fact that the essential cost of a film for cinematograph exhibition is not the intrinsic and manufactured cost and printing of the material, but the money employed in its production, which may be – according to the particular nature of the subject – anything from twenty to a hundred times the cost of a completed copy of a film.
>
> In America there is a vast field for the sale and hire of films immensely greater than in England, and the cost of production is recovered and a handsome profit realised within American territory. Surplus copies are produced for export, and the foreign rights sold to various countries, mainly England, which give a magnificent return to the American trader, as there are no further costs of production, and these are offered in competition against English films which have to bear the full and vital cost of their production, and have only the revenue of the English market to recoup them.[30]

This was confirmed by British producer Sidney Morgan of Renaissance Films, who averred there was 'one British firm that had spent enormous sums upon modern contingencies for film production only to be met with comparative failure, after really showing the trade that good pictures were possible under the best circumstances. The cost, however, had proved so enormous that the films were not marketable at a fairly remunerative price.'[31]

Another problem for British producers was the slow return on investment. The rise of the feature film and a market crowded with American films often meant a long gap between the completion of a film and its release: this left producers with capital locked up in films awaiting distribution. Cecil Hepworth blamed the problem on renters who stockpiled films:

> This was called 'block booking' and it transpired that booking dates receded further and further into the future until there were none to be had for eighteen months or two years . . . Anyway the result was the capital sunk in the making of a big film would not begin to come back to the maker until about two years afterwards. It can hardly be wondered at that so many makers preferred to keep to their old policy of small pictures and quick returns and so helped to build up and succour the very evil which was bringing about their own downfall.[32]

The Annual General Meeting of Kinematograph Manufacturers' Association in 1919 highlighted the problem of raising capital when returns were slow to accrue:

> At present a film which is ready for exhibition and which has cost some thousands of pounds, cannot be shown to the public and made available for commercial purposes until at least twelve months or perhaps fifteen months ahead, and instead of an improvement being shown in regard to this state of things, matters are gradually getting worse. The British Cinematograph Industry is vitally concerned in this question, primarily, of course, the manufacturer, for under the existing system it is practically impossible to attract British capital to the industry, owing to the unreasonable time that must elapse in securing an adequate return.[33]

While American films, which in most cases had already recovered their costs in the US market, were unaffected, British producers were disadvantaged as the long delays between production and release meant not only that they were accruing interest payments on borrowed money but also that their films ran the risk of being out of date by the time they were shown to the public. As *The Era* observed: 'To produce even quite a simple five-reel subject in Great Britain costs at the very least about £1,500, while the average cost is probably about double that . . . [It] not infrequently happens that a first-class and elaborately produced British film has to be released such a long time after its trade show, that the feminine fashions in it are hopelessly out of date.'[34]

With most of the early film-making pioneers having left the industry before the First World War, the concerns involved in production in the 1910s tended to be second-generation companies established between 1908 and 1916. For Low: 'The most marked change among the producers themselves was the disappearance of that individuality which had previously distinguished one British production company from another.'[35] The major producers of the 1910s were the Charles Urban Trading Company and Hepworth Manufacturing Company, both survivors of the early years, and the British and Colonial Kinematograph Company (established in 1908), Barker Motion Photography (1909), the London Film Company (1913), the Broadwest Film Company (1914) and the British Actors' Film Company (1916). The major British renters – the Gaumont Film Company, Ideal Films (1911) and Butcher's Film Service (1915) – were also active in production: Gaumont invested £30,000 in building a studio at Shepherd's Bush which opened in 1915.[36] Wardour Films – registered in 1916 with an initial capital of £15,000 – joined the ranks of the larger renters.[37] Low avers that the registered capital of new companies set up during the war 'was usually in the neighbourhood of £10,000'.[38] Most production companies were private concerns: the London Film Company and Broadwest were the first to make public share issues. The Standard Feature Film Company – incorporated in 1913 with capital of £1,000 as 'manufacturers, producers and dealers in cinematograph films' – was a representative example of the smaller companies that proliferated during the war: it produced around a dozen films before its dissolution in 1919.[39]

Gerry Turvey's history of the British and Colonial Kinematograph Company (B&C) offers a case study of how the fortunes of a particular company 'reflected general developments in British cinema at the time'.[40] B&C was set up as a private company in 1908 by Albert Henry Bloomfield and initially specialised in topical non-fiction films in the manner of the Charles Urban Trading Company. From 1909 it moved into fiction subjects and enjoyed popular success with series films featuring recurring characters, notably naval hero Lieutenant Daring and highwayman Dick Turpin. Turvey argues that without a public share issue, B&C 'was expanding through the management's careful husbanding of company resources, the ploughing back of income, the reinvestment of profits, and occasionally, through whatever loans it could secure from a bank'.[41] In 1913, when control of the company passed to managing director J. B. McDowell, B&C signalled a shift towards the production of longer and more expensive films such as *The Battle of Waterloo* (1913). B&C enjoyed its greatest success between 1913 and 1916, but following McDowell's departure and the appointment of Edward Godal as managing director in 1918 the company failed to keep pace with its competitors and went into liquidation in 1924. Turvey concludes that 'B&C became a major player in the British cinema industry between 1908 and 1916 and remained a minor player from 1919 to 1924'.[42]

Ironically the most successful British film of the war years was produced outside normal commercial contexts. *Battle of the Somme* (1916) was produced under the auspices of the Topical Committee for Films, a trade body comprising several of the major producers and renters which had succeeded in persuading the War Office to allow officially sanctioned cinematographers to shoot actuality footage at the front (hitherto most war films had been fictionalised dramas rather than documentaries). From late 1915 a series of short actuality subjects were produced, but the footage shot by camera operators Geoffrey Malins and J. B. McDowell of the early phase of the British summer offensive on the Somme was considered so good that it was edited into a five-reel feature. *Battle of the Somme* was released in London on 21 August 1916 and followed in other major cities a week later.[43] All contemporary and historical accounts indicate that *Battle of the Somme* had a quite extraordinary reception from the public – even more so than *The Birth of a Nation* – and it seems to have been regarded as an act of patriotism to see the film. Nicholas Reeves estimates that it was seen by 20 million people in its first six weeks on release: he also provides evidence that it attracted people who were not regular cinema patrons or might even have been making their first visit to the cinema.[44]

Historical accounts of *Battle of the Somme* have usually focused on its authenticity – a few sequences (including the famous shots of British troops going 'over the top' and advancing through No Man's Lands) turned out to have been reconstructed behind the lines – but its distribution and exhibition are also of significant interest. *Battle of the Somme* was released by William Jury's Imperial Pictures on behalf of the War Office, which collected a share of the rental fees starting at 40 per cent in the first week and 35 per cent in the second. There are reports of packed cinemas and of the film being held over by exhibitors. This meant that other films would have been delayed or even cancelled to show *Battle of the Somme*. As *The Times* observed:

> Big profits are undoubtedly being made by the cinema proprietors, but a good deal is to be said for those who have been among the first to show the film. Cinema programmes have to be approved months ahead of the actual exhibition, and the proprietors who last week in London, and this week in the country, are paying the top hiring fees for the war pictures, are directly adding that fee to the cost of a programme already announced. Films which had previously been booked are not being used, although they have to be paid for. The State, it should be said, as a result of the success of the pictures, benefits by the collection of an increased amount of entertainment tax.[45]

Entertainment Duty (or 'Mr McKenna's Amusement Tax' as it was dubbed by the trade) had been introduced in March 1916: this applied to each cinema ticket sold on a sliding scale starting at a halfpenny on seats of two pence or less. *Battle of the Somme* was one of the first 'big' films released after the introduction of the duty.

The War Office's share of receipts for *Battle of the Somme* was donated to war charities. There are conflicting sources for its receipts. Low contends that '*The Battle of the Somme* [sic] had the extraordinary number of two thousand bookings and raised about £30,000.'[46] This may be an underestimate, however, as a contemporary newspaper article reported that the first week's gross receipts alone 'have been at least £30,000'.[47] In September 1917 it was reported that £60,000 had been handed over to charities by the War Office Cinematograph Committee, which had taken over the work of the Topical Committee for Films: this figure includes two other feature-length actuality films in the same mode as *Battle of the Somme*: *The Battle of the Ancre and the Advance of the Tanks* (1917) and *The German Retreat and the Battle of Arras* (1917).[48] Another report indicated that the War Office received £71,096 from the release of official films during the year ending 31 July 1918.[49] In contrast the bi-weekly newsreel produced under the aegis of the Cinematograph Committee but sold on a commercial basis, *War Office Official Topical Budget*, earned a modest profit of £6,280 during the year ending 22 June 1918.[50]

By the later years of the war there was a marked divergence between the optimism of the trade press and the experiences of individual producers. The editorials of the *Kine Year Book* are replete with hyperbole about the prospects of the industry. It declared that 1916 'has been the most momentous in the history of the kinematograph industry . . . Unquestionably, the trade is in a more solid position than has previously obtained. The weeding-out process has undoubtedly left our ground clearer and better.'[51] The following year the *Year Book* claimed: 'On the financial side, the industry is in a more solid position than it ever before occupied . . . So far as the producing side is concerned, the progress made continues to be greater each succeeding year, and we on this side may fairly claim that our producers are now putting out work which compares favourably with the best American product.'[52] However, Cecil Hepworth suggested in his memoirs that the latter claim 'is one of those thoughts which are fathered so prolifically by wishes'.[53] Reflecting on the founding of Hepworth Picture Plays in 1919 with a capital of £100,000, Hepworth wrote:

> Hepworth Pictures Plays Ltd made an issue on November 1st of £2,500 debentures, part of a series already registered, and again in December, 1920, of £10,000 similar debentures. It will I think be obvious that underneath the record of these things there must have been the heave and throb of big difficulties; a feeling of premonition of heavy trouble in store for us. There was a pressure in the air which we did not understand and we worked on as best we could in spite of it.[54]

However, another issue for £250,000 in 1922 was under-subscribed and this spelled the end for Hepworth: 'I had been warned that this might be so and that the high reputation of the firm might not be proof against the choice of a date when the money market was depressed. But I felt that it must be risked, and I alone am to blame for the result.'[55]

Hepworth was the last survivor of the pioneer generation of British filmmakers: his longevity in the industry suggests that the conventional view that he failed to adjust to changes in film style and industry practices needs to be reconsidered. His retirement following the collapse of Hepworth Picture Plays in 1924 seems in hindsight to mark a moment of changing of the guard in British cinema: the generation of new producers who emerged in the 1920s – including Herbert Wilcox and Michael Balcon – were businessmen who entered the industry through the expanding distribution sector and who would look to emulate the professional practices and production values of Hollywood which had by now firmly established itself, both economically and culturally, as the dominant film industry in the world.

Notes

1. 'The British Industry', *The Times*, 21 February 1922, p. 32.
2. *Parliamentary Debates: House of Commons*, 5th Series, vol. 203, 16 March 1927, col. 2044.
3. Rachael Low, *The History of the British Film 1914–1918* (London: George Allen & Unwin, 1950), p. 49.
4. *The Cinema: Its Present Position and Future Possibilities. Being the Report of and Chief Evidence taken by the Cinema Commission of Enquiry instituted by the National Council of Public Morals* (London: Williams and Norgate, 1917), p. 3.
5. The National Archives (TNA) INF 4/6: Minute on the Cinema Industry and its Relation to the Government (no date).
6. *The Cinema: Its Present Position and Future Possibilities*, p. 46.
7. 'Kinematograph Finance', *The Kinematograph & Lantern Weekly*, 24 September 1914, p. 23.
8. Ibid.
9. Kristin Thompson, *Exporting Entertainment: America in the World Film Market 1907–1934* (London: British Film Institute, 1985), p. 215.
10. *Kinematograph Year Book Diary and Directory 1917* (London: Kinematograph and Lantern Weekly, 1917), p. 21.

11. Ibid., pp. 416–19.
12. Ibid., pp. 317–29.
13. 'Los Angeles the Film Capital of the World', *Los Angeles Times*, 1 January 1916, pp. III–70.
14. On the structure of the US film industry in this period, see Richard Koszarski, *An Evening's Entertainment: The Age of the Silent Feature Picture, 1915–1928* (Berkeley: University of California Press, 1990), pp. 63–94.
15. *Kinematograph Year Book Diary and Directory 1917*, pp. 351–82.
16. Ibid., pp. 305–16.
17. Ibid., p. 20.
18. 'Civicus Britannicus', *The Bioscope*, 9 September 1915, p. 1274.
19. 'Films Good and Evil', *The Times*, 12 February 1916, p. 7.
20. 'Imports, Exports and Re-Exports on Kinematograph Films', *The Kinematograph & Lantern Weekly*, 23 March 1916, p. 9.
21. Low, *The History of the British Film 1914–1918*, p. 111.
22. 'The Suggested Film Blockade', *The Bioscope*, 10 February 1916, p. 451.
23. Thompson, *Exporting Entertainment*, pp. 66–7.
24. 'Trade From Our Shores', *Kinematograph Year Book Diary and Directory 1917*, p. 32.
25. 'New York or London?', *The Bioscope*, 5 April 1917, p. 5.
26. Thompson, *Exporting Entertainment*, p. 100.
27. Michael Hammond, *The Big Show: British Cinema Culture in the Great War 1914–1918* (Exeter: University of Exeter Press, 2006), pp. 128–53.
28. Low, *The History of the British Film 1914–1918*, p. 53.
29. 'It is for Enfland', *The Halifax Daily Guardian*, 19 January 1917, p. 3.
30. 'All British Films', *Pall Mall Gazette*, 6 March 1915, p. 5.
31. 'American Versus British Films', *The Kinematograph & Lantern Weekly*, 12 April 1917, p. 25.
32. Cecil Hepworth, *Came the Dawn: Memories of a Film Pioneer* (London: Pheonix House, 1951), p. 147.
33. 'The Problem of Release Dates', *The Bioscope*, 16 October 1919, p. 10.
34. 'The Block Booking Tyranny', *The Era*, 3 September 1919, p. 18.
35. Low, *The History of the British Film 1914–1918*, p. 56.
36. 'Unique Trade Show', *The Kinematograph & Lantern Weekly*, 16 December 1915, p. 891.
37. TNA BT 31/32229/145176: Certificate of Incorporation and Statement of the Nominal Capital of Bolton's Mutual Films Ltd, 27 September 1916. (The company changed its name to Wardour Films in 1919.)
38. Low, *The History of the British Film 1914–1918*, p. 51.
39. TNA BT 31/22182/135000: Certificate of Incorporation and Statement of Nominal Capital of the Standard Feature Film Company, 31 March 1913.
40. Gerry Turvey, *The B&C Kinematograph Company and British Cinema: Early Twentieth-Century Spectacle and Melodrama* (Exeter: University of Exeter Press, 2021), p. 4.
41. Ibid., p. 28.
42. Ibid., p. 327.
43. The production of *Battle of the Somme* has been well documented by film historians: see in particular Stephen Badsey, '*Battle of the Somme*: British war-propaganda', *Historical Journal of Film, Radio and Television*, 3: 2 (1983), pp. 99–115.

44. Nicholas Reeves, *Official British Film Propaganda During the First World War* (London: Croom Helm, 1986), pp. 15–16.
45. 'The Somme Films', *The Times*, 1 September 1915, p. 9.
46. Low, *The History of the British Film 1914–1918*, p. 29.
47. 'Somme Film Receipts', *Bolton Evening News*, 4 September 1916, p. 1.
48. 'More Official War Films', *The Evening Star and Daily Herald*, 24 September 1917, p. 3.
49. 'War Film Profits', *North Eastern Daily Gazette*, 25 August 1919, p. 3.
50. 'Battle Film Profits', *The Daily News*, 23 September 1918, p. 6.
51. 'A Retrospect of the Year', *The Kinematograph Year Book Diary and Directory 1917*, p. 19.
52. 'A Momentous Year for the Industry', *Kinematograph Year Book Diary and Directory 1918* (London: Kinematograph Publications, 1919), p. 19.
53. Hepworth, *Came the Dawn*, p. 161.
54. Ibid., p. 168.
55. Ibid., p. 186.

CHAPTER 3

The Road to Protection

In 1927 the British government introduced statutory protection for the film production sector in the form of the Cinematograph Films Act: this mandated that exhibitors and renters should offer by law a minimum quota of British film. The Quota Act, as it was widely known, was a response to a crisis in the mid-1920s that had brought the domestic film production industry close to collapse. American films had achieved a dominant market share in Britain: some estimates suggest that 'foreign' films accounted for 95 per cent of all those shown in British cinemas.[1] There was a growing recognition among politicians that cinema was a powerful medium of national projection: the continuing production of British films was therefore seen as necessary for presenting positive images of Britain and British life for audiences at home and abroad. Prime Minister Stanley Baldwin was one of those to recognise the importance of film for projecting Britain, telling the House of Commons in 1925:

> I think the time has come when the position of the Industry in this country should be examined with a view to seeing whether it be not possible, as it is desirable on national grounds to say that the larger proportion of films exhibited in this country are British, having regard to the enormous power which the film is developing for propaganda purposes, and the danger to which we in this country and our Empire subject ourselves if we allow that method of propaganda to be entirely in the hands of foreign countries.[2]

John Ramsden has shown that Baldwin gave 'a high priority' to the film industry and that 'the timing of his career corresponded exactly with the zenith of film as a source of information and an influence on attitudes in Britain'.[3]

The introduction of state protection for the film industry needs to be understood in the context of the economic situation in Britain in the 1920s. Britain had emerged from the war victorious but carrying heavy debts; its major manufacturing industries – steel, textiles, shipbuilding – were in long-term structural decline; it had lost a large proportion of its export markets, especially in South America and the Far East, to the United States; unemployment was high following post-war demobilisation and industrial tensions peaked with the General Strike of 1926. It did not help that the Conservative government in power between 1924 and 1929 remained wedded to orthodoxy in its economic and fiscal policy: this was exemplified by the return to the Gold Standard and maintaining an unrealistically high exchange rate of sterling against the US dollar in order to keep wages high and reduce the price of imported goods. The major debate during the 1920s was free trade versus protectionism: after the war there was growing pressure to protect key industries through imposing tariffs on imports.[4] The cinema industry reflected the wider picture of British industry insofar as the home market was exposed to American competition and the export market was small. Rachael Low provides evidence that in 1919 the average revenue of a British feature in the United States was around £800 compared to £15,000 for an American film in Britain.[5]

The end of the First World War had brought a new sense of optimism to the British cinema industry. The *Kine Year Book* reported that ninety-one British films were produced in 1919 and suggested that more capital was becoming available for production: 'Aided by large influxes of capital and much commendable enterprise, British producers have shown during 1919 that if their activities were necessarily curtailed during the years of war, they are now able to hold their own against the best that the world can produce, and their latest efforts have created a very favourable impression.'[6] In 1920 some 139 British films were produced and several large new producing and distributing concerns were established:

> A great deal of further interest in the financial side of the Industry has been evinced during the year, and it is a healthy sign that the capitalists are beginning to realise the potentialities of the motion-picture business in this country. A number of companies, for example General Film Renting Co., Ideal Films, British Famous Films, have received fresh accessions of financial support, while on the producing side the most important development was the successful flotation of the Stoll Pictures Productions, Ltd, with studios at Surbiton and Cricklewood, [which] has gone ahead till it has reached the foremost position as a purely British enterprise.[7]

The major new companies registered in the year included the Alliance Film Corporation (£1 million authorised capital), the General Film Renting Company (£600,000), British Foreign Films (£300,000) and Stoll Picture Productions (£400,000). Stoll would become the leading British producer of the early 1920s: its adaptations of the Sherlock Holmes stories of Sir Arthur Conan Doyle won critical and public acclaim at home and abroad.[8]

However, the trade's optimism disguised underlying structural weaknesses in the British cinema industry. For one thing each of the three sectors of the industry – production, distribution and exhibition – was still highly fragmented; this was in contrast to the US film industry, which by the 1920s was developing into a mature oligopoly where the process of vertical integration – the emergence of large companies with interests in each of the three sectors – contributed to the domination of the market by the 'Big Five'. In contrast the British film industry was made up of many smaller companies without anything approaching the same level of consolidation. The *Kine Year Book* for 1919 identifies twenty-three British producers and sixty-four renters: seventeen of the renters handled three quarters of all films. In total some 145 new companies were registered in 1918: most of these were on the exhibition side of the industry.[9] And for another thing the British industry was under-capitalised in comparison to its main competitor. In 1926 the statistician

Simon Rowson calculated that the total capital invested in all branches of the British industry was around £35 million: this was only 11 per cent of the £308 million (US$1,500 million) invested in the US industry.[10] While the Cinematograph Films Act would encourage more capital investment, the British industry still lagged a long way behind the United States. In 1930 the *Kine Year Book* estimated total investment in Britain at £70 million compared to £400 million for the United States.[11]

There were several reasons why investment was not readily forthcoming for British film production. One of those was that film production was a risky enterprise. Many of the new film concerns founded after the war did not survive for long: the *Kine Year Book* listed fifteen liquidations in 1921 and twenty-four in 1922. The Alliance Film Corporation, launched with much fanfare in 1919, was one of the casualties. Alliance's directors included Conservative MP and theatre impresario Sir Walter de Frece, publisher William Hutchinson and actors Gerald du Maurier and A. E. Matthews, and £229,855 of its authorised capital of £1 million was issued.[12] It paid £69,928 for the purchase of the Atlanta Film Syndicate and borrowed £25,000 from Lloyds Bank to purchase a site at Harrow Weald Park to build its own studio. It set out to produce 'super' films for the international market: it sold the American rights of *Carnival* for US$100,000, but other films did not find a US distributor and at an extraordinary general meeting on 30 December 1922 the shareholders voted to put the company into voluntary liquidation. *The Financial News* laid the blame on the trade depression of the early 1920s rather than any inherent failing on the part of the company itself:

> There seems, indeed, little reason to doubt that the Alliance Film Corporation was soundly conceived, and has very distinct dividend-earning possibilities. It is not very probable that in ordinary circumstances the difficulties met in financing the enterprise – difficulties which Sir Walter de Frece frankly laid before the shareholders – would have occurred. Circumstances, however, are far from ordinary. Even the film world and the picture houses have felt something of the wave of depression, and not in this country only.[13]

British producers also faced stiff competition from American films. There were several reasons why American films had a competitive advantage. One was the size of the American domestic market. In the mid-1920s there were five times as many cinemas in the United States (20,000) compared to Britain (4,000) and approximately four times as many tickets sold (80 million a week in America compared to 20 million a week in Britain).[14] This meant that American films were able to recover their production costs in their home market: American distributors could therefore offer their films in overseas markets at a cheaper rate than domestic producers and still make a profit. Britain was the largest overseas market for American films: it was estimated that 20 per cent of Hollywood's total revenues were earned in Britain.[15] The Americans were also supported by a powerful trade organisation in the form of the Motion Picture Producers and Distributors of America (MPPDA), which lobbied hard on behalf of the industry and had a close relationship with the US Department of Commerce.[16]

The real strength of American film interests in Britain was in the distribution sector. In 1920 a total of 878 films were offered for hire of which only 144 were British: the large majority of the remaining 734 (representing 83.6 per cent of the total) were American. Five American renters – Famous-Lasky, Fox, Vitagraph, Western Import and Goldwyn – offered 295 films of which only four were British, while the nine largest British renters – Butcher's, Film Booking Offices, Gaumont, the General Film Renting Company, Jury's Imperial, the London Independent Trading Company, Pathé, Stoll and Walturdaw – offered 322 films of which seventy were British.[17] American distributors were also able to exploit the popularity of their best films through restrictive practices such as blind and block booking: the former meant that exhibitors were obliged to take films unseen, the latter was the practice of making exhibitors accept all the films on offer in order to secure the most popular titles. *Reynolds's Illustrated News* aptly described this practice as one 'by which exhibitors have to take what they do not want in order to get what they do want'.[18]

There was also a widespread view that American films were simply better – in both their production and entertainment values – than British films. As S. G. Rayment observed:

> It is hardly too much to say that the ordinary British kinema-goer has been educated actually to prefer an American picture to a native one. Apart from the slick efficiency of direction in which even a second-rate director from the States is ahead of all but our very best, the long dominance of the American picture has developed an entirely artificial film-sense amongst our audiences, and just as the experienced showman will tell you that his crowd must have adventurous pictures, social dramas, slapstick, or whatnot, because they have been taught to expect them, so, generally speaking, do they appreciate just what they have been accustomed and thought to appreciate in the selection and treatment of stories, in which respect one might almost say that they feel that any pictures which are not constructed according to the American conventions fall short of the recognised standard.[19]

British films were often regarded as being narratively slow-paced and static in camera style when compared to the dynamic movement and fluid editing of American films. While revisionist British cinema scholarship, exemplified by the work of Andrew Higson and Christine Gledhill, has sought to rehabilitate British films of the 1920s, arguing that their pictorialism can be seen as a form of product differentiation, emphasising the literary and theatrical provenance of many British films, the fact remains that, with a few exceptions, these films were less successful with audiences than American movies.[20]

There were several industry initiatives in the early 1920s to promote British films. In 1921 a group of leading British renters led by A. C. Bromhead of the Gaumont Company and F. W. Baker of Butcher's Film Service formed the British National Film League, whereby they pledged 'to abolish "block-booking" and pool their output so as to ensure that one good British film per week could be supplied to any exhibitor'.[21] The League was an 'effort to regularise the British output': it proposed that films should be trade shown before their release and that every film should be booked on its merits rather than unseen. The *Kine Year Book* welcomed the initiative: 'It is obvious that this plan – founded on a combination of producers without any fusion of commercial interests whatever – can be made the basis of a general scheme of reform having the abolition of blind and block-booking and the reduction of the release period as its chief aims.'[22] The League also organised a series of 'British Film Weeks' in 1923–4. However, neither of these initiatives achieved any tangible results: there was no chance of significantly changing distribution practices without the co-operation of American renters, while the 'British Film Weeks' proved to be a damp squib as the films put forward by the trade were of such poor quality that they excited little interest.[23]

By the mid-1920s it was apparent that the British production sector was depressed to such an extent that it was being seen as a crisis. There had been a sharp decline in the volume of British production: the number of British feature films fell from 136 in 1921 to 95 in 1922, 75 in 1923, 56 in 1924, 45 in 1925 and only 37 in 1926.[24] The symbolic nadir came in November 1924, when all British studios were empty. As the *Kine Year Book* reported:

> In the field of British production there is a depressing account to be given . . . Fewer and fewer of our studios were kept in commission as the year wore on, more and more of our stars and directors found openings on the Continent and in America. At last, in November, we arrived at such a state of affairs that not a single foot of film was being exposed on any British floor. It was probably the first time since there has been an industry at all that this can be said.[25]

There was a view, not limited to the trade itself, that the British film production industry was on the verge of collapse. A leading article in the *Dundee Courier* entitled 'Saving Britain's Film Industry' is a typical example: 'About the desirability of saving the British cinema film industry from extinction by American competition there can be no two opinions in this country. The question is what means we should take to achieve this end.'[26]

The studio crisis coincided with the re-election of the Conservative Party following the fall of the minority Labour government. Stanley Baldwin had campaigned on a platform of no protection and had explicitly ruled out a general tariff. Baldwin's Chancellor of the Exchequer (Winston Churchill) was a free trader, while the President of the Board of Trade (Sir Philip Cunliffe-Lister) was an advocate of protectionism. By 1925 there was speculation in the trade press whether the film industry was eligible for protection under the Safeguarding of Industries Act, which imposed tariffs on imported goods that were sold at lower cost than British-produced equivalents. In May 1925 Conservative MP Sir Richard Wells asked, 'what steps it is proposed to take to prevent abnormal quantities of cinematograph films being imported into this country, in view of the new duties on these goods?'[27] (The McKenna Duties – introduced during the war, abolished in 1923 and reintroduced in 1925 – applied to imported film stock at a rate of 33.3 per cent.) The Board of Trade's own figures reported that Britain spent a total of £1,159,000 on imported film stock in 1924.[28]

The question of a more general enquiry into the state of the film production industry was raised by Conservative peer Lord Newton in April 1925. Newton put forward a motion to 'appoint a Departmental Committee to inquire into the causes of the present depression of the industry'.[29] Viscount Peel, the First Commissioner of Works, replied that the Board of Trade was already involved in 'searching investigations' into the industry. Newton raised the issue again a month later with a powerful speech during which he declared that 'the industry has now sunk to a condition in which British production of films is really little more than the renting and exhibition of foreign films, almost entirely American'. He also outlined several possible actions, including increasing duty on imported films, reciprocity agreements and the introduction of a quota for 'native-made films'. He also raised 'one further remedy, which I have also heard suggested – a practical remedy – and that is that some patriotic financier should be found who would provide the money to tide the industry over its difficulties'.[30]

Some of these measures were not politically possible. The government was reluctant to impose more tariffs beyond the reintroduction of the McKenna Duties, while a reciprocity agreement would be dependent upon the co-operation of American renters who did not show much interest in (or need for) British films. And the precarious nature of the industry made it unlikely that a 'patriotic financier' could be persuaded to bail it out. In 1920 the press baron Lord Beaverbrook, proprietor of the *Daily Express*, had briefly been a major shareholder in Provincial Cinematograph Theatres, but he had subsequently 'announced his intention of taking no further interest in the industry'.[31] The quota policy emerged almost by default. Quotas had been introduced with some success in Europe after the war. The one that was often cited in contemporary debates was the German *Kontingent* system. Germany had introduced a quota in 1921: initially it limited imports to 15 per cent of the negative footage produced in Germany. In 1924 this was changed to a system whereby renters had to handle one German film for each imported film. This had some success in maintaining a market share of around 40 per cent for German films in the 1920s.[32] However, Germany had a stronger domestic industry than Britain, including a large vertically integrated corporation in the form of UFA (Universum Film Aktiengesellschaft), which received state support.

There were several trade initiatives to attempt to find a workable solution. The Film Producers' Group of the Federation of British Industries (FBI) – an influential lobby group – held a conference on film production in May 1925: delegates included the FBI's President F. Vernon Willey, deputy director Charles Tennyson and Lord Newton. The FBI's proposals – included in a memorandum that was published in *Kine Weekly* – involved both the creation of what it called an 'assisted market' and the provision of capital:

> It is clear from these inquiries that any scheme must provide adequate capital and some assistance in securing a market for the films produced. Film production requires large capital, and in the present condition of the film market it is plainly impossible to expect capital to be forthcoming from ordinary channels on a scale adequate to restore British production to a satisfactory volume and standard.[33]

Its specific proposals were to create a protected market either by imposing 'a substantial import duty on foreign films released in Great Britain' or through the adoption 'in a modified form of the "Kontingent" system at present in force in Germany', and the provision of capital either through a government guarantee to meet necessary capital expenditure under the Trade Facilities Act of 1921 or the imposition of a levy on exhibitors from showing foreign films. It also suggested creating a finance company to administer the scheme and the 'establishment of a National Studio in order to reduce establishment charges of individual producing firms'. The national studio – which came to be referred to as a 'British Hollywood' – seems to have envisaged something similiar to UFA.

At the same time a Joint Trade Committee had been set up by the Cinematograph Exhibitors' Association and Kinematograph Renters' Society. It was concerned with reform of the release system – the abolition of blind and block booking was an issue where exhibitors and British renters were in agreement – and a quota scheme.[34] The committee's recommendations were published in the trade press in August 1925. They also included a recommendation that foreign interests should be blocked from acquiring control of British companies. The rationale for its proposals were threefold:

1. To increase the quantity and proportion of the British films screened in the United Kingdom and elsewhere;
2. To establish an industry under British control in the United Kingdom for the production of these films;
3. To encourage the production of such films as will directly or indirectly give employment to British labour at home, and increase the prestige of the British name, British institutions and British manufactured products at home and abroad.[35]

The specific proposals suggested introducing a minimum quota of British films for renters and exhibitors, starting at 10 per cent of total footage and rising to 25 per cent after three years. A 'British' film was understood as one where the producing company was British controlled, that was shot in a British studio and where 75 per cent of wages excluding the fees of the producer and one principal artiste were paid to persons living in Britain. The 'Ormiston Plan' – so known after CEA President Tom Ormiston – was approved by the CEA's General Council but rejected by a referendum of its members.[36]

Sir Philip Cunliffe-Lister had been involved in meetings with trade interests from the summer of 1925. In February 1926 he presented a paper on the film industry to the Cabinet urging that 'the Cabinet should authorise me to make an early announcement of the Government's policy with regard to the British film industry . . . the time has come when I feel I can formulate my proposals and when I feel a Government pronouncement imperative'.[37] The case that Cunliffe-Lister presented for supporting the industry prioritised its cultural and social significance with only a passing reference to its importance to trade:

> I can hardly emphasize too strongly the importance of establishing a British film industry. In Great Britain and throughout the Empire, nearly every film shown represents American ideas, set in an American atmosphere (and in American language). The accessories are American houses, American motor cars, American manufacturers, and so forth. I have no wish to attack or to malign the American industry, but cinematograph audiences are made up of the most impressionable sections of the community, and it seems to me of the utmost importance that they should see at least some proportion of British films – of importance for our prestige, for our trade, and – I am assured – for our morals. I am therefore convinced that a British film industry would be a national asset. But I am anxious not to underrate the difficulties, and not to undertake ambitious measures which might overweight an infant industry.[38]

Cunliffe-Lister went on to outline the reasons for American dominance and to summarise the options available. At this stage, the paper reveals, he did not favour a mandatory quota:

> To deal with this situation, I have been pressed to take immediate and drastic action and force a quota of British films on all exhibitors. But to do that would antagonise many of the exhibitors. They have a genuine and natural fear lest they might be compelled to show poor pictures, pictures which would not draw audiences. If that fear were realised, it might kill the movement for British films in the same way that the voluntary 'British film weeks' of 1923, by giving a chance to the worst films, did so much harm.[39]

Instead, he proposed that exhibitors should be asked 'to make a genuine voluntary effort to take as from a given date in the future an agreed proportion of British films' with the option of legislation to be left open if the trade interests were not able to reach agreement within a year. He also suggested that 'we should give our blessing to the idea of a national studio, provided a sound scheme with proper financial backing is put forward': to this end he seemed to hope that Lord Ashfield – Chairman of Provincial Cinematograph Theatres and himself a former President of the Board of Trade – might have been involved.[40]

In March 1926 Cunliffe-Lister tasked the trade with reaching a voluntary agreement, while maintaining that 'if voluntary efforts fail, I am authorised to say that the Government will not hesitate to seek such powers. But there are, I think – and I am authorised to speak for the Government to-day – obvious objections to seeking such powers if the end can be obtained without them.'[41] The Joint Trade Committee was reconstituted 'to further explore avenues towards a solution of the British film production difficulty'.[42] Discussions took place for several months but no agreement could be reached. In early August the Joint Trade Committee reported 'that there is now no possible chance of an agreed scheme being produced from within the industry itself'. *The Times* remarked: 'Such a confession of failure has been expected for some weeks now, and the report has caused no surprise.'[43] *Kine Weekly* called out the 'greedy and impolitic quibbling' between trade factions and described the outcome 'as abject a confession of incompetence as a Minister can have received from a responsible group of business men'.[44]

While the failure to reach a voluntary agreement made government action likely, Cunliffe-Lister did not move immediately. He wanted to wait until the Imperial Conference in London in November 1926. This was the latest in a series of occasional meetings between the heads of governments of the Dominions that had been running since 1911: the conference focused on both constitutional and economic matters – including the doctrine of Imperial Preference, of which Cunliffe-Lister was an advocate. Film quotas were on the agenda of an economic sub-committee at the London conference: it received evidence that the same problem as in Britain was prevalent throughout the Dominions. British Empire-produced films accounted for only 10 per cent of those shown in New Zealand, 8 per cent in Australia and a mere 1 per cent in Canada. The conference resolved 'that it is of the greatest importance that a larger and increasing proportion of the films exhibited throughout the Empire should be of Empire production' and supported 'the remedial measures proposed to the consideration of the governments of the various parts of the Empire with a view to such early and effective action to deal with the serious situation as they may severally find possible'.[45] The Imperial Conference was important in the framing of the Cinematograph Films Bill, as the definition of a 'British' film would be extended to include those produced anywhere in the British Empire.

In 1927 the Board of Trade moved ahead with statutory protection for the industry. Cunliffe-Lister's proposals were 'generally approved' by the Cabinet on 2 February 1927.[46] The Cinematograph Films Bill combined aspects of both the FBI's proposals (although the films bank had been dropped) and the 'Ormiston Plan'. The Bill was in four parts. Part I introduced clauses restricting blind booking and advance booking and stipulating that all films should be trade shown within six months of the rental agreement, and part II dealt with the process of registering films with the Board of Trade. Part III included the substantive clauses. The quota would be set initially at 7.5 per cent for both renters and exhibitors, rising to 25 per cent by the mid-1930s: the quota percentages were calculated on the total footage offered by renters and screened by exhibitors during the quota year. To be eligible for quota, the 'maker' of the film had to be a British subject (the 'maker' was defined as 'the person by whom the arrangements necessary for the production of the film are undertaken', which describes the role of the producer); the production company had to be 'constituted under the law of some part of the British Empire' and where 'the majority of the voting power of which is in the hands of persons who are British subjects'; the studio scenes must have been shot in a studio in Britain or the British Empire; the author of either the 'scenario' of the film or the 'original work' on which it was based should be a British subject; and a minimum of 75 per cent of salary costs – excluding the 'producer' (defined as 'the person responsible for the organisation of the scenes to be depicted on the film', which more accurately describes the role of the director) and one actor or actress (to allow the employment of foreign stars) – should be paid to British subjects or persons resident in Britain or the British Empire. Part IV included clauses for a Cinematograph Advisory Committee of eleven members: eight representatives of the trade and three 'independent' members.[47]

The Cinematograph Films Bill had its first reading in the House of Commons on 10 March 1927. Cunliffe-Lister's opening speech for the second reading on 16 March – the occasion for the major set-piece debate over the proposed legislation – rehearsed the now-familiar argument for the cultural significance of film:

> [The] cinema is to-day the most universal means through which national ideas and national atmosphere can be spread, and even if these be intangible things, surely they are among the most important influences in civilisation ... To-day films are shown to millions of people throughout the Empire and must ever so obviously influence the ideas and outlook of British people of all races. But only a fraction, something like 5 per cent, of the films which are at present shown in the British Empire are of British origin. That, as I submit and as the Imperial Conference held, is a position which is intolerable if we can do anything effective to remedy it.[48]

This might be seen as a pre-emptive attempt to deflect the debate away from the politically controversial subject of protectionism versus free trade onto the idea of film as a medium of national projection on which there was broad agreement across parties. Cunliffe-Lister also sought to present himself as a reluctant interventionist who had been obliged to bring forward legislation only following the failure to reach a voluntary agreement by the trade:

> If all sections of the trade, the producers, the renters and the exhibitors, could have agreed upon a combined voluntary effort which would have been effective, there would have been no need for Government action, and the Government were determined that an opportunity should be given to the trade to make such an effort. In view of some of the criticisms, I think it is only right that the House should realise that an attempt was made within the trade, and that that attempt failed in spite of the very genuine effort made by a large number both of exhibitors and renters.[49]

Cunliffe-Lister was evidently pushing some responsibility for the legislation onto the trade interests: 'I asked them to agree upon a voluntary scheme, but I made it clear that if the voluntary effort failed, the Government would not hesitate to seek compulsory powers.'[50]

The ensuing debate – which included tangential asides on such subjects as whether actors in British films should wear British-made clothes and whether the nationality requirement for original works applied to films based on the Bible – proved such a lively affair that it had to be adjourned to a second day. The main argument against the legislation was that it privileged the interests of producers over renters and exhibitors. The Labour Party opposed it on the grounds that it was 'a party Bill'. Labour leader James Ramsay MacDonald argued: 'It has been prompted and handed over almost Clause by Clause by one side engaged and interested in this controversy – the side of the producers, and not all of them, but one section of the producers.'[51] He averred that it 'puts a possible monopoly in the hands of a group of British film producers . . . He creates the monopoly, as the producers who are behind the Bill desire him to do, and he leaves it with them to fix their trade terms.'[52] Labour MP Harry Day, a theatre and cinema owner, called the Bill 'iniquitous . . . All that it does is to protect the producer who, it is acknowledged, cannot produce films in this country properly.'[53] Walter Runciman, for the Liberal Party, averred 'that this Bill has been devised by those who have a commercial interest in the British film industry, and have no consideration whatsoever for those who get either enjoyment or education out of attendance at the picture palaces.'[54] Arguments were made against the quota on the grounds that the same principle of minimum British content would never be applied to concert performances or music hall. However, there was support from the government benches. Sir Charles Oman, MP for Oxford, reminded the House: 'We are only trying to restore to the film industry the state of things which had existed before the War, not trying to introduce a wholly new and different status.'[55] And Reginald Applin, MP for Enfield: 'We have to get back into the film industry, and we cannot do it unless we have some manner of compelling renters and exhibitors to take at least a small proportion of British films.'[56] Others distanced themselves from the detail while accepting that some action was necessary. Sir Alfred Butt, a former theatre impresario, said: 'Personally, I do not like the Bill . . . [The President of the Board of Trade] has been forced to introduce a measure of his own initiative; and whilst it may be bad to start protecting any particular industry, I think the House ought to weigh up the evil and the remedy, and see which it is the more advantageous to accept.'[57] After the debate went to a second day, the second reading was passed by 243 votes to 135.

Cunliffe-Lister had accepted at several points during the debate that specific points of detail could be revised when the Bill went to Standing Committee. He was even prepared to reconsider some clauses himself. A memo to Chancellor of the Exchequer Winston Churchill suggested a form of Imperial Preference for imported negative film:

> I have been wondering whether it would not be possible to proceed further than I have done in the Cinematograph Films Bill with the recommendations of the General Economic Sub-Committee of the Imperial Conference on the methods which might be adopted to assist British Empire films, and to grant a preference of 100 per cent to films made within the Empire . . . At the present time the quantity of negative films imported – and it is only on *negative* films that I suggest a concession – complying with the existing regulations requiring 25 per cent of British Empire labour to obtain the one-third imperial preference, is only about 40,000 feet, so that the revenue involved is very small. It would, however, no doubt increase as the film-making industry in the Empire develops.[58]

Churchill agreed this suggestion, but a follow-up letter from the Board of Trade indicated that 'the President has now come to the conclusion that the best course would be to leave the position as it is and in the Finance Act of next year to exempt from duty films which comply with the definition of British as laid down in the Cinematograph Films Bill'.[59]

The Films Bill was widely debated in the press. The letters and commentary reveal that opinions were as polarised as they had been during the debate. Sir Oswald Stoll felt that the protection did not go far enough: he suggested that 'it ensures for all time that at least 75 per cent of the screen space and screen values in Great Britain in feature pictures will be reserved for non-British films'. He also highlighted a loophole in the proposal that production companies should be British controlled: 'A non-British combine is free to form a subsidiary company here with British capital, and in that guise to make the British pictures which will constitute the necessary quota. The capital need not control the company even if the shares be held by actual investors rather than by mere nominees.'[60] The *Daily Herald* published a letter from Harry Day – a participant in the Commons debate – arguing against the Bill: 'The general public is probably unaware how restrictive are the measures which the Government intends to impose on the trade. The Bill – which is at present in Committee – becomes daily more and more unpopular with those whom it professes to help.'[61]

The public discourse around the Films Bill highlighted two broader political issues: free trade versus protectionism, and attitudes towards America. The popular press – including the Rothermere and Harmsworth titles – were in favour of the Bill. For the *Sunday Pictorial*:

> The enemies of the Cinematograph Films Bill have appeared just as expected. They are either Americans who resent any modification of their virtual monopoly in this country, or they are British people who have, or imagine they have, large interests in American film companies. This opposition, however, is immaterial. The Bill is sound in principle and will certainly become law.[62]

And the *Daily Mail* asked:

> Why is it that opponents of the Cinematograph Films Bill are such 'dismal Jimmies' and are indulging in such gloomy prophecies about the future of the British film? . . . The fact is that many of the pessimists are interested parties. They are saying that British films are bad and can't succeed because *they want them to be bad and don't want them to succeed*. The foreign interests which have captured so large a share of the British film market have been busily working underground to keep their hold, and, if they can, to defeat the Government's Bill.[63]

The 'City Correspondent' of the *Daily Chronicle* suggested, somewhat facetiously, that the worst outcome of the Bill 'means that bad American films will be replaced by bad British films'.[64] This argument was rejected by *The Bioscope* as being 'without foundation':

> We are afraid that 'A City Correspondent' is writing without full knowledge of the facts of the situation. The Bill is certainly going to encourage quantity, but the

exhibitors' choice will be wide enough to ensure that only those British films which possess quality will be shown widely. If British companies try to produce on the cheap, hoping to make vast profits, they will be very seriously disappointed.[65]

And Labour MP Josiah Wedgwood told the press: 'The Cinematograph Films Bill is inspired by vulgar Balham-Tootingish hatred of America.'[66]

The Films Bill underwent a number of amendments during its Standing Committee stage. Indeed it spent so long in Committee that a *Times* leader could remark that it 'will have the distinction at all events of having secured in Committee more hours of Parliamentary time than were ever warranted by its importance'.[67] There were some 250 amendments, mostly on administrative matters. The most significant were that the quota was to be in force for ten years rather than twelve; the starting point for exhibitors' quota was reduced from 7.5 per cent to 5 per cent (this was in response to lobbying from exhibitors who argued that they should be offered some choice in which films to take from each renter) and the top end for both renters' and exhibitors' quota was set at 20 per cent by 1936 rather than 25 per cent; short films (under 3,000 feet) were not to be included in the quota; and the definition of a British film was changed to one that was made by a 'British company' (understood as one where a majority of the directors were British) rather than a 'British-controlled company'. A stipulation that exhibitors would be exempt from the quota if they could show they had been unable to secure a sufficient quality of British films was met with incredulity by *The Times*:

> None but LEWIS CARROLL could do justice to this conclusion of an Act of Parliament designed to initiate and provide for the enforcement of a quota. The section exhibits a damning realization by the Government that it is very unjust and unreasonable to compel a merchant to trade in goods which, but for the compulsion, he would reject – a realization, in short, that a quota Bill which does nothing to encourage high quality in the privileged and enforced supply is not defensible on any commercial principle.[68]

In contrast the *Daily Mail*, which supported the legislation, thought that 'the Cinematograph Films Bill has already been so emasculated that it seems now to depend entirely on its definition of a "British" film . . . A British film should not only be *financed and controlled by Britons but actually directed by a Briton from a scenario written by a Briton*.'[69]

The Cinematograph Films Bill passed its third reading by 223 votes to 125 and received royal assent on 22 December 1927. It came into effect on 1 April 1928 and would be in force until 31 March 1938. *Kine* editor S. G. Rayment felt that it 'will probably be found to be generally helpful, and it is to the credit of the President of the Board of Trade that he has so freely entered into consultations with the leaders of the Industry and has accepted representation from all sections'.[70] *The Financial Times* welcomed the quota as 'it is hoped that under the Cinematograph Films Act the production of British films will receive a fillip'.[71] However, *The Economist* was more cautious, on the grounds that the Act 'implied that, regardless of quality,

British films must be produced, [and] acted as an invitation to the company promoter and to the public to subscribe to any and every film company issue'.[72]

Later assessments of the Cinematograph Films Act – influenced by knowledge of the proliferation of low-cost 'quota quickies' in the 1930s – have tended to be rather jaundiced. Rachael Low, for example, contends that 'the quota did make room on the screens for British films of a sort, and thus did bring capital into the production industry . . . But it also led straight to the disastrous decline in quality which had clearly been foreseen by so many people.'[73] In truth, however, the concern that a guaranteed market for British films would inevitably lead to the production of low-cost and low-quality films had not been a major feature of the debate around the Cinematograph Films Bill. Margaret Dickinson and Sarah Street conclude that 'the mechanism adopted to combat the "Hollywood invasion" was not really appropriate as a means of establishing a flourishing British film industry which would be independent of American economic and cultural influence'.[74] By requiring American renters to produce or sponsor films for British quota, the Act drew American interests more closely than before into the production and financing of British films.

To some extent the Cinematograph Films Act was a political syllogism: there was a consensus that something needed to be done to support the ailing film production industry and the quota legislation became that something. The next two chapters will explore the financial and economic consequences of the Quota Act. On the one hand the Act did act as a stimulant to the British production sector – its primary aim – and as a catalyst for the injection of more capital into the industry; on the other hand many of the films produced in the expectation of guaranteed screen time were indeed of low quality. However, the real significance of the Act was not its immediate impact upon British film production but the principle that had been established: that the cinema deserved to be regarded as a vital national industry and that it merited some form of protection. It created a framework for statutory protection of the domestic production sector that, with various modifications, would remain in force for nearly half a century until it was finally removed in the 1980s.

Notes

1. *The British Film Industry: A Report on its History and Present Organisation, with Special Reference to the Economic Problems of British Feature Film Production* (London: Political and Economic Planning, 1952), p. 41.
2. *Parliamentary Debates: House of Commons*, 5th Series, vol. 185, 29 June 1925, col. 2084.
3. J. A. Ramsden, 'Baldwin and film', in Nicholas Pronay and D. W. Spring (eds), *Propaganda, Politics and Film, 1918-45* (London: Macmillan, 1982), p. 127.
4. W. R. Garside, 'Party Politics, Political Economy and British Protectionism, 1919–1932', *History*, 269 (1998), pp. 47–65.
5. Rachael Low, *The History of the British Film 1918–1929* (London: George Allen & Unwin, 1971), p. 79.

6. G. A. Atkinson, 'The Story of the Year', *Kinematograph Year Book Diary and Directory 1920* (London: Kinematograph Publications, 1920), p. 12.
7. Frank A. Tilley, 'The Story of the Year', *Kinematograph Year Book Diary and Directory 1921* (London: Kinematograph Publications, 1921), p. 11.
8. Nathalie Morris, 'An Eminent British Series: *The Adventures of Sherlock Holmes* and the Stoll Film Company, 1921–23', *Journal of British Cinema and Television*, 4: 1 (2007), pp. 18–36.
9. *The Kinematograph Year Book Diary and Directory 1919* (London: Kinematograph Publications, 1919), pp. 142–5, 158–9.
10. Margaret Dickinson and Sarah Street, *Cinema and State: The Film Industry and the British Government 1927–84* (London: British Film Institute, 1985), p. 10.
11. 'Capital Invested in the Film Industry', *Kinematograph Year Book Diary and Directory 1930* (London: Kinematograph Publications, 1930), p. 214.
12. The National Archives (TNA) BT 31/32328/160000: Certificate of Incorporation and Statement of the Nominal Capital of Alliance Film Corporation, 27 October 1919.
13. *The Financial News*, 2 May 1921.
14. These were the statistics quoted by Lord Newington in the course of a debate in the House of Lords. *Parliamentary Debates: House of Lords*, 5th Series, vol. 61, 14 May 1925, col. 273.
15. 'The Film World', *The Daily Chronicle*, 25 March 1927, p. 5.
16. Kristin Thompson, *Exporting Entertainment: America in the World Film Market, 1907–34* (London: British Film Institute, 1985), pp. 117–24.
17. Political and Economic Planning, *The British Film Industry*, p. 40.
18. 'The Case for British Films', *Reynolds's Illustrated News*, 20 March 1927, p. 14.
19. S. G. Rayment, 'The Story of 1924', *Kinematograph Year Book Diary and Directory 1925* (London: Kinematograph Publications, 1925), p. 12.
20. Andrew Higson, *Waving the Flag: Constructing a National Cinema in Britain* (Oxford: Clarendon Press, 1995), pp. 26–97; Christine Gledhill, *Reframing British Cinema, 1918–1928: Between Restraint and Passion* (London: British Film Institute, 2003), pp. 31–63.
21. 'Fighting American Films', *The Daily News*, 10 November 1921, p. 5.
22. 'The Story of the Year', *Kinematograph Year Book Diary and Directory 1922* (London: Kinematograph Publications, 1922), p. 1.
23. Olly Gruner, '"Good Business, Good Policy, Good Patriotism": The British Film Weeks of 1924', *Historical Journal of Film, Radio and Television*, 32: 1 (2013), pp. 41–56.
24. Dickinson and Street, *Cinema and State*, p. 13.
25. S. G. Rayment, 'The Story of 1924', *Kinematograph Year Book Diary and Directory 1925* (London: Kinematograph Publications, 1925), p. 11.
26. 'Saving Britain's Film Industry', *The Dundee Courier*, 3 July 1925, p. 4.
27. *Parliamentary Debates: House of Commons*, 5th Series, vol. 183, 7 May 1925, col. 1130.
28. 'Film Imports', *Kinematograph Weekly*, 2 July 1925, p. 44.
29. *Parliamentary Debates: House of Lords*, 5th Series, vol. 60, 29 April 1925, col. 1089.
30. *Parliamentary Debates: House of Lords*, 5th Series, vol. 61, 14 May 1925, cols 274–81.
31. Tilley, 'The Story of the Year', p. 10.
32. Thompson, *Exporting Entertainment*, pp. 106–7.
33. 'To Revive Production: FBI's Summary of the Rival Plans', *Kinematograph Weekly*, 6 August 1925, p. 38.

34. 'CEA and its committees', *Kinematograph Weekly*, 9 January 1925, p. 65.
35. '"Quota" Triumphs', *Kinematograph Weekly*, 5 August 1925, p. 28.
36. 'CEA States its "Plans"', *Kinematograph Weekly*, 17 September 1925, p. 73.
37. TNA CO 24/178/70: Cabinet Paper No. 69: 'The British Film Industry: Memorandum by the President of the Board of Trade', 16 February 1926.
38. Ibid., pp. 1–2.
39. Ibid., p. 3.
40. Ibid., p. 6.
41. 'Government and British Films', *The Bioscope*, 18 March 1926, p. 36.
42. 'Joint Trade Committee Meeting', *The Bioscope*, 1 April 1926, p. 18.
43. 'British Film Industry', *The Times*, 3 August 1926, p. 8.
44. '"The Times" and the Joint Committee's Failure', *Kinematograph Weekly*, 12 August 1926, p. 49.
45. TNA CAB 32/59: Imperial Conference: General Economic Sub-Committee, 13th Report, 18 November 1926.
46. TNA CO 32/397/41: Cabinet 6 (27), 'The Film Industry', 2 February 1927.
47. *Cinematograph Films: A Bill to Restrict Blind Booking and Advance Booking of Cinematograph Films, and to Secure the Renting and Exhibition of a Certain Proportion of British Films and for Purposes Concerned Therein*, AD 1927, 17 Geo 5.
48. *Parliamentary Debates: House of Commons*, 5th Series, vol. 203, 16 March 1927, col. 2039.
49. Ibid., col. 2042.
50. Ibid.
51. Ibid., col. 2052.
52. Ibid., col. 2053.
53. Ibid., col. 2073.
54. Ibid., col. 2062.
55. Ibid., col. 2066.
56. *Parliamentary Debates: House of Commons*, 5th Series, vol. 204, 22 March 1927, col. 258.
57. *Parliamentary Debates: House of Commons*, 5th Series, vol. 203, 16 March 1927, col. 2090.
58. TNA BT 64/1: P. Cunliffe-Lister to Winston Churchill, 13 April 1927.
59. Ibid.: Percy Ashley to C. J. T. S. Grylls, 18 May 1927.
60. 'The British Films Quota: Sir Oswald Stoll's View', *The Times*, 15 March 1927, p. 14.
61. 'Cinematograph Films Bill', *Daily Herald*, 16 May 1927, p. 4.
62. 'Film Bill Opposition', *Sunday Pictorial*, 20 March 1927, p. 5.
63. 'British Vitality and British Films', *Daily Mail*, 29 April 1927, p. 10.
64. 'The Film World: Better Films', *Daily Chronicle*, 25 March 1927, p. 5.
65. 'The Wrong Way', *The Bioscope*, 5 May 1927, p. 32.
66. 'Points of View', *Reynolds's Illustrated News*, 17 July 1927, p. 13.
67. 'The Films Bill Amended', *The Times*, 6 August 1927, p. 11.
68. Ibid.
69. 'Real British Films', *Daily Mail*, 14 July 1927, p. 8 (original emphasis).
70. S. G. Rayment, 'The Story of 1927', *Kinematograph Year Book Diary and Directory 1928* (London: Kinematograph Publications, 1928), p. 9.
71. 'British Trade Prospects', *The Financial Times*, 30 December 1927, p. 7.
72. 'Company Promotions of 1928 – An Inquest', *The Economist*, 17 August 1929, p. 317.
73. Low, *The History of the British Film 1918–1929*, pp. 105–6.
74. Dickinson and Street, *Cinema and State*, p. 33.

CHAPTER 4

Capitalisation and Consolidation

The late 1920s was a period of far-reaching change and transformation for the British cinema industry. A combination of factors – including the introduction of the Cinematograph Films Act, the advent of the commercial sound film, and the emergence of two large vertically-integrated combines with interests in production, distribution and exhibition – entirely transformed the structure of the industry. The establishment of British International Pictures (March 1926) and the Gaumont-British Picture Corporation (March 1927) saw the adoption in Britain of the model of industrial and economic organisation that had already become established in the US film industry. And the Cinematograph Films Act was the catalyst for the injection of large amounts of new capital into the production sector of the industry. *The Economist* calculated in July 1928 that public share issues of production companies worth over £2.4 million had been made since the introduction of the Films Bill in Parliament and that £1,936,750 of the total had been subscribed in cash.[1] S. G. Rayment noted in his review of the year for the *Kine Year Book*: 'Money, which has in past years fought shy of pictures except perhaps in the theatre end of the business, has flowed much more freely, and as a consequence there is a much more promising support available for production than ever before.'[2] *The Bioscope* – which had previously bemoaned the lack of capital investment in British production – was now equivocal about the entrance of major sources of finance-capital into the industry: 'This entrance of bankers as protagonists in the British film drama may be regarded as inaugurating a new phase of the business – a phase which follows the line of development of the American industry, where the individuality of showmen is being replaced steadily by the impersonal commercial machine.'[3]

The expansion of the production sector in the late 1920s is evident from the number of new companies set up either side of the Cinematograph Films Act. A total of 122 new production concerns were registered between January 1927 and December 1929.[4] While many of these were small concerns with only nominal capital, a fair number were more substantial outfits. As well as the two combines, those with authorised capital of at least £50,000 that made public share issues in the twelve months either side of the introduction of the Act were Whitehall Films (March 1927), British Filmcraft Productions (November 1927), the British Lion Film Corporation (November 1927), Burlington Films (January 1928), the

British and Dominions Film Corporation (February 1928), British Associated Cinematograph Films (February 1928), New Era National Pictures (February 1928), Welsh-Pearson-Elder Films (February 1928), British Screen Productions (March 1928), the Blattner Film Corporation (May 1928) and the British Colonial Film Corporation (June 1928).[5] In many respects the rapid expansion of the production sector in the late 1920s was reminiscent of the cinema-building boom before the First World War: a mushrooming of new concerns founded in order to cash in on apparently favourable conditions that attracted lavish investment from the public on the basis of highly speculative share prospectuses. *The Economist* was prompted to caution against the investment boom: it suggested that 'indefensible' share issues had been made 'for the most part by unproved companies inviting money from the public for the production of new films by untried organisations'. It felt that the Cinematograph Films Act had already given rise to unforeseen consequences:

> The Parliamentary supporters of the Films Act perhaps never considered the financial consequences of their well-meaning measure of protection for the British film industry ... [As] far as we know no one in Parliament foresaw the dangerous opportunity which the Films Act gave to the financial promoters of film companies. With the Government declaring that they must have British films at any price, an invitation was in effect given to the company promoters to get busy, and the public were in effect encouraged to subscribe money to any film promotion they offered.[6]

It soon became apparent – as it had before 1914 – that the film industry was not the pot of gold that its promoters claimed. In November 1929 *The Economist* reported that twelve new film companies with a total issued capital of £2,265,607 were now valued on the Stock Exchange at only £613,255: subscribers had lost nearly three quarters of their investments. Among the companies that had published their accounts, those trading at a loss included Whitehall Films (-£31,246), British and Foreign Films (-£37,457), the British Lion Film Corporation (-£14,303) and the British and Dominions Film Corporation (-£5,387). The biggest loss was sustained by Welsh-Pearson-Elder Films, whose accounts revealed receipts of only £11,629 against expenditure of £178,301. There were modest profits for the Blattner Film Corporation (£2,422), New Era National Pictures (£18,734) and Gainsborough Pictures (£14,185), though these were significantly less than the profits anticipated in the companies' prospectuses. The report was particularly critical of the promoters of film share issues as

> the prospectuses did not always make clear to the investing public that the first twelve months of a company's career are a period of initial development, during which little or no revenue was accrued from the films produced ... Unfortunately, the Films Act deluded the public into thinking that British films had only to be made, irrespective of quality, to bring in money.[7]

Many of the new production companies proved to be short-lived concerns: there were fifty liquidations in 1930 alone.[8] The reason most commonly advanced for their failure was the arrival of talking pictures. In this narrative the unexpected success of the 'talkies' took the industry by surprise and was responsible for putting many of the smaller producers out of business. The talkies arrived in Britain in the autumn of 1928 when Warner Bros.' *The Jazz Singer* (the first feature with synchronised sound and dialogue) and *The Singing Fool* were shown in London. British studios – including Elstree, Islington, Twickenham and Walton – installed sound equipment and the first British sound films were produced in 1929.[9] Initially there was some resistance to talkies: some critics regretted the demise of the silent film, which had achieved the maturity of an art form (a view associated with the journal *Close-Up*, which represented the voice of intellectual film culture in Britain in the late 1920s), while many exhibitors thought that sound would be a short-lived novelty. There were also technical problems to overcome: rival sound systems competed for a while until RCA and Western Electric became the industry norms. Nevertheless, it was soon apparent that the talkies were here to stay. By the end of 1929 there were 685 cinemas in the United Kingdom wired for sound: by the end of 1930 this figure had risen to over 2,500.[10] The rush to convert to sound left producers and distributors with unreleased silent films sitting on the shelf that suddenly were deemed to have little or no commercial value. At the end of 1929 it was estimated that British producers had a total of £894,340 invested in unreleased silent pictures: some of these were released with the addition of a musical soundtrack and billed as 'synchronised' films, although it is unlikely that many would have recouped the additional cost.[11] The smaller distributors were also affected: British Exhibitors Films had invested £15,000 in a silent picture entitled *To What Red Hell* but was left with a film that 'was quite valueless'.[12]

The case of Gainsborough Pictures exemplifies how the rapid adoption of talking pictures affected even the better-capitalised production units. Gainsborough had recapitalised in 1928 – it now held fully paid-up capital of £262,500 – and had returned a modest profit in 1929. In his speech to the Annual General Meeting in 1930, however, chairman C. M. Woolf explained that the company had 'considerable capital locked up in silent product':

> There were two courses and only two courses possible – either to jettison our silent films completed and partially completed, or to synchronise them with sound, music and dialogue sequences . . . We chose the lesser of two evils and converted our films, but before they could be converted and booked, the market was flooded with a large number of foreign all-talking productions, which exhibitors preferred to the synchronised variety.[13]

In 1928 Gainsborough had spent £120,258 on the production of six silent pictures: the cost of converting those films to synchronous sound was another £38,111.[14] However, the combined revenues of the same films (including both home and foreign markets) amounted to only £85,117.[15] Even allowing for a 'special amortisation' of £50,000 to write off its silent films, Gainsborough still recorded a loss of £49,807 for the year.[16]

In January 1930 *Kine Weekly*'s studio correspondent P. L. Mannock reported that 'we have arrived at a stage where not a single silent film is being made. The period of transition has been costly, painful and laborious . . . A year ago I predicted the collapse of more than one of the spate of new companies whose existence, so patently due to the Films Act, was one of promotion rather than prospect.'[17] However, the narrative that the failure of these companies was due in sole or large measure to the arrival of talkies may be contested. There is evidence that poor management and lack of sufficient trade expertise were often significant factors. The case of Whitehall Films is a good example. This company was registered in 1927 and its share issue of £200,000 was 'heavily oversubscribed'.[18] Its directors included three eminent persons – Sir Edward Bethune (retired general), Nicholas Gratton (Conservative MP) and war correspondent Sir Basil Clarke – who found themselves all at sea when their experienced managing directors (Charles Lapworth, Aldelqui Millar and Norman Pogson) resigned following a dispute over their remuneration. Whitehall Films acquired the distribution rights to several European pictures, including Carl Dreyer's *The Passion of Joan of Arc*, and produced three films of its own – *Juan Jose*, *The Inseparables* and *St George and the Dragon* – but it lost over £38,000 by underwriting a failed share issue in Union Cinemas and spent over twice its estimate of £25,000 on the acquisition of studios. In March 1930 the company was liquidated with a deficiency of £193,517. Brethune, the chairman of the board, blamed its losses on the 'disastrous effects of talking pictures on silent pictures'.[19] However, the Official Receiver attributed its failure to other reasons including 'the complete failure of the managing directors to work in unity, extravagant expenditure, the purchase of three foreign films without arranging for proper distribution, and liability incurred by the underwriting'.[20] Whitehall Films was the first major casualty but it would not be the last: New Era National Pictures, British Talking Pictures and British Filmcraft all followed in short order.

The arrival of talking pictures had initially seemed to herald even greater opportunity for investing in the film industry. There was a rush to launch new film companies in 1929 in order to profit from the popularity of talkies. In particular, several major new concerns were announced to produce multiple-language films: the practice of shooting different versions of the same film simultaneously utilising the same sets but with different casts and crews. The most ambitious was International Talking Screen Productions (ITSP), which was announced with much fanfare in April 1929. ITSP was set up to acquire the share capital of four existing companies and merge them into one: British Screen Productions, the Rayart Film Corporation of New York, and Staaken Filmwerke and Deutsche-Russische Film Alliance of Berlin. Its plan was to produce multiple-language films and its prospectus declared: 'Success in the film industry depends largely upon securing world markets for the films produced . . . The Company will be a unique organisation, being the first of its kind to control an International Film Industry comprising production and distribution in three of the principal revenue-producing countries of the world.'[21] However, investors proved wary: the £850,000 share issue was undersubscribed by nearly 90 per cent.[22]

World Studio Centre was a similar initiative: it was proposed by Sir Gordon Craig, managing director of British Movietonews, and distributor J. D. Williams with the ambition of producing '30 "original" (master version) pictures' a year in six languages.[23] In March 1930 the Lord Privy Seal was asked to provide a letter of support for the undertaking. A Treasury official noted that 'the City generally is prejudiced against the Br. Film Industry, but the Midland Bank are prepared to underwrite this scheme if the Govt would give the kind of encouragement involved in yr writing a letter on the lines of the attached draft'.[24] However, the Board of Trade advised against any declaration of official support:

> The enterprise could hardly be a success unless the English versions succeed in competing in the market with American productions, and it is very much to be doubted that whether the sudden throwing upon the market by a new organisation of a greatly increased number of British films would be good either for the new organisation or for the British industry in general.
>
> In any case, the enterprise is bound to be a speculative one. Neither the trade nor the public have yet forgotten the heavy losses sustained by investment in various new film producing companies about the time of the passing of the Films Act, and the Government would expose themselves to criticism for which there might be a good deal of justification if they attempted to encourage the now less willing public to repeat the experiment.[25]

Again, the World Studio Centre proved to be big on ambition but short on achievement: it does not seem to have produced any films. The multiple-language film experiment did not persist long into the 1930s: the strategy was not cost-effective due to the expense incurred in rewriting scripts and the alternative casts required for the different versions.[26]

In August 1931 *The Economist* reported:

> Most of the "bubble" promotions have disappeared or no longer count – the advent of the "talkies" gave them their *coup de grâce* – and the few survivors, together with the pre-Act companies, the Gaumont-British and British International Pictures and a few floating private enterprises, are now beginning to show results in quantity, even if the quality of British films has not yet achieved the level of the best American productions.[27]

The emergence of two heavily capitalised vertically-integrated combines can be attributed in large measure to the Cinematograph Films Act: the Act created the conditions for vertical integration insofar as the introduction of the quota placed groups with their own cinema circuits and distribution organisations at an advantage as they could guarantee a wide release for their own films which in turn made it easier to raise capital for production. To this extent the Act may be seen as a catalyst for the emergence of a British studio system in the 1930s: the two combines – supplemented by several smaller producer-distributors and independent producers – formed the nucleus of the British film production industry until the financing crisis of 1937 brought about further reorganisation.[28]

The two British 'majors' emerged from the same industrial and economic contexts in the late 1920s but they were quite different beasts. British International Pictures (BIP) was first registered as a private company in March 1926, a full two years before the quota came into force. The driving force behind it was John Maxwell, a Scottish solicitor who had entered the industry as an exhibitor before the war and had founded the distributor Wardour Films with Arthur Dent and J. A. Thorpe in 1923. Maxwell was backed by the Commercial Bank of Scotland and the District Bank. In January 1927 he joined the board of British National Pictures, which increased its capital in order 'to increase production to include a number of pictures designed for the British Empire market and to be made under the direction of Alfred Hitchcock'.[29] The share issue was underwritten by Wardour Films. A few months later BIP acquired the full share capital of British National – which owned the newly completed Elstree Studios, then the largest and best-equipped production facility in Britain – for a reported price of £100,000.[30] At this point it was stated that there was 'no possibility' of a public share issue. However, in November 1927 BIP offered £600,000 of share capital: this was to acquire control of Wardour Films on the grounds that '[the] rise and importance of the Company's output of pictures make it necessary for the Company to secure its own distributing organisation'.[31] It was reported 'that small and trade applications have received special consideration and will be alloted in full': this was Maxwell's strategy to maintain control of the corporation in which he was the largest single ordinary shareholder.[32]

BIP continued to expand. In August 1928 it acquired the whole share capital of First National-Pathé, another renting concern recently formed through the merger of First National and Pathé Frères.[33] BIP now controlled interests in production and distribution: the natural next step was to move into exhibition. In January 1928 Maxwell had registered Associated British Cinemas (ABC), again initially as a private company with capital of £50,000. BIP had a controlling interest in the new company. In November 1928 ABC went public with a share issue of £1 million of which three quarters was issued.[34] ABC was set up for the purpose of acquiring control of cinemas: it bought Savoy Cinemas (ten cinemas in London) and Scottish Cinema and Variety Theatres (twenty-four cinemas in Glasgow). Early in 1929 it increased its capital to £2 million and continued its programme of cinema acquisition so that by the end of the year it owned eighty-eight sites.[35] Maxwell was the dominant personality within the group: he was Chairman of BIP, Wardour Films and ABC. Maxwell was regarded as something of a dictator within the trade, though he looked to deny this: 'I am not the "Mussolini of British Film", by which title I have been described. I am a business man and a Scotsman, and although I have a certain admiration for Benito Mussolini I think that I do not talk quite so much.'[36] Like most British producers at this time, Maxwell was also keen to assert his patriotic credentials: 'I realised that hole-in-the-corner production was no good. British films had to be big enough to be worthy of our race. They had to have money behind them – lots of money.'[37]

At the outset BIP demonstrated evidence of a forward-looking production strategy. It embraced sound enthusiastically – Alfred Hitchcock's *Blackmail* (1929) was the first British talking picture to be released commercially – and it also pioneered co-productions with other European film industries through multiple-language films such as E. A. Dupont's *Atlantic* (1929) and Richard Eichberg's *The Flame of Love* (1930).[38] It also made the musical revue *Elstree Calling* (1930). *The Financial Times* held the company up as a success story:

> If all the British film-producing companies could boast an initial record comparable with that of British International Pictures, the so-called American menace would be non-existent. For there is no doubt that, far from signalising [sic] the eclipse of the industry in this country, the advent of the talking film has given British producers with the means and energy to exploit their advantage an opportunity to shine in film production superior to any which they have yet enjoyed.[39]

However, Maxwell was a fiscally cautious chairman: having built up his empire he became increasingly risk averse. Following its flirtation with international pictures in the late 1920s, BIP oriented its production towards the home market. In 1930 Maxwell told shareholders that 'they were now able to produce pictures quicker and more cheaply than ever before, and that the finished article had a special appeal to British audiences, shown by the best possible test – pay-box receipts greater than they had hitherto experienced'.[40]

Maxwell's fiscal conservatism was justified during the economic crisis of 1931 which led to the formation of the National Government: BIP nevertheless recorded a 'satisfactory' trading profit of £112,283 despite 'the effects of the financial crisis and the drastic remedies the Government had found it necessary to apply'.[41] These included raising the Entertainment Duty paid on cinema tickets from 11 per cent to 16.5 per cent. However, the group's revenues from exhibition were declining in the early 1930s: ABC's profits fell from £429,545 in 1931 to £371,444 in 1932 and £278,017 in 1933.[42] Maxwell planned to raise more debenture capital but this was cancelled when 'another large and important cinema debenture issue' (by the Gaumont-British Picture Corporation) was under-subscribed: he explained that 'we [were] required to alter our policy and find another means of dealing with the financial position'.[43] Hence the Associated British Picture Corporation (ABPC) was formed in 1933 as a holding company to take over the entire capital of BIP, Wardour Films and ABC. The effect of this restructuring was to put exhibition on an equal footing with production and distribution. In this the corporation was successful: ABPC's profits increased from £273,591 in 1934 to £370,753 in 1935 and £639,851 in 1936.[44]

By the mid-1930s ABPC had authorised capital of £4 million, of which £3,550,000 had been issued, while its assets in two studios (Elstree and Welwyn) and 290 cinemas were estimated at £10.5 million. The capital was made up of £2 million in £1 preference shares and 6.2 million ordinary shares at 5s.

The largest ordinary shareholder was John Maxwell with 2,096,000 shares: most of the other major shareholders were nominee companies for various banks including the Commercial Bank of Scotland (460,000), the Clydesdale Bank (360,000), the National Provincial Bank (190,000) and the Royal Bank of Scotland (161,000). The rest of the shares were held in small blocks by individuals including the usual *eminences grises* such as retired politician Sir Clement Kinloch-Cooke, shipbuilder Sir Harold Yarrow and tobacco magnate Sir Ernest Wills. ABPC also held loans equivalent to its issued capital in the form of a £3.5 million 5 per cent debenture in favour of the Law Debenture Corporation.[45] While its production strategy may have been unambitious, ABPC's finances were based on a solid foundation that would enable it to weather the crisis of the late 1930s.

The Gaumont-British Picture Corporation (GBPC) was a larger and more ambitious undertaking than British International/Associated British. It is clear that GBPC was set up with the specific intention of creating a vertically-integrated studio organisation on the Hollywood model. As *The Financial Times* observed in June 1928:

> The natural advantages in the way of profit earning inherent in properly organised and economically conducted combinations can hardly fail to strengthen the earning capacity of the undertaking in its new form . . . It is believed to be the only large combine in England that operates on the same lines as the giant United States organisations.[46]

GBPC was registered as a public company in March 1927 with issued capital of £2.5 million: it was set up 'primarily to acquire and operate the following important businesses which occupy a very prominent position in the Film industry of this country': the Gaumont Film Company, Ideal Films and the W & F (Woolf & Freedman) Film Service as well as twenty-one 'important picture theatres' including the Marble Arch Pavilion and Shaftesbury Avenue Pavilion in London's West End.[47] Gaumont was one of the oldest film companies in Britain – it was a major distributor and also owned its own studio (Shepherd's Bush) – and had been run for nearly thirty years by Alfred and Reginald Bromhead. Ideal Films and the W & F Film Service were also distributors: the latter – of which C. M. Woolf was managing director – was a particularly valuable asset as it handled popular American fare including the films of comedian Harold Lloyd as well as some of the higher-end British films produced by Gainsborough Pictures.

The financial backing for the new combine was always somewhat opaque. The main shareholders were the Ostrer brothers, merchant bankers who had invested in the Gaumont Company and held controlling interests in Ideal Films, the W & F Film Service and a small cinema circuit (Bicolour) with eight theatres in London and others in the provinces, which they sold in return for a large shareholding in GBPC. Indeed, the establishment of GBPC was really a means of consolidating the Ostrers' growing interests in the industry: *The Financial Times* observed that '[by] this transaction the Messrs Ostrer Brothers become the largest film producers and renters in the country'.[48] The Ostrers were financiers rather than film-makers:

Isidore, the eldest, was regarded as the financial 'brains', middle brother Mark looked after the sales aspect of the organisation and younger brother Maurice was a production executive. They were initially content to leave the day-to-day management of the combine in the hands of others. Hence Alfred Bromhead became the first chairman of GBPC, Reginald Bromhead was the managing director and C. M. Woolf was in charge of distribution.

It was soon apparent that GBPC had ambitions for further expansion. It increased its capital through further share and debenture issues in order to fund the acquisition of three cinema circuits in 1928: Denman Picture Houses, the General Theatre Corporation and Provincial Cinematograph Theatres. Denman Picture Houses was a recently registered public company with a capital of £1 million which operated ninety-six cinemas: GBPC became a majority shareholder and entered into an agreement whereby it would act as general manager of the Denman circuit in return for 10 per cent of profits. The General Theatre Corporation had authorised capital of £2 million and operated fifty-six cinemas: GBPC swooped to acquire it in its entirety following a poor public response to the initial share issue, which was attributed to its board not including anyone with trade experience.[49] However, the most important acquisition was Provincial Cinematograph Theatres (PCT), which operated some seventy-five cinemas including the showcase Tivoli in London. In November 1928 GBPC outbid Associated British Cinemas to acquire the Standard Film Company, the holding company of PCT. The purchase of PCT was worth £1.5 million and following the other acquisitions 'will result in over 300 British theatres being placed under the control of a company with a capital exceeding £14,000,000'.[50] There were some voices who felt that in its rush to expand its exhibition interests GBPC had paid too high a price: *The Economist* later suggested that 'the Gaumont-British group has had the advantage of strong cash resources and the oldest established theatre circuit in the country – that of Provincial Cinematograph Theatres – but has become over-capitalised by the purchase at high prices of other theatre circuits – in particular those of General Theatres and Denman Picture Houses'.[51] However, Alfred Bromhead justified the expansion to shareholders on the grounds that the directors 'became convinced of the desirability of enlarging the corporation's sphere, so as to command, if possible, a dominant situation in the principal branches of the business'.[52]

From April 1928 GBPC also entered into a financing and distributing arrangement with Michael Balcon's Gainsborough Pictures. There were already close links between the two companies: Gainsborough's films had been distributed by the W & F Film Service since 1926, while both Maurice Ostrer and C. M. Woolf sat on Gainsborough's board. The tie-up between the two companies has usually been seen as the large combine taking over the smaller production company, with Gainsborough becoming to all intents and purposes 'a wholly-owned outpost of the Gaumont-British empire'.[53] In fact, Gainsborough operated as a semi-autonomous unit for three and a half years until GBPC acquired outright control at the end of 1931. It produced around six to eight films a year which were mostly financed fifty-fifty by Gainsborough and either W & F or Ideal Films.[54]

For Gainsborough the arrangement brought more secure distribution – it had previously negotiated with W & F on a film-by-film basis – and access to a large and expanding cinema circuit, including prestigious theatres in the West End, while for GBPC it brought a steady supply of 'quality' rather than quota films. *The Bioscope* averred that Woolf and Maurice Ostrer were 'well known in the world of film finance, while Michael Balcon is among the most progressive of the younger producers behind British film to-day. His sound commercial perception has identified him with post-war British film activity in both the distributing and producing [*sic*].'[55] In 1930 Gainsborough produced eight features: four were profitable – the most successful by some distance being *Journey's End* – and four made a loss.[56]

In 1929 the Ostrers moved to consolidate their control of Gaumont-British. A rumour in the City that an American interest – subsequently identified as the Fox Film Corporation – was on the brink of acquiring a large shareholding in GBPC prompted a brief power struggle between the Ostrers and the Bromheads. In June 1929 there were press reports that William Fox had made 'overtures' for the purchase of shares 'which may result in the Fox Company acquiring a controlling interest in the Gaumont-British Picture Corporation'.[57] This was denied by Alfred Bromhead, although an extraordinary general meeting of shareholders was called in order to amend the Articles of Association so that foreign nationals would be barred from becoming directors of GBPC.[58] *The Bioscope* published an editorial letter addressed to the Bromheads supporting their stance and implicitly critical of the Ostrers:

> [Not] everyone now financially associated with the GBP Corporation has, perhaps, the same personal interest and sense of responsibility in maintaining absolute purity of control. Such people might be tempted to try, in one of the more dubious ways familiar to professional manipulators, to secure these ends which you have so clearly set your face against at the present juncture . . . It is, we repeat, from this angle particularly gratifying to the trade as a whole that you are standing as a solid bulwark at the head of your Corporation to protect the Company, the trade and the country from alien influences.[59]

However, the congratulations were premature. The Ostrers responded by offering cash for 1.3 million ordinary shares for sixpence above their trading value.[60] The Bromheads resigned from the board in August 1929: Isidore Ostrer became the chairman, Mark vice-chairman and C. M. Woolf managing director. At the same time the Ostrers transferred their shares to a private holding company known as the Metropolis and Bradford Trust.

The confusion over the ownership of GBPC persisted. In April 1930 the *Kine* noted: 'Ever since the Ostrer Brothers acquired a large share interest in the Gaumont-British Picture Corporation, the question as to the actual control of the Corporation has been an intriguing one, and even now is unresolved so far as the public is concerned.'[61] In June 1930 the *Daily Mail* reported that '[active] control of the Gaumont-British Picture Corporation and all its allied companies [has] passed into the hands of the Fox Film Corporation'.[62] However, the report was not correct. Fox's shareholding was not in GBPC but in the Metropolis and Bradford

Trust. This was presumably a way of circumventing GBPC's revised Articles of Association which prevented foreign nationals from holding directorships or voting in respect of their shares. Control of the Trust itself was vested in 10,000 voting shares, of which 4,950 were held by the Ostrers, 4,950 by Fox and 100 by the chairman Lord Lee of Fareham.[63] Lord Lee, who effectively held the casting vote in the event of a disagreement between the other parties, averred that 'the constitution of the Metropolis and Bradford Trust Company, and my appointment as its chairman, were specifically devised to preserve British control, and there is no intention of surrendering this control to any foreign interest'.[64]

The *contretemps* over alleged American control reignited the whole question of US influence over the British film industry so soon after the introduction of the Cinematograph Films Act. It was particularly acute given that GBPC was now by some distance the largest film corporation in Britain: any loss of control would have represented a serious impediment to the development of British cinema as a national project. The question would not go away. In April 1931 Conservative MP J. R. Remar alleged that US interests 'are Americanising the entertainment industry in this country': he specifically cited Fox and Gaumont-British.[65] It was against this background that in May 1931 Isidore Ostrer instructed his solicitors to sound out the Board of Trade about making 'a gift to the Nation of the Ostrer voting shares in the Metropolis and Bradford Trust'.[66] The Board of Trade was perplexed by this offer. It clarified that the complex Articles of Association of the Metropolis and Bradford Trust were such 'that Fox cannot get control of the Corporation without Ostrer, and Ostrer cannot give control of the Corporation to any other American interests without Fox'.[67] The Permanent Under-Secretary at the Board of Trade speculated about Ostrer's motives:

> It is impossible not to suspect that the offer is in some way related to the rivalry between Gaumont British and British International Pictures. The latter is an admittedly British concern, whereas the nationality of the former has been under considerable suspicion. We know that the leaders of BIP have considered how they could obtain some sort of State recognition in order to make borrowing more easy, and it may be that Mr Ostrer has lighted upon an ingenious plan with the same aim, which he considers difficult for the Government to reject. If the Government refuses his offer, he can say that he is no longer called upon to preserve British control and that he is at liberty to sell to those who offer him most money... On the other hand, if the Government accept the offer, he can use it for purposes of publicity.[68]

It was also suggested that Ostrer might have been looking for a public show of support from the government in order to head off an impending lawsuit by the Fox interests.[69] In the event, the Board of Trade decided to thank Ostrer for his offer but felt that it should be entirely his decision whether or not he wanted to sell the shares or place them in trust.[70]

GBPC continued to expand its exhibition interests: in 1930 it acquired a 'substantial share interest' in United Picture Theatres for a reported £50,000.[71] Indeed, the corporation had perhaps expanded too rapidly for its own stability at a time when the conversion to sound necessitated an overhaul of production facilities and cinemas. GBPC had recorded a trading profit of £412,344 in its first full year of operation, but this fell to £284,724 in 1929 and £317,077 in 1930. In 1930 Isidore Ostrer assured shareholders that 'their corporation was definitely unwilling to take second place in production to any other company operating in the kingdom': he cited *High Treason*, *Journey's End*, *Rookery Nook*, *Alf's Button*, *Splinters* and *The Great Game* as evidence of its commitment to quality.[72] In 1931 GBPC undertook a major refurbishment of Shepherd's Bush – the first film shot at the reopened studios was the thriller *Rome Express* (1932) – and consolidated all production under the direction of Michael Balcon.[73] In the early 1930s its profits improved – £502,057 in 1931, £490,301 in 1932 and £462,612 in 1933 – but the corporation's complicated internal structure and the heavy debts of some subsidiaries made investors wary. In 1933, for example, a new debenture issue was under-subscribed by 60 per cent. As *The Economist* remarked: 'Further simplification and consolidation of the structure of the Gaumont-British group would help the investor in making a decision as regards any further issues of new capital which may be made.'[74]

The capital structure of GBPC was similar to ABPC but the total was nearly twice as large. In the mid-1930s its authorised capital amounted to £6,250,000 divided into 3,250,000 preference shares at £1 each and 5 million ordinary shares: £2.5 million at 10*s.* and £500,000 at 5*s.* The Metropolis and Bradford Trust effectively controlled the company through owning a majority of the ordinary shares (2,915,000). Other large shareholders in GBPC included Bishopsgate Nominees, the Prudential Assurance Company, Midland Bank, Royal Bank of Scotland and several investment trusts. However, GBPC was carrying heavier debts: these included debentures totalling over £5 million and a secured overdraft from the National Provincial Bank that in November 1936 stood at £1,149,785.[75]

Unlike its main rival, GBPC embraced a bold production strategy that set its eyes on the lucrative American market: this necessitated investing in production values. Balcon seems to have been the main driver of this policy. He told a colleague that 'my heart is tied up in America just as much as yours because I do know that success for the output stands or falls by its success in that market . . . I am indeed sincere about this because if I am determined about anything it is to leave no stone unturned to adjust our picture point of view so as to obtain that market without losing what we have.'[76] In his report to the directors at the end of 1934, Balcon was keen to impress upon them that 'it is necessary to bear in mind that in order to obtain a firm grip on the American market our pictures must bear comparison, not only with the average Hollywood product, but with the outstanding American films; this is our problem in a nutshell and it cannot be solved without spending more.'[77] The provisional production programme for 1935 envisioned fourteen films at a total estimated cost of around £926,000: individual projects ranged between £30,000 and £100,000.[78]

Although some Gaumont-British films achieved success in the American market, such as *The 39 Steps*, *Evergreen* and *Chu Chin Chow*, the strategy overall did not return the results that Balcon had hoped.[79] In 1935 GBPC announced a record profit of £720,433, but this was largely due to its exhibition interests: it had to put aside £200,000 against anticipated losses on production and distribution.[80] Early in 1936 the Bank of England reported:

> The Gaumont Company is at present seriously pressed for finance but unless plans which are now being considered for the internal reconstruction of their capital set-up can be brought to a satisfactory result it will be quite impossible for them to raise further finance. This would enable Fox Films to exercise the necessary pressure to achieve their end.[81]

In July 1936 it was reported that the Ostrers were again considering selling their shares: Sir Edward Spears, the Conservative MP for Carlisle, claimed that 'American interests have purchased the share capital of Gaumont-British Limited'.[82] Yet again this turned out to be incorrect: negotiations between the Ostrers and Fox chairman Joseph M. Schenck had stalled. *Kine* reported a New York source that 'the Ostrer brothers were not unanimous on the end sum to be paid, one of them standing out against the deal'.[83] At this point John Maxwell came forward with a cash offer of £1,250,000 for the Ostrers' shares in the Metropolis and Bradford Trust. However, the Articles of Association of the Metropolis and Bradford Trust determined that the consent of any party holding over 25 per cent of voting shares was needed for the transfer of a majority of shares: this allowed the Fox interests to block the sale of the Ostrers' shares. Maxwell was left with 250,000 non-voting shares, a seat on the Gaumont-British board and a five-year first option on the voting shares if Fox approved their sale in the future.[84] Maxwell launched a lawsuit against the Ostrers, only to withdraw it following his resignation from the board when he refused to accept the company's accounts.[85]

With its financial position deteriorating, GBPC's response was to adopt a strategy of retrenchment. In November 1936 Isidore Ostrer announced that the company would not be paying a dividend due to the rising costs of production and the failure to sell pictures in the United States: 'I am satisfied that we have now proved it impossible to recover from the home market alone the full cost of quality films ... We are, therefore, faced with the choice of abandoning our efforts in the American market in favour of a programme of cheaper films for the home market only, or abandoning film production altogether.'[86] In March 1937 Gainsborough Pictures reported a loss of £98,182, which it blamed on rising costs and that 'several films in stock at the close of last year did not realise the valuation placed upon them in the valuation for that year'.[87] In 1937 GBPC temporarily ceased production at Shepherd's Bush and concentrated its film-making activities at Islington under head of production Edward Black (Michael Balcon left at the end of 1936 to head MGM's British production unit). Its production strategy followed its rival ABPC by switching to films budgeted in the expectation of returns mostly from the home market: these included a series of popular vehicles for comedians such as Will Hay and the Crazy Gang.[88]

At the height of the production boom of the mid-1930s the two combines were jointly responsible for around a quarter of British films. They were complemented by several other production concerns which also came into being as a consequence of the Cinematograph Films Act. The British Lion Film Corporation was one of the more successful of the Quota Act companies. It was established in December 1927 by the popular author and playwright Edgar Wallace with the intention of making films of his work: its first film was *The Ringer* (1928). British Lion had authorised capital of £200,000, although its share issue was not fully subscribed. It bought a one-stage studio at Beaconsfield and early in 1929 produced an all-talking picture, *The Clue of the New Pin*, which was trade shown before BIP's *Blackmail*, although it was not released until later in the year and attracted little interest as it was deemed technically inferior.[89] British Lion incurred losses for its first three years and was probably lucky to survive the transition to talking pictures. By the end of 1931 it had lost £92,766 and took the unusual step of reducing its capital by that amount: the loss was to be borne by preferred shareholders.[90] Following Wallace's death in 1932, while he was in Hollywood working on the script of *King Kong*, control of British Lion passed to managing director S. W. Smith and production manager Herbert Smith who steered it away from an exclusive diet of Wallace adaptations and broadened its portfolio to include dramas and comedies. British Lion's survival was to some extent a consequence of the failure of other quota producers and choosing not to go down the 'quickie' route: it distributed American second features and made up its British quota by producing a small number of British first features around the £20,000 mark (comparable to the costs of BIP's films).

The British and Dominions Film Corporation was founded by Herbert Wilcox in 1928 with an authorised capital of £500,000, of which half was initially issued.[91] Wilcox had support from the City – his backers included several millionaire businessmen, including Sir Harry McGowan of Imperial Chemical Industries and Sir Hugo Hirst of the General Electric Company, and the bankers Otto and Ernest Schiff – which made British and Dominions a more secure investment than other film concerns in the eyes of subscribers. Wilcox was one of the new generation of modern producers: he travelled to Hollywood to study production techniques and studio management. British and Dominions owned its own studio (Imperial Studios at Elstree), which it equipped for sound and rented out to other producers. Its capital outlay meant that it operated at a loss for its first two years, but Wilcox evidently had more of a plan for the longer term than most of the bubble companies and by 1931 recorded a profit of just over £50,000. The trade press welcomed the news:

> This splendid news cannot fail to provide a stimulation to the British industry. It proves definitely that British and Dominions have, following the initiation of a sound financial policy by Hubert T. Marsh, the Company's managing director, overcome what appeared to be almost insuperable difficulties and are now able to "enter the straight" among the foremost British production concerns.[92]

The British and Dominions Film Corporation produced 124 films between 1928 and 1938. In the early 1930s its output included both low-cost quota pictures for an American distributor (Paramount) and higher-cost films released by the W & F Film Service. In 1933 United Artists (UA) guaranteed a loan of £15,000 from Lloyds Bank towards the production of *That's A Good Girl*.[93] This prefaced a distribution agreement between UA and British and Dominions: UA felt that British and Dominions 'are producing superior British made motion pictures which are proving to be profitable box-office attractions for the exhibitors to whom they are licensed'.[94] Wilcox enjoyed success with the costume pictures *Nell Gwynn* and *Peg of Old Drury*, but increasing costs – those films were reported to have cost £80,000 or more – squeezed the profit margins. In February 1936 Imperial Studios was gutted by a fire, after which British and Dominions invested in a new facility at Pinewood Studios. In 1937 C. M. Woolf told the Bank of England that 'British Dominions have no money . . . They would have to get rid of their United Artists contract before starting production again.'[95]

Associated Talking Pictures (ATP) was registered by theatre producer Basil Dean in May 1929 with the aim of producing sound films of literary and theatrical properties. It had an inauspicious start when its initial capital issue of £125,000 was under-subscribed: Dean and his fellow directors – who included philanthropist Stephen Courtauld and managing director Reginald Baker – were left having to offer personal guarantees to the National Provincial Bank for an overdraft facility up to £110,000.[96] According to Dean's memoir, his first film, an adaptation of John Galsworthy's *Escape* (1930), cost £42,762 and was a box-office flop.[97] Like Wilcox, Dean travelled to Hollywood to study film production techniques and was open to recruiting American technicians. ATP initially produced at the small British Lion studio at Beaconsfield, but in 1931 it opened its own studios at Ealing – the first in Britain to be built specifically for the production of sound films, at a cost of £247,000.[98] In 1932 ATP entered into a co-production deal with RKO Radio Pictures for the production of four higher-end quota films at an average cost of around £25,000.[99] ATP also hired out studio space to tenant producers – including the Gloria Swanson vehicle *Perfect Understanding* for United Artists and Ludovico Toeplitz's *The Dictator* – and in 1933 set up its own distribution arm (Associated British Film Distributors). Its most successful in-house productions were a cycle of star vehicles for the Lancastrian music hall star Gracie Fields, including *Sally in Our Alley*, *Looking on the Bright Side*, *Love, Life and Laughter*, *Sing As We Go* and *Look Up and Laugh*. However, ATP was trading at a loss throughout the 1930s and did not pay any dividends: it was effectively bankrolled by its own directors.[100]

By the early 1930s the structure of the new British cinema industry had taken shape: the two combines and a number of medium-sized concerns formed the nucleus of the domestic production sector and were responsible for around half of all British features. The remainder was provided by low-budget quota producers and by ambitious independent production units such as Alexander Korda's London Film Productions. The capitalisation of the film industry in the wake of the Cinematograph Films Act had seen banks and investment trusts take up a significant position in the industry. John Maxwell and the Ostrers were the biggest individual shareholders in the two major combines and exerted considerable personal influence over British film production. But the real financial control was shifting from the individuals and entrepreneurs who had built the industry to the bankers and moneymen whose capital was needed for the industry to grow.

Notes

1. 'British Film Finance', *The Economist*, 14 July 1928, p. 74.
2. S. G. Rayment, 'The Story of 1927', *Kinematograph Year Book Diary and Directory 1928* (London: Kinematograph Publications, 1928), p. 12.
3. 'Enter the Bankers!', *The Bioscope*, 7 August 1929, p. 14.
4. Margaret Dickinson and Sarah Street, *Cinema and State: The Film Industry and the British Government 1927–84* (London: British Film Institute, 1985), p. 39.
5. New Era National Pictures and British and Foreign Films were both set up in order to take over existing concerns. The others in the list were new companies.
6. 'British Film Finance', *The Economist*, 14 July 1928, p. 74.
7. 'British Film Finance', *The Economist*, 30 November 1929, p. 1027.
8. *Kinematograph Year Book Diary and Directory 1931* (London: Kinematograph Publications, 1931), pp. 153–7.
9. For a summary of the transition, see Laraine Porter, 'The Talkies Come to Britain: British silent cinema and the transition to sound, 1928-30', in I. Q. Hunter, Laraine Porter and Justin Smith (eds), *The Routledge Companion to British Cinema History* (London: Routledge, 2017), pp. 87–98.
10. Rachael Low, *The History of the British Film 1918–1929* (London: George Allen & Unwin, 1971), p. 206.
11. 'British Film Finance', *The Economist*, 30 November 1929, p. 1028.
12. The National Archives (TNA) BT 64/86: Non-Fulfilment of Quota – Submission Under Section 23 (2): British Exhibitors Films Ltd: Buleraig and Davis (solicitors) to Board of Trade, 27 June 1929.
13. British Film Institute (BFI) MEB A/68: Gainsborough Pictures: Draft Chairman's Speech for Annual General Meeting, 15 October 1930.
14. Ibid.: Note of conversion of costs, 9 October 1930. The films were *The Return of the Rat* (original cost £29,327, plus conversion cost £4,950), *Taxi for Two* (£13,022 + £6,252), *City of Play* (£17,287 + £7,045), *The Wrecker* (£14,692 + £2,293), *The Crooked Billet* (£15,657 + £4,995) and *Balaclava* (£29,763 + £3,329, and another £9,246 for an 'all-dialogue version').
15. Ibid.: Gainsborough Pictures: Schedule of Profit and Losses on Productions – 30 June 1930. The total revenues (including domestic and foreign markets) for the six films were: *The Return of the Rat* (£16,477), *Taxi for Two* (£10,047), *City of Play* (££5,529), *The Wrecker* (£9,834), *The Crooked Billet* (£15,509) and *Balaclava* (£27,721).
16. Ibid.: Gainsborough Pictures (1928) Ltd: Accounts and Schedules, 30 June 1930.
17. 'Will British Films Improve?', *Kinematograph Weekly*, 2 January 1930, p. 67.
18. 'Whitehall Films, Limited', *The Bioscope*, 10 November 1927, p. 16.
19. 'Whitehall Films: Stormy Meeting', *The Scotsman*, 25 June 1929, p. 6.
20. 'Whitehall Films £193,517 Deficiency', *The Bioscope*, 9 April 1930, p. 30.
21. 'International Talking Screen Productions', *The Yorkshire Post*, 9 May 1929, p. 19.
22. 'International "Talkies" Under-subscribed', *The Bioscope*, 29 May 1929, p. 43.
23. 'The Big Multi-Lingual Group', *Kinematograph Weekly*, 6 March 1930, p. 31.

24. TNA BT 56/28: E. H. Marsh to Lord Privy Seal, 5 March 1930.
25. Ibid.: Draft note for the Lord Privy Seal regarding a British Centre for the Production of International Talking Pictures (no date).
26. Kristin Thompson, 'The Rise and Fall of Film Europe', in Andrew Higson and Richard Maltby (eds), *'Film Europe' and 'Film America': Cinema, Commerce and Cultural Exchange 1920–1939* (Exeter: University of Exeter Press, 1999), pp. 56–81.
27. 'British Film Finance', *The Economist*, 15 August 1931, p. 314.
28. See, for example, Tom Ryall, 'A British Studio System: The Associated British Picture Corporation and the Gaumont-British Picture Corporation in the 1930s', in Robert Murphy (ed.), *The British Cinema Book* (London: British Film Institute, 1997), pp. 27–36.
29. 'Wardour and British National', *The Bioscope*, 13 January 1927, p. 46.
30. 'Elstree Studios Change Hands', *The Bioscope*, 14 April 1927, p. 23.
31. 'British International Pictures', *The Bioscope*, 17 November 1927, p. 6.
32. 'British International Pictures', *Western Mail*, 26 November 1927, p. 14.
33. 'Pathe-Freres Acquisition', *The Financial Times*, 16 August 1928, p. 5.
34. 'Maxwell's Theatres Issue Next Week', *The Bioscope*, 21 November 1928, p. 30.
35. Low, *The History of the British Film 1918–1929*, p. 45.
36. 'The Future of British Films', *The Fife Free Press*, 24 November 1928, p. 5.
37. Ibid.
38. Andrew Higson, 'Polyglot Films for an International Market: E. A. Dupont, the British Film Industry, and the Idea of a European Cinema, 1926–1930', in Higson and Maltby (eds), *'Film Europe' and 'Film America'*, pp. 274–301.
39. 'A Film Example', *The Financial Times*, 1 July 1929, p. 6.
40. 'British International Pictures, Limited', *The Economist*, 25 August 1930, p. 378.
41. 'British International Pictures, Limited', *The Economist*, 24 September 1932, p. 566.
42. 'British Film Finance', *The Economist*, 7 October 1933, p. 676.
43. 'Associated British Cinemas', *The Financial Times*, 2 October 1933, p. 7.
44. F. D. Klingender and Stuart Legg, *Money Behind the Screen: A Report Prepared on Behalf of the Film Council* (London: Lawrence and Wishart, 1937), p. 32.
45. Ibid., pp. 30–1.
46. 'Gaumont-British', *The Financial Times*, 15 June 1928, p. 8.
47. 'Gaumont-British Corporation, Limited', *The Financial Times*, 8 April 1927, p. 14.
48. 'Gaumont-British Pictures', *The Financial Times*, 26 March 1927, p. 7.
49. Low, *The History of the British Film 1918–1929*, p. 44.
50. 'Large Film Amalgamation Proposal', *The Financial Times*, 28 November 1928, p. 9.
51. 'British Film Finances', *The Economist*, 24 September 1932, p. 553.
52. 'Gaumont-British Picture Corporation', *The Financial Times*, 27 September 1928, p. 4.
53. Philip Kemp, 'Not for Peckham: Michael Balcon and Gainsborough's International Trajectory in the 1920s', in Pam Cook (ed.), *Gainsborough Pictures* (London: Cassell, 1997), p. 29.
54. BFI MEB B/19: Gainsborough Pictures: Agenda (no date but including a letter dated 30 November 1932).
55. 'Gainsborough Pictures', *The Bioscope*, 12 December 1928, p. 172.
56. BFI MEB A/68: Gainsborough Picture: Schedule of Profit and Losses on Production, 30 June 1930. The profitable films were *Armistice* (+£741), *Woman to Woman* (+£1,595), *Sugar & Spice* (+£459) and *Journey's End* (+£13,370), while the loss-makers were *South*

Sea Bubble (-£2,276), *The Gallant Hussar* (-£735), *First Born* (-£1,093) and *A Light Woman* (-£309).
57. 'US & Our Cinemas', *Daily Mail*, 22 June 1929, p. 11.
58. 'Gaumont Pictures: British Control Assured', *The Scotsman*, 3 August 1929, p. 6.
59. 'Messages from "The Bioscope"', *The Bioscope*, 24 July 1929, p. 31.
60. 'Gaumont British Control', *The Bioscope*, 24 July 1929, p. 26.
61. 'Gaumont Riddle', *Kinematograph Weekly*, 24 April 1930, p. 23.
62. 'Fox Company Secure Control of British Film', *Daily Mail*, 7 June 1930, p. 17.
63. Some contemporary reports suggest that the Ostrers and Fox each held 4,750 voting shares, leaving 500 divided equally between the five directors: Isidore Ostrer, Maurice Ostrer, R. B. McDonald, F. H. Pummitt and Lord Lee. McDonald and Pummitt were representatives of the Fox Film Corporation. Hence the Ostrers and Fox *de facto* controlled 4,950 voting shares each with the remaining 100 held by Lee.
64. 'Not Controlled by Fox', *The Bioscope*, 21 June 1930, p. 5.
65. *Parliamentary Debates: House of Commons*, 5th Series, vol. 251, 21 April 1931, col. 786.
66. TNA BT 64/86: Lawrence, Messer & Co. to President of the Board of Trade, 22 May 1931.
67. Ibid.: Minute by Mr Hutchinson, 3 June 1931.
68. Ibid.: Minute by Sir Patrick Hamilton, 25 June 1931.
69. 'English Bankers Deny Fox Control of British-Gaumont Theatres', *Variety*, 20 May 1931, p. 5.
70. TNA BT 64/86: W. B. Brown to Messrs Lawrence, Messer & Co., 29 July 1931.
71. 'Gaumont and United P.T.', *Kinematograph Weekly*, 1 May 1930, p. 80.
72. 'Gaumont-British Picture Corporation Limited', *The Economist*, 4 October 1930, p. 638.
73. 'British Studios To-day', *The Bioscope*, 14 October 1931, p. 19.
74. 'British Film Finance', *The Economist*, 7 October 1933, p. 676.
75. Klingender and Legg, *Money Behind the Screen*, pp. 23–7.
76. BFI MEB C/55: Michael Balcon to Jeffrey Bernerd, 8 January 1934.
77. BFI MEB C/28: Report to the Managing Directors on the 1935 Programme by M. E. Balcon, 15 December 1934.
78. Ibid.: Programme: Shepherd's Bush, 1935. The films identified by title are *The 39 Steps* (£48,000), *The Tunnel* (£85,000), *King of the Damned* (£65,000), *The Passing of the Third Floor Back* (£45,000) and *Soldiers Three* (£60,000). The last was started but never completed.
79. John Sedgwick, 'Michael Balcon's Close Encounter with the American Market, 1934–1936', *Historical Journal of Film, Radio and Television*, 16: 3 (1996), pp. 333–48.
80. 'M. Ostrer's Warning on Film Costs', *Kinematograph Weekly*, 3 October 1935, p. 14.
81. Bank of England Archive (BEA) SMT 2/31: Note of a meeting between the Governor and Claud Serocold, 30 January 1936.
82. *Parliamentary Debates: House of Commons*, 5th Series, vol. 314, 16 July 1936, col. 2237.
83. 'Financial Moves Behind G-B Deal', *Kinematograph Weekly*, 1 October 1936, p. 3.
84. 'Finance Details of G-B Deal', *Kinematograph Weekly*, 22 October 1936, p. 16.
85. 'John Maxwell Resigns from GB Board', *Kinematograph Weekly*, 14 July 1938, p. 5.
86. 'Gaumont-British Picture Corporation', *The Financial Times*, 3 November 1936, p. 4.
87. 'Gainsborough Pictures', *The Financial Times*, 2 March 1937, p. 7.
88. Sue Harper, '"Nothing to Beat the Hay Diet": Comedy at Gaumont and Gainsborough', in Cook (ed.), *Gainsborough Pictures*, pp. 80–98.

89. Low, *The History of the British Film 1918–1929*, p. 194.
90. 'British Lion Reduces Capital', *The Bioscope*, 4 November 1931, p. 26.
91. 'British and Dominions Film Corporation', *The Yorkshire Post*, 15 February 1928, p. 16.
92. 'British & Dominions £50,649 Trading Profit', *The Bioscope*, 23 December 1931, p. 5.
93. Media History Digital Library, Centre for Film and Theatre Research, University of Wisconsin – Madison: United Artists Corporate Papers: Adjourned Meeting of the Board of Directors of United Artists Corporation, 30 January 1934.
94. Ibid.: Annual Meeting of the Stockholders of United Artists Corporation, 2 April 1934.
95. BEA SMT 2/34: Evidence of C. M. Woolf, 7 May 1937.
96. BEA SMT 2/39: 'Associated Talking Pictures' (no date).
97. Basil Dean, *Mind's Eye* (London: Hutchinson, 1973) p. 145.
98. BEA SMT 2/34: R. P. Baker to E. H. D. Skinner, 27 May 1937.
99. 'New RKO Studios for London', *The Bioscope*, 1 April 1931, p. 13.
100. Rachael Low, *The History of the British Film 1929–1939: Film Making in 1930s Britain* (London: George Allen & Unwin, 1985), p. 159.

CHAPTER 5

Quota Production in the Early 1930s

The main purpose of the Cinematograph Films Act had been to support the domestic production sector by creating conditions favourable to investment in British films. On one level the introduction of the quota can be adjudged to have been successful as the volume of British production did indeed increase over the following years. In August 1927 the *Daily Express* suggested that 'the Compulsory Films Bill [*sic*] has given birth to a £1,000,000 production programme'.[1] A total of 131 British 'long' films (over 3,000 feet in length) were registered with the Board of Trade during the first year of the quota in 1928–9. While the total fell to ninety-six the following year, as British studios converted to the production of talking pictures, the overall trend thereafter was upwards: the total number of British films increased from 125 in 1930–1 to a high of 228 in 1937–8 before the production sector again contracted at the end of the decade.[2] Other statistical evidence indicates that more British films were being made than required by the legislation. The total British footage registered by renters exceeded the statutory minimum for every year of the operation of the Act. In 1929, for example, British films made up nearly 20 per cent (against a statutory minimum of 7.5 per cent) and rose to a high of 26.6 per cent in 1936 (against a statutory 20 per cent).[3] It was a similar picture for exhibitors' quota: British films accounted for 21.6 per cent in 1932 (against a statutory 10 per cent) and reached a high of 27.9 per cent in 1937 (against a statutory 20 per cent).[4] In 1934 the Board of Trade concluded that the relative stability of the production sector and the increasing public interest in British films could both be attributed to the Cinematograph Films Act: 'It may be said at once that the policy embedded in the Act has been distinctly successful and that the machinery devised has worked with a minimum of friction to the trade . . . Moreover, the British cinema-going public began to show a distinct preference for the British film as soon as it reached a point where its entertainment value was equal to that of the United States film.'[5]

All the renters operating in Britain were required to offer a minimum amount of British film to meet their quota obligations: the amounts per renter varied according to the total amount of imported footage. It followed that the American renters, who each had full catalogues of their own films, tended to have higher quota liabilities than British renters who imported fewer foreign films. The excess of quota footage offered in the early 1930s was due to British renters who routinely registered more than required to meet their statutory obligations. The statistician

Simon Rowson calculated that in the quota year 1933–4, British renters exceeded their statutory quota by 169 per cent: nine British renters registered 522,000 feet of British quota footage against a total statutory requirement of 194,000 feet. Table 5.1 compares the quota liabilities of the major British and American renters with the actual footage offered.

There was a stark difference between British renters, all but one of which registered more quota footage than required, often significantly more, and American renters, most of whom registered the bare minimum of quota footage to meet their obligations, the one exception being United Artists. Rowson concluded that

> nearly every British company produced its British films in quantity far in excess of their statutory liability, and probably entirely without any regard to that liability. The British firms were, in fact, concerned with the development of the new home industry; the foreign firms had no such interest and were concerned only with such a technical compliance with the Act as to permit the exploitation of their own imported films.[6]

Table 5.1 Quota liabilities and total quota footage registered by major British and American renters in the quota year 1 April 1933–31 March 1934

RENTER	QUOTA LIABILITY	QUOTA REGISTERED
British renters		
Associated British Film Distributors	10,000 ft	67,000 ft
Associated Producing and Distributing Co.	8,500 ft	16,000 ft
British Lion Film Corporation	11,000 ft	39,000 ft
Butcher's Film Service	10,000 ft	28,000 ft
Equity British Films	10,000 ft	11,000 ft
Gaumont-British Film Distributors	44,000 ft	206,000 ft
Pathé	32,000 ft	37,000 ft
Producers Distributing Co.	22,000 ft	12,000 ft
Wardour Films	18,000 ft	109,000 ft
American renters		
Columbia	37,000 ft	37,000 ft
First National Film Distributors	45,000 ft	46,000 ft
Fox Films	65,000 ft	66,000 ft
Metro-Goldwyn-Mayer	98,000 ft	98,000 ft
Paramount Film Service	108,000 ft	108,000 ft
Radio Pictures	88,000 ft	89,000 ft
United Artists	59,000 ft	90,000 ft
Warner Bros. Film Distributors	49,000 ft	50,000 ft

Source: Simon Rowson, 'A Statistical Survey of the Cinema Industry in Great Britain in 1934'.

The standard narrative of British cinema of the 1930s is that a large proportion of domestic production consisted of cheaply made, low-quality films that were produced solely to meet the quota. There is much anecdotal evidence of the proliferation of what came to be known as 'quota quickies'. As early as 1929, *Kine Weekly* studio correspondent P. L. Mannock noted 'the premium which is now artificially placed on indifferent "quickie" production by renters clamouring for the British films necessary for their continuance in business . . . It is a scandal that slapdash films should have any artificial premium.'[7] A year later and the situation had worsened: 'A deplorable and rather sinister consequence of the shortage of quota films available . . . has been the demand for British films of any grade. Shoddy, contemptible and cheap pictures have been hurriedly made, and old films formerly too bad to show have been raked out of the vaults simply to enable American firms to comply with the law.'[8] In 1933 Basil Dean of Associated Talking Pictures highlighted 'the shoddy rubbish which is made for quota purposes on lines which actually put a premium on slapdash inefficiency'.[9] Arthur Jarratt, senior film booker for the Gaumont cinema circuit, felt that it 'was to be regretted that so many theatres showed this class of quota film. Millions of theatre patrons could only judge British films from the deplorable specimens of quota product they were compelled to see.'[10] And Michael Balcon wrote in his memoirs that quota quickies 'brought the name of British films into disrepute. For many people "a British film" became the rubbishy second feature you had to sit through, or avoid, if you went to see a Hollywood picture.'[11] The notoriety of the quota quickies has exerted a strong influence on the historiography of British cinema of the 1930s. In his influential account of the film culture of the decade *The Age of the Dream Palace*, for example, Jeffrey Richards argues that the reason for the poor critical reputation of British films was 'the lingering memory of the "quota quickies", a truly awful flood of cinematic rubbish produced to fill the requirements of the statutory British film quota'.[12]

A narrative emerged that it was American renters seeking to fulfil their quota liability at the lowest possible cost who were to blame for the 'quickies'. It was even suggested that the American companies deliberately produced bad British films in order to enhance the appeal of their own films. Sir Ernest Gordon Craig of British Movietonews suggested that 'the Films Act has failed in its task of rehabilitating an efficient and flourishing condition of British film production' and suggested that 'American distributing houses have used lower-grade British pictures in their quota and had created the idea that it was impossible to make good ones'.[13] And Geoffrey Mander, the Liberal MP for Wolverhampton East, averred that 'the American interests in this country have been producing films at a cost of only £3,000 or £4,000 – deliberately and necessarily of a very low quality – in order to stamp them as bad'.[14] There was a persistent rumour that American renters had 'fixed' the price of their quota films at a level that militated against quality. In its evidence to the Moyne Committee in 1936, for example, the Association of Cine-Technicians stated: 'Some companies are alleged to have purposely made bad pictures in order to show up the superiority of American productions . . . It is widely alleged that after the passing of the Cinematograph Films Act, 1927, all the American distributing organisations in Great Britain signed an agreement amongst themselves at a special meeting in Paris not to pay more than £1 per foot for quota pictures made for them by other organisations.'[15]

There was never a formal definition of 'quota quickie', but the figure of £1 a foot came to be understood as the yardstick for low-cost quota production. Distributors would rent second features at a fixed price rather than on a percentage of box-office receipts; therefore, they would look to pay producers an agreed price based on the length of the film. Michael Powell, who cut his teeth directing low-cost quota pictures for American producer Jerome Jackson in the early 1930s, explained in his memoirs that £1 per foot 'was the normal visible cash payment by the American distributors to independent British producers'.[16] This was confirmed by Adrian Brunel, who had directed several major films for Gainsborough Pictures in the 1920s, including *Blighty* and *The Constant Nymph*, but who in the early 1930s was slumming it at Wembley Studios:

> The man to help me was Hugh Perceval, then in charge of Fox British, and through him I got my first assignment with George Smith, an experienced and businesslike film executive who was bringing cheap production to a fine art. His aim was to give the best value for little money. The price paid for these quickies was £1 per foot, out of which the producer had to get his profit. It resulted in frighteningly low budgets – as, it was claimed by British producers, was the intention of the American distributors, who, in order to discredit British production and undermine our quota regulations, had fixed this maximum price for the British films required to fulfil their quota obligations.[17]

The profit margin for quota producers was therefore very tight and depended on being able to deliver the films for less than the amount paid by distributors. Anthony Havelock-Allan, who produced several dozen British quota films for Paramount in the mid-1930s, explained in his interview for the BECTU Oral History Project that Paramount would contract films for around £6,500: 'Sometimes if something was especially good we would try and bargain for a little more money than the £6,500. But in the main what we were doing was making them for £5,000, £5,500. Somehow we managed to make an average of £600 or £500.'[18]

The absence of an official definition of quota quickies makes it difficult to establish with any precision the proportion of British films that fell into this category. Some estimates suggest that quota quickies accounted for around half of all British films. Rachael Low, for example, contends that 'half the enormous number of British films turned out by British studios up to 1937 were produced at minimum cost simply to exploit the protected market or, at worst, to comply with the law'.[19] And John Sedgwick suggests that 'more than 50 per cent of domestic films may be described as "quota quickies" – films made solely to satisfy the renters' and exhibitors' "quota" requirements under the 1927 legislation'.[20] However, it is possible that these estimates are exaggerated. Contemporary estimates suggest a more nuanced picture with more films in an intermediate range between clear first features and quickies. In his evidence to the Moyne Committee, for example, Simon Rowson offered this assessment of the 178 British films registered in the quota year 1934–5:

> Out of the first group of 100 pictures about 14 were intended for the world market, and most of these were exported to America earning in the majority of cases a small contribution only for the ultimate benefit of the British producer. Of the second group of 78 pictures, about 30 may have earned some revenue from foreign markets and possibly about 10 showed a credit balance on exploitation in America. It appears, therefore, that excluding 'quota quickies' about 50 to 60 pictures were made without any designs on the foreign market. The average cost of this group of pictures must have been £15,000–£20,000... This class of picture is rendered possible by protection based on the quota principle, and would probably be unable to survive any protection-system which compelled them to compete on equal terms for dates with the pictures coming from abroad.[21]

This challenges the common assumption that all films produced to exploit the quota were low-cost quickies: Rowson identified a group of films – possibly comprising up to a third of all British production – whose existence could be attributed to the Cinematograph Films Act but were not quota quickies.

The most complete source for the costs of British film production in the early 1930s is a ledger compiled by the Board of Trade in 1933 documenting the statutory costs of 158 of the 159 films registered for renters' quota during the quota year 1 April 1932 to 31 March 1933.[22] The statutory cost was the amount the distributor had to declare in production unit and artistes' salaries (excepting any exempted individuals under clause 27 (3) of the Cinematograph Films Act) in order to qualify for renters' quota. The ledger was compiled as part of a consultation carried out by the Board of Trade into the idea of introducing a minimum cost test for British quota films. The Board of Trade reckoned the statutory cost as usually between 50–60 per cent of the total picture cost: therefore it is possible to estimate the cost range of each film from the statutory cost. For example, *The Good Companions* (1933) – produced by the Gaumont-British Picture Corporation and the highest-cost film registered by a British renter during the year – had a statutory cost of £32,406: this would suggest a total picture cost somewhere in the range between approximately £54,000 and £65,000. The average statutory cost of all the films included in the ledger was £7,251: therefore, the average total cost of a British quota picture was somewhere in the range of £12,000 and £14,500.

The average cost disguises a wide range of variations. The most expensive film in the ledger is United Artists' *Perfect Understanding* (1933) at a statutory cost of £70,010: this film – a vehicle for Hollywood star Gloria Swanson made by her own production company at Ealing Studios – was over twice the cost of the next most expensive film (*The Good Companions*). The lowest-cost film is also something of an outlier: *The Third Gun* (1932) – produced by British Sound Film Productions for Universal Pictures – had a barely credible statutory cost of £55 (although at 3,250 feet it only just crept into the 'long' film category). The lowest-cost full feature (over 5,000 feet) during this quota year was *On Thin Ice* (1933) produced by Hallmark Productions for Equity British Films with a statutory cost of £222. The ledger indicates that the films registered by British renters were on average nearly twice the cost of those registered by American renters: the average statutory cost of the seventy-five films registered by British renters was £9,718 compared to £5,021 for the eighty-three films registered by American renters.

Considering the range of costs indicates that there were relatively few films at the upper end (see Table 5.2): only seven above a statutory cost of £20,000 and only two of those above £30,000. A total of thirty-eight films (24 per cent) cost above £10,000 compared to forty-six (29 per cent) in the medium range between £5,000 and £10,000 and seventy-four (47 per cent) below £5,000. The spread of costs reveals a concentration of films in the medium- and lower-cost range: 120 films (76 per cent) cost below £10,000. A notable feature of Table 5.2 is that American-backed quota films were in a preponderance only in the lower-cost range under £5,000.

The ledger does not specifically identify films as quota quickies. However, an accompanying memorandum explains that the Board of Trade reckoned a statutory cost of £55 per 100 feet to be equivalent to a final picture cost of £100 per 100 feet (or £1 per foot).[23] The statutory costs per 100 feet recorded in the ledger range from a top end of £899 (*Perfect Understanding*) to a low of £4 (*On Thin Ice*). One third (52 of 158) of films in the ledger had a statutory cost of £55 per 100 feet or below: this is less than the estimates by Low and Sedgwick that quickies accounted for around half of all British films. Three quarters of the films in this range were short featurettes: thirty-nine films in the ledger were shorter than 5,000 feet and eleven of those were under 4,000 feet. The running time of a 4,000-foot film was 44 minutes. The proliferation of the featurette in the early 1930s was a consequence of the demand for films that would allow exhibitors to run two full programmes each evening from around 6 p.m. Such films were 'just long enough to pass as features under the Films Act – but just short enough to form useful second items to run in the film bill and help out the quota'.[24]

Table 5.2 Cost range of British quota films registered in the quota year 1 April 1932–31 March 1933

COST RANGE	FILMS	BRITISH/AMERICAN RENTERS
Over £30,000	2	1 British; 1 American
£20,000-£30,000	5	4 British; 1 American
£15,000-£20,000	12	10 British; 2 American
£10,000-£15,000	19	18 British; 1 American
£5,000-£10,000	46	26 British; 20 American
Under £5,000	74	14 British; 60 American

Source: The National Archives BT 64/97: Particulars of British Films Acquired by Renters during the Quota Year 1932–3.

The ledger is particularly illuminating for what it reveals about the strategies of the major British producers. The Gaumont-British Picture Corporation produced twelve films at an average statutory cost of £18,577: these included four films produced by Gaumont-British at Shepherd's Bush (*Rome Express, After the Ball, The Midshipmaid, The Good Companions*) at an average statutory cost of £23,784 and eight films produced by its Gainsborough Pictures subsidiary (*Soldiers of the King, Love on Wheels, Jack's the Boy, The Man From Toronto, Marry Me, There Goes the Bride, The Faithful Heart, White Face*) at Islington Studios at an average statutory cost of £15,974.[25] The Gaumont-British group had nine of the top twenty-five highest-cost films and five of the top ten. The ledger confirms that the Gaumont-British group dealt exclusively in first features: its lowest-cost feature (*White Face*) had a statutory cost of £9,586 – indicating a final picture cost in the range between £16,000 and £19,200 – and the average picture cost was in a range between £31,000 and £37,200, which was around 2.5 times the average cost of British films in 1932–3. Gaumont-British's costs were broadly comparable to a middle-ranking Hollywood studio such as Warner Bros. or RKO.

British International Pictures spent a similar amount on film production – the combined statutory cost of its programme for 1932–3 was £239,723 compared to £224,930 for Gaumont-British – but it produced more films at lower cost. Overall, the costs of BIP's films were slightly above the average for British quota films: this was consistent with its strategy of economical production for the home market. BIP produced twenty-five features at an average statutory cost of £9,202 (and five featurettes at an average statutory cost of £3,357): the average feature cost would therefore be somewhere between £15,000 and £18,500. This was the range identified by Simon Rowson as films that benefited from the protection offered by the Quota Act without being 'quickies'. BIP's most expensive film was *Maid of the Mountains* (1932) at a statutory cost of £17,308: this was less than the average cost for the Gaumont-British group but still well above the average for British films. The case of *Number Seventeen* (1932) is noteworthy. This was the last film from BIP's star director Alfred Hitchcock before he left the studio. It has sometimes been suggested that Hitchcock resented being assigned to directing a low-cost quota feature and that the studio's lack of ambition was the cause of his leaving.[26] Hitchcock himself claimed that *Number Seventeen* was produced as a quota picture for an American renter:

> The American companies had contracted to release films that were a hundred per cent British: they were called 'quota pictures' and were usually made very cheaply. When British International Pictures took on some of these films at the Elstree Studios for one of the American renters, I agreed to produce one or two. My idea was to turn over the direction to [Benn W.] Levy, who was a friend and was quite well known as a playwright.[27]

However, this is not correct: *Number Seventeen* was released not by one of the American renters but by Wardour Films. The idea that it was a quota quickie may have arisen from its relatively short length (5,756 feet). But *Number Seventeen* was no quickie: in fact, it was the studio's second most expensive film of the year at a statutory cost of £15,202 and in the top twenty highest-cost quota films of the year from all producers.

After the two combines, the British and Dominions Film Corporation was the largest producer: it produced nineteen features at an average statutory cost of £10,637. B&D's films fell into two distinct categories. It produced thirteen films for the W&F Film Service at an average statutory cost of £12,412 and six films for Paramount Film Service at an average statutory cost of £5,627. The statutory costs of the films for the British renter W&F ranged between £23,942 for *Yes, Mrs Brown* and £7,096 for *The Flag Lieutenant*, while the range for the American renter was between £9,662 for *The Barton Mystery* and £4,392 for *Discord*. This would suggest that American renters were paying on average significantly less than British renters for quota films from the same producer. London Film Productions, newly established in 1932, produced five films – one for Ideal Films (*Wedding Rehearsal*) and four for Paramount (*Money Means Nothing, Men of Tomorrow, Strange Evidence, Counsel's Opinion*) – at an average statutory cost of £9,218: the film for the British renter was again the most expensive (£13,766). The British Lion Film Corporation found a niche in the production of quota films that were not quickies: it produced four features in 1932–3 – *The Flying Squad* (£7,912), *Sally Bishop* (£11,261), *Where Is This Lady?* (£11,427) and *King of the Ritz* (12,828) – at costs comparable to the middle range of BIP's output. It also produced one featurette (*Yes, Madam*) for an American renter (Fox) at a significantly lower cost (£3,378).

The economic determinants of the British film industry following the Cinematograph Films Act created the conditions for the emergence of production units geared specifically to quota production. Julius Hagen's Twickenham Studios, set up in 1928, for example, operated as 'a miniature mass production machine ... often with one film shot during the day and another at night'.[28] Twickenham Studios had a close relationship with Real Art Productions, a £100 company formed in April 1931 which over the following five years produced a total of forty-five quota films, all produced by Hagen, mostly for American renters. In 1932–3 Real Art Productions contracted eleven films for four American renters – United Artists (two), the Fox Film Corporation (two), MGM (one) and RKO Radio Pictures (six) – at an average statutory cost of £3,355.[29] Most of these films had a statutory cost between £57 and £66 per 100 feet (the UA films were higher at £85–£88). Hagen also produced occasional higher-cost films: *The Lodger* (1932) – a talkie remake of the Gainsborough/Hitchcock film of 1926 – was produced at Twickenham by J. H. Productions at a statutory cost of £9,950 and released by the W&F Film Service.

Sound City Films – the production arm of Norman Loudon's Sound City Studios, a new studio facility that opened at Shepperton in May 1932 – produced five films for MGM at an average statutory cost of £1,805: the highest-cost film was *The Golden Cage* (£48 per 100 feet) with the other films all between £20–£27 per 100 feet.[30] These films were all squarely within the quickie category. Sound City Films also produced one film for British renter Butcher's Film Service (*Watch*

Beverley) at a statutory cost of £1,811 (£25 per 100 feet). Evidence that low cost did not necessarily mean low quality can be found in *Kine Weekly*'s verdict that 'Butcher's found themselves again with a first-rate British proposition and despite the relatively short period that has elapsed since the Trade show a very substantial harvest of contracts has already been gathered'.[31] Loudon, the managing director of Sound City, wound up the production unit after a few years and focused instead on turning the studios into a rental facility for independent producers. He explained that 'by renting stages from this company producers could enjoy the advantages of a vast studio undertaking without being saddled with the whole of the general overheads'.[32] In 1935 Sound City made a profit of £53,000 and was estimated to have been the production base for one fifth of all British quota films.[3]

Linda Wood has argued that quota quickies represented an economically determined mode of low-cost production that played an important role in sustaining the British film industry in the 1930s: they provided employment, kept studios busy and provided valuable experience for British technicians that in the longer term would contribute to the improvement in quality of British films during the Second World War.[34] The imperative was for streamlined production: quota quickies were often shot in as little as two weeks and under conditions of strict budgetary economy. Adrian Brunel explained how film-makers adapted to the conditions of low-budget production in an article for *The Era* in 1934:

> I cannot refrain from a personal note here, as my own experience in making seven 'quickies' during the last year provides me with a moral. I believe that it is possible to make good entertainment (without any particular spectacular or production qualities, I need hardly say) for the modest sums I have had at my disposal – and I have been fortunate in having a brilliant partner who has a gift for making each farthing expended do the work of another producer's penny – but I do not believe that it is possible for any unit to be infallible. A cheap production that does not hit its mark can be a very sorry affair, and although an experienced 'quickie' unit can achieve marvels, it cannot guarantee results.[35]

George Pearson, an experienced silent director who made several quickies during the 1930s, explained that the 'feverish and restless environment' of quota production militated against quality: 'To make a talking film with only £6,000 to meet the cost of studio space, subject, script, director, technicians, film stock, lights, artistes, overheads and end up with a profit needed a spartan economy and a slave-driving effort. All vaunting ideas of film as an art had to be abandoned.'[36]

The Board of Trade ledger provides ample evidence that British film-makers were capable of turning out films for much less than £1 per foot. And that sometimes – at least judging by the 'reviews for showmen' published in *Kine Weekly* – they were able to rise above their low-budget status. For example *Here's George* (1932) – produced by Tom Arnold at Cricklewood Studios for the Producers' Distributing Corporation – had a statutory cost of £2,358 (£41 per 100 feet): *Kine* found it 'a refreshing British comedy which has all the promise of a popular success'.[37] It added that the film 'was exceptionally well received at the London Trade show and big returns are expected when the film is released on Boxing Day'.[38] *Hiking With Mademoiselle* (1933) – a four-reeler directed by Edward Nakhimoff for International Productions – had a statutory cost of £987 (£29 per 100 feet): *Kine* thought it 'an excellent supporting offering for most halls'.[39] And the four-reeler *Heroes of the Mine* (1933) – directed by the legendary low-cost specialist Widgey Newman for Delta Films at a statutory cost of £604 (£12 per 100 feet) – was praised for its realism: it was a 'useful supporting feature' and was reported by its distributor Butcher's Film Service to have 'made an auspicious start with a three-figure circuit booking'.[40]

The Board of Trade ledger broadly confirms the narrative that American renters were responsible for most of the quota quickies. Not only were the average costs of American-sponsored quota films notably lower than British-financed films, but American renters offered more films in the lowest-cost range: some 48 per cent (40 of 83) of American-sponsored films had a statutory cost of £55 per 100 feet or less compared to only 13 per cent (10 of 75) of the British-financed films. A caveat should be lodged here insofar as American renters handled more films in the shorter featurette class: indeed, some renters – notably Fox and Warner Bros. – offered entirely or mostly featurettes. A memorandum accompanying the ledger records that '[a] large number of films were acquired by them which reflected little credit on British production' and that 'it was undoubtedly the policy of many renters to acquire indifferent films as cheaply as possible'.[41] However, a closer analysis of the ledger reveals a more complex picture with some significant variances between different renters. The average statutory cost of the films offered by United Artists (£12,440), for example, was over six times the average of Universal (£2,006) and four times the average of First National (£2,992).

United Artists stood apart from the other US distributors insofar as it produced no films of its own and so relied upon independent producers for all its product. The Board of Trade felt that UA 'on the whole have acquired better pictures than most US renters, although their expenditure has been by no means lavish ... They can certainly be regarded as doing their share.'[42] UA offered nine films from eight producers with an average statutory cost of £12,440. However, this figure is distorted by one exceptional high-cost picture: *Perfect Understanding* (£70,010). This film was shot by Gloria Swanson's British-registered production company at Ealing Studios. Swanson raised the finance by selling her stock in UA to the corporation.[43] UA's next most expensive film cost barely a tenth of the Swanson picture: *No Funny Business* (John Stafford Productions) had a statutory cost of £7,426. Without *Perfect Understanding*, the average statutory cost of UA's British films falls to £5,244: this was closer to the average for the American renters.[44] All bar one of UA's films were above the statutory cost of £55 per 100 feet that marks the unofficial threshold of a 'quickie': the exception was *Money for Speed* (Hallmark Films, 1932) which had a statutory cost of £41 per 100 feet.

After United Artists, Paramount was the American distributor with the highest average cost: it offered twelve British quota films at an average statutory cost of £7,817. Paramount had a close relationship with the British and Dominions Film

Corporation: its British subsidiary was based at B&D's studio at Elstree and it also contracted quota pictures from B&D. Paramount British Pictures produced three films: *Lily Christine* (£18,910), *Down Our Street* (£5,891) and *Insult* (£7,486). *Lily Christine* – a vehicle for American star Corinne Griffith – was twice the cost of any of the other Paramount films: the average statutory cost falls to £6,809 excluding that film. Paramount's other British films were contracted from London Film Productions (four films at an average statutory cost of £8,081) and B&D (six films at an average statutory cost of £5,627). None of Paramount's films was really in the 'quickie' category: the lowest statutory costs were for *The Barton Mystery* (£63 per 100 feet), *Discord* (£67 per 100 feet) and *The Crime at Blossoms* (£69 per 100 feet). Paramount's British managing director J. C. Graham told the Moyne Committee that Paramount had initially produced its own British quota films in a higher-cost range but was forced to move to lower-cost films due to the increasing amount of quota footage required under the Act:

> After the quota law was put into effect we took a stage, and began to bring personnel here as much as we could under the restrictions of the law, and we produced in one year pictures ranging in cost from £30,000 to about £70,000. I think those were the figures, and we lost money on that, on the whole lot, and we had to stop ... That one year we did eight pictures, and we found it did not pay, that it was a big loss, and it was heavier on us than our capital would stand, so we dropped down to a lower grade of picture in price, because the law was going up in quantity.[45]

MGM and RKO were both somewhere in the middle of the cost range for the American renters. MGM registered eight British films at an average statutory cost of £4,385. The Board of Trade noted that MGM have 'varied their policy from time to time. They have acquired at times good pictures and at others sheer rubbish.' The highest-cost film was *Diamond Cut Diamond* (£19,884), produced by Eric Hakim at Elstree Studios with American star Adolphe Menjou. However, excepting *Diamond Cut Diamond*, the average statutory cost of MGM's quota pictures falls to only £2,171 and the average statutory cost per 100 feet to £38. Most of these were produced by Sound City Films, but there were also films from Real Art Productions (*A Tight Corner*) and Westminster Films (*Born Lucky*). MGM's British managing director Sam Eckman Jr claimed that spending more did not necessarily guarantee better films:

> I admit I have discovered that based on production facilities, spending £20,000 to £25,000 for a film made by the companies that want to make films for us are no better than the films for which we spent £7,000 to £10,000. I have discovered that the companies that are willing to make films for us and that spend £20,000 to £25,000 to make them can make no better films than other companies who spend £7,000 to £10,000. They lack the ability even though they have the money and even though we take them.[46]

RKO 'acquire a number of cheap second features from various sources but, on the other hand, they distributed in 1932/3 some very good films made by Associated

Talking Pictures'. RKO released ten British films which can be divided into two distinct groups. Four films – *The Sign of Four* (£12,472), *The Impassive Footman* (£8,928), *Love on the Spot* (£7,218) and *Looking on the Bright Side* (£27,582) – were produced at Ealing Studios under a co-production arrangement with Associated Talking Pictures.[47] The average statutory cost of those films was £14,050, well above the average for a British quota film, although this figure was inflated by the Gracie Fields vehicle *Looking on the Bright Side*, which cost twice as much as any other. RKO's lower-cost quota films were provided by Real Art Productions: the average statutory cost of those films was £2,930 and the cost per 100 feet ranged between £57 and £66.

The Fox Film Corporation and Warner Bros./First National both focused on featurettes for much of their British quota. Fox was 'mostly producing short second features, four reelers, to form complete programmes with larger US features'. This meant that it had to offer more films to make up its quota footage. It handled eleven films from eight producers including Real Art Productions, George Smith and Harvey Cohen. All were four-reelers and the average statutory cost was £2,009: the Board of Trade calculated the average cost as £55 per 100 feet. Warner Bros. Film Distributors and First National Film Distributors were both part of the same corporation: the two were so closely linked as to be to all intents and purposes the same distributing organisation. Warner Bros. set up its own British production unit at Teddington Studios in 1931, headed by American producer Irving Asher, in order to produce its own quota films rather than acquiring them from external contractors.[48] *The Bioscope* reported that Warner intended to invest £200,000 in its British production programme.[49] However, the Board of Trade ledger reveals that the twenty films offered by Warner Bros. and First National in the quota year 1932–3 had a total statutory cost of £54,554: this suggests total expenditure on film production somewhere between £91,000 and £109,000. Warner opted to offer most of its quota footage through featurettes: only three films – *Illegal* (£6,399), *The Blind Spot* (£7,693) and *The Thirteenth Candle* (£2,331) – were longer than 6,000 feet.

However, the worst offender among the American renters as far as the Board of Trade was concerned was Universal Pictures:

> Universal are the black spot. So far as films made in this country are concerned, they only acquire rubbish. In silent days they adopted the policy of buying up – presumably for a very small amount – the English rights of Indian films, but the introduction of the talkies has dried up this source. They have now turned their attention to Australia and are obtaining a number of films from there which are quite good on the low comedy side, but are unbelievably poor on the dramatic side.[50]

The acquisition of Indian and Australian films was consistent with the Cinematograph Films Act which allowed films produced in the British Empire to be included in the quota. In 1932–3 Universal registered thirteen films at an average statutory cost of £2,006: these included six features and seven featurettes. Four of the features were Australian, including three produced by Efftree Productions of Melbourne – *A Sentimental Bloke* (£5,264), *Diggers* (£2,209) and *His Royal Highness* (£5,013) – and *Down on the Farm* (£3,156) from Cinesound Productions. The other two features included one made in Britain (*Betrayal*) and one acquired from India (*Toll of Destiny*). The latter film was shot as a silent in 1930 (its original title was *Karmano Kaher*): it was picked up for quota by Universal and released as a silent/sound hybrid with a synchronised soundtrack. Its exceptionally low statutory cost (£545) no doubt reflects cheaper labour costs in India but does not allow like-for-like comparison with British-made films. *Kine Weekly* averred that it was 'poorly produced' with 'very weak story and pictorial values ... The fact that it is a Quota picture constitutes the only appeal of this picture.'[51]

The Board of Trade data therefore confirms the anecdotal evidence that most of the cheaper quota pictures in the early 1930s were offered by American renters. However, there are some qualifications. United Artists and Paramount were exceptions insofar as their quota films were on average in the middle of the cost range for British films and were comparable to British renters such as Wardour Films and the British Lion Film Corporation. RKO adopted a two-tier strategy with a clear distinction between its higher-end films and lower-cost films that were nevertheless still above the unofficial level of £1 per foot that defined the quota quickies. MGM, Fox, Warner Bros./First National and Universal were responsible for the bulk of the 'quickies': collectively they offered 75 per cent (39 of 52) of the films at a statutory cost of £55 per 100 feet or less. It was therefore certain American renters rather than all American renters who were responsible for the low-cost British quota films of the early 1930s.

Notes

1. 'Compulsory Films Bill', *Daily Express*, 12 August 1927, p. 5.
2. Rachael Low, *The History of the British Film 1929–1939: Film Making in 1930s Britain* (London: George Allen & Unwin, 1985), p. 276.
3. Ibid., p. 280.
4. Ibid., p. 281.
5. The National Archives (TNA) BT 64/98: R. D. Fennelly, 'Cinematograph Films Act', November 1934.
6. Simon Rowson, 'A Statistical Survey of the Cinema Industry in Great Britain in 1934', *Journal of the Royal Statistical Society*, 99: 1 (1936), p. 111.
7. 'British Production News', *Kinematograph Weekly*, 14 February 1929, p. 44.
8. 'Will British Films Improve?', *Kinematograph Weekly*, 2 January 1930, p. 67.
9. 'More British Films – but Good Ones', *Kinematograph Weekly*, 30 March 1933, p. 4.
10. 'Arthur Jarratt Criticises Quota "Quickies"', *Kinematograph Weekly*, 7 June 1934, p. 1.
11. Michael Balcon, *Michael Balcon Presents ... A Lifetime of Films* (London: Hutchinson, 1969), p. 28.
12. Jeffrey Richards, *The Age of the Dream Palace: Cinema and Society in Britain 1930–1939* (London: Routledge & Kegan Paul, 1984), p. 3.
13. 'Amend the Quota Act', *Kinematograph Weekly*, 16 January 1930, p. 37.

14. *Parliamentary Debates: House of Commons*, 5th Series, vol. 241, 22 July 1930, col. 1947.
15. TNA BT 55/3: Association of Cine-Technicians: Evidence submitted to the Board of Trade Committee into the position of British Films, 13 May 1936.
16. Michael Powell, *A Life in Movies: An Autobiography* (London: William Heineman, 1986), p. 214.
17. Adrian Brunel, *Nice Work: The Story of Thirty Years in British Film Production* (London: Forbes Robertson, 1949), pp. 165–6.
18. 'Anthony Havelock-Allan: Part 1', 20 June–3 July 1990, *The British Entertainment History Project*: https://historyproject.org.uk/interview.anthony-havelock-allan (available June 2023).
19. Low, *The History of the British Film 1929–1939*, p. 115.
20. John Sedgwick, 'The Market for Feature Films in Britain, 1934: A Viable National Cinema', *Historical Journal of Film, Radio and Television*, 14: 1 (1994), p. 28.
21. TNA BT 55/3: Committee on Cinematograph Films: Memorandum of Evidence by S. Rowson, June 1936.
22. TNA BT 64/97: Particulars of British Films Acquired by Renters during Quota Year 1932–3. This handwritten document was probably compiled by Board of Trade official R. D. Fennelly whose name is attached to the accompanying memorandum. It lists the films by renter and includes for each the date of registration, the producer, the length in feet, the statutory cost and the statutory cost per 100 feet. The one film for which no cost information is provided is *Till the Bells Ring* (1933) produced by British Sound Film Productions for independent distributor A. L. Bayley. The ledger lists *Old Spanish Customers* (1932) under MGM though in fact it was distributed by Wardour Films.
23. Ibid.: R. D. Fennelly, 'Quality Test for British Films' (undated but c. October 1933). All unreferenced quotations in this chapter are from this memorandum.
24. 'British Studios Today', *The Bioscope*, 12 February 1930, p. 23.
25. This does not include the documentary feature *With Cobham to Kivu* (1932), which was atypical for the Gaumont-British group.
26. James Chapman, 'Hitchcock's *Number Seventeen* (1932) and the British Film Quota', *Historical Journal of Film, Radio and Television*, 43: 4 (2023), pp. 1183–91.
27. François Truffaut, with Helen G. Scott, *Hitchcock* (London: Paladin, rev. edn 1986), p. 104.
28. Low, *The History of the British Film 1929–1939*, pp. 174–5.
29. The Real Art Productions films in the 1932–3 quota year were *The Shadow* (£7,702) and *Puppets of Fate* (£5,748) for United Artists, *Double Dealing* (£2,848) and *A Safe Proposition* (£2,776) for Fox, *A Tight Corner* (£2,885) for MGM, and *The Face at the Window* (£2,712), *The World, the Flesh and the Devil* (£3,153), *The Iron Stair* (£2,677), *Called Back* (£2,752), *The Medicine Man* (£2,728) and *Excess Baggage* (£3,538) for RKO.
30. The films were *Reunion* (£1,985), *She Was Only a Village Maiden* (£2,485), *The Wishbone* (£2,689), *Side Street* (£1,175) and *The Golden Cage* (£2,701).
31. 'Butchers Booming', *Kinematograph Weekly*, 24 November 1932, p. 31.
32. 'Company Meeting', *The Times*, 24 August 1936, p. 18.
33. Derek Threadgall, *Shepperton Studios: An Independent View* (London: British Film Institute, 1994), pp. 4–23.
34. Linda Wood, 'Low-Budget British Films in the 1930s', in Robert Murphy (ed.), *The British Cinema Book* (London: British Film Institute, 1997), pp. 48–57.

35. '"Quota" Films and the Lesson of the German "Kontingent"', *The Era*, 3 January 1934, p. 9.
36. George Pearson, *Flashback* (London: George Allen & Unwin, 1957), p. 193.
37. *Kinematograph Weekly*, 22 September 1932, p. 37.
38. 'PDC's "Independence Day" Anniversary', *Kinematograph Weekly*, 1 December 1932, p. 32.
39. *Kinematograph Weekly*, 16 March 1933, p. 13.
40. 'Butcher's String of Winners', *Kinematograph Weekly*, 27 October 1933, p. 27.
41. TNA BT 64/97: 'Quality Test for British Films'.
42. Ibid.
43. Tino Balio, *United Artists: The Company Built by the Stars* (Madison: University of Wisconsin Press, 1976), p. 84.
44. Other than *Perfect Understanding*, the UA films were *His Lordship* (Westminster Films, £3,855), *Men of Steel* (Langham Productions, £5,166), *Puppets of Fate* (Real Art Productions, £5,166), *Daughters of Today* (FWK Productions, £5,148), *The Shadow* (Real Art Productions, £5,703), *Money for Speed* (Hallmark Productions, £2,734), *Matinee Idol* (Wyndham Films, £5,901) and *No Funny Business* (John Stafford Productions, £7,426).
45. Board of Trade, *Minutes of Evidence Taken before the Departmental Committee on Cinematograph Films* (London: HMSO, 1936), p. 99 (968-8).
46. Ibid., p. 105 (1084).
47. 'US Cash for Pictures Made Here', *Sunday Dispatch*, 13 September 1931, p. 3.
48. Steve Chibnall, 'Hollywood on Thames: The British Productions of Warner Bros.–First National, 1931–1945', *Historical Journal of Film, Radio and Television*, 39: 4 (2019), pp. 687–724.
49. 'Warner's £200,000 for British Production', *The Bioscope*, 2 September 1931, p. 16.
50. TNA BT 64/97: 'Quality Test for British Films'.
51. *Kinematograph Weekly*, 19 May 1932, p. 25.

CHAPTER 6

Korda and the City

Alexander Korda was 'the man who made the world conscious of British films'.[1] Korda was the most successful British producer of the 1930s and came to be regarded as something of a talisman for the British film industry: his fortunes also reflected the course of a turbulent decade characterised by a cycle of boom and bust.[2] It was the spectacular success of Korda's *The Private Life of Henry VIII* (1933) that put British cinema on the international map: it is also credited with encouraging investors to back British film production in the expectation that other films would repeat its success, especially in the American market. Three years of highly speculative investment followed, after which the bubble burst and the banks and insurance companies that had financed the boom found themselves facing large losses. While this general narrative is uncontested, however, there is some debate as to the extent of Korda's responsibility for the financial crisis that hit the film industry in 1937. Lady Yule, the co-founder of British National Films, was critical of the knighthood awarded to Korda in 1942: 'The knighthood could not have been given for services to the British film industry. Korda had lost the industry, or the Prudential Assurance Company, over three million.'[3] George Perry, while not blaming Korda directly, contends that the 'extravagant success' of *The Private Life of Henry VIII* 'set in train a period of excessive speculation with City firms falling over themselves in the rush to get a stake in the new booming industry'.[4] Sarah Street suggests that Korda bore much of the responsibility for the financial problems of the industry insofar as 'Korda's profligacy influenced the City's negative attitude towards production probably more than any other company'.[5] Rachael Low, in contrast, argues that Korda played a minimal role in the crisis of 1937 and lays the blame instead on a group of companies headed by another émigré, Max Schach, 'whose expensive failures did far more to discredit British production as an investment than the picturesque extravagance of Korda'.[6] While Kevin Gough-Yates absolves the producers themselves of much of the blame and argues that 'the bubble was created less by film makers than by banks and financial houses eager for easy money'.[7]

A Hungarian émigré, Korda based himself in Britain from 1932 after a peripatetic film-making career that had previously included both Europe and Hollywood. Korda directed one British quota picture for Paramount Pictures (*Service for Ladies*) before setting up as an independent producer. He registered London Film Productions (LFP) as a private company in May 1932 with a nominal capital of £100: Korda and Conservative MP Captain A. C. N. Dixey were the managing directors, while the veteran actor George Grossmith was chairman of the board. In 1932–3 LFP made seven features (mostly for Paramount) at a total cost of £245,476: *Wedding Rehearsal* (£42,080), *Man of Tomorrow* (£30,922), *That Night in London* (£33,428), *Strange Evidence* (£28,350), *Counsel's Opinion* (£25,424), *Cash* (£22,694) and *The Girl from Maxim's* (£62,578).[8] Even at this stage Korda was evidently orienting towards the production of 'quality' films: all LFP's films cost significantly more than the average for a British film in the 1932–3 quota year. LFP increased its capital by private share issues to £20,000 in November 1932 and then to £80,000 in April 1933.[9]

The Private Life of Henry VIII was the breakthrough for Korda and for London Films. It was recognised at the time as a landmark in quality film production for Britain: *Picturegoer* called it 'the best production that has ever been turned out from a British studio – and there are no exceptions'.[10] There are different accounts of the film's origin: Korda's version was that he was inspired to make it after hearing a London cabbie singing the music hall refrain 'I'm 'Enery the Eighth I Am', while others credit actress Elsa Lanchester with noticing her husband Charles Laughton's likeness to Holbein's portrait of Henry.[11] The historical subject matter was consistent with previous Korda films including *The Prince and the Pauper* in Austria and *The Private Life of Helen of Troy* in Hollywood. Korda's nephew Michael Korda later presented the success of *The Private Life of Henry VIII* as a happy accident:

> Alex himself never thought of *Henry VIII* as a classic – in fact he went out of his way to prevent it being presented as one. He knew better than anyone that the film was a hasty attempt to put together all the elements that were available to him on a shoestring budget. Once he had succeeded, much to his own surprise, he spent the rest of his life selling the film, borrowing against it, buying it back and re-releasing it throughout the world.[12]

It is curious that Michael Korda, who elsewhere in his memoir is keen to assert his uncle's vision and tenacity, does not allow him greater credit for *The Private Life of Henry VIII*. Far from being hastily assembled, *The Private Life of Henry VIII* was in fact a highly planned and entirely conscious attempt to produce a 'quality' British film for the world market. Its success – including with critics and audiences – was no accident.

For one thing *The Private Life of Henry VIII* was no 'shoestring' production. LFP's records indicate that the final cost of the film was £93,710.[13] This was over five times the average cost of a British-financed quota feature in 1932–3 (around £17,900). Korda was able to raise the production finance by borrowing against a distribution contract with United Artists: when the film ran over budget a completion loan was provided by Italian bankers Ludovico and Giuseppe Toeplitz, secured against the producer's share of the US receipts.[14] It was a calculated gamble by Korda as *The Private Life of Henry VIII* was too expensive to recover its cost from the domestic market alone. As the journal *World Film News* observed at the time: 'The risk in making ambitious films is a very considerable one for England. The home market is small. It is not sufficient to return with any certainty the cost of a film like *Henry VIII*, and it is incapable of returning the cost of [MGM's] *Mutiny on the Bounty*.'[15] In the event *The Private Life of Henry VIII* did exceptionally good business in Britain: it is estimated to have been the second most popular box-office attraction of 1933 (behind the Hollywood-made 'British' film *Cavalcade*).[16] Its distributor's receipts of £81,825 from the home market were equivalent to 87 per cent of the cost of production – this was a large percentage for a such a high-cost film but nevertheless also demonstrates the extent to which Korda had gambled on accessing the world market.

It was the international release of *The Private Life of Henry VIII* that made it such an outstanding success. Again, this was no accident. Korda co-ordinated a series of premières at prestigious locations in different capital cities: these included a 'World Première' at the Lord Byron Cinema in Paris on 1 October 1933 and an American première at the Radio City Music Hall in New York on 12 October before its West End première at the Leicester Square Theatre on 24 October. *The Private Life of Henry VIII* did exceptional business for a British film in the United States. It was reported to have set a record for the Radio City Music Hall with a one-day gross of US$18,400 and returned a distributor's gross of US$469,646 (equivalent to approximately £104,365) from the United States where it was UA's seventh top-grossing release of 1933.[17] Some sources claim that Korda made a profit of over £500,000 from *The Private Life of Henry VIII*, although this is something of an exaggeration. LFP's records indicate that after four years it had earned distributor's receipts of £210,000 in total: this would suggest a profit somewhere in the region of £100,000 following repayment of the production cost and distributor's fees and expenses.[18] Even so this still represented a profit of more than 100 per cent against the cost of production – a huge margin by the standards of the film industry and especially so for such a high-cost film.

The success of *The Private Life of Henry VIII* was extraordinary in every respect: it returned a higher profit than any previous British picture for which financial records exist. It also proved to be a non-recurring phenomenon insofar as none of the subsequent attempts to emulate it – including by Korda and by other producers – came near to matching its success. Korda cannot be held responsible for the policies of other producers who budgeted their films in the expectation of significant revenues from the United States or for the banks who loaned money to unproven film-makers. And Korda was different from other independent producers in several important respects. One was that he adopted a portfolio strategy that spread the risk across a programme of films: his major films over the next six years included *Catherine the Great* (1934), *The Private Life of Don Juan* (1934), *The Scarlet Pimpernel* (1934), *Sanders of the River* (1935), *The Ghost Goes West* (1935), *Rembrandt* (1936), *Things to Come* (1936), *The Man Who Could Work Miracles* (1936), *Knight Without Armour* (1937), *Elephant Boy* (1937), *The Divorce of Lady X* (1938), *The Drum* (1938) and *The Four Feathers* (1939). Following *The Private Life of Henry VIII*, Korda secured a long-term distribution deal with United Artists which guaranteed access to the US market.[19] Another difference was that Korda, unlike many producers who had only nominal capital and financed their production activities through loans, sought to build up the capital reserves of London Films. LFP made a series of further share issues in 1934 and 1935. The additional capital was 'to be utilised partly in connection with the erection of studios, partly in developing the Hillman colour process and also partly in connection with the general development of the company'.[20] By 1936 LFP's authorised capital amounted to £825,000 of which £428,799 had been issued.[21] A third important difference was that Korda built his own studio facility (Denham Studios): this would enable him to streamline his production activity (hitherto Korda had been a tenant at the British and Dominions studio at Elstree) and to rent out stages to other producers. Denham was a modern studio with five stages built at a cost of £1 million: it opened in May 1936 and was said to be home to 'half the crack technicians of Europe'.[22]

By January 1937 LFP had increased its authorised capital to £2,238,549. The biggest shareholder was the Prudential Assurance Company, which held a majority of the preferred shares (250,000) and 25,000 ordinary shares, while other significant investors were Lloyds Bank Nominees (1 million ordinary shares), London Film Productions Trust (397,701), Midland Bank Nominees (325,000), Clydesdale Bank Nominees (90,000) and the insurance company C. T. Bowring & Co. (90,000). The largest personal shareholding was held by banker Leopold Sutro (27,500 preferred shares) whose interests were represented on the board by his son John: in total the Sutro family interests held 49,000 shares. LFP also held loans and debentures amounting to £1,502,853: these included five loans from the Prudential Assurance Company (£1,113,200 in total), Lloyds Bank (£263,073) and the United Artists Corporation (£100,000).[23] Denham Securities was formed in January 1936 with share capital of £52,800 to arrange financing for independent producers at Denham.[24]

The role of the Prudential Assurance Company in film finance – and in particular its investment in LFP – requires explanation. As Michael Korda observed:

> Oddly enough, the first major investor attracted by the success of *Henry VIII* was that doughty, conservative bastion of British finance, the Prudential . . . Exactly how Percy Crump and Sir Connop Guthrie were persuaded to gamble the Pru's hard-earned money on Alex remains something of a mystery. Alex's friends in the City and the government certainly helped . . . In any event, the Pru agreed to finance London Films and to enable Alex to build Denham Studios.[25]

The Prudential was one of the largest providers of personal life and accident insurance in the world: it had pioneered cheap insurance policies for the working classes (with premiums as low as a penny a week) and was reckoned to insure a third of the population of the United Kingdom. It was also cash rich and was looking to invest across a range of businesses and industries: in 1934 the Prudential held assets of £290 million and its investments ranged from government bonds to property mortgages and shares in the railway and shipping industries.[26] There are different accounts of how the Prudential, which had built its reputation on conservatism in its investment portfolio, got involved in such a speculative business as the film industry. One explanation was political pressure. According to Michael Korda:

'The British government, concerned that the Prudential might invest abroad, encouraged the giant insurance company "to take a position" in the British film industry, which obviously needed financing, and which, on the evidence of *Henry VIII*, seemed likely to offer substantial profits.'[27] However, there is no hard evidence that this was the case and in any event the Prudential already held significant foreign investments, especially in the British Dominions.

Another explanation is that Korda and the Prudential came into each other's orbit when Korda was interested in a company (Gerrard Industries) in which the Prudential already held a substantial interest. Gerrard Industries was developing an experimental colour process invented by George Hillman that promised to be less expensive than rival processes such as Technicolor. *The Financial Times* reported in September 1934:

> It is now an open secret that the Prudential Assurance Company has guaranteed fully £300,000 new money for the energetic exploitation of the Gerrard Company's unique colour film process, which is claimed to be inexpensive as well as far in advance of former methods. It is hoped that the first full-length picture will be produced by the London Film Productions Company, which has made such a coup in securing Mr Alexander Korda's services.[28]

In the event the Hillman process lost out to the Technicolor Corporation of New York, which successfully developed its three-strip colour process and collaborated with Pioneer Pictures in the production of the first colour feature film in 1935: *Becky Sharp*. Gerrard Industries did not lose out: it invested £45,320 in Technicolor's British subsidiary and its managing director Kay Harris became the managing director of Technicolor Limited.[29] In the meantime Sir Connop Guthrie joined the board of London Films as the Prudential's representative.

Initially, at least, all seemed to go well for Korda. London Films recorded its first profit (a modest £3,755) in 1934: the accounts indicate that LFP had earned net film revenue of £137,309, mostly from *The Private Life of Henry VIII*.[30] The following year film revenues amounted to £449,424 (43 per cent of which was for *The Private Life of Henry VIII*) and LFP returned a profit of £80,011. At this point LFP's accounts were anticipating a profit on the three films completed in 1934 (*The Private Life of Don Juan*, *The Scarlet Pimpernel* and *Sanders of the River*). The annual report recorded:

> [The] residual value of *The Scarlet Pimpernel* is considerably less than the figure at which it appears in the Balance Sheet, but against this we should mention that *The Private Life of Henry VIII* appears in such Accounts at the nominal value of £1, although expected still to produce substantial revenue . . . Taking the completed productions of the Company altogether they stand in the Accounts at a figure substantially less than it is estimated they will earn collectively.[31]

LFP adopted the Hollywood accounting practice of including anticipated revenues from films as assets on its balance sheet. It would also write off films after (usually) two years, even if, as with *The Private Life of Henry VIII*, they were still earning revenue. In January 1936 it reported an estimated profit of £70,943 for the previous year 'assuming that revenues est. by sales dept will be received & that film *Tarass Boulba* [sic] will be completed before March 1936 at cost of no more than £50,000'.[32] However, in May 1936 a balance sheet submitted to the Prudential indicated that LFP was showing a loss of £375,128 on film production.[33]

There were several reasons for LFP's deteriorating financial position. The underlying reason was that most of Korda's films lost money. A ledger of film costs and revenues to April 1937 indicates that LFP had spent a total of £1,443,954 on film production since 1933 but had received only £1,159,143 in receipts from distribution (see Table 6.1). The ledger divides the films into two groups. Group I – comprising *The Private Life of Henry VIII*, *Catherine the Great*, *The Private Life of Don Juan*, *The Scarlet Pimpernel*, *Sanders of the River* and *The Ghost Goes West* – cost £785,189 in total and collectively returned £896,289. There were significant profits for *The Private Life of Henry VIII* and *The Scarlet Pimpernel* and a small one for *The Ghost Goes West*, while *Catherine the Great* and *Sanders of the River* both made modest losses and *The Private Life of Don Juan* a significant loss. However, the five Group II films – *Moscow Nights*, *Things to Come*, *The Man Who Could Work Miracles*, *Rembrandt* and *Men Are Not Gods* – cost £658,765 in total but returned only £262,854. The only profitable film in this group was the modestly budgeted (by Korda's standards) *Moscow Nights*. But there were significant losses for *Things to Come*, *The Man Who Could Work Miracles*, *Rembrandt* and *Men Are Not Gods*. It was not just the losses that affected the balance sheet but the fact that actual revenues were often significantly less than the amount anticipated in the accounts even for successful films: the revenues of

Table 6.1 Production costs and distributors' receipts of feature films produced by London Film Productions, 1933–6

FILM	PRODUCTION COST	RECEIPTS
The Private Life of Henry VIII (1933)	£93,700	£210,000
Catherine the Great (1934)	£127,868	£127,000
The Private Life of Don Juan (1934)	£114,239	£53,700
The Scarlet Pimpernel (1934)	£143,521	£204,300
Sanders of the River (1935)	£149,789	£143,200
The Ghost Goes West (1935)	£156,062	£158,039
Moscow Nights (1935)	£52,536	£83,865
Things to Come (1936)	£244,028	£119,500
The Man Who Could Work Miracles (1936)	£133,104	£20,400
Rembrandt (1936)	£138,945	£36,141
Men Are Not Gods (1936)	£93,362	£2,948

Source: Prudential Group Archive Box 2357: London Film Productions: Cost of production and receipts to 24 April 1937.

The Scarlet Pimpernel (£204,300) were some way short of the £250,000 anticipated, while the anticipated revenues of £175,000 for *The Private Life of Don Juan* (actual revenue £53,500) and £300,000 for *Things to Come* (actual revenue £119,500) were both highly optimistic.[34]

A caveat needs to be lodged here insofar as Korda's films did not lose money on account of being bad films. Most of them were popular and were regarded as 'hits'. John Sedgwick's statistical analysis of popular preferences in Britain suggests that *Catherine the Great* was the fourth most popular film in 1934, *The Scarlet Pimpernel* third and *Sanders of the River* sixth in 1935, and *The Ghost Goes West* sixth and *Things to Come* ninth in 1936.[35] The issue was more that they were too expensive to recover their costs from the domestic market alone. All the films after *The Private Life of Henry VIII* returned a lower percentage of their cost from the home market: *The Scarlet Pimpernel* (78 per cent), *Sanders of the River* (65 per cent), *The Ghost Goes West* (54 per cent), *Catherine the Great* (46 per cent), *Things to Come* (28 per cent), *Rembrandt* (24 per cent) and *The Private Life of Don Juan* (16 per cent) demonstrate the extent to which the films were dependent upon international receipts.[36] However, returns from the all-important US market were disappointing overall: the most successful in terms of US distributor's receipts were *The Scarlet Pimpernel* (US$376,866), *Catherine the Great* (US$282,083) and *The Ghost Goes West* (US$156,722).[37]

The combination of increasing production costs and shortfalls in revenue meant that by the mid-1930s Korda was facing a severe liquidity crisis. This was the context in which the Prudential, already the biggest equity investor in London Films, made a series of loans to the company between August 1935 and January 1937. The first loan (12 August 1935) was for £82,200 and was specifically for LFP to buy shares in Technicolor Limited: this seemed to all parties a good investment given that Technicolor had now proven its quality and Korda was already planning on making films using the process. A second, much larger loan of £500,000 (6 December 1935) was to support LFP's production programme for 1936 for which Korda did not have sufficient capital. The third loan of £250,000 (12 October 1936) was specifically for the production of two films – *I, Claudius* and *Lawrence of Arabia* – which were each forecast to cost around £125,000. It was evident by now that the Prudential was concerned about pumping more money into LFP. Ernest Lever, the joint secretary of the Prudential, stated in no uncertain terms 'that yet again an estimate put forward by the Company has been vitiated and after full consideration, it was resolved that no further production should be commenced after *I, Claudius* until July 1937 and the position should then be reviewed in the light of the existing circumstances'.[38] However, on 4 January 1937 the Prudential made another two loans to LFP amounting to £281,000 in total: the purpose was not stated, but it is probably no coincidence that this latest advance came at precisely the time that Twickenham Film Studios had filed for bankruptcy.[39] Twickenham was a smaller operation than LFP but had a similar set-up insofar as it included both a production arm and a studio company. A list of secured loans put LFP's total indebtedness at £1,498,705.[40]

It was not just film-making costs that accounted for LFP's expenditure. LFP had particularly high salary costs and overheads: Korda was paid a salary of £9,000 per year (after tax) and had an 'entertainment allowance' of £3,000. This was in addition to his producer's fee per picture and percentage of the profits.[41] Korda had a tendency to buy or option properties that would be counted as company assets even if they were not made into films. Some money was expended on what looks suspiciously like patronage. He offered Winston Churchill £10,000 as an advance against a 25 per cent share of the profits of a film to mark the Silver Jubilee of King George V for which Churchill was to write the scenario: Korda ended up paying Churchill £2,750 for a draft of the unmade film along with another £2,000 to write several short subjects which were also never made.[42] And there were also a number of unrealised films that incurred significant expenditure before they were abandoned. A schedule of aborted films in September 1937 includes *I, Claudius* (£131,865), *Lawrence of Arabia* (£24,834), *Cyrano de Bergerac* (£35,000), *Taras Bulba* (£27,275) and *Conquest of the Air* (£39,430).[43] To be fair, Korda cannot be blamed for the abandonment of *I, Claudius* and *Lawrence of Arabia*. The former, based on the novel by Robert Graves, was intended as a third major vehicle for Charles Laughton following *The Private Life of Henry VIII* and *Rembrandt* directed by Josef Von Sternberg. It was abandoned several months into shooting due to injuries sustained by co-star Merle Oberon in a motor car accident.[44] And *Lawrence of Arabia* – Korda's biopic of the enigmatic soldier-scholar T. E. Lawrence and his role in the Arab Revolt – was a victim of political circumstances: the location shooting in Palestine was cancelled due to local unrest and Korda eventually bowed to pressure from the Foreign Office not to proceed with the film as it presented Turkey in a negative light.[45]

Another problem for Korda arose in relation to tenant producers at Denham. At the end of 1936 LFP had contracts with Capitol Film Productions and Trafalgar Film Productions to provide studio space and managerial services for three years at a total cost of £112,000 per year. It was also in negotiation with other producers including British Cine Alliance, Atlantic Film Productions, Victor Saville and Erich Pommer: 'All these are understood to be very anxious to enter into contracts and the only impediment would appear to be finance. If they are successful in obtaining outside finance and fulfil their contracts, the rentals and other receipts to be received during the ten months under review should amount to about £120,000.'[46] The problem for Denham was that the financial crisis that hit the film industry early in 1937 was felt most acutely by the sort of independent producers who were looking to emulate Korda in the production of high-budget international pictures. A list of debtors dated 2 January 1937 included Atlantic Film Productions (£8,863), British Cine Alliance (£3,303), Capitol Film Corporation (£14,904), New World Pictures (£14,289) and Pendennis Pictures Corporation (£36,215).[47] There was also a suggestion of antipathy between Korda and some clients. A memorandum in the Prudential Archive records: 'There is no doubt whatever that certain producers of good standing who have received financial assistance with Prudential money in the past have fallen foul of Korda for various reasons and can be ruled out as tenants at Denham while Korda is associated with the management of the studios.'[48]

The empty stages at Denham so soon after it had opened meant that Korda had to increase LFP's output in order to keep the studios operational. This was inevitably the cause of further tension with the Prudential, which wanted him to cut back on production. Korda's solution was ingenious: he sold the rights to many of the properties optioned by LFP to other producers – thereby realising some of the asset value held on LFP's books – who would produce the films at Denham 'for London Film Productions' with distribution handled by United Artists. The first films under this arrangement were *Fire Over England* (1937), produced by Erich Pommer's Pendennis Pictures, and Victor Saville's *Dark Journey* (1937). Saville would make another three films over the next two years – the others were *Storm in a Teacup* (1937), *Action for Slander* (1937) and *South Riding* (1938) – and a new tenant company Denham Productions would make three: *The Squeaker* (1937), *Paradise for Two* (1937) and *The Challenge* (1938). Korda was credited as executive producer of most of these films. The share of the budget provided by LFP varied: it advanced 40 per cent for *Fire Over England* (total cost: £162,093) and half the cost of a second Erich Pommer production, *Farewell Again* (£77,958), but advanced only 10 per cent for *Action for Slander* (£77,353) and *South Riding* (£83,714) and 7.5 per cent for *Dark Journey* (£125,508) and *Storm in a Teacup* (£73,358).[49] The remainder of the finance was arranged through Denham Securities. Even so LFP had earmarked £844,250 for film production in 1937 – including its own films and those by associated producers – for which it had only £400,000 arranged.[50]

It was clear that the honeymoon period between Korda and the Prudential was well and truly over. With his main investor unwilling to provide any further additional funding, Korda now looked to America to raise further finance. In the summer of 1937 he visited the United States to negotiate a number of financing deals. The Prudential Archive records that he borrowed US$500,000 from the Bank of America secured against the world receipts of *Knight Without Armour*: this was used to repay part of the outstanding loan to the Prudential.[51] Korda was effectively mortgaging the future of his company against anticipated revenues of future films. He also involved in what became a protracted negotiation to buy a controlling interest in United Artists in association with American independent producer Samuel Goldwyn. Korda had been a member of United Artists' board since 1935. Korda and Goldwyn were both providing much of UA's prestige product: their aim was to secure better terms and (for Korda) better distribution. In May 1937 they secured an option on the shares held in UA by three of its original founding members – Mary Pickford, Charlie Chaplin and Douglas Fairbanks – for a sum reported to be equivalent to £1.2 million (US$5 million). *Kine Weekly* described it as a 'stupendous deal'.[52] The option was confirmed at a special meeting of UA's stockholders.[53] However, when Goldwyn pulled out of the deal later in the year, Korda was unable to raise sufficient funds to take up the option before it expired. The Prudential was involved in the negotiations in the autumn but was unwilling to provide the full amount, while an attempt to form an investment syndicate came to nothing due to the City's dented confidence in the film industry. The deal was abandoned late in the year: it was reported that either Pickford or Chaplin had rejected a revised offer from Korda.[54]

Korda's relationship with United Artists was also becoming strained. He blamed LFP's financial woes on the under-selling of its films in the American market and repeatedly requested a revision of the terms of his distribution contract with UA to allow him to produce or direct films for other distributors. He told UA that 'he believed the selling of English made pictures in the United States had been poorly handled and that he was in a quandary as to what to do'.[55] Korda's grumbling came to a head in December 1937 when he wrote to the UA board to complain about 'your failure to secure anything like a fair or adequate return for these pictures, particularly in the United States' and suggesting that LFP would be forced to cease production unless the distribution contract were revised:

> The liquidation of London Film Productions will of necessity terminate the relationship which our contract purports to set out and will necessitate my seeking other employment in the making of pictures. After the experience of London Film Productions under the present distribution contract it is obvious that capital for the production of further pictures in England will not be forthcoming if the product is to be distributed under the unfavorable setup which now exists.[5]

It is possible that Korda may have raised the spectre of liquidation in order to apply pressure to the Prudential: Sir Connop Guthrie was also a member of UA's board. The Prudential did not want to see LFP go out of business as it would be unable to recover any of its investment. UA replied 'that the same could not be accepted by the corporation in that it contained certain charges which the corporation of course denies': Korda subsequently withdrew his letter only to resubmit it when Goldwyn – who had a similar agreement but was not complaining about the handling of his films – would not agree to Korda's terms.

At the start of 1938 LFP reported a modest profit for the previous year (£16,506), but it was carrying heavy debts. Much now depended on the performance of the two major films completed during 1937: *Knight Without Armour* (£309,295) and *Elephant Boy* (£152,361).[57] *Knight Without Armour* was Korda's most expensive film to date: its high cost was due in large measure to the fees paid to stars Marlene Dietrich (US$250,000) and Robert Donat (£25,000). *Elephant Boy* had started out as a project by documentarist Robert Flaherty who shot reels of footage in India which then had to be edited into a narrative by Korda's brother Zoltan. *Elephant Boy* nearly broke even (its total receipts were £151,708); there are no receipts recorded for *Knight Without Armour* but it is generally held to have been a heavy loss-maker.[58] Korda sought to diversify his production output and to reduce costs. He had already signalled his intention to prioritise more films at lower cost: 'It will not be so necessary to make costly "freak" pictures to break in. A steady supply of British films, most of them with British stories, will result as a future supply . . . The risks are less, and the prospects reasonably assured.'[59]

LFP's production programme for 1938 indicated lower budgets: the highest-budgeted film was *Over the Moon* (£155,000) followed by *The Drum* (£110,000), *The Divorce of Lady X* (£96,000), *The Return of the Scarlet Pimpernel* (£89,000), *The Squeaker* (£89,000), *Prison Without Bars* (£80,000) and *The Playboy* (£79,000).[60]

However, LFP was now carrying total indebtedness of £1,881,259 and the company was unable to meet the interest payments on its loans.[61] A memorandum by the Prudential's joint secretary Percy Crump in August 1938 recorded:

> The fact that we have lost a great deal of money through our association with Korda must be faced . . . His engaging personality and charm of manner must be resisted. His financial sense is non-existent and his promises (even when they are sincere) are worthless . . . Korda is a very dominant man and dangerous to converse with owing to his powers of persuasion.[62]

The situation had reached a point where the Prudential had to act. It put together a plan to ensure that Korda had sufficient funds to continue in business while imposing strict financial control to rein in his excesses. E. H. Lever devised a restructuring and refinancing package for LFP that involved setting up a new and entirely separate studio company to take control of Denham. LFP would transfer most of its share interest in the studio company to the Prudential 'in part satisfaction of this liability'. The intention, clearly, was to sideline Korda from the running of Denham Studios: 'It is not thought desirable that Korda should act in any personal capacity in this company, in fact there are certain definite disadvantages in his doing so.' (A handwritten addendum states: 'Korda should be eliminated from personal interest.') It was estimated that the annual cost of running the studios would be around £200,000, which would mean producing around fifteen films a year to break even:

> Assuming the studios to be fully occupied for 9 months out of 12 with five pictures on the floor each taking 12 weeks shooting time it would mean that some 15 pictures would be produced in that period, so that the average picture would have to bring in about £13,500 in income to the Studio Company to break even. This figure is a very reasonable one and should be quite a practical proposition. In the past such income has averaged £17,500 per production.[63]

However, this plan was posited on maintaining the same level of production as in the previous two years. By 1938 the volume of British production had reduced significantly: 103 British features were completed in 1938 compared to over 200 in each of the two previous years. In April 1938 *Kine Weekly* reported that no new films were starting at Denham.[64]

A revised version of the plan was approved by the Prudential in November 1938. The aim from the Prudential's point of view was to bring about a 'material reduction' in the amount of its investment leading 'ultimately to a complete realisation of the investment should this be desired'.[65] A separate company was to be formed to take over the running of Denham Studios; Prudential would cancel some of its loans to London Films in return for shares and a mortgage on of the 'empire trilogy' directed by Zoltan Korda following *Sanders of the River* and *The Drum* – had already been completed at a cost of £193,238 and the rights transferred to the new company. The loan had been provided by the Bank of America, whose London manager expected it would return a profit:

> United Artists, the distributors of 'Four Feathers', estimate that the theatre receipts from this picture in the United States and Canada will amount to $950,000 (other foreign countries $300,000), which will be converted into sterling and thus liquidate our loan, together with estimated receipts of £225,000 in Great Britain, the surplus going to the producer to be invested in subsequent pictures made at Denham.[74]

It was an accurate estimate: *The Four Feathers* returned distributor's receipts of £231,458 in Britain and US$801,564 from North America.[75] It was Korda's most successful film since *The Private Life of Henry VIII*. The Prudential recognised that 'the real value to Korda of this picture is the amount which he can borrow on it. Having raised a substantial sum on it, say £100,000, it is extremely doubtful whether he could raise a second loan on it.'[76]

Korda – never one to rest on his laurels – promptly embarked upon the most complex and ambitious film of his career: a lavish Technicolor production of *The Thief of Bagdad* that went into production at Denham in April 1939. Korda raised a loan of US$600,000 from the London branch of the Bankers Trust of New York secured against the UK receipts plus 25 per cent of the profits.[77] The Prudential was concerned that 'the production [is] in danger of being for Korda a "reputation" picture'.[78] Michael Powell, one of the three directors assigned to *The Thief of Bagdad* alongside Ludwig Berger and Tim Whelan, averred that Korda 'wanted a great, big, colourful extravaganza, and he was determined to get it'.[79] *The Thief of Bagdad* was around nine-tenths complete by the end of August 1939. However, immediately upon the outbreak of the Second World War, Korda shut down production of the film and set Powell and others to work on a hastily conceived propaganda vehicle called *The Lion Has Wings* (1939), which was shot in six weeks and released within three months. *The Lion Has Wings* was made with the co-operation of the Royal Air Force in return for which it was agreed that the Treasury should share in the receipts of the film.[80] The Treasury did not put up any money for the film, which Korda financed from his own resources. Michael Korda claimed that his uncle 'cashed in his life insurance policies to finance it'.[81] The Bank of America loaned £15,000 towards the production.[82] *The Lion Has Wings* was a hodge-podge of newsreel footage and dramatised studio scenes, but it was a box-office hit on account of being the first 'war' picture released after the outbreak of war. The Treasury's share of the receipts amounted to £25,140.[83]

However, Korda was once again short of capital. His application for a revolving credit from the Bank of America fell through when the bank was not allowed to 'swap' dollars between London and New York due to the imposition of wartime controls on currency exchange.[84] In November 1939 Alexander Korda Film Productions raised £347,000 through an issue of redeemable notes secured against the company's assets.[85] At the same time Korda took the decision to complete *The*

Thief of Bagdad in America: the war prevented him from sending a unit to Egypt as planned so the exteriors were shot in Arizona in 1940. In the spring of 1940 Korda was able to raise loans in America secured (as the Prudential had predicted) against *The Four Feathers*. The Security National Bank of Los Angeles and the Bankers' Trust Company of New York made loans totalling US$3.6 million (approximately £900,000): this was seen as signalling Korda's intention to move his production base to Hollywood.[86] *The Thief of Bagdad* was completed and released at the end of 1940: it became United Artists' biggest film of 1941 with a distributor's gross over US$1 million. United Artists had guaranteed a minimum of US$600,000 to Alexander Korda Film Productions, though there seems to have been some delay in remitting this back to Britain.[87] Korda produced two very successful films in Hollywood: *That Hamilton Woman* (1941) – released in Britain as *Lady Hamilton* and reportedly Winston Churchill's favourite film – and *The Jungle Book* (1942) before returning to Britain to recommence his activities there in 1943.

Korda – who had become a naturalised British subject in 1936 – was undoubtedly the most visionary British producer of his era. He was responsible for producing a cycle of films distinguished by their technical excellence and artistic ambition: London Film Productions was the only British producer of the 1930s whose films matched the production values and showmanship of the very best that Hollywood had to offer. However, such quality came at a cost. Korda had spent over £3 million on film production during the 1930s: the home market was too small and access to the American market – despite the success there of *The Private Life of Henry VIII*, *The Scarlet Pimpernel* and *The Four Feathers* – was not sufficient to guarantee consistently profitable returns for such high-cost films. So where does this leave the question of Korda's responsibility for the boom and bust of the British film production industry in the 1930s? On the one hand, Korda was certainly profligate in his expenditure on production (although he was by no means the only culprit in this regard) and he consistently overestimated the likely profits of his films. His visionary talents as a producer were not matched by competence in the nitty-gritty business of studio management. On the other hand, Korda had demonstrated that it was possible under the right circumstances for British films to succeed in the world market. His philosophy of 'international' films was established by the success of *The Private Life of Henry VIII*:

> I might put it epigrammatically and say I believe that international films are what good directors make. And though I have made many bad films in my life I always hope to be a good director. But perhaps the phrase 'international film' is a little ambiguous. I do not mean that a film must try to suit the psychology and manners of every country in which it is going to be shown. On the contrary, to be really international a film must first of all be truly and intensely national. It must be true to the matter in it.[88]

Korda had flair and was prepared to take economic and cultural risks: this set him apart from other producers who lacked one or other of those characteristics. And, for all the difficulties he created for his backers in the City, Korda was able to continue securing finance when others had fallen by the wayside. In particular, his success in raising finance in the United States when British sources had all but dried up pointed the way forward for the British film industry, which after the Second World War would come to depend increasingly upon American distributors for the provision of production finance. To that extent Korda was not only a visionary, he laid the foundations for later generations of British international film production including the epics of David Lean and the James Bond films.

Notes

1. 'The Private Life of Alexander the Great', *Picturegoer Weekly*, 18 January 1936, p. 13.
2. See Rachael Low, *The History of the British Film 1929–1939: Film Making in 1930s Britain* (London: George Allen & Unwin, 1985), pp. 165–73, 218–29. The best biography of Korda remains Karol Kulik, *Alexander Korda: The Man Who Could Work Miracles* (London: W. H. Allen, 1975). See also Charles Drazin, *Korda: Britain's Only Movie Mogul* (London: Sidgwick & Jackson, 2002).
3. *The Diaries of Robert Bruce Lockhart, Volume II: 1939–1945*, ed. Kenneth Young (London: Macmillan, 1980), p. 455.
4. George Perry, *The Great British Picture Show* (London: Pavilion Books, 1985), p. 76.
5. Sarah Street, 'Alexander Korda, Prudential Assurance and British Film Finance in the 1930s', *Historical Journal of Film, Radio and Television*, 6: 2 (1986), p. 17.
6. Low, *The History of the British Film 1929–1939*, p. 208.
7. Kevin Gough-Yates, 'Jews and Exiles in British Cinema', *The Leo Beck Institute Year Book*, 37: 1 (1992), p. 520.
8. Prudential Group Archive (hereafter Prudential) Box 2358: London Film Productions: Balance Sheet, Profit and Loss Account and Supporting Schedules, 30 April 1934.
9. '£80,000 Capital Increase for London Film Productions', *Kinematograph Weekly*, 13 April 1933, p. 5.
10. *Picturegoer Weekly*, 17 February 1934, p. 24.
11. Greg Walker, *The Private Life of Henry VIII: A British Film Guide* (London: I. B. Tauris, 2003), pp. 11–12.
12. Michael Korda, *Charmed Lives: A Family Romance* (London: Allen Lane, 1979), pp. 100–1.
13. British Film Institute (BFI) London Films Collection Box 5: Memorandum by Sir David Cunynghame, 7 January 1946.
14. Media History Digital Library, Centre for Film and Theatre Research, University of Wisconsin-Madison: United Artists Corporate Records (MHDL/UA): Adjourned Minutes of the Board of Directors of United Artists Corporation, 30 January 1934.
15. 'Korda and the Big Time', *World Film News*, 1: 9 (December 1936), p. 3.
16. John Sedgwick, *Popular Filmgoing in 1930s Britain: A Choice of Pleasures* (Exeter: University of Exeter Press, 2000), p. 264.
17. Sarah Street, *Transatlantic Crossings: British Feature Films in the United States* (London: Continuum, 2002), pp. 48–9.
18. Prudential Box 2357: London Film Productions: Cost of Production and Receipts to 24 April 1937.
19. 'UA to Handle London Film Product', *Kinematograph Weekly*, 25 May 1933, p. 1.
20. 'London Film Big Capital Rise', *The Financial Times*, 13 October 1934, p. 7.

21. Bank of England Archive (BEA) SMT 2/39: Memo – London Film Productions, 31 December 1936.
22. 'Denham Gets On With the Job', *World Film News*, 1: 4 (July 1936), p. 6.
23. Prudential Box 2357: London Film Productions: Shareholders as at 2 January 1937.
24. BEA SMT 2/39: Memo – Denham Securities (no date).
25. Korda, *Charmed Lives*, pp. 105–6.
26. R. W. Bernard, *A Century of Service: The Story of the Prudential 1848–1948* (London: Prudential Assurance, 1948), p. 129.
27. Korda, *Charmed Lives*, p. 106.
28. 'The Fruits of Endeavour', *The Financial Times*, 20 September 1934, p. 1.
29. 'Reports and Notices', *The Economist*, 12 October 1936, p. 733.
30. Prudential Box 2358: London Film Productions: Balance Sheet, Profit and Loss Account and Supporting Schedules, 30 April 1934.
31. Ibid.: London Film Productions: Account for the Year Ended 27 April 1935, 29 July 1935.
32. Ibid.: London Film Productions: Report and Schedules, 27 January 1936.
33. Ibid.: London Film Productions: Balance Sheet and Supporting Schedules, 2 May 1936.
34. Ibid.: Memorandum with Regard to Cash Budget for the Ten Months Ending 31 December 1936, Schedule A, 24 February 1936.
35. Sedgwick, *Popular Filmgoing in 1930s Britain*, pp. 264–76.
36. Ibid., p. 234.
37. Street, *Transatlantic Crossings*, p. 55.
38. Prudential Box 2354: London Film Productions Executive Board Minutes, 19 November 1936.
39. 'Twickenham Film Group Failure', *The Financial Times*, 15 January 1937, p. 5.
40. Prudential Box 2357: London Film Productions: Secured Loans as at 2 January 1937.
41. Prudential Box 2358: London Film Productions: Balance Sheet, Profit and Loss Account and Supporting Schedules, 30 April 1934.
42. Martin Gilbert, *Prophet of Truth: Winston S. Churchill 1922–1939* (London: William Heinemann, 1976), p. 589.
43. Prudential Box 2357: London Film Productions: Schedule of Productions, 25 September 1937.
44. Michael Korda suggests that Merle Oberon's accident 'was a heaven-sent opportunity to dispose of *I, Claudius*', which was running over schedule and consequently over budget due to the dysfunctional relationship between star Charles Laughton and director Josef Von Sternberg. See *Charmed Lives*, p. 118.
45. Jeffrey Richards and Jeffrey Hulbert, 'Censorship in Action: The Case of *Lawrence of Arabia*', *Journal of Contemporary History*, 19: 1 (1984), pp. 154–67.
46. Prudential Box 2357: London Film Productions: Memorandum with Regard to Cash Budget for the Ten Months Ending 31 December 1936, 24 February 1936.
47. Ibid.: London Film Productions: Renters' Balances, 2 January 1937.
48. Ibid.: Linklaters & Paives to C.W.A. Ray, 24 March 1938.
49. Ibid.: London Film Productions: Summary of Interests in Other Companies' Productions, Cost to 13 November 1937. The document also lists a 50 per cent contribution to *The Return of the Scarlet Pimpernel* (£98,742), though in the event this was a wholly London Films production.

50. Ibid.: London Film Productions: Statement Showing Method by which 1937 Programme is being Financed, 12 October 1937. This schedule lists ten films with their estimated costs: *The Squeaker* (£92,500), *First and Last* (£80,500), *Kiss Me Goodnight* (£82,250), *The Challenge* (£40,000), *The Divorce of Lady X* (£98,000), *The Drum* (£136,000), *Over the Moon* (£100,000), an unnamed 'Bergner-Czinner Picture' (£90,000) and the ultimately unmade *Lawrence of Arabia* (£125,000).
51. Prudential Box 2354: London Film Productions Executive Board: Minutes of the 25th Meeting, 5 June 1937.
52. 'Bid for UA Control', *Kinematograph Weekly*, 3 June 1937, p. 3.
53. MHDL/UA: Minutes of a Special Meeting of the Stockholders of United Artists Corporation, 24 May 1937.
54. 'Korda-United Artists Deal Breakdown', *Kinematograph Weekly*, 16 December 1937, p. 15.
55. MHDL/UA: Minutes of a Special Meeting of the Board of Directors of United Artists Corporation, 28 July 1937.
56. Ibid.: Alexander Korda to United Artists Corporation, 10 December 1937, included with the Minutes of the Meeting of the Board of Directors of United Artists Corporation, 11 December 1937.
57. Prudential Box 2358: London Film Productions: Report of the Directors and Statement of the Company's Accounts for the Period 3 January 1937 to 1 January 1938.
58. Kulik, *Alexander Korda*, p. 205.
59. 'Korda Talks on £1,200,000 UA Deal', *Kinematograph Weekly*, 17 June 1937, p. 3.
60. Prudential Box 2358: London Film Productions: Estimated Final Costs. Handwritten annotations suggest that the projected costs of *The Drum* and *The Divorce of Lady X* were subsequently adjusted upwards to £160,000 and £105,000.
61. Ibid.: London Film Productions: Balance Sheet, 1 January 1938.
62. Prudential Box 2357: Percy Crump, 'London Film Productions', 2 August 1938.
63. Ibid.: Linklaters & Paives to C.W.A. Ray, 24 March 1938.
64. 'The Studio Situation', *Kinematograph Weekly*, 21 April 1938, p. 3.
65. Prudential Box 2352: London Film Productions: Mr E. H. Lever's Re-Organisation Scheme, 4 November 1938.
66. Ibid.
67. 'Denham and Pinewood in Amalgamation', *Kinematograph Weekly*, 1 December 1938, p. 29.
68. '£750,000 Denham and Pinewood Company', *Kinematograph Weekly*, 5 January 1939, p. 18.
69. BEA SMT 2/42: 'British Features' Ledger, 1 April 1938–30 November 1939.
70. 'Columbia Will Spend £600,000 More in 1939', *Kinematograph Weekly*, 12 January 1939, p. 101.
71. Prudential Box 2358: London Film Productions: Balance Sheet and Profit and Loss Account, 31 August 1940.
72. Michael Powell, *A Life in Movies: An Autobiography* (London: William Heinemann, 1986), p. 299.
73. Prudential Box 2352: Alexander Korda Film Productions: Rough Balance Sheet, 28 September 1940.
74. BEA EC 4/248: Robert E. Dorton to G. F. Bolton, 4 October 1939.

75. Prudential Box 2352: Alexander Korda Film Productions: Rough Balance Sheet, 28 September 1940; Street, *Transatlantic Crossings*, p. 68.
76. Prudential Box 2358: London Film Productions: Comments on Part II of Scheme (no date).
77. BEA EC 4/249: Memorandum – Alexander Korda Film Productions Ltd, 20 August 1941.
78. Prudential Box 2358: London Film Productions: Comments on Part II of Schedule.
79. Powell, *A Life in Movies*, p. 231.
80. The National Archives (TNA) TS 27/474: Agreement between the Treasury and Alexander Korda Film Productions, 14 November 1939.
81. Korda, *Charmed Lives*, p. 137.
82. 'Mortgages and Charges', *Kinematograph Weekly*, 12 October 1939, p. 11.
83. TNA INF 1/199: Receipts from Commercial Distribution of Films: Summary of Statement Prepared for the Public Accounts Committee, May 1944.
84. BEA EC 4/248: Dorton to H. A. Siepmann, 25 September 1939.
85. 'Alexander Korda Film Productions', *The Financial Times*, 23 November 1939, p. 1.
86. Kulik, *Alexander Korda*, pp. 240–2.
87. Prudential Box 2352: E. H. Lever to H. G. Boxall, 25 March 1941.
88. 'Alexander Korda and the International Film', *Cinema Quarterly*, 2: 1 (1933), pp. 13–14.

CHAPTER 7

Boom and Bust

The history of British film production in the 1930s is generally characterised as a cycle of boom and bust. Korda's success with *The Private Life of Henry VIII* was the starting gun for other producers who sought to emulate his ambitious strategy of international films. The expansion of the British production sector in the mid-1930s is evident from the number of new production concerns registered: these rose from 46 in 1932 and 64 in 1933 to 86 in 1934 and 108 in 1935.[1] For the first time in the history of the industry, producers seemed to find raising their finance easy. In 1935, for example, the *Evening News* reported: 'The British film business is growing so fast that it is finding itself short of nearly everything it requires – except money . . . It is estimated that £2,500,000 will be spent on British films this year.'[2] John Maxwell, the ever-cautious chairman of the Associated British Picture Corporation, was moved to warn against excessive speculation: 'British film production seems to be looked upon as a sort of new Klondyke – a land flowing with easy money for all and sundry. Large sums of money are being spent extravagantly and wastefully, with the result [that] costs are being forced up all round.'[3] Maxwell's warning went unheeded, but he was proved right when the bubble burst in 1937 and City investment in the film industry all but dried up. The decade ended with a highly publicised trial in which the Westminster Bank brought an action against a group of insurance companies for the non-repayment of guaranteed loans to producers amounting to over £1 million. The biggest, though by no means only culprit, was the Austrian émigré Max Schach, who borrowed heavily, spent extravagantly and lost money prodigiously. Naomi Collinson contends that Schach 'nearly managed to wreck the British film industry, set the biggest names in the City at each other's throats, and without even turning up in court created so much chaos in the King's Bench Division that at times the proceedings were reminiscent of the trial scene in *Alice in Wonderland*'.[4]

To some extent the mid-1930s production boom recalled the similar boom following the Cinematograph Films Act: a mushrooming of new production concerns looking to exploit what seemed to be favourable economic and industrial conditions. There were, however, some important differences. Most of the new production units of the mid-1930s were private companies that did not make public share issues. And – no doubt inspired by the success of *The Private Life of Henry VIII* – they set their sights on the production of 'quality' pictures for the international market rather than quota quickies. As well as Korda's London Film Productions, the major new production units of the mid-1930s included British and Continental Film Productions (incorporated January 1934), Tower Film Productions (March 1934), Toeplitz Productions (June 1934), British National Films (July 1934), Capitol Film Productions (July 1934), Erich Pommer Productions (March 1935), Garrett-Klement Productions (March 1935), Grosvenor Sound Films (May 1935), Criterion Film Productions (June 1935), British Cine Alliance (June 1935), Bergner-Czinner Productions (August 1935), Cavalcade Film Corporation (November 1935), Atlantic Film Productions (November 1935), Trafalgar Film Productions (January 1936), Buckingham Film Productions (February 1936), Pall Mall Productions (April 1936) and Victor Saville Productions (April 1936).

Accounts of the problems of the film industry in the 1930s have focused on the role of spendthrift foreign producers. A notable feature of this period was the influx of European émigré and exile film-makers into the British film industry: Paul Czinner, Marcel Hellman, Otto Klement, Erich Pommer, Max Schach and Ludovico Toeplitz were among the many who fled central Europe and settled in Britain following the rise of National Socialism. Some accounts lay the blame for the industry's woes at the door of the 'continentals'. Ernest Betts – the *Sunday Express* film critic who, rather ironically, was employed as a story advisor by Max Schach in 1936 – later wrote that 'many get-rich-quick promoters, some from the continent, joined forces with City under-writers in wild-cat production schemes'.[5] John Maxwell was one of the British producers who felt they faced 'unreasonable competition' from the émigré producers. He told the Moyne Committee in 1936: 'These foreign producers who have come over here get millions from Insurance companies to chuck about, and they do chuck it about while it lasts and before the inevitable bankruptcy supervenes. We native British producers working with tight belts because we intend to continue in business and pay dividends to our shareholders suffer from this unreasonable competition.'[6] At times the hostility towards émigrés took on an anti-Semitic character. An example can be found in the diaries of former diplomat Robert Bruce Lockhart, who recorded on 23 August 1938:

> Last night [Stanley] Bayliss-Smith, who is a leading chartered accountant and represents the creditors in some of the big cinema finance messes in this country, says the cinema industry here has cost the banks and insurance companies about £4,000,000. Most of this lost by Jews – like Korda and Max Schacht [*sic*]. Latter already lost a packet for German Government before Hitler. Has now done same here. In Bayliss-Smith's opinion, and he would not say so lightly, Korda is a much worse man than Schacht. Schacht is just a slick Jew who sees financial moves ahead of the other fellow. Korda is a crook and, according to Bayliss-Smith, an evil man.[7]

Evidence that anti-Semitism also existed at an institutional level can be found in the records of the Bank of England: 'At present the industry in this country is nearly entirely in the hands of Jews – and foreign ones at that – who own most of the theatre circuits and most of the distribution companies and production companies themselves, though there are notable exceptions in the latter branch of the industry.'[8]

Some of the émigré producers were adept at ingratiating themselves with members of the establishment: the boards of production companies were populated by many *eminences grises* – including politicians, retired generals and society figures – who often had little or no knowledge of the film industry. For producers the presence of well-connected 'names' was a means of securing introductions to banks and finance houses as well as meeting the legal requirements for their films to be eligible for British quota. When Italian producer Ludovico Toeplitz set up Toeplitz Productions in 1934, for example, he persuaded Sir Henry Cassie Holden to become its chairman: Holden's father had been Chairman of the Midland Bank.[9] Many of those who sat on company boards of directors did so for a combination of pecuniary and patriotic reasons. For example, Major Henry Procter, Conservative MP for Accrington and chairman of several of the companies in Max Schach's Capitol group, believed that a prosperous British film industry was 'vital to this country and essential to our Imperial relations, and it will give us an opportunity of selling our culture and showing what Britain stands for not only in our own Dominions but in the rest of the world'.[10] The support of such luminaries was advantageous to foreign producers who often faced prejudice from traditional finance sources.

Another explanation for the cycle of boom and bust is that it had less to do with the extravagance and behaviour of individual producers, regardless of their nationality, but rather was a consequence of the unstable fiscal structure of the industry. In particular, there was a marked increase in film production financed by short-term money. In January 1937, just before the whole system of film finance collapsed, *Kine Weekly* observed:

> During recent months almost any would-be film producer has been able to form a small company with a capital of £200 and immediately raise, say, £30,000 to £50,000 in order to finance a picture. The system is interesting, and is made possible mainly because certain insurance companies facing a big loss of marine insurance business endeavoured to replace this by financing the film Trade . . . It was owing to the fact that films take a long time to produce and to realise that this business reached the proportions it did before its weaknesses were exposed.[11]

Most lenders were willing to advance around £50,000 to £60,000 for the production of a single picture. Political and Economic Planning later observed 'that £60,000 became a kind of "magic figure" and films which were to cost more than this were suspect by the financiers regardless of the content proposed. From then until 1937 loans for "quality" productions aimed at a world market were taken up on an ever-increasing scale.'[12]

This was also the conclusion reached in a contemporary survey of film finance by sociologist F. D. Klingender and documentary film-maker Stuart Legg, published in 1937 as *Money Behind the Screen*.[13] Klingender and Legg mined the trade and business press to document the total advances to British producers during 1936 through bank loans, mortgages and debentures. They estimated that the total amount advanced to film producers (excluding the two combines and other 'studio the assets of the studio company; Korda would continue production under the guise of a new production company; and London Films would receive shares and redeemable notes in the new production company in return for transferring its assets and rights including the completed but as yet unreleased *The Four Feathers*. Lever accepted that the plan depended upon Korda making a success of his production programme:

> It will be obvious that the plan will only be completely successful if Korda makes a success of his new company and in view of the fact that the assets which it is proposed to transfer to the new company will do no more than set it going, it is equally obvious that Korda, being deprived any further financial assistance from the Prudential, will be compelled in due course to find finance from other sources if he is to carry on.[66]

Lever's plan included a clause that the new studio company set up to manage Denham was 'to be amalgamated with the company owning Pinewood Studios (such amalgamation already agreed in principle)'. Pinewood was another modern new complex that had opened shortly after Denham: the two studios were within twelve miles of each other and therefore the merger was a pragmatic response to the declining volume of British production in the late 1930s. A month later it was formally announced that 'the two largest studios in Europe' were to merge under the banner of Denham & Pinewood (D&P) Films.[6]

D&P Films was set up in January 1939 with a capital of £750,000: the Prudential's share was £428,540 converted from its shareholding in London Films, with Guthrie and Lever representing the Prudential on the board.[68] Pinewood's studio manager Richard Norton was the managing director of the new company. The rationalisation of capacity at the two studios saw all production activity concentrated at Denham where the tenant producers included MGM's British unit and British producers G&S Films and Harefield Productions. G&S Films produced three films in 1939 – *The Arsenal Stadium Mystery* (£41,488), *On the Night of the Fire* (£71,926) and *A Window in London* (£48,473) – for General Film Distributors.[69] Harefield Productions was a Korda company set up to produce British quota films for Columbia Pictures: LFP's contract with United Artists prevented Korda from producing for another distributor so the solution was for Irving Asher – an American producer who had previously headed Warner's British production unit at Teddington – to produce 'for London Film Productions' with Korda as executive producer.[70] The first two Harefield Productions films were *Q-Planes* (£67,502) and *The Spy in Black* (£46,882).[71] Michael Powell, who directed *The Spy in Black*, later claimed that Harefield was a way of providing employment for LFP contract artistes such as Conrad Veidt and Valerie Hobson.[72]

Korda's main effort now focused on Alexander Korda Film Productions, which was incorporated in March 1939 with a capital of £200,000 and secured loans of £464,039.[73] Korda was effectively being allowed to resume production with a clean sheet but without any further investment from the Prudential, which held a share interest but would not make any cash advances. *The Four Feathers* (1939) – the last enterprises' such as Alexander Korda, Herbert Wilcox and Julius Hagen) was slightly over £4 million. The sums varied, but one common factor was that loans were often significantly in excess of the capital held by the producers themselves. Klingender and Legg elaborated:

> The rapid expansion during the last eighteen months of British independent production on a scale more ambitious than that of mere quota 'quickies' has led to a financial situation which bears all the characteristics of a highly speculative trade boom. As we have seen, these production units are almost without exception private companies, with relatively insignificant capital resources of their own. The great bulk of the production cost incurred by them is secured by means of insurance policies against the non-payment of bank overdrafts with specified limits, varying from £1,500 to £450,000 on single guarantees. The security offered is the highly problematical one of the expected returns from films about to be produced or in the process of production.[14]

The combines also borrowed money for production, but this was against secured capital. In 1936, for example, GBPC had a total secured capital of £6,250,000 and loans of around £6.5 million, while ABPC had secured capital of £3,550,000 and loans of £3,509,000. In contrast, the seventeen best capitalised new production units set up between 1932 and 1936 held total capital of £1,035,000 but had borrowed nearly five times that amount (£5,035,000).[15]

The facility for independent producers to raise production finance was made possible by the provision of distribution contracts. In 1933 *Kine Weekly* reported that '[a] scheme is afoot in the City whereby anyone with a renter's contract for distribution can secure finance for film production': it indicated that 'a large corporation' with 'ample resources' was behind the scheme whereby production loans would be repaid from the distributor's gross receipts.[16] The company in question was United Artists. UA differed from the other US distributors insofar as it relied upon independent producers for all its product. Its distribution guarantee had enabled Korda to raise the cash budget for *The Private Life of Henry VIII*. The typical distribution contract guaranteed to return a minimum amount to the producer within a specified period (usually twelve months after the film's release) and offered the producer 25–30 per cent of profits after the distributor had recovered their fee and costs.[17] At the height of the production boom in 1936, United Artists provided distribution guarantees for independent British producers worth £2.5 million in total: these included London Film Productions (six films for £1.2 million), Erich Pommer Productions (two films for £300,000), Trafalgar Film Productions (two for £250,000), Criterion Film Productions (two for £200,000), Garrett-Klement Productions (two for £150,000), Atlantic Film Productions (one for £100,000), Victor Saville (two for £160,000) and Herbert Wilcox (two for £80,000).[18]

The other major sponsor of independent British producers in the 1930s was General Film Distributors (GFD). This company was set up by former Gaumont-British distribution chief C. M. Woolf in May 1935 with an authorised capital of £275,000.[19] Woolf told the Bank of England that GFD would usually advance 70 per cent of the agreed production cost (the advance would be paid upon delivery of the negative) with the producer responsible for finding the balance and liable for overcosts: if GFD had to advance additional funds beyond the amount originally agreed this would be recouped by charging a higher distribution fee.[20] In 1936 GFD made advances to seventeen films with a combined cost of over £900,000: these included films produced by the Capitol Film Corporation (four films for an estimated £332,200), Herbert Wilcox (four for £253,800), Cecil Films (two for £169,200), the City Film Corporation (four for £118,200), British National Films (one for £38,200), Grafton Films (one for £22,800) and J. G. and R. B. Wainwright (one for £22,600).[21] An advantage of GFD for producers was that the advance upon delivery of the negative meant that the bank loan could be repaid sooner rather than waiting for recoupment from the box office, which often took twelve months to run off. A memorandum written for the managing director of the British General Insurance Company recorded that GFD 'is very substantial and is reported to be a very strong Company and a very successful one'.[22]

The provision of a distribution contract allowed producers to raise their finance from commercial lenders. In 1936 the Bank of England reported that '[the] financing of film production had until now been carried out by the Clearing Banks, the underlying security for their advances being insurance policies'.[23] The usual process of securing finance was for the producer to borrow the cash from a bank (usually at an interest rate of 4.5 per cent): the loan was to be repaid from the producer's share of the receipts on which the bank or its nominee held a mortgage until the loan was repaid. Otherwise, the bank had no financial stake in the film: its interest in the enterprise ended upon repayment of the loan. The major clearing banks – Barclays, District, Lloyds, Midland, National Provincial and Westminster – were all involved in the provision of film loans. A ledger held by the Commercial Union Archive reveals that at 31 July 1938 total production loans to independent producers amounted to £4,127,146. The biggest lender by some distance was the Westminster Bank, which made 98 loans totalling £2,594,662 towards the production of seventy-nine films. The next biggest lenders were the National Provincial Bank (21 loans totalling £280,250) – the National Provincial was also a major creditor for the Gaumont British Picture Corporation and Associated Talking Pictures, District Bank (11 loans totalling £280,400), Barclays Bank (11 loans totalling £228,500), Martins Bank (6 loans totalling £237,380), Midland Bank (5 loans totalling £191,500) and Lloyds Bank (11 loans totalling £175,754). The ledger also includes two foreign banks – Chase National Bank of New York (10 loans totalling £78,800) and Banque Belge (3 loans totalling £49,000) – which lent money to British producers.[24]

The example of Martins Bank reveals how banks assessed the risks of film loans.[25] In January 1936 Criterion Film Productions – set up by American actor Douglas Fairbanks Jr in association with émigré producers Marcel Hellman and Paul Czinner – requested loans for three films: the bank agreed on condition that each loan should be limited to £60,000 and security provided in the form of guarantees from insurance companies.[26] Six weeks later the maximum was increased to

£69,000 per loan and the production company indicated 'that instead of financing three films consecutively for that amount, the full amount, namely £210,000, may be required at one time. The guarantee of the various insurance companies will be increased correspondingly.'[27] The bank's Standing Committee minutes do not reveal the titles of the films, but they were probably *Accused*, *Crime Over London* and *Jump for Glory*, all released in 1936. However, Martins Bank was a cautious lender that limited its advances to the film industry. In November 1936 it recorded that it had received applications 'which would involve further considerable advances to finance other films. After discussing the matter, the General Manager had argued that the customers should be informed we should prefer to see some of the present advances run off before considering a new application.'[28]

As most independent producers had only nominal capital, the lending banks naturally required security for their loans. This was the context in which insurance companies became involved in the film business as guarantors of production loans. In August 1935, for example, Garrett-Klement Productions – a collaborative venture between Robert Garrett and Otto Klement described as 'film agents and producers' – borrowed £48,000 from the Pall Mall branch of Barclays Bank secured against the guarantee of the London Assurance Company.[29] The bank register does not name the film, but it would have been either *A Woman Alone* or *The Amazing Quest of Mr Bliss*. As the business developed, the insurance companies moved from guaranteeing the full amount of loans to forming syndicates where each party would guarantee part of the loan and therefore share the risk. For example, the British General Insurance Company felt that 'in the acceptance of this business we must act cautiously. On this score we seldom accept more than £5,000 [on] any one risk . . . This is quite small compared with what some of the other Companies are accepting, but in view of the special nature of the business, the caution which we have insisted upon is undeniably desirable.'[30]

The large amounts of money flowing into the industry in the mid-1930s could not fail to attract attention. In February 1936 the *Daily Express* noted the 'very large business being done in film insurance': it estimated the amount of the business as being between £3 million and £5 million.[31] In April 1936 *Kine Weekly* published a front-page article highlighting 'a group of mystery financiers who are providing hundreds of thousands of pounds of capital for kinematograph productions in this country'. It reported that a company known as Aldgate Trustees held mortgages and charges in favour of various insurance companies amounting to over £1.5 million. All that was known about the company, however, was that it had been set up in July 1935 and that its three directors were Frank Ellis, a member of Lloyd's, insurance broker Leopold Watkins and chartered accountant Stanley Bayliss-Smith of Casselton Elliott & Co.[32] *Kine* concluded that Aldgate Trustees 'represent a powerful and wealthy group . . . [who] so far have succeeded in maintaining complete anonymity'.[33]

Archival records shed light on the 'mystery' of Aldgate Trustees. It was in fact simply a trustee company set up by insurance brokers Glanvill, Enthoven & Co. in order to handle their growing film insurance business. Glanvill, Enthoven &

Co. was a well-established firm of brokers and the only one with a partner (Mr L. St John Austin) considered to be an expert on the film industry. A memorandum written for the managing director of the British General Insurance Company early in 1936 explained:

> As you are aware, we have confined our acceptance of this business to one source, namely Messrs Glanvill, Enthoven & Co., and although other Brokers have endeavoured from time to time to interest us in this business, we continue to confine our acceptance to this firm of Brokers. Our reason for doing so is that the business is still in its experimental stage and we have quite satisfied ourselves that Messrs Glanvill, Enthoven & Co., appreciating the possibilities of this business, have been very exacting in their enquiries, and the organisation which they have set up is very complete and very thorough.[34]

Two of the directors of Aldgate Trustees, Ellis and Watkins, were also partners in Glanvill, Enthoven & Co. They initially acted as agents for the insurance underwriters, but the growth of the business made it desirable to set up a separate trustee company. Aldgate was 'purely a trustee holding company and the only duty which it owed to Underwriters was to keep the securities and enforce them in case of need'.[35] A legal opinion recorded that Aldgate Trustees 'was regarded as a section of Glanvill, Enthoven & Co.'[36]

The basis on which the Aldgate system worked was that for each loan there would be two contracts – a deed of assignment and a guarantee – in addition to the distribution contract between the producer and the distributor.[37] The bank would advance an agreed amount to the production company which the producer would undertake to repay by a specific date (usually twelve months after the date of the loan, although loan periods could be extended): the producer would assign to the trustees all sums received from its share of receipts until the bank's advances were repaid. For example, Aldgate held two charges amounting to £140,000 in favour of Toeplitz Productions, secured against the producer's rights in *The Dictator* (1935) which Toeplitz produced for Gaumont-British Distributors.[38]

The producer most closely associated with Aldgate Trustees was Max Schach, whose role in the crisis would attract a good deal of controversy. Schach had production experience from the pre-Nazi German film industry, where he had produced films at UFA and Emelka Studios of Munich before heading up Universal Pictures' European operations. Following the Nazi accession to power, Schach came to Britain and set up as an independent producer with Capitol Film Productions in July 1934. The directors were Schach (managing director), fellow émigré Karl Grune (with whom he had worked in Germany in the 1920s), Louis Neel and Henry Procter.[39] Schach co-produced *Abdul the Damned* (1935) in association with British International Pictures.[40] BIP and Capitol each put up half of the £50,000 budget: Schach borrowed £15,000 from the Westminster Bank towards his share of the cost.[41] *Abdul the Damned* – a historical drama about the 'Young Turk' movement before the Great War – was directed by Karl Grune and was well received by critics in London and New York. BIP's Walter Mycroft described it as 'an artistic rather than a commercial success'.[42]

For a number of reasons – partly because he arrived in Britain at the height of the production boom, partly because his board included well-connected individuals from the worlds of politics and finance and partly due to his own powers of persuasion – Schach had no difficulty in raising finance. Schach himself told the trade press that raising finance 'was the easiest part of the whole business . . . Now I have the money I must make the pictures. That is not so easy . . . And every one of the films must be worthy of world distribution.'[43] *The Bystander* observed that Schach 'believed in himself and had a knack of making others believe in him too'.[44] Following *Abdul the Damned*, Schach upscaled his ambitions. In August 1935 Capitol Film Productions was reconstituted as the Capitol Film Corporation with an authorised capital of £125,000: Beverley Baxter (Conservative MP and former editor of the *Daily Express*) joined the board of directors in February 1936. Schach was managing director and Henry Procter was chairman. Capitol leased space at the British and Dominions Film Corporation's studios at Elstree. It secured distribution guarantees from General Film Distributors which advanced 37.5 per cent towards the production costs of four films: *When Knights Were Bold*, *The Marriage of Corbal*, *Love in Exile* and *Land Without Music*.[45] United Artists agreed to distribute the same films and a fifth (*Mademoiselle Docteur*) in North America.[46] Between September 1935 and June 1936 Capitol borrowed a total of £555,000 from the Westminster Bank towards the production of thirteen films.[47]

However, the ease with which Schach was able to borrow would also prove to be his undoing as he looked to expand his production interests. In June 1935 he joined Herman Fellner in setting up Cecil Films with an authorised capital of £1,000: its directors were Schach, Fellner, Neel, Procter and B. O. Schonegevel. Cecil Films produced two pictures for GFD – *Public Nuisance No. 1* and *Dishonour Bright* – for which Westminster Bank loaned £70,000. Capitol had already borrowed £15,000 for *Public Nuisance No. 1*: this charge was transferred to Cecil Films. Cecil's 'second series' comprised four films – *Lilac Domino*, *Jericho*, *International Quartet* and *No Other Tiger* – at a total budget of £220,000. National Provincial Bank advanced £110,000 for *Lilac Domino* and *Jericho*, Westminster Bank the same amount for *International Quartet* and *No Other Tiger*. In total Cecil borrowed £290,000 for the production of six films with a further £157,000 in additional provision loans.[48]

Trafalgar Film Productions followed in January 1936: its registered capital was £25,000 and its directors were Schach, Neel, Procter and Baxter. Trafalgar 'became associate producer to make films for United Artists which will be released throughout the world'.[49] Trafalgar borrowed £468,000 from the Westminster Bank towards the production of six films: *Pagliacci*, *Dreaming Lips*, *Love From a Stranger*, *Mademoiselle Docteur*, *Wheat* and *Little Lady of the Big House*. A loan in respect of *Mademoiselle Docteur* had already been procured by Capitol: in the event the film was produced by another company (Grafton Films). The last of the Schach companies was registered in February 1936: Buckingham Film Productions had the same directors and £25,000 registered capital of which nothing was issued. It borrowed £100,000 from the District Bank for two films (*Jericho* and *The Stars Look Down*) and £14,000 from the Chase National Bank of New York towards a third (*The Beggar's Opera*). In the event only one of those films was ever made: the Paul Robeson vehicle *Jericho* at Pinewood for GFD. In total Schach had borrowed £1,589,000, of which the Westminster Bank had loaned £1,128,000.[50]

Schach's notoriety in accounts of the financing crisis is such that it is necessary to lodge the caveat that the Capitol group was one of the best capitalised of the independent producers. In January 1936, at the height of the production boom, *Kine Weekly* suggested that Schach 'has built his house on the rock of sound finance'.[51] However, this impression was illusory. For one thing very little of the authorised capital of Schach's companies was actually issued: only £3,917 10s. of a total authorised capital of £176,000 was paid up.[52] Schach had been able to raise finance for a programme of films before any revenue had been earned: the bank and insurers had gambled on an unknown quantity. However, Schach turned out to be a spendthrift producer who was unable to control production costs. It did not help that he paid over the odds for talent: Richard Tauber reportedly received £60,000 for *Pagliacci* and Elisabeth Bergner £50,000 for *Dreaming Lips*.[53] Table 7.1 lists the estimated budgets and final costs of twelve films produced by the Schach group. The average overcost was an extraordinarily high 60.9 per cent, with *Dreaming Lips* (127 per cent), *Love from a Stranger* (119.5 per cent) and *Pagliacci* (112 per cent) all costing over twice the budget estimate.[54]

Table 7.1 Estimated budgets and final production costs of feature films produced by the Capitol group, 1936–7

FILM	BUDGET	PRODUCTION COST
Dishonour Bright (Cecil, 1936)	£45,000	£86,419
Dreaming Lips (Trafalgar, 1937)	£78,000	£177,398
For Valour (Capitol, 1937)	£35,000	£60,873
Jericho (Buckingham, 1937)	£50,000	£62,000 (to 31/03/1937)
Land Without Music (Capitol, 1936)	£45,000	£73,400 (estimated)
Lilac Domino (Cecil, 1937)	£65,000	£35,955 (to 31/03/1937)
Love from a Stranger (Trafalgar, 1937)	£78,000	£171,249
Love in Exile (Capitol, 1936)	£60,000	£61,800 (estimated)
The Marriage of Corbal (Capitol, 1936)	£60,000	£103,800 (estimated)
Pagliacci (Trafalgar, 1936)	£78,000	£165,608
Public Nuisance No. 1 (Cecil, 1936)	£45,000	£65,125
When Knights Were Bold (Capitol, 1936)	£60,000	£61,600 (estimated)

Source: Aviva Group Archive CU 540/1: Schedule of Films Produced by the Capitol Group, 28 June 1937.

Some trade commentators realised that the whole structure of film finance was built on insecure foundations. *World Film News* – successor to *Cinema Quarterly* as the voice of progressive film culture in Britain, and which adopted a more critical position towards the industry than the trade press – cautioned in July 1936 that 'British film production faces impending troubles of some magnitude... The problem facing the production companies at the moment is gross over-expenditure on film production and on overheads. It is generally admitted in the film trade that a collapse is imminent and that it may come at any time within the next six months.' It suggested that loans had been made too indiscriminately and alleged that 'certain film companies in this country obtained money on false pretences'.[55] Some of the new production units set up during the boom were already experiencing difficulties. In May 1936, for example, a group of unsecured creditors brought a petition for the compulsory winding-up of the City Film Corporation. This had been founded two years earlier by Harry Hughes and Basil Humphreys: it was a £100 company that between May 1935 and May 1936 registered fifteen charges totalling £285,600 – mostly held by Aldgate Trustees – secured against contracts with various British distributors.[56] City Film Corporation could not be described as a spendthrift producer: its most expensive film was *You Must Get Married* (£59,000) and other films for which costs are recorded were *Tropical Trouble* (£26,000), *The Improper Duchess* (£16,800) and *King of the Castle* (£12,400).[57] However, at the time of the winding-up order the total charges against the company amounted to £225,000.[58]

Some trade voices – perhaps to allay the fears of an imminent crisis – attempted to downplay the extent of the problems. An article in the *Sunday Dispatch* in December 1936 suggested that 'there was a crazy period a few years back, when many film companies went in for what is known in the City as "crazy finance"... It is unfortunate that a large and important industry should have had so murky a financial past, but happily the days of the mushroom film companies are almost over.'[59] *The Economist* suggested that the extent of loans to the film industry had been overstated:

> It does not follow, when a charge of say £1,000,000 has been registered, that the whole of this sum has been, or ever will be, eventually borrowed. It merely records an arrangement by which a series of advances will be made, in rotation, for a succession of pictures, provided that certain conditions – for each picture in turn – are satisfied. Equally misleading are bold statements that forty or fifty new production companies have been registered in recent months. Many of these companies are, in fact, designed to produce only a single picture. Others register merely the aspirations of promoters, which will never be realised.[60]

But for once *The Economist* had missed the point: many production companies had indeed taken up the full amount of the bank advances. And it was the single-picture companies that were most likely to go bankrupt: creditors for the larger concerns were more inclined to want to maintain them as going concerns in order to recoup at least some of their loans.

It was early in 1937 when the bubble finally burst. The first major casualty was Julius Hagen's Twickenham group – comprising J. H. Productions, Twickenham Film Distributors and Twickenham Studios – which filed for bankruptcy in January 1937.[61] Twickenham Studios had been founded in 1931 with capital of £15,000 raised through a debenture in favour of the Westminster Bank. It had started out as a streamlined quickie factory, but from the mid-1930s Hagen reoriented it towards medium-cost first features.[62] In 1936 it produced seven pictures at a total cost of £245,600: *Broken Blossoms* (£49,000), *Spy of Napoleon* (£40,800), *Dusty Ermine* (£40,000), *The Man in the Mirror* (£34,200), *In the Soup* (£29,200), *Juggernaut* (£28,200) and *Eliza Comes to Stay* (£24,800).[63] These budgets were modest in comparison to the films of Korda or Schach, but nevertheless Hagen still lost £11,500 on production and distribution in 1936. The Westminster Bank called in the Official Receiver. The Twickenham group's total liabilities at the time of liquidation amounted to £138,590. Hagen attributed its demise 'to lack of working capital; to heavy production and overhead expenses; to the proceeds of film distribution not realising the amounts anticipated; and to depreciation in the value of assets'. However, the Official Receiver rejected this explanation and instead attributed blame 'to the omission of the directors to make proper provision for capital necessary, to the excessive optimism of Mr Hagen regarding the value of film production and to heavy salaries paid to the directors, particularly Mr Hagen'.[64] Hagen was declared bankrupt with debts of £416,947: he died in 1940 at the age of fifty-six.[65]

It was the Twickenham collapse that precipitated the crisis in film finance. Campbell Dixon, the film correspondent of the *Daily Telegraph*, reported that '[a] sensation was caused in the film world last night by the report that a receivership has been applied for by a well-known independent British producer. Simultaneously comes another report that two of the "Big Five" banks have decided to lend no more money to independent film producers.'[66] Twickenham's collapse had a domino effect on the British film production industry as other liquidations followed in its wake. Early in March E. H. Lever of Prudential Assurance told Bank of England Governor Montagu Norman that he 'sees chaos & drama ahead'.[67] British Artistic Films declared bankruptcy in April 1937: it was showing losses of £19,111, of which half was in respect of one film: *Gypsy Melody* (1936). The company had borrowed £17,500 from Barclays Bank to produce this film, which ended up costing £27,812. Only £7,135 of the bank advance was repaid.[68] The company's failure was attributed 'to inadequate cash working capital, which necessitated borrowing money at heavy interest, [and] to the non-receipt from RIP of £13,750 which the company claimed was payable in accordance with the terms of their guarantee under the distribution agreement'.[69] John Clein Productions was wound up in July 1937 with liabilities of £35,000: it was a £100 company that borrowed £27,000 from Lloyds Bank towards the production of *The Mill on the Floss* (1936), which was budgeted at £30,000 but cost £47,464. The film was completed, but the liquidation of the distributor (National Provincial Distributors) left the producer unable to repay the bank.⁷⁰ Another casualty in November 1937 was Grosvenor Sound Films, which showed liabilities of £48,522. Grosvenor had made five films at modest cost – *Hyde Park Corner* (£18,600), *The Cardinal* (£19,100), *The Gay Adventure* (£22,200), *Take a Chance* (£25,800) and *Midnight Menace* (£32,100) – but collectively they lost over £37,000.⁷¹ Criterion Film Productions followed in January 1938: it had repaid only £84,386 of the £207,000 borrowed from Martins Bank.⁷² Criterion was one of five producers to be put into receivership in just one week: the others – Beaumont Film Productions, London and Continental Pictures, London Screen Plays and Oxford Films – were all one-picture companies.⁷³

However, the biggest shock waves were caused by Max Schach's Capitol group. By April 1937 Schach was known to be in trouble. A Board of Trade official reported:

> The Schach Group, which involves several smaller production Companies including Capitol, Cecil, Trafalgar and Buckingham, representing £1½ million were in difficulties a week ago. The Insurance Companies had made an investigation utilising two Accountants . . . These concerns made highly-priced pictures of the £100,000 type and had been too extravagant and even so failed to market them in America.⁷⁴

Most of Schach's films were frothy Ruritanian musicals and costume pictures: they were well made in themselves but evidently not to the taste of audiences and they struggled to secure bookings. At a time when 1,500 theatrical bookings were considered necessary for a film to recover its costs in the home market, the total bookings for *Dishonour Bright* (1,171), *Land Without Music* (999) and *Southern Roses* (795), all released by General Film Distributors, would have been deemed poor, while *Pagliacci* (553), *Dreaming Lips* (449) and *Love From a Stranger* (325), released by United Artists, were very poor indeed.⁷⁵

The insurers' audit of the financial affairs of the Capitol group revealed a very sorry state of affairs. The group as a whole had borrowed £1,432,000, but as at 31 March 1937 it had repaid only £154,781: the insurance underwriters were anticipating total losses of £751,781 against their guarantee policies.⁷⁶ The audit also revealed that Schach's accounting practices – which involved transferring charges between different companies and in some cases borrowing money for the same film twice – were somewhat irregular to say the least. William A. Crump, the solicitors acting for Aldgate Trustees, put Schach on notice 'to draw attention to the very serious irregularities which have been disclosed with regard to the disposal of these loans . . . It is now apparent that a large number of the advances made by the Banks have not been applied to the films for which the advance was made but have been utilized in completing other films of the company.'⁷⁷ It emerged that the Capitol group had taken out thirty-six loans towards the production of twenty-seven films but had completed only sixteen of them. Six films had not even started production and another (*Mademoiselle Docteur*) had been produced only in a French version. *Kossack* (formerly *Taras Bulba*) 'was rejected by the distributor and has not been remade ... The advance of £35,000 is therefore lost.'[78] United Artists loaned £4,600 for the completion of *Love from a Stranger* and £6,000 for completion of *Lilac Domino*.[79] At the same time it received a request from Aldgate Trustees to repay the Westminster Bank loans in respect of *Pagliacci*, *Love from a Stranger* and *Mademoiselle Docteur*.[80]

The problem for both the Westminster Bank and the insurers was that they had so much invested in the Capitol group that liquidation was not an option. A meeting of the bank and insurers on 22 April 1937 recorded that 'if the Companies are to be wound up, it was obvious that a very large loss indeed would have to be made by the Insurance Companies' and therefore it was 'the desire of all concerned, if not to eliminate at any rate to ameliorate such heavy loss'.[81] It was agreed to advance a further £127,000, of which £74,510 was for the completion of three films – *Jericho*, *Lilac Domino* and the English version of *Mademoiselle Docteur* – with the balance to pay creditors and make interest payments.[82] Aldgate Trustees appointed Stanley Bayliss-Smith as chairman and managing director of all companies in the Capitol group: Schach remained in a nominal role as director of production.[83]

The most immediate effect of the financing crisis was a sudden loss of confidence in the film industry from investors. *Kine Weekly* reported in August 1937: 'The City is still busy sorting out the mess brought about by last year's indiscriminate lending to mushroom film production companies. Whereas at that time it was possible to obtain fresh finance quite readily, it is now one of the most difficult things in the world to raise a loan.'[84] The difficulty of raising finance led to a decline in production output: British studios that had been full to capacity in 1935 and 1936 now found themselves with empty stages. Norman Loudon, the managing director of Sound City, averred that a consequence of the crisis 'is that studios have fewer tenants, and a further corollary is that there will be a shortage of British films in the future'. Sound City made a profit of £35,729 in 1937, but it put aside £20,000 of that to cover bad debts as 'certain of our debtors in the Trade were very seriously affected as a result of the financial stringency and were unable, for the time being at any rate, to meet their obligations to this company'.[85] The full effects of the crisis were seen in 1938 when Sound City's revenue fell by £94,000, which was attributed to the withdrawal of insurance finance and to the reduction of renters' quota under the Cinematograph Films Act of 1938.[86]

The City in the meantime was picking up the pieces and facing up to the extent of its losses. In June 1937 a group of Lloyd's underwriters commissioned insurance solicitor W. A. Crocker 'to investigate the problem of film production insurance'. Crocker had previously undertaken an investigation of losses in the fire insurance market that had resulted in bringing fire-raisers to trial. According to *The Financial Times*, Crocker was charged specifically to investigate Lloyd's producer indemnity policies: this was a guarantee to repay the bank in the event that a producer did not recover their costs from their share of the distributor's receipts.[87] The aim of the investigation seems to have been as much to limit the underwriters' liabilities as to uncover the underlying reasons for the crisis. G. A. Atkinson, editor of *The Era*, was incredulous:

It is not easy to understand why professional underwriters should have lost money. They are accustomed to estimating risks, and unlike the general public they are in a position to get the 'low down' on practically every form of expenditure. It shakes one's confidence in Lloyd's as an institution to find that such recklessness exists among its ranks.[88]

The Crocker report was never published, but there was much speculation about its content. *Kine Weekly* reported that it 'is alleged to contain sensational revelations regarding last year's film finances'.[89] It was rumoured that the reason the report was not made public was that it was so damning of the insurance companies themselves. *Reynolds's News* suggested: 'It is now most unlikely that the Crocker secret report on the financing of British film by Lloyd's underwriters will result in legal action, however ample the grounds. Reason is that if the full facts were stated, some of the underwriters might be chaffed mercilessly by their friends in the City. They prefer to cut their losses.'[90]

The extent of the liabilities incurred by insurance companies on film loans is revealed in a ledger held by the Commercial Union Archive. Some sixteen insurance companies had total liabilities of £3,407,943 relating to guarantees for film loans (Table 7.2). Over half the total liability was held by three insurers – British Oak, Switzerland & General and the Union of Canton – whose 'position is rendered more serious by the fact that up to the present their reinsurance cover under an Excess Policy at Lloyds is seriously in dispute'.[91]

Table 7.2 Total liabilities of insurance companies holding guarantee policies for film loans, 1937

INSURANCE COMPANY	LIABILITY
British General	£313,478
British Oak	£811,749
Canton Triton Insurance	£7,334
Commercial Union	£33,750
General Accident Fire and Life	£35,388
Guildhall Insurance	£268,715
Liverpool Marine and General	£123,553
Indemnity Marine	£196,312
Northern Insurance	£211,735
Provincial	£1,500
Ralli Bros. Insurance Company	£127,801
Sea Insurance Company	£134,160
Switzerland & General	£296,194
Union Insurance Society of Canton	£692,572
Andrew Weir	£141,056
TOTAL	£3,407,943

Source: Aviva Group Archive CU 550/5: Insurers Statement of Total Liabilities.

This was the context in which the Westminster Bank brought a legal action against fifteen insurance companies for non-repayment of its loans: the case – brought in the King's Bench Division before Mr Justice Singleton – lasted for six days in May 1939. The proceedings were widely reported in the press: to this extent the case made public the full extent of the chaos and confusion that prevailed in the provision of film finance. Sir Stafford Cripps KC, acting for the bank, focused on the relationship between the Capitol group and 'a firm of well-known brokers in the City' (Glanvill, Enthoven & Co.) who would approach insurers to issue guarantee policies that would allow the producer to borrow from the bank:

> Some ingenious person in the City of London devised a way by which the necessary money could be raised by these various companies without any difficulty, and this method had given rise to the present actions ... The producing company who desired to raise money would get into contact with the Brokers, and tell them what the requirement was. It might be that they desired to raise two loans of £50,000 in order to produce two named films. Thereupon the Brokers would go to a number of underwriters in the marine underwriting market and ask them whether they would be prepared to issue guarantee policies for some share of the total amount of £50,000.
>
> The Brokers assumed that these policies could persuade some bank to advance the cash against the security of the policies. Relying on the security of the guarantee given by the marine underwriters, the bank would advance the cash. After the first few dealings in that way it appeared that it became nearly automatic for these companies to adopt this procedure and get as much money as they wanted.[92]

Cripps explained how, when repayment became due, the insurance policies and loans would be extended. In that way the system of film finance became self-perpetuating:

> Apparently at the time, no one seemed to think there was any risk that this very delightful state of affairs would ever come to an end. The companies were getting as much money as they wanted. That enabled them to give the distributing companies a very favourable deal indeed. The actors were able to charge the most fabulous fees and the underwriters got a great deal of lucrative business at a time when the market was very dull. Glanvills were doing very well indeed out of it by reason of their commissions from underwriters and from the companies, and the bank was finding a safe use for its money at a decent rate of interest with the guarantee of most substantial insurance companies behind it.[93]

There were, however, Cripps argued, two flaws in the system. One was the 'incompetent and inefficient management of the producing companies', the other was 'a complete failure by Glanvills to watch the interests of the underwriters as they were expected to by the underwriters themselves'.

The affairs of the Capitol group featured so prominently in the Westminster Bank case that it is important to remember that it was not Schach who was on trial. Nor for that matter were Glanvill, Enthoven & Co., who had facilitated the provision of loans but were not themselves responsible for either the loans or the insurance policies. The insurers felt they were being made the scapegoats and brought a counter suit against the bank. The case hinged on the interpretation of the insurance policies and the responsibilities of the bank and the underwriters. The bank's case was that the policies were guarantees of repayment and that the insurers were liable to repay loans when the producer defaulted, whereas the underwriters argued that the policies were to guarantee delivery of the films and that the bank had failed to disclose the full facts relating to the production companies prior to issue of the policies. In the event, the case was settled out of court: the details of the settlement were not made public but it was speculated that the bank accepted an offer from the underwriters to repay most of the outstanding loans.[94]

Rachael Low contends that Schach should bear much of the responsibility for the film finance crisis of the late 1930s:

> Schach's impact on British production was as crucial in its way as that of Korda. But unlike Korda he contributed nothing to the industry. Preferring to use visiting European and Hollywood stars and top technicians, he hired established British studios and used their infrastructure, and such British talent as he did employ was taken away from other companies. With his fellow directors Neel, Procter and Baxter, he used the Aldgate system to finance many independent producers and directors whose expensive failures did far more to discredit British production as an investment than the picturesque extravagance of Korda.[95]

Schach certainly exemplified the worst excesses of extravagance that bedevilled the British film industry in the 1930s. His management was undisciplined and his accounting practices were dubious in the extreme. All that said, Schach was a product of the system rather than the cause of it: he simply exploited it more systematically than other producers. The underlying cause of the crisis was not that individual producers lacked budgetary discipline (although some evidently did), or that too many films were produced with unrealistic expectations of their appeal to the American market (although this was certainly true for many), but rather that the whole system of film finance based on short-term loans was unsound. Schach and others were no doubt responsible for poor management, but that was as much an outcome of the system that enabled it rather than the fault of the producers themselves.

Notes

1. Linda Wood, *British Films 1927–1939* (London: BFI Library Services, 1986), p. 128.
2. 'British Films Held Up', *Evening News*, 5 August 1935, p. 5.
3. 'Money Wasted on Films', *The Scotsman*, 29 August 1935, p. 2.
4. Naomi Collinson, 'The Legacy of Max Schach', *Film History*, 15: 3 (2003), p. 376.
5. Ernest Betts, *The Film Business: A History of British Cinema 1896–1972* (London: George Allen & Unwin, 1973), p. 102.

6. Board of Trade, *Minutes of Evidence Taken Before the Departmental Committee on Cinematograph Films Together with Appendices and Index* (London: HMSO, 1936), p. 108 (1136).
7. *The Diaries of Robert Bruce Lockhart Volume I: 1915–1938*, ed. Kenneth Young (London: Macmillan, 1973), p. 392.
8. Bank of England Archive (BEA) SMT 2/31: Memorandum – 'The Cinema Industry', 30 January 1936.
9. 'Rise of New British Companies', *The Yorkshire Post*, 9 October 1934, p. 8.
10. *Parliamentary Debates: House of Commons*, 5th Series, vol. 328, 4 November 1937, col. 1241.
11. 'City Financiers Start Spring Cleaning', *Kinematograph Weekly*, 14 January 1937, p. 13.
12. *The British Film Industry: A Report on its History and Present Organisation, with Special Reference to the Economic Problems of British Feature Film Production* (London: Political and Economic Planning, 1952), p. 69.
13. The research first appeared as a series of articles in the journal *World Film News* early in 1937 under the byline of 'the Film Council': the first – and most substantial – article was 'Secrets of British Film Finance', *World Film News*, 1: 10 (January 1937), pp. 18–23. See also 'Flora and Fauna of the British Film Industry', *World Film News*, 2: 6 (September 1937), p. 19.
14. F. D. Klingender and Stuart Legg, *Money Behind the Screen: A Report Prepared on Behalf of the Film Council* (London: Lawrence and Wishart, 1937), p. 48.
15. Ibid., p. 54.
16. 'Sinews of War', *Kinematograph Weekly*, 20 July 1933, p. 4.
17. Prudential Group Archive Box 2352: E. H. Lever, 'United Artists Corporation', 6 April 1938.
18. 'United Artists' £2,500,000 British Programme', *Kinematograph Weekly*, 13 August 1936, p. 36.
19. 'General Film Distributors', *The Financial Times*, 29 May 1935, p. 5.
20. BEA SMT 2/34: Interview with C. M. Woolf, 7 May 1937.
21. BEA SMT 2/30: 'Films – Large Renters – Cost Form C'. 'Form C' was the audited return which itemised statutory costs (excepting excluded foreign artistes). General Film Distributors handled seventeen features in 1936 at a combined statutory cost of £465,700: the costs of individual films ranged between £8,400 (the City Film Corporation's *The Improper Duchess*) and £52,000 (Capitol's *Love in Exile*). The Bank of England reckoned the 'Form C' cost to be half the final picture cost.
22. Aviva Group Archive (hereafter Aviva) CU 540/1: 'Film Guarantees', 13 January 1937.
23. BEA G14/80: Extract from Minutes of the Committee of Treasury, 3 June 1936.
24. Aviva CU 540/6: Film Financial Guarantee Policies: Statement of Ultimate Loss on Loans.
25. Martins Bank was one of the largest private banks in Britain: it had been a limited company since 1891 and was acquired by the Bank of Liverpool in 1918 but maintained the Martins name. It was a major lender to cinema properties, especially the Odeon Group.
26. Barclays Group Archive: Martins Bank Standing Committee No. 3 (ACC 80/581): Criterion Films Ltd, Curzon Street Branch, 27 January 1936.
27. Ibid.: Criterion Films Ltd, 11 March 1936.
28. Ibid.: Film Companies, 26 November 1936.

29. Ibid.: Barclays Bank Advance Registers 1934–35 (140/79), 28 August 1935.
30. Aviva CFU 540/2: 'Film Guarantees', 30 January 1936.
31. 'British Films: Renewed Activity and Finance', *Daily Express*, 21 February 1936, p. 5.
32. Aldgate Trustees may have been so called due to its proximity to Aldgate Underground station on the Circle Line: its registered address was on Throgmorton Avenue.
33. 'Millions for Film Production: Mystery Financiers Unlimited Backing for British Pictures', *Kinematograph Weekly*, 9 April 1936, p. 1.
34. Aviva CU 540/2: 'Film Guarantees', 30 January 1936.
35. Aviva CU 540/1: 'Film Insurance: Notes' (no date).
36. Ibid.: 'Opinion' – Stephen Chapman, 28 June 1937.
37. BEA SMT 2/35 includes blank copies of two deeds of assignment and two guarantee agreements (the lender is the Westminster Bank) procured by Simon Rowson, who explained: 'The first provided finance for three pictures to be distributed by a certain renting company. The second provided for a further three pictures to be distributed by a second renting company, reserving to the Underwriters any residual values in connection with the first contract to be retained by them as collateral necessary for advances made under the second contract.' Rowson to Evelyn Bunbury, 11 June 1937.
38. BEA SMT 2/39: Statement of the Charges Registered During the Two Years Ending 30 June 1936. *The Dictator* is one of several instances where the details recorded in the ledger are somewhat opaque. The first charge (16 October 1935) was for £120,000 in respect of two films named as *The Love Affair* and *The Dictator*. However, there was no such film as *The Love Affair*: the working title of *The Dictator* was *The Love Affair of the Dictator*. The second charge (11 March 1936) was for £20,000 in respect of exploitation of 'the above film'.
39. 'The Men Behind Capitol Films', *Kinematograph Weekly*, 18 October 1934, p. 54.
40. 'B.I.P.'s "Dandy" Ten', *Kinematograph Weekly*, 18 September 1934, p. 36.
41. Aviva CU 540/1: 'Westminster Bank Limited: Notes on Discovery of Documents' (no date).
42. Walter Mycroft, *The Time of My Life: The Memoirs of a British Film Producer*, ed. Vincent Porter (Lanham, MD: Scarecrow Press, 2006), p. 146.
43. 'Who is This Max Schach?', *Kinematograph Weekly*, 13 February 1936, p. 24A.
44. 'Max Schach Makes Good Again', *The Bystander*, 20 January 1937, p. 98.
45. 'Woolf Deal with Schach?', *The Era*, 22 May 1935, p. 6.
46. Media History Digital Library, Centre for Film and Theatre Research, University of Wisconsin – Madison: United Artists Corporate Records (MHDL/UA): Minutes of Organization Meeting of the Board of Directors of United Artists Corporation, 22 July 1936.
47. Aviva CU 540/2: Capitol Film Corporation and Associated Companies: Schedule of Bank Advances and Ultimate Losses.
48. Ibid.
49. 'A New Film Co.', *The Scotsman*, 5 February 1936, p. 2.
50. Aviva CU 540/2: Capitol Film Corporation and Associated Companies: Schedule of Bank Advances and Ultimate Losses.
51. 'Capitol Steps Out into the Front Rank', *Kinematograph Weekly*, 19 January 1936, p. 209.
52. Aviva CU 540/1: 'Opinion' – Stephen Chapman, 28 June 1937.
53. Low, *The History of the British Film 1929–1939*, pp. 203–4.

54. The schedule also includes – somewhat confusingly – *Moscow Nights* (1935), produced by Korda's London Film Productions.
55. 'British Film Industry Faces Crisis', *World Film News*, 1: 4 (July 1936), p. 5.
56. BEA SMT 2/39: Statement of the Charges Registered During the Two Years Ending 30 June 1936.
57. BEA G95/7: 'Films – Form C Costs – General Film Distributors – City Films'.
58. 'Winding Up of City Films', *Kinematograph Weekly*, 21 May 1936, p. 27.
59. 'No More "Crazy" Finance for Film Trade', *Sunday Dispatch*, 6 December 1936, p. 17.
60. 'British Film Finance', *The Economist*, 13 February 1937, p. 343.
61. 'Twickenham Film Group Failure', *The Financial Times*, 15 January 1937, p. 5.
62. Linda Wood, 'Julius Hagen and Twickenham Studios', in Jeffrey Richards (ed.), *The Unknown 1930s: An Alternative History of British Cinema, 1929–1939* (London: I. B. Tauris, 1998), pp. 37–55.
63. BEA G95/7: 'Films – Form C Costs – Twickenham Distributors'.
64. *Kinematograph Year Book Diary and Directory 1938* (London: Kinematograph Publications, 1938), p. 239.
65. Low, *The History of the British Film 1929–1939*, p. 236.
66. 'Film Industry Sensations', *The Daily Telegraph*, 8 January 1937, p. 14.
67. BEA ADM 34/26: Diary of Montagu Norman 1937: Entry for 3 March 1937.
68. Aviva CU 540/6: Film Financial Guarantee Policies: Statement of Ultimate Losses on Loans.
69. 'British Artistic Films: Receiver's Analysis', *Kinematograph Weekly*, 16 September 1937, p. 34.
70. '£30,000 Picture Costs £47,464', *Kinematograph Weekly*, 8 July 1937, p. 18.
71. BEA SMT 2/39 includes costs and receipts for three films produced by Grosvenor Sound Films and distributed by Pathé Pictures. In each case Pathé advanced 62.5 per cent of the budget with Grosvenor providing the balance and being responsible for any overcost. *Hyde Park Corner* (1936) cost £18,572: its distributor's receipts were £17,055 which following deduction of expenses (£3,115) left £13,940 to be divided between the producer (65 per cent) and distributor (35 per cent). Grosvenor received £9,061 against its investment of £6,975. *The Cardinal* (1936) cost £19,139 and returned distributor's receipts of £5,888 which following deduction of expenses (£2,170) left £3,717 to be shared between producer and distributor. Grosvenor received £2,416 against its investment of £7,369. *The Gay Adventure* (1936) cost £22,202: its distributor's receipts were £6,322 which following deduction of expenses (£2,618) left £3,704 to be shared between producer and distributor. Grosvenor received £2,407 against its investment of £9,702.
72. Aviva CU 540/6: Film Financial Guarantee Policies: Schedule of Ultimate Losses on Loans.
73. Ibid.: Beaumont Film Productions had borrowed £20,000 from Westminster Bank for *Toilers of the Sea* of which only £38 had been repaid (the film was belatedly released by Columbia Pictures in 1939): London and Continental Pictures had borrowed £22,500 from Westminster Bank for *Dreams Come True* and had repaid just £24; London Screen Plays had repaid nothing of the £22,500 it borrowed from Lloyds Bank for *Olympia Honeymoon*; and the full £27,000 advanced by Banque Belge to Oxford Films for *My Partner Mr Denis* was also outstanding.
74. BEA SMT 2/33: Interview with Mr Fennelly, 26 April 1937.

75. Aviva CU 540/6: Capitol Group of Companies: Progress Report 31 March 1937 to 17 July 1837 and Position as at 17 July 1937.
76. Aviva CU 540/2: William Templeton to Norman Walker, 6 April 1937.
77. Aviva CU 540/1: William A. Crump & Sons to L. A. Neel, Max Schach and A. B. Baxter, 15 April 1937.
78. Ibid.: Schedule of Films Produced by the Capitol Group, 28 June 1937.
79. MHDL/UA: Minutes of Special Meeting of the Board of Directors of United Artists Corporation, 28 July 1937.
80. Ibid.: Minutes of the Meeting of the Executive Committee of United Artists Corporation, 9 July 1937.
81. Aviva CU 540/6: Memorandum of Interview Re: Capitol Film Corporation Ltd, 22 April 1937.
82. Ibid.: Capitol Group of Companies: Progress Report 31 March 1937 to 17 July 1937 and Position as at 17 July 1937.
83. 'Film Magnate Leaves His Post', *Daily Herald*, 1 December 1937, p. 11.
84. 'Caution in the City', *Kinematograph Weekly*, 12 August 1937, p. 28.
85. 'Production and the Financial Crisis', *Kinematograph Weekly*, 23 September 1937, p. 3.
86. 'Films Act's Effects on Sound City', *Kinematograph Weekly*, 1 December 1938, p. 3.
87. 'Film Losses by Lloyd's Underwriters', *The Financial Times*, 15 June 1937, p. 5.
88. 'British Film Losses', *The Era*, 17 June 1937, p. 1.
89. '£5,000,000 Loans for Production', *Kinematograph Weekly*, 2 December 1937, p. 5.
90. 'History of Today', *Reynolds's News*, 19 December 1937, p. 10.
91. Aviva CU 540/5: W. L. Templeton to Lewis, 'Film Guarantees' (no date).
92. '£1,000,000 Lawsuit Over Film Finance', *The Financial Times*, 2 May 1939, p. 9.
93. Ibid.
94. 'Big Film Suit Settled', *The Financial Times*, 9 May 1939, p. 7.
95. Low, *The History of the British Film 1929–1939*, pp. 207–8.

CHAPTER 8

The Bank of England and the Film Industry

From the mid-1930s the Bank of England found itself – much against its will, it must be said – drawn into the British film industry. Montagu Norman, the Governor of the Bank of England for nearly a quarter of a century between 1920 and 1944, was famously hostile to the industry, as Herbert Wilcox found out when he joined Montagu and Lord Portal for lunch:

> At lunch I met Montagu Norman, who succeeded in embarrassing me as never before . . . Introductions over, Portal started to outline the Universal deal when Norman broke in with: 'Wyndham, you're surely not going to interest yourself in that awful film industry? . . . It's no good, Wyndham! It's unsound. And those dreadful people are not your class. Keep out of it.'[1]

Wilcox's anecdotal account of Norman's antipathy is corroborated by documents held by the Bank of England Archive. A Governor's note of July 1935 in respect of a suggestion to employ Lord Portal as chairman of a film combine, for example, records that 'for my part I thought this film business attracted mucky people – at any rate in certain positions – and was not in the least the sort of job which Portal would be wise to undertake'.[2] And Norman's appointments diary records a meeting in June 1936 with merchant banker Francis Goldsmith and Herbert Tritton, president of the Equitable Life Assurance Company – one of the companies involved in making loans to film producers – where he told them 'that no "Film" Bills are good here'.[3]

Despite the Governor's well-known antipathy, however, it was due in some measure to his stewardship of the Bank of England that the film industry came within its orbit. Norman is widely credited for overseeing the completion of the process whereby the Bank of England was transformed from its original role as private banker to the government to a modern central bank: he saw the Bank's primary role as being to support the fiscal stability of the banking sector which during the interwar period had significantly increased its loans to business customers.[4] The economic fall-out of the Wall Street Crash – which brought about the abandonment of the Gold Standard and the temporary imposition of currency controls – prompted the Bank to set up a subsidiary body known as the Securities Management Trust in 1929. Its role was to support industry, not through direct intervention in the management of specific companies but rather by creating frameworks for restructuring and rationalisation where this became necessary.

For example, the Securities Management Trust was responsible for the establishment of the Lancashire Cotton Corporation in 1929 and the Cotton Spindles Board in 1936.[5] Norman would also use his influence with the financial institutions of the City of London to encourage mergers where this would create more stable businesses: the discussion over Lord Portal was in respect of a suggestion to merge the Gaumont-British Picture Corporation and London Film Productions from Sir Connop Guthrie of Prudential Assurance, which had investments in both companies. However, Norman's interests focused on traditional industries – coal, tin, oil, steel, cotton and tobacco – and he preferred to keep the film industry at arm's length.

Norman's first contacts with the film industry were in an informal capacity. It was Claud Serocold, a stockbroker with the firm Cazenove and Ackroyds who sometimes acted in the role of an unofficial go-between for the Bank of England and the City, and whose clients included Sir Connop Guthrie, who had consulted him over Portal's possible availability for the proposed Gaumont British-London Films merger. Portal was a paper magnate whose company provided the paper for banknotes: Norman replied that 'in spite of long association, we claimed no right over Portal's activities'.[6] Early in 1936 Serocold met Norman again 'to report, for the Governor's information, the present situation regarding matters in the film industry'. The meeting focused on the deteriorating situation of the Gaumont-British Picture Corporation and the possibility that the Ostrers might sell their shares to an American company (Twentieth Century-Fox), but it also touched upon wider issues affecting the industry at large. A memorandum, unsigned but very probably by Serocold, suggested that more competent fiscal management was a prerequisite for bringing greater stability to the industry:

> Sooner or later, it appears imperative that this great money-making and production industry, which is also a very large employer of labour, should be, if possible, guided into more responsible and respectable hands than it is at present; but, in order to do that, it will be necessary for some big City house to become identified with it, not so much from the point of view of the actual finding of money, but from that of, by its advice and reputation, satisfying the public that at least they will be getting a fair deal for their money.[7]

The record of the meeting between Norman and Serocold suggests that the ownership and control of the film industry was regarded as a matter of national interest:

> The British Government are anxious that the film industry in this country should be in British hands. They realise that second only to the Wireless the films provide the most important means of propaganda at present available . . . The time has arrived, however, when it is necessary that they should have the backing of some respectable and responsible City house. Mr Serocold stated that he had spoken to Barings and Rothschilds both of whom are at present disinclined to accept such a position. He enquired whether the Bank, if moved to do so by the Government, would be willing to use their influence to secure responsible City backing for the Company.[8]

This was therefore one of those occasions where Norman was asked to leverage his influence with the City of London to support an industry, though on this occasion it came to nothing. The idea of involving one of the large London merchant banks was probably less to do with the provision of finance for individual producers than to provide some sort of financial guarantee that would reassure other investors.

A month later Alexander Korda contacted the Bank in regard to the impending renewal of the Cinematograph Films Act. This came shortly before the Board of Trade's appointment of the Moyne Committee to review the operation of the Act: it might have been that Korda feared he would be excluded from giving evidence or that he mistakenly thought the Bank of England would be involved with the committee. Korda submitted a ten-page memorandum outlining his view of the issues affecting the industry. While it was hardly the 'impartial point of view on the highly complicated and very debatable question of the Quota Act' that Korda claimed, his memo effectively summarised the positions of the different trade interests:

> In my opinion the Quota Act should not only be maintained, but should be revised with a view to affording even greater protection to the British film industry. The problem is very complex. The American film companies will raise great obstacles. Even the British companies will not be unanimous in their opinion as to the drafting of the new act. The cinema exhibitors will say that they are faced with ruin if any further restrictions are made. The big British companies having large holdings in cinemas will side with the American companies and with the owners of individual cinemas. Their objections, which I don't want to enumerate here, must all collapse under close scrutiny. The cinema owner will do better business if more popular British pictures are produced, than he will do with purely or chiefly American films. Naturally, the British film industry itself would grow under increased protection with infinitely greater rapidity in the next three years than it has in the past three years. The ire of prejudice is broken and all that is required for its success now is further effort.[9]

Korda's memorandum was strong on diagnosis of the problems but notably vague as regards practical solutions. Its chief interest as a historical document is the general information it includes in relation to film revenues and shares of the British market. Korda put total box-office revenues at £50 million a year (more than the £42 million calculated by Simon Rowson in his 'A Statistical Survey of the Cinema Industry in 1934') and reckoned that a single feature might gross 'anything between £3,000 and £200,000'. The combined producers' share of box-office receipts (after exhibitors and distributors had taken their shares) was around £10 million but 'only £1,500,000 or less remains in Gt Britain as revenue from British pictures'. He cited MGM as an example of how American companies were able to exploit the quota: the company released around forty of its own films each year, produced at a total cost of £3 million and which earned between £1.5 million and £2 million in the British market. This meant that the company could spend around

£50,000 on twelve British films to meet its quota and still earn a large profit from the British market. Korda suggested (somewhat speculatively) that an increase in the quota to 50 per cent would double the receipts returned to British producers for the distribution and exhibition of their own films in the home market: he felt that the increased production capacity of the British industry would be able to meet this demand.

Korda's memorandum met with a mixed response inside the Bank of England. Sir Edward Peacock, one of the Bank's directors, said that he 'found it very interesting indeed. I think it is an able presentation of an important matter'.[10] However, Norman was equivocal: he felt that Korda's memorandum was 'well put together, interesting, and mostly convincing', but added that 'I am utterly ignorant of Films in every shape and form' and that 'I should need a deal more information from many angles before I could have any opinion or give any advice about the Quota!'[11] As the Moyne Committee was appointed shortly afterwards to put forward proposals for the renewal of the quota, Norman was able to let the matter drop.

None of these early attempts to involve the Bank of England in the film industry bore any fruit: Norman was able to keep the Bank from any dealings with the 'mucky people'. However, the financing crisis of 1937 precipitated by the collapse of Twickenham Studios was so severe that the Bank was obliged to take an interest. From the beginning of the year Ernest Lever, the joint secretary of the Prudential Assurance Company and one of the City contacts with whom Norman had frequent personal meetings, approached the Bank to solicit its support in petitioning the government to provide financial assistance for the film production industry. Norman's diary records several meetings with Lever. On 3 March 1937 Lever said that he would like to see 'wider co-ordination from above, perhaps legislation'; on 7 September Lever 'pleaded for Film help, I say nothing doing, await new Act'.[12] On 15 March 1937 Lever wrote a long letter in which he laid out the case for the establishment of a film bank, suggesting that its capital should be provided by a consortium of insurance companies and joint stock banks:

> [Although] ultimately such a bank should be a purely lending institution run on conservative and economic lines it should in the early stages of the building up of the industry take some part of the real risks of film production and might in some form or other be the channel through which the Government could give the industry direct financial support if it decided to do so.
>
> I should make the provision of such finance contingent upon the industry energetically continuing to put its house in order and as a first step to this I would urge that steps be taken to concentrate the production side of the business into two or three strong groups and to encourage a much closer collaboration than has been the case in the past.[13]

Lever always claimed in his correspondence to be acting in the interests of the film industry as a national enterprise rather than specifically advocating on behalf of the Prudential and London Films. However, the Bank was sceptical of this claim: 'He [Lever] may have lost more than he cares to say and wants to lessen his commitments on the production side . . . He rather spoils his case for the independent producer in his anxiety for the Prudential and although the difficulties of Pinewood and Denham reflect the real difficulty of the "independent", a safe and satisfactory way of giving assistance to these people has not so far emerged.'[14]

In February 1937 Norman had asked Gordon Munro and Alfred Wagg to undertake an informal investigation of the film industry: Munro was a City director and Wagg was chairman of the investment bank Helbert, Wagg & Co. Norman's diary records a meeting at the end of February in which he advised them to 'avoid sieve of publicity, or good guessing; make report as preliminary, on safe items & leave dangerous items over for consideration later'.[15] The formal letter requested '[a] general examination of the Film Industry', including '[the] need, if any, for a general consolidation of the industry or of particular sections of the industry'.[16] The terms of the enquiry and the suggestion of 'general consolidation' were consistent with the role of the Securities Management Trust. Munro and Wagg were joined by two Bank of England officials: Evelyn Bunbury and Ernest Skinner (Skinner was Norman's private secretary and secretary to the Securities Management Trust). In early April, however, the scope of the enquiry was extended when Norman was asked formally by Sir Horace Wilson, the Chief Industrial Adviser to the National Government and a close ally of Chancellor of the Exchequer (and soon-to-be Prime Minister) Neville Chamberlain, for the Bank 'to arrange for a general investigation of the Film Industry in this country'.[17] As Norman had already instigated the Bank's own enquiry, it clearly made sense for him to extend its scope rather than start over again.

A meeting of representatives of the Bank of England and Board of Trade with Munro and Wagg on 8 April 1937 set the terms of the enquiry: it was tasked specifically with gathering evidence 'on which a financial group could be approached to form a Syndicate or Company for the purpose of meeting the temporary financial difficulties of the film producers' and 'to consider what form the proposed organisation should take and how its temporary constitution can be fitted in with the proposed Film Bank to be formed later'.[18] The Board of Trade was willing to consider the possibility of providing some sort of financial support for the film industry only if it could be demonstrated that it was absolutely necessary: it was also mindful that any official assistance would require legislation and that a stop-gap arrangement might be necessary in the short term. Before the enquiry had taken evidence, Gordon Munro put forward a memorandum suggesting the formation of a syndicate with two thirds of its capital subscribed by banks and insurance companies and one third from 'other quarters': the syndicate would fund 50 per cent of the cost of a film (the other 50 per cent coming from the distributor) to be paid upon delivery of the negative.[19] That a finance organisation of some kind was under consideration was evidently common knowledge in the industry at large. John Corfield, the managing director of British National Films, had wind of it. He wrote to Wagg in respect of 'a movement on foot in the City, backed by an important group of Insurance Companies, for the financing of British Film Production on new and approved lines' and reported: 'From the information which I have in my possession, this movement has received the tacit approval of certain Banks and Insurance Companies. According to my information the Prudential Assurance Co. is one of the prime movers behind the scheme, and a verbal enquiry has been addressed to us whether we should be prepared to participate in the scheme or not.'[20]

The Bank of England enquiry was conducted over the course of April and May 1937. It took the form of a series of interviews with representatives of the trade: these were mostly the heads of British distribution companies but also included Ernest Lever and Lord Portal (in his capacity as chairman of the General Cinema Finance Corporation). A suggestion that Aldgate Trustees should be invited came to nothing. Several of those interviewed were less alarmist about the state of the industry than Lever. S. W. Smith (British Lion Film Corporation) suggested that the impression of a bankrupt industry 'was true only up to a point. Bad finance had been the cause: money had been too easy to obtain and the money which had been so obtained had gone into the wrong hands, mainly those of the independent producers.'[21] R. P. Baker (Associated British Film Distributors) also identified the cause of the problem as 'a class of person attracted by the speculation and glamour of the film business. Some have gone out, others will doubtless come in.'[22] And F. W. Baker (Butchers Film Service) argued that film production was more economically conducted when producers were working with a cash budget, as 'if production were done on the guarantee basis without sufficient supervision it usually meant that the renters found that the estimated costs had been exceeded and had to advance further money in order to make good the money involved by the guarantee'.[23]

The interview with C. M. Woolf (General Film Distributors) was particularly revealing. He suggested that it was 'safe to make to a figure of £40/75,000. Such pictures gross £110,000 in this country: £10,000 in the Colonies and £3/5,000 from foreign exhibition.' GFD had contracts with independent producers at Pinewood Studios for which it advanced up to 70 per cent of the cost (Woolf mentioned Grosvenor Sound Films and J. W. Wainwright) and with Gaumont-British with whom it shared production costs on a fifty-fifty basis. He explained that 'GFD do not control or supervise the making of pictures which they finance but they keep in touch with what is going on and insist on speeding up, etc, where necessary'. Woolf blamed the industry's problems on the proliferation of inadequately financed production units:

> Urged the Bank to do nothing that would involve them in loss because if the industry were to have another crash it would be the end. Small people are not wanted and are the cause of all the trouble. But he would like to see the worth-while independents continue as such if we could find the way. There were any number of independent producers who can produce good pictures. Pheonix mentioned by name.[24]

However, Woolf's acumen was called into question by other testimony. Lord Portal indicated that 'Woolf was a good man ... but his financial sense was so bad that he, [Paul] Lindenberg and others connected with GFD had formed a small company called the General Cinema Finance Corporation which looked after the finances of GFD'.[25]

The trade representatives were in accord that the root of the difficulties lay with the provision of easy finance to untried producers: many of these had already ceased production (Woolf averred that 'City were out of business: Cecil finished: and Capitol "I should say are out".'). There also seems to have been a consensus that sufficient finance was available for production and that producers who could spread their risks across a portfolio of films were better placed to weather the storm than single-picture units. Butchers and British Lion were largely unaffected by the crisis as they specialised in lower-cost films for the home market that could be expected to recover their costs provided they were economically produced. In this respect the evidence of Simon Rowson, who acted as a consultant for the enquiry (he was paid an honorarium of 100 guineas), was particularly important. He calculated that a film produced for £30,000 would need to earn distributor's receipts of £37,500 in order to break even, assuming a distribution charge of 15 per cent: therefore a programme of thirty films at an average cost of £30,000 and returning £40,000 each should return an overall profit of £75,000. Rowson's proposal for a film bank was based on five assumptions:

1. Producers associated with the distributing company (a) have a reputation for successful picture making, or (b) have sufficient equity available to guarantee financiers against loss and completion.
2. The test of *successful* picture making is found in [the] relationship between cost and gross renters' receipts, ignoring for present purposes the handicaps of (a) heavy finance costs, (b) too onerous distribution terms, (c) uneconomic production methods of a unitary compared with programme production, (d) extravagance. The object is to try and ascertain if the productions might have been profitable in the proposed new organisation.
3. Finance will be much less costly than hitherto, and not entirely on banking terms.
4. Distributor is prepared – subject to safeguards – to make finance advances during production, and to reduce distribution charges to lowest possible rate and permitting of pro-rata recoupment of production cost from distribution receipts.
5. Producers must be prepared to submit to distribution control before and during production.[26]

Rowson envisaged a scheme whereby production finance would be channelled through the distributor: interest charges would be reduced and the distribution contract for those participating in the scheme would be standardised.

As well as interviews with trade representatives, the Bank of England enquiry also gathered an archive of financial information that provides a fairly comprehensive overview of the structure of the British film industry in the mid-1930s. The two major combines were the best capitalised outfits: the Gaumont-British Picture Corporation (£6,250,000) and Associated British Picture Corporation

(£3,525,000). The other major producers and studios – Associated Talking Pictures (£61,546), British and Dominions Film Corporation (£500,000), the British Lion Film Corporation (£141,383), London Film Productions (£428,799) and Sound City Films (£231,013) – amounted to only 14 per cent of the combined capital of the two combines.[27] After the combines, the best capitalised concern was a newcomer to the industry: the General Cinema Finance Corporation. This was incorporated in March 1936 for the purpose of acquiring 90 per cent of the share capital of General Film Distributors.[28] GCFC had an initial capital of £1,125,000 subscribed by major investment trusts and individuals: its four directors were Lord Portal, J. Arthur Rank (heir to a Yorkshire flour milling dynasty), Paul Lindenberg (managing director of the merchant bank S. Japhet & Co.) and chartered accountant Leslie Farrow. *World Film News* noted that GCFC was backed by 'some of the most successful figures in the world of English capital-finance'.[29] In June 1936 GCFC acquired a large shareholding in Universal Pictures: General Film Distributors therefore became the only British renter to handle the films of one of the major Hollywood studios.[30]

The enquiry confirmed the report of the independent 'Film Council' – published in 1937 as *Money Behind the Screen* – that most British film production was financed by short-term loans. Table 8.1 summarises a document itemising loans and charges registered by producers, and their trustees, in the two years to 30 June 1936. The total loans (excluding the two combines) amounted to £2,290,287, and £1,567,950 of that amount (over 68 per cent of the total) was in favour of Aldgate Trustees.[31]

While the enquiry was still underway, another narrative was unfolding behind the scenes. It was common knowledge that Ernest Lever was lobbying politicians to solicit their support for government intervention in the film industry. Munro reported on 23 April that Lever had met Sir Joseph Ball, Director of the Conservative Party Research Department and a close political ally of Neville Chamberlain, and was 'most anxious to impress upon JB the urgency of the situation and to see whether JB could get anybody to do something quickly'.[32] A few days later Munro recorded: 'Mr Lever rang me this morning. He continues to be very upset that the Government and/or Bank of England are not able to say or do anything, at once, either directly to help the emergency that exists in Film Production, or to restore some measure of confidence among otherwise would-be helpers from the financial point of view.'[33] Lever's claim to be acting in the general interest of the film industry does not bear much scrutiny. On 6 May Bunbury reported a meeting with Lever 'at his urgent request' when Lloyds Bank had refused to make any further loans to London Film Productions: the production company needed £400,000 to complete films already in production and another £1.5 million to continue with its planned programme beyond July. Lever was evidently hoping that the Bank of England could use its influence to persuade Lloyds or one of the other joint stock banks to bail out LFP. However, Bunbury was disinclined to offer support for one company rather than the sector

Table 8.1 Loans and charges registered by producers, and their trustees, in the two years to 30 June 1936

PRODUCER	CHARGE (DATE)	TRUSTEE
Alexander Film Productions	£3,000 (2.9.1935)	Mrs Florence Lewis
	£191.11s.5d. (20.4.1936)	David Jamilly
Albury Studios	£900 (5.4.1935)	Stella Richard
B&N Films	£9,000 (23.10.1934)	Patrick O'Brune
British & Continental Film Productions	£61,100 (12.12.1935)	Francis Cork
British Lion Film Corporation	£10,000	Satisfied (8.12.1935)
	£125,000	Aldgate Trustees
British International Pictures	£100,000	Branch Nominees
Capitol Film Productions	£12,500 (16.12.1935)	Equity Law & Life Assurance
Carnival Films	£3,000 (22.5.1935)	Sir Harold V. Mackintosh
	£2,000 (13.7.1935)	Sir Harold V. Mackintosh
	£1,000 (12.2.1936)	Sir Harold V. Mackintosh
Cecil Films	£45,000) (27.8.1935)	Aldgate Trustees
	£150,000 (27.3.1936)	Aldgate Trustees
City Film Corporation	£2,500 (31.5.1935)	M.R.S. Kaidakara
	£4,450 (25.6.1935)	F.C. Ellis & L.H. Watkins
	£5,000 (8.7.1935)	F.C. Ellis & L.H. Watkins
	£30,000 (13.7.1935)	F.C. Ellis & L.H. Watkins
	£8,000 (17.9.1935)	Aldgate Trustees
	£50,000 (20.11.1935)	Aldgate Trustees
	£51,000 (1.1.1936)	Aldgate Trustees
	£86,000 (28.1.1936)	Aldgate Trustees
	£6,000 (19.3.1936)	Aldgate Trustees
	£5,000 (19.3.1936)	Aldgate Trustees
	£2,000 (27.3.1936)	Aldgate Trustees
	£3,000 (6.4.1936)	Aldgate Trustees
	£1,900 (9.4.1936)	Aldgate Trustees
	£15,000 (7.5.1935)	Aldgate Trustees
Concordia Films	£14,000 (28.5.1935)	Sound City Films
	£6,000 (28.5.1935)	Sound City Films
	£33,942 (25.11.1935)	J. B. Ellis/Bertha Jennings

(*Continued*)

Table 8.1 Loans and charges registered by producers, and their trustees, in the two years to 30 June 1936

PRODUCER	CHARGE (DATE)	TRUSTEE
Criterion Film Productions	£50,000 (7.10.1935)	Aldgate Trustees
	£20,000 (27.11.1935)	Aldgate Trustees
	£5,000 (30.4.1935)	Aldgate Trustees
	£207,000 (15.4.1935)	Aldgate Trustees
Crusade Films	£2,750 (18.6.1935)	Fully met
	£560 (11.7.1935)	Fully met
	£3,810 (1.10.1935)	Fully met
	£500 (22.10.1935)	Fully met
	£500 (21.11.1935)	Fully met
Embassy Pictures	£6,000 (20.5.1935)	F.C. Ellis & L.H. Watkins
Leslie Fuller Productions	£20,000 (11.1.1935)	Not stated
Gaiety Films	£4,905 (24.5.1935)	John Inghamilton
	£1,090 (16.7.1935)	Stanley Lupino
	£1,090 (16.7.1935)	Alec W. Hendry
	£1,090 (11.10.1935)	Stanley Lupino
Gaumont-British Picture Corporation	£30,000	Guardian Assurance Co.
	£6,500,000	Law Debenture Corp.
Grosvenor Sound Films	£27,500 (21.6.1935)	F.C. Ellis & L.H. Watkins
IFP Films	£100,000 (19.8.1935)	Aldgate Trustees
	£3,000 (2.6.1936)	Aldgate Trustees
Fred Karno Film Company	£11,000 (10.9.1935)	Aldgate Trustees
Lupino Lane Productions	£3,000 (28.10.1935)	Not stated
Lupino Lane Productions	£500,000 (13.3.1935)	Prudential Assurance
	£25,000 (23.5.1935)	F. G. Minster Ltd
Stanley Lupino Productions	£20,000 (26.8.1935)	Aldgate Trustees
	£1,000 (15.10.1935)	Stanley Lupino
	£2,100 (11.11.1935)	Aldgate Trustees
	£500 (13.11.1935)	Stanley Lupino
	£1,000 (13.11.1935)	Mrs R.M.A. Henry
	£2,100 (13.11.1935)	London Screenplays
New Ideal Pictures	£60,000 (13.8.1935)	Aldgate Trustees
	£5,000 (21.11.1935)	Aldgate Trustees
	£5,000 (5.12.1935)	Aldgate Trustees

(*Continued*)

Table 8.1 Loans and charges registered by producers, and their trustees, in the two years to 30 June 1936

PRODUCER	CHARGE (DATE)	TRUSTEE
Progress Pictures	£8,000 (26.6.1934)	Gerald F. Court
Radius Films	£26,000 (1.8.1935)	Aldgate Trustees
Sound City Studios	£100,000 (5.12.1935)	Equity Law & Life Assurance
John Stafford Productions	'All moneys owing'	Aldgate Trustees
Time Pictures	£6,000 (25.7.1935)	C.T. Bowring & Co.
	£10,000 (1.8.1935)	Not stated
Toeplitz Productions	£120,000 (18.10.1935)	Aldgate Trustees
	£20,000 (11.3.1936)	Aldgate Trustees
Twickenham Film Studios	£30,000 (10.1.1935)	Satisfied
UK Films	£58,000) (18.3.1936)	Aldgate Trustees
J. G. and R. B. Wainwright	£30,000 (13.9.1935)	Aldgate Trustees
Herbert Wilcox Productions	£330,000 (2.9.1935)	Aldgate Trustees

Source: Bank of England Archive SMT 2/39: Statement of the Charges Registered during the two years ending 30 June 1936.

as a whole ('To deal with any individual case at this juncture will make the pursuit of our enquiry difficult and may prejudice the case we may be able to make for dealing with the problem as a whole') and in any event was not sympathetic to the Prudential's plight ('There is a degree of unanimity amongst those we have seen of extravagance, irresponsible management and lack of control in LFP and amazement that the Prudential should have done what they have done').[34]

The LFP/Prudential crisis escalated in early June. The Prudential had decided not to make any further advances to Korda: Lever told the Bank of England that unless Korda could find other sources of finance it was likely either that LFP would be put into liquidation or that its assets would be sold to an American company. Lever was no doubt playing on knowledge that the government was keen that control of the film industry should remain in British hands. Bunbury was so concerned that Lever would try to use the predicament of LFP to leverage support from the Bank that he wrote a personal letter to Norman:

> I see great danger in our being put in a false position through the insistent applications from one quarter and another on behalf of that Company. Frankly I would not help with our present knowledge . . . Only a properly equipped Film Bank could handle the LFP and I greatly doubt whether any such Bank would or should help on the present set up. I think LFP must find their own solution.[35]

Bunbury subsequently reported that he had learned from a Mr Parker of Lloyds Bank that Lloyds had agreed to advance £140,000 to Denham Securities for the completion of films currently shooting but would make no further advances thereafter.[36] However, on 11 June Lever wrote to Bunbury: 'I thought you should know that the immediate financial difficulties of "London Films" have been overcome through the help of American finance. I think it is very regrettable that said help had to be obtained, but there was no alternative in view of the hostile attitude of the British banks.'[37]

It was evidently a sore point for Lever that the Bank of England had not been able to provide any concrete assistance. He even went so far as to suggest that the Bank had been deliberately obstructive. Bunbury wrote again to Norman:

> Munro told me that Lever had been to see Nigel Campbell in a purely personal capacity and had mentioned to Nigel Campbell that he could not convince himself that the Bank of England had not in some way or another influenced the Joint Stock Banks to slow down on finance for film production. He mentioned that in one particular case (I presume this must be Glyn Mills) negotiations had taken place on what Lever termed gilt-edged security and that this particular Bank had said that they might consult the Bank of England and that subsequently the Bank had turned down the proposition under consideration. Lever further told Nigel Campbell that he had taken the business to one of the American Banks who had given his Company the facilities asked for without any trouble.[38]

While there is no direct evidence that the Bank of England ever advised banks to cut back on their loans to the film industry – and in this regard it should be pointed out that Norman was adamant that it was not the Bank's role to advise the banks on their commercial activities – the Governor's antipathy towards the film industry was no secret.

Even before the enquiry was completed, there were strong indications of the likely form its report would take. The enquiry was not persuaded that film production was in quite the sort of 'crisis' that was being claimed. A memorandum of 20 May 1937 states:

> The Aide-Memoire pre-supposed a crisis in production of such a nature as could [only] be remedied by some stop-gap financing that would avoid a Government subsidy which would have to await legislation . . . Actually, we have found no such position. Production has fallen off but the production so affected was largely fortuitous – the result of cheap money. While the better concerns have no doubt been affected by the ebb and flow, they are not financially embarrassed at the moment. The exception is the LFP. They have also demanded help.[39]

'A sound industry should finance itself, otherwise production needed to satisfy the quota must be subsidised', Skinner recorded separately. 'No reason why the Bank of England should provide the subsidy which like all subsidies, and particularly so, might be limitless.'[40]

An 'interim report' was presented on 22 May 1937. It weighed up the pros and cons of a film bank, concluding that the industry's needs would not be met by short-term remedies: 'No evidence has been given of the need for stop-gap finance as distinct from a general plan in the case of any individual concern apart from the LFP, and there has been no indication that any immediate crisis owing to lack of finance would be revealed in the affairs of such other persons as may yet be interviewed.'[41] It noted that 'a large number of independent producers have been eliminated as the result of the curtailment of the sources of easy finance' and that the 'known and suspected difficulties of certain prominent British Companies, is causing some anxiety regarding the future in the matter of the sufficiency of British production'. It laid the blame for the current crisis on irresponsible lending ('the methods employed by the City over the last few years have been uninformed and injurious'), but at the same time felt that the diminishing supply of capital had weeded out the lesser producers ('the shake out has been beneficial in so far as it has involved mainly those people who have neither substance nor a knowledge of production'). It suggested that 'the industry would not survive another crisis and any financial assistance should only be made under stringent conditions to people of substance' and urged a fiscally conservative approach insofar as 'any Film Financial Organisation ought to take the same attitude towards the Film Industry as Banks do towards Industry in general. Banks should take no special risk in respect of films. There was no support for Mr Lever's suggestion that the Film Financial Organisation should take the last position.'[42]

The report went on to explain how the peculiar conditions of the film industry were not conducive to the establishment of a film bank:

> There are certain fundamental aspects of this Entertainment and Publicity business which are not to be found in other commercial or industrial undertakings:
>
> (a) It is essentially personal – dependent frequently on one individual for its success or failure.
> (b) There is no straight line product; each film is different – every film is a personality.
> (c) There is no definite relationship between cost and market value. Market value, i.e. Box Office takings, is not established in the majority of cases for 8–12 months after completion of the negative.
> (d) The price of a seat in the cinema buys equally a 'Rolls Royce' or an 'Austin 7'.
>
> These factors – to which must be added the need for Research – underline the necessity for adequate permanent capital for producers and any Financial Organisation to ensure averaging the results of a series of films over a sufficiently long period.[43]

The report then suggested that the question of the industry's need for secure long-term capital was beyond its terms of reference:

> [It] would appear from the nature of the evidence so far obtained that the Enquiry passed from the particular position of an Interim Financial Organisation visualised in the Aide-Memoire of the 8th April to the general position and that any Financial Organisation would have to be placed on a permanent footing from the beginning. This conclusion places the problem on a fundamentally different footing from that which the Enquiry by the Bank of England was entered upon.[44]

The report did not categorically rule out some form of 'special assistance', but it batted the idea back into the government's court by suggesting that financial support for the industry could not be separated from the quota legislation: 'The wider problem is necessarily more dependent upon the Government policy and decisions in the matter of the Films Act, and this indicates the difficulty of conducting contemporaneously with the Quota discussions an independent enquiry into the practicability, scope and character of any Financial Organisation.'[45]

On 7 June 1937 Norman wrote a 'secret memorandum' on film finance to Sir Horace Wilson summarising the enquiry's conclusions. It amounted in effect to a list of problems that would need to be addressed in setting up a film bank. One was that if the organisation replaced the existing system of borrowing production finance against distributors' guarantees then it would only cover the so-called 'senior' money (the proportion – usually 60–70 per cent of the budget – that was first to be repaid to lenders from the producer's receipts):

> Finance on commercial terms by any Film Finance Organisation would to a large extent be mainly a substitution for existing finance, and in so far as it would be senior money or senior security and on reasonable terms, it would require that the balance be put up by the borrower. The extent to which finance on such terms could be availed of will depend on the ability of the borrowers to find the necessary junior money.[46]

Another problem was finding people with the right experience to run it:

> Without independent expert personnel with a knowledge of the Industry and of the people in it, no Film Finance Organisation could succeed. No such personnel can be found outside the Industry itself. To take personnel from the Industry means taking men from one of the few successful concerns which could ill-afford to spare them.[47]

And there was also a concern that any further adverse developments in the film industry might leave the government and the Bank exposed:

> Once special support should have been given to a Film Finance Organisation, withdrawal would be difficult since sentiment plays so large a part. Further, money could only be obtained at present on the basis of HMG or the Bank of England if reasonable rates are to be charged for accommodation; this is a permanent moral position and a potential commitment over and above any initial financial stake which the Bank of England might have to put up.[48]

He concluded with a clear steer against a film bank: 'The Bank of England should only attempt to take steps (a) if the finance for the new quota legislation be not there, or (b) if after some experience of the working of the new Act it should be clear that financial assistance was necessary to maintain the quota.'[49] Norman was therefore pushing back the whole issue until the new Cinematograph Films Act came into effect, evidently in the hope that the new quota legislation would render the film bank unnecessary.

Norman had successfully warded off (for the time being at least) the suggestion that the Bank of England should take a position in relation to the film industry. This should not be seen as due solely to his personal distaste for the 'mucky people' who populated the film business. There was clearly a sense in which the film industry was not like other businesses. It had several unusual features: the cost of the product did not necessarily guarantee its success; it involved a high capital investment for a product that was more than usually dependent upon public taste; it took a relatively long time for returns on investment; and even for successful films the return on investment was usually modest in relation to the capital involved. At the heart of the Bank of England's reluctance to organise support for the film industry was the concern that once it was 'in' it would be difficult to get 'out'. Indeed, the Bank's main reason for not taking its enquiry any further was that it might create unrealistic expectations. As Ernest Skinner commented: 'For the Bank of England to take any further steps by way of enquiries would imply that something was likely to be done and I have no confidence that any further enquiries would disclose a practicable basis for any worth-while Film Bank on commercial lines.'[50]

The Bank of England's highly jaundiced view of the film industry persisted. A few months after the conclusion of its enquiry, Sir Edward Peacock reported that Rothschilds had been approached on behalf of the Prudential to loan money to United Artists: 'Film finance has been so queer and dirty that my instinct was to say: "Don't look at it". But those who ask us are people we hesitate to refuse so I've said: "Look further into it, but we shall probably have to refuse."'[51] And when the Bank was asked to suggest nominees for a City representative on the Cinematograph Films Council – the new advisory body set up following the Cinematograph Films Act of 1938 – it was reluctant to get involved: a handwritten note records that 'I believe it's a rotten job which no good energetic man should take or be advised to take.'[52]

Notes

1. Herbert Wilcox, *Twenty-Five Thousand Sunsets: The Autobiography of Herbert Wilcox* (New York: A. S. Barnes, 1969), pp. 106–7.
2. Bank of England Archive (BEA) SMT 2/31: Note of Meeting between the Governor of the Bank of England and Claud Serocold, 27 July 1935.
3. BEA ADM 34/25: Diary of Montagu Norman 1936: entry for 4 June 1936.
4. Elizabeth Hennessy, *A Domestic History of the Bank of England* (Cambridge: Cambridge University Press, 2012), p. 10.
5. Martin Daunton, *Wealth and Welfare: An Economic and Social History of Britain 1851–1951* (Oxford: Oxford University Press, 2007), p. 118.
6. BEA SMT 2/31: Note of Meeting between the Governor and Claud Serocold, 27 July 1935.
7. Ibid.: Memorandum – 'The Cinema Industry', 30 January 1936.
8. Ibid.: Note of a Meeting with Claud Serocold, 30 January 1936.
9. Ibid.: Alexander Korda, 'Memorandum on the Film Quota Act', 18 February 1936.
10. Ibid.: Sir Edward Peacock to Montagu Norman, 25 February 1936.

11. Ibid.: Norman to Peacock, 3 March 1936.
12. BEA ADM 34/26: Diary of Montagu Norman 1937: entry for 3 March 1937; entry for 7 September 1937.
13. BEA SMT 2/33: E. H. Lever to Gordon Munro, 15 March 1937.
14. Ibid.: 'Interview with Mr Lever', 21 April 1937.
15. BEA ADM 34/26: Diary of Montagu Norman 1937: entry for 24 February 1937.
16. BEA SMT 2/33: Montagu Norman to A. R. Wagg, 22 February 1937.
17. BEA SMT 2/40: Extract from the Minutes of the Committee of the Treasury, 7 April 1937.
18. BEA SMT 2/33: Aide-memoire – 'Film Finance', 9 April 1937.
19. Ibid.: 'Film Finance', 16 April 1937.
20. Ibid.: John Corfield to Alfred Wagg, 27 April 1937.
21. Ibid.: Summary of interview with S. W. Smith, 19 May 1937.
22. BEA SMT 2/34: Summary of Interview with R. P. Baker, 8 May 1937.
23. Ibid.: Summary of Interview with F. W. Baker, 4 May 1937.
24. Ibid.: Summary of Interview with C. M. Woolf, 7 May 1937.
25. BEA SMT 2/33: Summary of Interview with Lord Portal (no date).
26. Ibid.: Simon Rowson to E. J. Bunbury, 4 May 1937.
27. BEA C48/326: List of Capital Issues of Film Companies, April 1937.
28. The National Archives (TNA) BT 31/434851: Agreement between General Cinema Finance Corporation and General Film Distributors, 8 April 1936.
29. 'Secrets of British Film Finance', *World Film News*, 1: 10 (January 1937), p. 21.
30. 'Woolf Outlines Policy of His Organisation', *Kinematograph Weekly*, 28 May 1936, p. 45.
31. The Aldgate total includes the charges in the names of F. C. Ellis and L. W. Watkins.
32. BEA SMT 2/33: 'Films', 23 April 1937.
33. Ibid.: 'Films', 27 April 1937.
34. BEA SMT 2/34: E. J. Bunbury to Montagu Norman, 6 May 1937.
35. BEA SMT 2/35: Bunbury to Norman, 1 June 1937.
36. Ibid.: Bunbury to Norman, 4 June 1937.
37. Ibid.: E. H. Lever to Bunbury, 11 June 1937.
38. Ibid.: Bunbury to Norman, 10 June 1937.
39. Ibid.: Memorandum, 20 May 1937. The memorandum is unsigned but was presumably written by either Bunbury or Skinner, or possibly both.
40. Ibid.: Note by Skinner, 19 May 1937.
41. BEA SMT 2/40: 'Films: Interim Report to the Governor', 7 June 1937, p. 2.
42. Ibid., pp. 2–3.
43. Ibid., p. 4.
44. Ibid., p. 5.
45. Ibid.
46. Ibid., p. 1.
47. Ibid., p. 2.
48. Ibid.
49. Ibid., p. 4.
50. BEA SMT 2/35: Note by Skinner, 9 June 1937.
51. Ibid.: E. R. Peacock to B. G. Catterns, 1 August 1937.
52. Ibid.: handwritten addendum (no initials) to a note by Skinner, 21 May 1938.

CHAPTER 9

Renewing the Quota

The Cinematograph Films Act of 1927 had a lifespan of ten years: the legislation was due to expire on 31 March 1938. From the mid-1930s the most pressing issue facing the film industry was the renewal of the quota. There were several – and sometimes competing – imperatives. British producers were strongly in favour of the renewal and strengthening of the quota legislation. Distributors were more equivocal, with the American renters operating in Britain the most vocal in their opposition to the quota. Exhibitors wanted good-quality films regardless of origin: their main concern was to eliminate the low-cost 'quota quickies' that had brought British films into such disrepute. In truth there was never any real likelihood that the quota would not be renewed: the increased volume of British film production since the Cinematograph Films Act suggested that the quota had succeeded in its primary aim. As a Board of Trade official observed in 1933: 'The present Act works exceedingly well and under the protection afforded by it British production has made far more progress than the sponsors of the Act dared to expect. Where an Act is clearly fulfilling its main function and no overwhelming case has been made for amending it, there is everything to be said for leaving it untouched.'[1]

The first review of the operation of the Cinematograph Films Act had been conducted by the Cinematograph Films Advisory Committee in 1929. The committee maintained that it 'considered that the usages and practices of the industry should conform to the requirements of the Act, rather than that the Act should be modified to meet the requirements of the industry'. Nevertheless, it identified two areas where it felt the legislation stood in need of modification. One was that the fines imposed for default in renters' quota were 'insignificant compared with the value of films and constitutes no deterrent': it recommended that renters should have to 'carry forward' quota defaults to the following year and that the legislation should be amended to allow for the withdrawal of the renter's licence after two years rather than three. The other was to relax the British labour conditions ('We consider that it would be of substantial assistance to British film production if more latitude were given to British makers in the employment of foreign personnel of the front rank') and specifically the requirement that the scenario writer should be British ('We must regretfully admit that there are few British scenario writers in the front rank of their profession, this being the technique in which this country is most deficient').[2] The Board of Trade was evidently sympathetic to these proposals. An internal minute suggested that some renters 'will deliberately incur the maximum penalty at present provided for non-compliance by the quota provision, rather than comply with them, the penalty being negligible in comparison with the advantage to be gained by non-compliance'.[3] (It tended to be the smaller independent British renters who defaulted: American renters usually fulfilled their minimum quota obligations and no more.) Another minute recorded: 'The first proposed amendment concerning the "scenario writer" is clearly right. This man [*sic*] is nowadays at any rate not the person whom the Act intended to indicate and there is no advantage in requiring him to be a British subject or of British domicile.'[4] However, there was no appetite to revise the Act so soon after its introduction. William Graham, President of the Board of Trade, told the committee's chair that 'I have been obliged to come to the conclusion that – quite apart from the merits of these proposals, about which I hope to have a talk with you when you call – it would be quite impossible for me to ask the Government to add to their legislative programme in the near future'.[5]

The Cinematograph Films Advisory Committee made only passing reference to the problem of 'quota quickies', noting 'a tendency on the part of American renters to confine themselves to securing as cheaply as possible the prescribed length of British film with little regard to quality'.[6] However, by 1930 it was clear that this was the main concern about the Quota Act, especially for producers and exhibitors. The trade's attention turned to how to rid the industry of low-cost 'quickies'. An idea that gained traction in the early 1930s was the introduction of a minimum cost threshold for quota films: a final picture cost of anywhere between £10,000 and £15,000 was variously suggested. A joint deputation of producers and exhibitors proposed a minimum cost of £150 per 100 feet and an overall picture cost of £10,000.[7] Liberal MP Sir Geoffrey Mander suggested a minimum cost threshold of £12,000.[8] Sir Gordon Craig, the managing director of British Movietonews and the short-lived World Studio Centre, advocated a 'minimum cost of £15,000 in order to enforce quality'.[9] However, there were also objections to the idea of a minimum cost, whatever the amount. *The Economist* pointed out there was not necessarily a correlation between cost and quality:

> Mr Mander's mistake, however, is in supposing that the cost of production is any criterion of entertainment values. There have been British films produced at a cost of £40,000 which have been rejected by exhibitors as worthless for exhibition. There have, on the other hand, been British films costing only £5,000, which have had an extraordinary success with the public.[10]

Kine Weekly's P. L. Mannock raised another objection: that a minimum cost would not guarantee the budget being spent on production values rather than on 'graft' (inflated salaries): 'No one, for example, can deny that *Shooting Stars* or *The Lily of Killarney* could not have been improved by a greater expenditure of money. On the other hand, *Tip Toes* and *Champagne*, made at a total cost of £65,000, are heartbreaking because that sum represents the cost of about four really good films.'[11]

The next formal review of the Cinematograph Films Act was undertaken at its own initiative by the CFAC in 1935. It focused on contraventions of the 'blind' booking clauses and the proliferation of quota quickies. The report highlighted the 'gentleman's agreements' between renters and exhibitors through which contracts were drawn up after films had been accepted: it explained 'that no offence is committed until an agreement has been made and that evidence of the offence can normally be obtained only from one of the parties to the agreement. Naturally, neither is willing to confess.'[12] It suggested increasing penalties for non-compliance to include the withdrawal of licenses. In response to the quickies, it proposed a cost threshold whereby 'the conditions of eligibility for the registration of films as British should be not less than £2 a foot'.[13] However, the report was not unanimous. C. P. Metcalfe, an independent exhibitor, submitted a minority report recommending the abolition of all booking restrictions and the introduction of a quality test rather than one based on cost:

> A cost test such as is recommended by the Committee would prevent certain types of films which do not earn large sums at the box office, but which are nevertheless in demand by many Cinemas, from being imported, as the cost of quota against them would be prohibitive.
>
> It would put a premium on extravagance, put some of the smaller producers out of business, would restrict expansion and would tend to create monopolies by preventing new production units from coming into existence, unless they were very heavily financed.[14]

A Board of Trade official minuted: 'Clearly this Report will not help the Government to decide whether the main provisions of the Cinematograph Films Act be continued (with or without amendments) or should be allowed to lapse.'[15] The same official informed the Permanent Under-Secretary of State Sir Horace Hamilton: 'The present report is the result of a self-imposed task. The Advisory Committee were never asked by the Board to consider the legislative position. In fact it was always felt to be unfortunate that they should enter upon this field.'[16]

Early in 1936 the Board of Trade decided to appoint a departmental committee 'to consider the position of British films, having in mind the approaching expiry of the Films Act, 1927, and to advise whether any, and if so what, measures are still required in the public interest to promote the production, renting and exhibition of such films'.[17] The committee was chaired by Lord Moyne of Bury St Edmunds. Moyne, as Walter Guinness, of the brewing dynasty, had been a Conservative MP between 1907 and 1931 and a former Minister of Agriculture and Fisheries. Following his peerage, Moyne had chaired a parliamentary committee on slum clearances and sat on the Royal Commission on the constitution of Durham University. The other members of the committee were A. C. Cameron (a governor of the British Film Institute and one of the contributors to the 1932 report *The Film in National Life* by the Commission on Educational and Cultural Films), Joseph Stanley Holmes (Liberal National MP for Harwich), J. J. Mallon (an economist who was warden of the East End charity Toynbee Hall), and two members of the Cinematograph Films Advisory Council, Eleanor Plumer (academic and warden of the Mary Ward Settlement) and Sir Arnold Wilson (Conservative MP for Hitchin).[18] The committee met fifteen times and took both written and oral evidence from a range of witnesses. The Board of Trade's R. D. Fennelly and statistician Simon Rowson provided factual data on the operation of the quota and the economics of the film business. Other witnesses included representatives of the Film Producers' Group of the Federation of British Industries, the Association of Cine Technicians, the Cinematograph Exhibitors' Association and the Kinematograph Renters' Society, while John Grierson, Paul Rotha and Harry Bruce Woolfe spoke for the producers of non-fiction films.

The different – and often opposing – concerns of the various trade interests became apparent during the course of the enquiry. About the only point on which all witnesses agreed was that the quota quickies were damaging to the reputation of the British film industry; but there was no consensus on the remedy. The memorandum submitted on behalf of producers stated that they 'are unanimously convinced that the complete or partial withdrawal of the protection afforded to this Industry by the present Act would be disastrous'.[19] A supporting annex attributed the expansion of the British production sector since the introduction of the Quota Act to the protection it offered: the production capacity of the industry had grown from nineteen stages totalling 105,211 square feet in 1928 to seventy stages totalling 795,557 square feet by 1935. The producers supported the introduction of a minimum cost threshold and suggested that for 'long' films this should be either a total picture cost of £15,000 or a statutory cost of £7,500: they also advocated the abolition of blind and block booking and for legislation to prevent quota films being screened in so-called 'dead' hours.[20]

The Association of Cine Technicians was similarly 'of the opinion that the growth and present size of the British Film Industry, with the consequent employment to thousands of British persons, is almost entirely due to the "Quota Act"'.[21] It recommended a minimum cost of £12,000 for any film over 6,000 feet and £2 per foot for films under 6,000 feet and with no more than 30 per cent of the budget to be spent on producers' and directors' fees, scenarios and studio overheads. It was in its evidence to the Moyne Committee that the ACT claimed US renters had conspired to keep the cost of their quota pictures artificially low:

> It is widely alleged that after the passing of the Cinematograph Films Act, 1927, all the American distributing organisations in Great Britain signed an agreement amongst themselves at a special meeting in Paris not to pay more than the £1 per foot for quota pictures made for them by other organisations . . . [If] a 6,000 foot picture was required, the producer's plan was to get what profit he could by producing a picture for as much below the figure of £6,000 as possible.[22]

The ACT also repeated claims that quota quickies were sometimes shown by exhibitors to empty cinemas in order to comply with the letter of the law: the evidence they submitted was articles from *The Era*. This was the origin of the oft-repeated claim that quota quickies were shown in the mornings to cleaners before cinemas had opened to the public.[23]

The Cinematograph Exhibitors' Association took a very different position. It argued for 'a substantial reduction of quota': it was also strongly in favour of relaxing the conditions of the legislation which it felt were unnecessarily restrictive, especially in regard to penalties for defaults. The CEA's argument was posited on the assertion that the quota had not guaranteed quality. Its evidence included its members' ratings of films. In 1935, for example, the CEA reviewed the 178 British quota films shown to the trade and found that significantly under half (73) were 'good first features', while the remainder comprised 41 'varying second features', 31 described as 'inferior' and 33 deemed 'definitely unshowable'. The CEA's evidence also highlighted the difference between the cinemas owned by the combines and independent exhibitors who were denied the opportunity to show the best British films due to bars (the agreement between renters and exhibitors that certain cinemas would have exclusivity in specified areas) and were obliged to take the lower-quality films to meet their quota. However, the CEA rejected the idea of a cost threshold for quota pictures:

> We are not in favour of the suggested solution of cost as a basis of qualification as we are not convinced that it will be the means of increasing production. On the contrary, we anticipate that the introduction would be followed by a considerable decrease. The figure which has been mooted, namely £2 per foot, is of little value. A good film generally costs in the making to-day from £25,000 to £30,000 at least. If either of these figures be instituted the effect would not be to produce more British pictures, but would shut out from this market a considerable number of foreign films – which it would no longer pay to import on account of the attendant expenses of acquiring British quota.[24]

In essence the CEA was concerned that a cost threshold would not bring about the necessary increase in quality but would jeopardise the supply of superior American films.

The delegation from the Kinematograph Renters' Society included representatives of both British and American renters. The former were represented by John Maxwell of the Associated British Picture Corporation, whose evidence reflected his role as chairman of one of the two large combines and focused as much on production and exhibition as distribution. He supported an adjusted version of the quota that would prioritise quality over quantity, explaining that it was not possible to step up production while maintaining quality:

> My own company has tried to increase the number of pictures beyond the 20 or so that we handle each year, but has found it impossible to get the talent and skilled personnel necessary to do so. When we did try in one or two years to largely increase the output we found several of the pictures were of such poor quality, that we hastily abandoned the idea and confined ourselves to the figure mentioned above.[25]

Maxwell was speaking from the perspective of the combines: the increase in the volume of British production during the early and mid-1930s had been driven largely by independent producers not attached to one of the combines. Maxwell rebutted the CEA's argument that independent exhibitors were disadvantaged as circuit bookings alone were insufficient for a film to return a profit: 'A successful picture, to be a successful picture, has got to get around 1,500 playdates, or bookings . . . The most I can give it in my own theatres is about 200, so obviously the other 1,300 playdates have got to come from independent exhibitors.'[26]

The representatives of American renters – Sam Eckman of MGM, J. C. Graham of Paramount and D. E. Griffiths of Warner Bros. – were at pains to deny responsibility for the quota quickies. They argued that the proliferation of low-cost quota films was an inevitable outcome of industrial and economic conditions. In particular, the high level at which renters' quota was set meant that the US distributors, who imported most of their Hollywood films to Britain, were obliged to prioritise quantity over quality. Griffiths highlighted the difficulty of producing sufficient films to meet the quota: 'The law which compels such a large footage to be made makes it impossible to acquire such a large footage of quality . . . I have a studio that cost £200,000. I have spent nearly one million pounds over a period of years.'[27] Eckman highlighted the dearth of skilled technicians in Britain compared to the United States and also suggested that some British producers were unwilling to release their films through MGM: he said 'the Company I represent has on many occasions made an attempt to get the better British films, but the British companies are reluctant to distribute through our agency because their attitude is that we have so many, if I may say so, outstanding films of our own, that we could not possibly lend our best efforts to the distribution of their films'.[28]

Simon Rowson's evidence included the most detail about the provision of production finance. His memorandum highlighted the under-capitalisation of the British industry and the consequent problems of reliance on short-term money:

> There is another subject to which I feel I must draw your attention because it gives me concern for great anxiety. I refer to the relation between the capital employed in film production in this country, and to the fears which I share with many people in the trade that this capital is seriously inadequate. In America, it is estimated that the capital employed for production is about £20 million . . . Though no accurate estimate of capital in the British production industry has been made, I feel certain that this figure is very greatly in excess of the capital actually available. The consequence of this under-capitalisation is the extensive resort to short-date capital in every one of the large variety of aspects known to the resourceful financier. Such finance is very dear money, and apart from other serious inconveniences represents a further charge on the cost of production.[29]

Rowson argued for retention of the quota ('I know of no authoritative opinion in support of the view that British interests would be served if the Quota were permitted to expire with the present Act in 1938'). He proposed the reduction of renters' quota to 15 per cent rising 2.5 per cent every two years to a maximum of

25 per cent, with exhibitors' quota reduced to 12.5 per cent and increasing on a similar basis. He suggested a cost threshold of £1 a foot but was willing to support 15 shillings a foot increasing to £1 a foot after a few years.[30]

Some of the evidence received by the committee was not included in the published evidence. There was some confidential financial data including a summary of receipts of the overseas distribution of British films for the major production groups for the year ending 31 March 1936. The most successful by some distance was London Film Productions, which had earned £202,000 from overseas distribution, followed by the Gaumont-British Picture Corporation (£143,000) and the British and Dominions Film Corporation (£50,920).[31] These figures were probably provided in the context of the possibility of reviving the discussion of a reciprocity agreement with American companies over the distribution of British films in the United States. The oral evidence presented by Alexander Korda and Sir Connop Guthrie of the Prudential Assurance Company was also not published so as not to prejudice their current negotiations with United Artists. Guthrie insisted that American trade interests were actively seeking to destabilise the British film industry as a prelude to taking it over:

> Sir Connop said emphatically that the USA film industry is out to ruin the British film industry. The Government should make it very clear to the American interests that they are not going to be allowed to control the British industry. The exhibitors should be asked to support efforts which are made to increase British film production. If they do not, they will at no distant date be in dire straits themselves.[32]

Guthrie provided no evidence for his assertions – the only significant American interests in the British film industry at the time were Fox's non-voting shareholding in Gaumont-British and the fact that some American distributors owned non-circuit showcase West End cinemas – but it seems likely that he was raising the spectre of American control in an effort to persuade the government to provide more direct financial support for the film industry. He 'was emphatic that the Government should see that the industry is placed on its feet by some means or other' and 'that if the film industry today were handled by the Government in the same manner as the steel industry finance would be forthcoming without difficulty'.[33]

The Moyne Committee submitted its report to the Board of Trade in November 1936. It was a wide-ranging report – perhaps more so than had been expected – and included some unexpected recommendations. It began with a general statement of the cultural and political significance of the film industry:

> The cinematograph film industry is to-day one of the most widely-used means for the amusement of the public at large. It is also undoubtedly a most important factor in the education of all classes of the community, in the spread of national culture and in presenting national ideas to the very large numbers to whom its appeals are almost unlimited. The propaganda value of the film cannot be over-emphasised. It is rivalled only by that of Broadcasting and the Press.[34]

The discursive language employed here recalls the arguments advanced in support of the Cinematograph Films Bill in 1927. It also provides some context for the report's opening section on 'Foreign Influences on the British Film Industry':

> We have received evidence which suggested that, owing to the increasing strength of the home industry, foreign interests are adopting means which are tending to prevent a further expansion of the output of British films and are, moreover, endeavouring to obtain a further measure of control of the production and exhibition as well of the distributing sides of the industry.[35]

This perspective seems to have been influenced by the confidential evidence of Sir Connop Guthrie: the published evidence barely touches upon foreign control of the British film industry, and Fennelly had explicitly stated that the amount of American capital invested in the production sector was minimal. Nevertheless, Moyne's first recommendation was that 'the Government should keep a close watch on transfers of interests in British producing, renting and exhibiting units with a view to prevent control passing abroad'. The report then turned its attention to the question of production finance:

> The evidence given before us made it clear that the British film production industry has an insufficient supply of capital for its needs and that the cost of production of British films has been increased by the necessary money being obtainable only at a high rate of interest. The more prominent financial houses have, we understand, generally speaking been disinclined to come to its assistance. Lack of finance is a powerful factor in enabling foreign interests to obtain control and is certainly an impediment to the industry's continued and satisfactory expansion.[36]

Moyne's second recommendation, therefore, was that a body 'should be created by financial interests to finance the film production industry in this country, in approved cases, on reasonably cheap terms': this was the origin of the idea of a film bank subscribed by financial institutions in the City that the Bank of England was asked to consider in 1937.

When it came to the renewal of the quota, the committee's primary purpose, its report argued that in order to support the continued growth of the industry 'a steadily increasing protection is in our view a *sine quâ non*. The evidence has been virtually unanimous in favour of a continuation of the legislation of the Act of 1927 as the most suitable method of protection. This Act has, in essence, proved to be framed on sound lines.'[37] It recommended setting exhibitors' quota at 15 per cent and renters' quota at 20 per cent for 'long' films with phased increases up to a maximum of 50 per cent, and the introduction of a separate quota for short films under 3,000 feet set at 10 per cent for exhibitors and 15 per cent for renters. It accepted the narrative that it was the American renters who were mostly responsible for the quota quickies. It rejected the idea of a minimum cost test on the grounds that 'the cost of a film is not necessarily any criterion of its value' and the widely quoted figure of £2 per foot would represent a 'serious handicap' for smaller producers.[38] Instead, it proposed a 'quality test' that 'would be concerned normally only with the entertainment value and general merits of a film'.[39] Other recommendations included removing the British nationality requirement for the author of a scenario and strengthening the prohibition of block booking (which had persisted in some cases through informal 'gentleman's agreements') by applying a penalty to any renter who engaged in the practice. Perhaps the most eye-catching recommendation, however, was to set up a statutory administrative organisation for the film industry: this body 'which might be called the Films Commission' would be responsible for the administration of film policy including the institution of the 'quality test' for quota films. Its members would be appointed by the government and should be independent of the trade.[40]

While many of the Moyne Committee's recommendations were uncontentious, the proposal for a statutory Films Commission was fiercely opposed within the trade. A *Kine Weekly* editorial indicated just how radical the idea seemed:

> If the proposals – particularly those referring to the financing of the business and the supervision of an all-powerful Commission – had been made by a Committee appointed by a Labour Government, the whole of the Industry would have risen in its wrath. 'Socialism' would have been raised. Members of the Commission would have been savagely called 'Kommisars'. We should have heard talk of passive resistance; and all the powers would have been evoked to fight for the privilege of minding our own business.[41]

World Film News outlined the responses of the different trade interests:

> All sections agree regarding as impracticable the notion that the industry's problems can be solved by a body consisting solely of persons without expert knowledge of the film trade. The renters fear – and they are to some extent supported in this by the producers – that any control by an outside body over the financing and production of films will have the effect of discouraging prospective investors. And they regard a quality test for films as impracticable in view of the diversity of taste they must necessarily cater for.[42]

The Economist thought the Films Commission was as a good idea in principle but cautioned: 'Unless the members appointed have considerable experience of the trade, the Commission will not inspire that confidence in the trade and the public which is essential if it is to realise the good intentions of its sponsors.'[43]

The Board of Trade invited trade responses to the Moyne Committee's report: several months of discussion followed. The trade generally welcomed renewal of the quota, although the CEA baulked at the proposal that exhibitors' quota should rise to 50 per cent, which 'has caused considerable apprehension among our members, who realise its impracticabilities'.[44] It turned out that the Board of Trade itself was not particularly keen on the establishment of a Films Commission, which it cautioned 'would have the grave disadvantage that a Minister should have to be responsible in Parliament for the acts of a body over which he would not have effective control'.[45] At the same time, however, the developing financial crisis in 1937 suggested that some form of regulation might be necessary. The Board of

Trade suggested that the industry itself might 'set up some body which can serve as a focusing point for matters affecting the trade as a whole and which can deal with some of the problems which arise between the various sections'.[46] The outcome was the establishment of a Joint Trade Committee that would represent the different trade interests, with the Board of Trade asked to appoint an arbitrator to resolve disagreements.[47] However, a schism was already opening up within the CEA whose General Council supported the introduction of a quality test (similar in principle to the Association's own rankings of films) but where the representatives of the major circuits were more inclined towards a minimum cost.[48] R. D. Fennelly recorded 'that there is little hope of the divergent views being reconciled without a strong lead team from outside and that the Government must proceed to formulate their own proposals . . . The exhibitors seem to be on rather a bad wicket as it can be argued their agitation is one in support of foreign films against British films.'[49]

In May 1937 Oliver Stanley succeeded Walter Runciman as President of the Board of Trade. Stanley, who had some knowledge of film matters from his previous role as a Home Office minister, where he had steered the Sunday Entertainments Bill through Parliament, put forward a White Paper (a draft version of proposed legislation) in July 1937. It proposed extending the quota for ten years: exhibitors' quota for long films was to start at 15 per cent rising to 25 per cent and renters' quota was to start at 20 per cent rising to 30 per cent. The quota for short films would be set at 5 per cent rising to 15 per cent for exhibitors and 10 per cent rising to 20 per cent for renters. However, the Moyne Committee's proposal of a quality test for quota films was rejected in favour of a cost test:

> The advantage of the viewing test are obvious, but it has one grave disadvantage. Whether or not a film is registered for quota would depend on the personal judgement of the viewing authority, given only after the film has been produced . . . The cost test, on the other hand, has the merit of certainty. A producer would know before production commenced that if he spent a certain amount his film would qualify for renters' quota and he could arrange his finance on that basis.[50]

The White Paper proposed that the minimum cost should be set at a statutory cost (i.e. the salary costs paid to British technicians and artistes) of £7,500 (reckoned as equivalent to a total picture cost of £15,000) for long films: there would be no cost threshold for shorts. The White Paper also took on board one of the ideas suggested to the Moyne Committee but not included in its report: the introduction of a 'double quota'. It proposed that a film with a statutory cost over three times the minimum threshold (£22,500, equivalent to a picture cost of £45,000) could be counted twice for renters' quota: this was in order 'to encourage British producers to make a proportion of higher quality films to compete with those of other producers in a world market'.[51] Another recommendation was that a renter who spent at least £20,000 on acquiring the foreign distribution rights of a British long film should be allowed to count it towards their quota. Finally, the White Paper suggested that the departmental committee was 'surprised by the measure of disagreement between the three branches of the cinematograph films industry' but accepted that in the absence of any consensus the Films Commission would not be a practicable body: the Films Commission was therefore dropped and it was proposed that 'the administration of any future Act should remain in the hands of the Board of Trade, assisted by an Advisory Committee constituted on lines similar to those on which the present Advisory Committee is constituted'.[52]

The Economist felt that the White Paper 'has, in the main, followed the line of least resistance by including those proposals which are likely to assume least opposition in the industry'.[53] However, the trade interests were again divided. The CEA opposed the cost test as it 'would be [so] easily avoided by foreign interests that such a test would serve little or no useful purpose'.[54] The CEA's General Secretary W. R. Fuller argued that the statutory £7,500 cost test 'represents a break figure which has no particular application to any actuality of film production'.[55] The KRS also argued for the removal of the cost test for renters' quota and to drop the proposals regarding blind and block booking. However, a Board of Trade official noted 'that they were without their Secretary and now decline to make representation in writing means, I presume, that the KRS as a whole is not unanimous on the subject. It seems impossible to satisfy even one of the three sections of the trade.'[56] And the ACT took against the double quota provision 'as (a) it would probably mean on balance the lowering of employment, and (b) it might tend towards the production of extravagant "white elephant" pictures rather than good ones, and would reduce the actual number of pictures made.'[57]

It was at this stage that the opposition of American renters to the proposed legislation became apparent. The Motion Picture Producers and Distributors of America – the powerful US trade association that unlike its British counterparts was both united and well connected politically – was becoming more interested in overseas markets during the 1930s.[58] At this time overseas markets accounted for over a third of the US film industry's revenues: Britain (and the British Empire) was by some distance the biggest of those markets and according to some estimates accounted for around 50 per cent of all Hollywood's foreign earnings.[59] The MPPDA lobbied for a reduction in renters' quota and argued that 'they be permitted to discharge their quota obligations by the production of a smaller number of pictures of high quality', and further suggested a higher threshold for the minimum cost on the ground that the proposed minimum of £15,000 'will not result in the production of quota pictures of high quality but will merely perpetuate quota productions of mediocre quality'. The MPPDA used the opportunity of the financing crisis that had hit the British production sector in 1937 to assert the importance of American investment:

> Competent observers are of the opinion that if, through the operation of the quota law as amended, the American companies were to come into the market in Great Britain for the studio space, equipment and technical services necessary to produce a reasonable number of films of the type suggested, it would put an end immediately to the present severe crisis that prevails in the larger studios, would unfreeze

the present frozen channels of film finance, and would give the stimulus to British production as a whole without which recovery from the present crisis may prove impossible.[60]

The MPPDA was supported by the US State Department, which at the time was involved in negotiating an Anglo-American Trade Agreement: the existence of the quota sat uneasily with the trade agreement that placed an emphasis on free trade and economic liberalism.

The MPPDA saw an opportunity to influence the new legislation to the advantage of the American companies. Its London representative Fay Allport met Oliver Stanley and put forward its own suggestion to extend the proposed double quota provision:

> The renters, while they would like to obtain an extra quota credit for every £15,000 they spent on a film, seem prepared to accept the jump from £15,000 to £45,000 for a double quota film. They urge, however, that films costing £60,000 and over (i.e. £30,000 in labour costs) should count for treble quota... Apparently the view of the Americans is that when it comes to making a film which they would hope to rent at a reasonable return, both in this and the United States market, at least £60,000 must be spent. From the point of view of producing better pictures there is something to be said for the proposal, but it would no doubt be strongly opposed by the exhibitors and the trade unions who do not in any case like double quota proposals as tending to reduce the supply of films.[61]

A treble quota arrangement would work to the American companies' advantage in two particular respects. Firstly, it would allow them to meet their quota obligations with fewer films: a renter currently obliged to offer, say, twelve British films would in theory be able to offer only four films at treble quota. Secondly, as the American companies would be spending more on their British quota films, they would have a better chance of marketing those films successfully in the United States. The MPPDA's intervention should therefore be seen as a deliberate attempt to influence the production contexts in Britain to the advantage of its own members. The Board of Trade was sympathetic to the treble quota as it would encourage American companies to produce higher-quality films in Britain.

The Cinematograph Films Bill presented to Parliament in November 1937 included provision for both double and treble quota. Eligibility for renters' quota was set at a statutory cost of £1 per foot with a minimum statutory cost of £7,500; double quota was set at £3 per foot with a minimum statutory cost of £22,500; and treble quota was set at £5 per foot with a minimum statutory cost of £37,500. It also proposed the establishment of a Cinematograph Films Council in place of the Cinematograph Films Advisory Committee. The Board of Trade was keen that the cost of the Council should not be borne by public funds:

> The Trade takes this Council very seriously and it seems probable that it will be called upon to do a considerable amount of work, though at this stage one cannot easily estimate how much the annual cost is likely to be... Our general view is that

as the Trade have asked for this Council they should pay for it and that the cost should come out of the registration and licence fees.[62]

A proposal by Labour MP Tom Williams to reintroduce the Films Commission as suggested by the Moyne Committee was defeated at the Standing Committee stage. However, by far the most contentious aspect of the legislation was the treble quota. This had not been included in the White Paper: its inclusion in the Bill took the trade by surprise. There were concerns from both independent British producers (who feared that they would be priced out of access to the larger studios by American companies producing higher-cost films) and from exhibitors (who were concerned that the treble quota applied only to renters and would mean fewer British films would be available for exhibitors). G. A. Atkinson, editor of *The Era*, went so far as to label the Films Bill 'a betrayal of Britain':

> The industry knows that it is designed to promote the making of foreign films in Britain ... It extinguishes the national British film because it extinguishes the independent producer, and may eventually extinguish the independent distributor and exhibitor ... Every corporate trade body or association of employment is united in its opposition to this fantastic measure. It represents the biggest legacy of trouble that any Government of recent years has invited.[63]

The CEA lobbied MPs to oppose the treble quota on the grounds that it 'may seriously imperil the Cinematograph Films Bill, which we have hitherto supported'.[64] The treble quota was in fact withdrawn during the report stage, only to be reintroduced for the Bill's third reading.[65]

While the Bill was progressing through Parliament, the US Embassy was lobbying the Foreign Office that the new legislation should be delayed until the conclusion of the Anglo-American Trade Agreement. A Foreign Office memo records:

> [The] Americans did not really understand our Parliamentary difficulties and thought that these could easily be put on one side if the Government made up their minds to do so. Mr Stanley, on the other hand, was definitely of the impression that to ask Parliament to agree a postponement of the legislation at the request of the US Government would be to court a rebuff and was not practical politics.[66]

Lord Halifax, the Foreign Secretary, reported on a meeting with the newly arrived US ambassador Joseph Kennedy to Oliver Stanley: 'Having begun about something else, he got on to films and said that the Bill, as it at present stands, will not in fact achieve either what we presumably want or what the Americans want.' Halifax added that Kennedy 'struck me as being reasonable and anxious to help, though no doubt in the process of helping us, they also hope to help themselves ... He is a wary fellow and seems genuinely anxious to be friendly, and I fancy he is pretty close to the President.'[67] R. D. Fennelly drafted a carefully balanced reply in which he stated that the government intended 'to secure certain amendments during later stages in the progress of the Bill which it is thought will go a long way towards meeting the important wishes of the United States renters' – in practice the amendments amounted to the restoration of the treble quota and a small adjustment to the quota credit for acquiring the foreign distribution rights of single quota films – while at the same time making it clear 'that any suggestion that HMG were in receipt of formal representations from the US Government on the subject of the Bill while it was still under consideration by Parliament might well destroy any sympathy Parliament might have for the proposals and might have a serious effect on the attitude of Parliament towards the impending trade negotiations'.[68]

A late spanner was thrown into the works when the House of Lords proposed an amendment that would set renters' quota at 20 per cent rather than 15 per cent during the first year of the new legislation. Yet again this suggestion exposed differences between sections of the trade. The amendment was welcomed by the producers who felt that it 'should be of material advantage to the Production Industry of this Country... Producers are also of the opinion, after further examination of the figures of production and estimated production, that there should be no difficulty in fulfilling the quotas as they now stand in the Bill as amended.'[69] However, for the renters, who had been preparing their next year's programmes on the assumption of a 15 per cent quota, the amendment came as a shock. Allport reported the 'grave concern' of the American renters and that 'their opinion [is] that such an increase is highly undesirable from the standpoint of British and American film interests alike'. He argued that it would undermine one of the key aspects of the new legislation insofar as it would mean the production of more 'quickies' to make up the difference:

> It is the intent of the impending Act that quota pictures should reflect credit on the British producing industry. The multiple credit features of the Bill will in time open the way for the production of quota pictures of this type to the extent that renters are permitted to utilise these provisions.
>
> Months are required, however, for the production of pictures of this type. It is recognised in the industry that under the best conditions a minimum of six to eight months is required for the production of a major picture. A creditable programme picture can seldom be produced in less than four months. Where the facilities are limited, even larger periods are required.[70]

The CEA similarly felt that the amendment 'is extraordinarily unwise' though for a different reason: it feared that 'if ... the renters make exclusively the expensive type of film our margin of choice would be reduced'.[71] Oliver Stanley responded that the Lords' amendments 'were carried against the advice of the representatives of the Government'.[72] When the Bill came back to the House of Commons, the 15 per cent renters' quota was restored.

The new Cinematograph Films Act came into effect on 1 April 1938. On the same day Adrian Brunel wrote to Prime Minister Neville Chamberlain: 'In my view the Films Bill is as much a weakening of Britain's power and influence, as if we had handed over four-fifths of our press to German and Italian control and agreed to cancel our re-armament programme ... Films are of vital national importance, and to reduce our output from 225 pictures a year to about 70 at such a time as the present (instead of increasing it) seems the height [of] unwisdom.'[73] The Association of Cine Technicians similarly commented in its annual report for 1938 that the Act was 'fundamentally unsound in that the basis of the Act is not primarily concerned with the development of a flourishing British film industry independent of foreign control'.[74] However, Alexander Korda told a *Financial Times* correspondent that 'the new Cinematograph Films Act would be beneficial to that part of the industry which catered for the home market. He added that in his view the success of the British film industry in the future depended not so much on its activities in the home market as on its ability to capture a fair share of the world market.'[75]

The Cinematograph Films Act of 1938 exemplified how the British government's film policy had changed since 1927. While protection of the domestic production industry through the quota remained the primary objective of the legislation, the operation of the quota itself had been significantly revised. The minimum cost threshold for renters' quota was intended to remove the curse of the quota quickies – to this extent it would prove to be largely successful – while the introduction of double and treble quota credits was intended to encourage the production of higher cost British films. The first year of the new legislation saw a significant reduction in the volume of British quota films: 103 films were registered in the quota year 1938–9 compared to 228 in the quota year 1937–8. However, the average cost of British films was estimated to have increased from £25,000 to £55,000, with 10 treble quota pictures, 21 double quota, 47 single quota and 23 below the threshold for renters' quota and registered for exhibitors' quota only.[76] The next chapter will assess the impact of the new Cinematograph Films Act on British film production and the provision of film finance.

Notes

1. The National Archives (TNA) BT 64/97: 'R. A.' to W. Hoskin, 20 October 1933.
2. TNA BT 64/86: Sir Lawrence Guillemand to President of the Board of Trade, 19 November 1929.
3. Ibid.: Minute by Mr Hamilton, 23 November 1929.
4. Ibid.: Minute by Percy Ashley, 10 December 1929.
5. Ibid.: William Graham to Sir Lawrence Guillemand, 27 January 1930.
6. Ibid.: Guillemand to President of the Board of Trade, 19 November 1929.
7. 'New Quota Revision Proposals', *The Bioscope*, 7 May 1930, p. 23.
8. *Parliamentary Debates: House of Commons*, 5th Series, vol. 236, 18 March 1930, col. 1886.
9. 'Amend the Quota Act', *Kinematograph Weekly*, 16 January 1930, p. 37.
10. 'The Future of British Films', *The Economist*, 16 August 1930, p. 312.
11. 'The Fetish of Expenditure', *Kinematograph Weekly*, 6 March 1930, p. 36.
12. TNA BT 64/88: Cinematograph Films Advisory Committee: Report on Quality Test for British Films.
13. Ibid.
14. Ibid.: Recommendation by Mr C. P. Metcalfe (no date).
15. Ibid.: Minute by 'W.R.P', 2 December 1935.

16. Ibid.: 'W. P.' to Sir Horace Hamilton, 11 December 1935.
17. *Parliamentary Debates: House of Commons*, 5th Series, vol. 310, 26 March 1936, col. 96.
18. Margaret Dickinson and Sarah Street, *Cinema and State: The Film Industry and the British Government 1927–84* (London: British Film Institute, 1985), pp. 55–6.
19. Board of Trade, *Minutes of Evidence Taken Before the Departmental Committee on Cinematograph Films together with Appendices and Index* (London: HMSO, 1936), p. 35.
20. Ibid., p. 38.
21. Ibid., pp. 71–2.
22. Ibid., p. 78.
23. 'Charwomen and Quota Films', *The Era*, 10 July 1935; 'Film Without an Audience', *The Era*, 6 November 1935.
24. Board of Trade, *Minutes of Evidence*, p. 82.
25. Ibid., p. 97.
26. Ibid., p. 102.
27. Ibid., p. 105.
28. Ibid., p. 99.
29. Ibid., p. 115.
30. Ibid., p. 114.
31. TNA BT 55/3: 'Very Confidential: Receipts from Overseas Distribution of Films during 12 Months Ending 31 March, 1936'. The total of £143,000 for Gaumont-British was broken down into the 'Empire market' (£82,000) and 'Foreign market' (£61,000 excluding US).
32. TNA BT 64/92: Minutes of the 10th Meeting of the Moyne Committee, 20 July 1936.
33. Ibid.
34. *Cinematograph Films Act, 1927: Report of the Committee Appointed by the Board of Trade*, Cmd. 5320 (November 1936), p. 4 (3).
35. Ibid., p. 11 (23).
36. Ibid., p. 12 (27).
37. Ibid., p. 13 (34).
38. Ibid., p. 20 (56).
39. Ibid., p. 20 (58).
40. Ibid., p. 35 (97).
41. 'Moyne and the Industry', *Kinematograph Weekly*, 3 December 1936, p. 4.
42. 'A Common Flag for British Films', *World Film News*, 2: 1 (April 1937), pp. 13–14.
43. 'Films and Fans', *The Economist*, 5 December 1936, p. 456.
44. 'Lord Moyne', *Kinematograph Weekly*, 21 January 1937, p. 7.
45. TNA BT 64/89: Draft Memorandum for Cabinet (no date).
46. 'Lord Moyne Discusses Committee's Work', *Kinematograph Weekly*, 11 March 1937, p. 36.
47. 'Film Conference', *The Financial Times*, 5 May 1937, p. 11.
48. 'Vigorous Debate on Quota Policy', *Kinematograph Weekly*, 24 June 1937, p. 6.
49. TNA BT 64/89: Minute by R. D. Fennelly, 29 May 1937.
50. *Proposals for Legislation on Cinematograph Films*, Cmd. 5529 (July 1937), p. 3 (5).
51. Ibid., p. 5 (8).
52. Ibid., p. 10 (24).
53. 'The Film Quota', *The Economist*, 31 July 1937, p. 234.

54. TNA BT 64/90: 'Views of Exhibitors on the White Paper Proposals', 22 September 1937.
55. Ibid.: W. R. Fuller to Oliver Stanley, 8 October 1937.
56. Ibid.: Minute by W. Palmer, 29 September 1937.
57. TNA BT 64/89: George H. Elvin to R. D. Fennelly, 1 July 1937.
58. Dickinson and Street, *Cinema and State*, pp. 94–5.
59. H. Mark Glancy, *When Hollywood Loved Britain: The Hollywood 'British' Film, 1939–45* (Manchester: Manchester University Press, 1999), p. 20.
60. TNA BT 64/90: MPPDA: 'Analysis of the Summary of Proposals Approved by the Board of Trade on July 29, 1937, as the basis of the new Films Act', 3 August 1937.
61. Ibid.: Note of Meeting between a Delegation of American Renters with Oliver Stanley, 15 November 1937.
62. Ibid.: R. D. Fennelly to N. G. Loughname, 22 November 1937.
63. 'Why the Films Bill is a Betrayal of Britain', *The Era*, 4 November 1937, p. 1.
64. 'CEA Canvasses MPs Against Treble Quota', *Kinematograph Weekly*, 24 February 1938, p. 9.
65. 'Treble Quota Not Dead Yet', *Kinematograph Weekly*, 3 March 1938, p. 17.
66. TNA BT 64/91: Gladwyn Jobb, 'Films Bill', 7 February 1938.
67. Ibid.: Lord Halifax to Oliver Stanley, 10 March 1938.
68. Ibid.: Draft Reply by R. D. Fennelly to Sir R. Lindsay (no date).
69. TNA BT 64/92: M. Neville Kearney to Board of Trade, 24 March 1938.
70. Ibid.: F. W. Allport to Oliver Stanley, 16 March 1938.
71. Ibid.: W. R. Fuller to Oliver Stanley, 17 March 1938.
72. Ibid.: Oliver Stanley to George Buchanan MP, 24 March 1935.
73. Ibid.: Adrian Brunel to Neville Chamberlain, 1 April 1938.
74. 'ACT Annual Report: Films Bill Declared "Unsound"', *Kinematograph Weekly*, 5 May 1938, p. 29.
75. 'British Films in Need of World Markets', *The Financial Times*, 4 April 1938, p. 7.
76. 'First Year of the Films Act', *The Economist*, 15 April 1939, p. 126.

CHAPTER 10

Recovery and Revival

The period between the introduction of the new Cinematograph Films Act in April 1938 and the outbreak of the Second World War in September 1939 was a period of relative optimism for the British film production industry. R. B. Marriott, the studio correspondent of *The Era*, wrote in March 1939: 'More money is being found for British film production . . . The aloofness of the City, which has been causing headaches for some time, is rapidly vanishing. Once again we are finding that finance is being made available for the extension and strengthening of the industry.'[1] There had been a clearing out of the inexperienced producers whose extravagance had contributed to the crisis; banks and insurance companies had become much more cautious when it came to lending to untried producers; and the growth of the J. Arthur Rank group had brought a degree of fiscal stability to the industry without yet prompting concern over the emergence of a nascent monopoly. The production sector had contracted by around half: the number of long films registered for British quota fell from 228 in 1937–8 to 103 in 1938–9.[2] However, there was a general sense that the quality of British films had undergone significant improvement. Marriott suggested that the success of recent British films – he mentioned *Pygmalion*, *Sixty Glorious Years*, *The Citadel* and *The Lady Vanishes* – 'has gone a long way towards restoring City confidence' in the industry: he felt that 'we can assert with confidence that faith is with us again – a vital, creative faith in British films . . . And this restoration of finance and faith should lead to even greater prosperity than ever before.'[3] The newly established statutory body the Cinematograph Films Council was more measured in tone but still felt that the outlook for British production was optimistic:

> [We] have some reason for believing that the tide has turned. The year that has just elapsed has witnessed the production of British films of the highest quality. This is demonstrated not only by the production of certain films at great cost, which have enjoyed wide popularity, but also by a high general average of merit. The minimum cost provision of the Act of 1938 has, doubtless, contributed to this result; but we are satisfied that the main source of the improvement lay in the fact that the financial lesson of the boom years had been learned and that those engaged in production were resolved to ensure that the quality of the picture justified its cost.[4]

Even the perennially cautious John Maxwell could tell shareholders of the Associated British Picture Corporation in 1939 that the company's accounts 'showed a position of quite considerable strength'.[5]

There were encouraging indications that more capital was becoming available for film production. The Cinematograph Films Council reported that a total of £5.7 million had been invested in film production in the first year following the Cinematograph Films Act, 1938.[6] An article in *The Financial Times* in June 1939 suggested that outside the two combines there were now three groups of producers in Britain. The first were production units financed directly by American parent companies: these were MGM British at Denham Studios, the Warner Bros. unit at Teddington Studios, and Twentieth Century Productions (the British subsidiary of Twentieth Century-Fox) which relocated from Wembley to Islington when the latter studios were vacated by Gainsborough Pictures. The second group were independent producers supported by distribution contracts with major US or British renters: these included Alexander Korda (United Artists), Herbert Wilcox (RKO) and Gabriel Pascal (General Film Distributors). The third group were smaller British producer-distributors such as Associated Talking Pictures, the British Lion Film Corporation and Butcher's Film Service. The article suggested that the last group 'assume a national importance far beyond their size' as they were outside the orbit of the combines but were also independent of American interests. However, they were less well-resourced than the units associated with the major distributors, and they tended to produce lower-cost films.[7]

A particular feature of the late 1930s was the increasing level of American investment in British film production. This included the provision of production finance as well as distribution contracts. For instance, the Bank of America, already a major supporter of the US film industry, had started making loans to British producers. The manager of its London branch told the Bank of England that it was filling a gap left by British banks:

> At this particular time we are using $678,566.63 (£150,000) of our dollar capital, necessitated in part through our financing Alexander Korda and Herbert Wilcox productions. In this connection permit me to mention that the reason we have these loans is because English banks do not want the business, also, that we have fairly recently advanced these two producers some £700,000 all of which has been spent in this country. As a matter of fact several of the best pictures produced in England could not have been made but for our loans.[8]

Korda and Wilcox both had close links with American distributors, which was no doubt instrumental in securing the backing of US lenders. The major British films supported by the Bank of America included Wilcox's *Sixty Glorious Years* (1938) and Korda's *The Four Feathers* (1939) and *Over the Moon* (1939). However, despite the success of his brace of Queen Victoria biopics (*Victoria the Great* had preceded *Sixty Glorious Years* in 1937), Wilcox had to go to Hollywood for his next film, *Nurse Edith Cavell* (1939). He told the press: 'The inability of the City to discriminate between what are good and bad propositions in the film business has made every film producer a financial outcast. The attitude to films in New York is entirely different from the attitude in London.'[9]

The overall trend in the British production sector in the late 1930s was towards fewer but more expensive films. In March 1939 Marriott noted that films due to start shooting over the next few months 'are nearly all to cost more than usual'.[10] This is borne out by statistical evidence. The Bank of England Archive holds a ledger itemising the costs of 172 British long quota films released in the eighteen months following the introduction of the Cinematograph Films Act, 1938.[11] The ledger reveals that the average statutory cost of a British long film in 1938–9 was £24,078: this was nearly 3.5 times the average statutory cost of a film in the same category in 1932–3 (£7,251). The average statutory cost was therefore above the threshold for double quota (£22,500). It should be noted that there were fewer films in the featurette class than in 1932–3: films under 5,000 feet accounted for only 9 per cent of the total compared to nearly 30 per cent earlier in the decade. As ever the average disguises a wide range of costs: the most expensive film in the ledger is Twentieth Century-Fox's *We're Going To Be Rich* with a statutory cost of £112,905 (the Bank of England estimated the total picture cost at £169,358), while the cheapest full feature is the Irish-made *Blarney* at a statutory cost of £4,836.[12] American renters now accounted for just under a third of all British quota films (55 of 172) compared to 53 per cent in 1932–3, but they were spending significantly more on their films: the average statutory cost of American-sponsored pictures was £39,917 compared to £16,503 for British-financed films. The average statutory cost of American renters' films was therefore above the level for treble quota: this suggests that the aim of encouraging them to spend more on their British quota films had been successful.

The Bank of England ledger indicates a wider range of costs than in the early 1930s, when the majority of quota films were in the middle- and lower-cost categories. Table 10.1 breaks down the films in each quota category by British and American renters. Treble quota pictures accounted for 12.2 per cent of the total and double quota pictures for 20.3 per cent; therefore, nearly a third of all films were either double or treble quota. This was probably more than even the most optimistic forecasts during the drafting of the 1938 Act. American renters were responsible for nearly three quarters of treble quota pictures, and over half the Americans' quota films were double or treble. It was British renters who now

Table 10.1 Cost range and quota status of British quota films registered between 1 April 1938 and 30 November 1939

COST RANGE	FILMS	BRITISH/US RENTERS
Treble quota (statutory cost over £42,500)	21	6 British; 15 American
Double quota (statutory cost over £22,500)	35	20 British; 15 American
Single quota (statutory cost over £7,500)	78	51 British; 27 American
Exhibitors' quota (statutory cost under £7,500)	38	38 British

Source: Bank of England Archive SMT 2/42: British Features from 01.04.1938 to 30.11.1939.

offered more films in the lower-cost categories: British renters were responsible for 65 per cent of the single quota pictures and all the films below the statutory £7,500 threshold for renters' quota. This is a complete reversal of the situation in the early 1930s when the large majority of American-sponsored films were towards the lower end of the cost range.

It might *prima facie* seem surprising that the American renters offered as many treble quota pictures as double quota. However, this can be explained in two ways. First, the Cinematograph Films Act allowed half of renters' total quota footage to be derived from treble quota films, with the remainder from any combination of single and double quota films: this made it more advantageous for renters to offer treble quota films. A second possible explanation for the relatively high proportion of treble quota pictures was a peculiar quirk of the film market. The Bank of England estimated that there were 'very broadly' three classes of British film: those with a total cost between £25,000 and £35,000 ('Apart from a few lucky hits, this has no hope of circulation outside this country, but it should earn a profit in the circulation here'), those costing between £70,000 and £80,000 ('This is rather a high cost to be covered by normal home circulation alone, and rather too low to be sure of appeal in the USA'), and those costing over £100,000 ('In competent hands this should be able to reach the USA market, and earn well there. But if the film does not get its market in the USA, there is a heavy loss.').[13] Hence the double quota range (a statutory cost between £22,500–£37,499, equating to a picture cost in the range £45,000–£75,000) was above the threshold at which a film would be deemed likely to recoup its cost from the British market but below the level where it would have a reasonable chance of success in the United States: on that basis a double quota picture might be less viable than a treble quota picture. It was treble quota films that were held more likely to appeal in the US market. United Artists, for example, estimated that *The Four Feathers* would earn distributors' receipts of £225,000 in Britain with another US$950,000 (£211,000) in North America.[14]

Otherwise, the Bank of England data highlights how the landscape of film finance had changed since the early 1930s. Of the top ten most expensive British features, nine were wholly or partially financed by American distributors: *We're Going To Be Rich* (£169,358), *A Yank at Oxford* (£167,870), *Over the Moon* (£160,488), *Goodbye, Mr Chips* (£152,239), *The Four Feathers* (£144,929), *Keep Smiling* (£142,220), *Shipyard Sally* (£137,853), *The Citadel* (£135,236) and *Sixty Glorious Years* (£124,512). Only one wholly British-financed film was in the top ten: *Jamaica Inn* (£128,331). The reason for the production of more high-cost films by American companies was undoubtedly the new Cinematograph Films Act: the Americans had suggested the treble quota and had evidently planned their British production strategies around it. Half of their quota could be derived from treble quota films and reciprocity credits (the clause that allowed a renter who bought the foreign distribution rights to a British quota film for a minimum of £20,000 to gain additional quota credit: for example, if they paid £20,000 for the foreign rights of a double quota film they could count it towards their quota twice).[15] In practice this meant that a distributor handling around forty to forty-five American features (the average annual output of each of the major Hollywood studios in the late 1930s) would need only four or five British films at double or treble quota.

MGM and Twentieth Century-Fox were the Hollywood studios that responded most proactively to the changing production and economic contexts. They both produced films in Britain on the same scale and at the same expense as their Hollywood productions. MGM had hitherto bought mostly low-cost films from British quota producers such as Julius Hagen and George King. However, early in 1937 the studio changed tack entirely, announcing that it was to set up its own British production unit at Denham Studios that would concentrate on high-end British product. This decision was made pre-emptively in anticipation of the new quota legislation.[16] *Variety* reported that MGM 'plans to export as many American names to stud the Anglo-American casts as local production commitments will permit. Idea is to lend marquee strength as one means to insure b.o. on both sides of the big pond.'[17] Michael Balcon, who relinquished his role as head of production for the Gaumont-British Picture Corporation at the end of 1936, was appointed as MGM's British production chief. Balcon's memoirs describe a contest for creative control between Denham and Culver City:

> The plan was that I should spend six months in Hollywood before we started our first British picture. This was to be *A Yank at Oxford* and the programme to follow that consisted of two best-selling novels, A. J. Cronin's *The Citadel* and James Hilton's *Goodbye Mr Chips* – all excellent material. A draft treatment of *A Yank at Oxford* was sent over from Hollywood. A number of studio writers had worked on it, including, incidentally, Hugh Walpole, but I did not like it. I took Sidney Gilliat from GB and he went to work on a new treatment. Mayer then sent over one of his writers – Leon Gordon – whom I did not need or want – to work with Sidney.[18]

The three British films produced by MGM's British unit – *A Yank at Oxford* (£167,870), *The Citadel* (£135,236) and *Goodbye, Mr Chips* (£152,239) – were all at the top end of the cost range for British films and were on a par with its features produced in California.[19]

The first of the MGM British films, *A Yank at Oxford* (1938), was also the first film to be registered for treble quota under the Cinematograph Films Act: it provides an exemplary case study of the political and cultural economies of quota production in the late 1930s. *A Yank at Oxford* gives every impression of having been budgeted to meet the statutory legal requirement for treble quota. An American star (Robert Taylor) and director (Jack Conway) were the two persons exempted from the labour costs which amounted to £104,500: this was well above the statutory labour requirement for treble quota of £37,500. The Board of Trade noted that 'the percentage of British labour, after excluding two aliens, is 92 per cent, which is a much higher figure than we were led to believe was possible in the course of our discussions with the American renters and is particularly noteworthy in view of the high quality of the film which has been produced'.[20] The high percentage for British labour was due in some measure to the high salary paid to Balcon as producer (£11,520) and to the fact that British cast members – including Griffith Jones (£3,100), Edmund Gwenn (£2,775), Maureen O'Sullivan (£2,750) and Vivien Leigh (£2,500) – were all paid more than their American co-star Lionel Barrymore (£1,969).[21] The highest salary for a non-excluded 'foreign' participant was for screenwriter Leon Gordon (£5,933), but the schedule of costs also included five British writers (Sidney Gilliat, Roland Pertwee, Angus MacPhail, Michael Hogan and Ben Travers) whose total remuneration amounted to £11,436.[22]

Balcon did not last long at MGM British: he felt undermined by the American end of the operation and left to become head of production at Ealing Studios in 1938. He was replaced by Victor Saville. *The Citadel* (1938) was very much Saville's project: he had optioned the rights to A. J. Cronin's novel (which he now sold to MGM) and produced it with an imported American director (King Vidor). Saville also had a tense relationship with the Americans: he wanted to direct *Goodbye, Mr Chips* (1939) but again had to accept a director approved by the studio (Sam Wood). He also chaffed at MGM's managerialism, though his memoirs also attest to the studio's investment in talent:

> However, much as MGM might fight to save a buck, they were profligate in the sums of money they paid authors and writers. Although permission had to be sought from an executive before retaking a close-up, that same executive thought little of assigning a writer at great cost to rewrite a screenplay that an author of equal talent had just completed, and if thought necessary, yet another author and another writer. I had never been used to such extravagance.[23]

It was nevertheless a successful formula: all three MGM British productions were successful at the box office. *Kine Weekly*'s chief reviewer R. H. 'Josh' Billings reported that *A Yank at Oxford* was one of two 'runners up' at the box office in 1938 (behind *Snow White and the Seven Dwarfs*) and *The Citadel* was second in 1939.[24]

However, MGM was not able to supply all its British quota from its own production unit. In the quota year 1938–9 its minimum quota requirement was 89,000 feet: its two treble quota pictures registered during the year – *A Yank at Oxford* and *The Citadel* – accounted for nearly two thirds of that total.[25] The studio therefore still needed other British films to make up its quota. In 1938 MGM entered into a co-production arrangement with Gainsborough Pictures, whereby it would contribute 20 per cent of the production costs in return for home and foreign distribution rights.[26] This arrangement produced three films: *The Lady Vanishes* (£59,238), *Climbing High* (£58,527) and *Ask a Policeman* (£35,030). The statutory costs of *The Lady Vanishes* (£39,492) and *Climbing High* (£39,018) were at the bottom end of the treble quota range, while *Ask a Policeman* (£23,353) was at the bottom end of double quota. MGM was able to meet its quota in the first year of the 1938 Act with just four films: *A Yank at Oxford, The Citadel, The Lady Vanishes* and *Climbing High*.[27]

Twentieth Century-Fox also invested heavily in British production in the late 1930s. Fox's British unit was based at Wembley Studios where initially it had turned out low-cost featurettes, but a new direction was signalled by *Wings of the Morning*

(1936) and *Dinner at the Ritz* (1937), both produced by Robert Kane under the banner of New World Productions. These films indicated that Fox had decided to move towards higher-cost films before the new Quota Act came into force. *Dinner at the Ritz* cost a total of £68,600 but nearly missed out on being eligible for quota as the British labour costs were calculated at a fraction under the statutory 75 per cent. New World claimed in mitigation that foreign labour costs were pushed up because co-stars Paul Lukas (Hungarian) and Romney Brent (Mexican) were contracted for longer than expected due to scheduling around the availability of star 'Miss Annabella' (the French actress who was one of the two excluded individuals alongside director Harold D. Schuster). However, the Board of Trade was not impressed by this argument:

> We have had trouble with the 75 per cent requirement in the case of practically every film which this Company have made. They ought by now to know our attitude and if we have to take the stand that the British labour costs are below 75 per cent of the whole cost I think we ought now to refuse to register as a British film, unless they can show substantial reasons why we should exercise our discretion under Section 27 (3) (iv).[28]

In the event, the Board of Trade agreed to make an exception for *Dinner at the Ritz* as the British labour costs were within less than 1 per cent of the minimum allowed.

Following the 1938 Act, Fox made a strategic decision to upgrade all its British production. In August 1938 head of production Darryl F. Zanuck announced that 'three British films planned this year will budget at two million five hundred thousand [dollars] for triple quota status'.[29] Its three highest-cost films – *We're Going To Be Rich* (£169,358), *Keep Smiling* (£142,220) and *Shipyard Sally* (£137,858) – were all vehicles for Gracie Fields, at the time Britain's most popular (and highly paid) film star.[30] The high costs of the films were due in large measure to the salaries paid to Fields (£50,000 per film) and director Monty Banks (£25,000): their combined remuneration accounted for 44.2 per cent of the cost of *We're Going to Be Rich*, 52.7 per cent for *Keep Smiling* and 54.4 per cent for *Shipyard Sally*. It is tempting to speculate that Fields' salary may have been inflated in order to ensure that the films met the statutory British labour costs: Banks (presumably the excluded technician) was an Italian national, so the American producers Robert Kane (*We're Going To Be Rich*) and Samuel G. Engel (*Keep Smiling*) would be included in the statutory costs. Quite why Fox executives believed that the earthy Lancashire music hall star would appeal to American audiences is a mystery that no film historian has ever been able to explain.[31]

Like MGM, Fox could not meet its quota solely from its own unit. At the end of 1938 Fox announced a deal with Gainsborough Pictures whereby its British subsidiary Twentieth Century Productions would produce at Islington Studios under the supervision of Maurice Ostrer and Edward Black. The films 'will be developed in a manner making them worthy of world release through Twentieth-Fox channels'.[32] Twentieth Century Productions completed five films before the outbreak of the Second World War – *So This is London* (£47,342), *Inspector Hornleigh* (£38,067), *A Girl Must Live* (£40,922), *Where's That Fire?* (£36,335) and *Inspector Hornleigh on Holiday* (£38,067) – all within the double quota range.

United Artists was in a different position to the other American distributors as it was reliant upon independent producers for all its product. UA's tie-up with Alexander Korda meant that it had access to a regular supply of high-end films for its British quota that it could also offer as first features in the American market. In April 1938 UA announced a change to the terms of its standard distribution contract whereby profits would be shared equally between producer and distributor.[33] In 1938–9 it released seven British films: six were London Films or Alexander Korda productions – *The Drum* (£110,348), *The Challenge* (£37,920), *Prison Without Bars* (£39,203), *The Four Feathers* (£144,929), *Over the Moon* (£160,488) and *The Lion Has Wings* (£22,311) – and one was from a newly formed producer Aldwych Films: *An Englishman's Home* (£41,759). *The Drum*, *The Four Feathers* and *Over the Moon* all comfortably exceeded the threshold for treble quota, while *The Challenge*, *Prison Without Bars* and *An Englishman's Home* were towards the lower end of the double quota range. *The Lion Has Wings* was an unusual case: a propaganda film about the Royal Air Force produced by Korda within six weeks of the outbreak of the Second World War. Its lower cost was due in part to its stars (Ralph Richardson, Merle Oberon) working for nominal fees and to the inclusion of documentary and newsreel footage.

Paramount and Columbia both adopted a policy of product diversification in the wake of the 1938 Act. In August 1938 Paramount announced 'an elaborate programme of British production' under the direction of David Rose.[34] It released six British films over the next year. These included two treble quota pictures from British producers – Paul Czinner's *Stolen Life* (£71,223) and Herbert Wilcox's *A Royal Divorce* (£56,259: the statutory cost of £37,506 was just over the minimum threshold) – and one double quota from a new independent unit Two Cities Films: *French Without Tears* (£44,117). The rest of Paramount's British films were single quota pictures – *This Man is News* (£11,807), *This Man in Paris* (£19,936) and *The Silent Battle* (£19,632) – produced by Pinebrook Films: Pinebrook was a co-operative venture specialising in low-cost films where technicians and artistes worked for lower salaries in return for a share of the producer's receipts.[35] The Association of Cine Technicians felt that the wages paid for *This Man is News* were unduly low: the statutory cost (£7,871) was close to the minimum threshold for renters' quota.[36] Columbia was a newcomer to the British production scene, having previously either released its films through an independent British distributor or picking up eligible Commonwealth films. Following the 1938 Act it changed its strategy, releasing five British quota films in 1938–9: these included Korda's *Twenty-One Days* (£65,211) and three produced at Denham Studios by Irving Asher: *Q-Planes* (£67,503), *The Spy in Black* (£46,882) and *Ten Days in Paris* (£36,447).[37]

The remaining American studios – RKO Radio Pictures and Warner Bros. – did not embrace the higher-cost strategy to the same extent, though nevertheless they did adjust their British production programmes in response to the new legislation. The ledger includes nine RKO films. Other than one 'super', Herbert Wilcox's *Sixty Glorious Years* (£124,512), for which Wilcox raised his finance against RKO's distribution guarantee, RKO's films were towards the lower end of the single quota range: *His Lordship Regrets* (£15,224), *His Lordship Goes to Paris* (£15,224), *Weddings Are Wonderful* (£15,166), *Flying Fifty-Five* (£16,254), *The Saint in London* (£29,864), *Meet Maxwell Archer* (£15,626), *Shadowed Eyes* (£17,058) and *Blind Polly* (£15,318). Most of RKO's British quota films were produced by George Smith at Walton or Isleworth: the exceptions were *The Saint in London* and *Meet Maxwell Archer*, both produced by William Sistrom at Rock Studios.[38]

Warner Bros. was the most prolific American producer in Britain in the 1930s. All its British quota films were produced by its unit at Teddington Studios: they were handled by two renters – Warner Bros. Film Distributors and First National Film Distributors – though to all intents and purposes the two organisations were one and the same. Teddington was closed temporarily following the death of head of production Ralph Ince in a car crash in 1937: it reopened under the management of Jerry Jackson following the passing of the 1938 Act.[39] Warner's strategy was to produce the required quota footage at minimum cost. Warner Bros. Film Distributors released eight British films in a cost range between £11,859 (*His Brother's Keeper*) and £31,059 (*Everything Happens to Me*), while First National released eleven in a range between £11,762 (*Confidential Lady*) and £39,524 (*The Good Old Days*). The latter was the only film to meet the threshold for double quota with a statutory cost of £26,349.

British distributors handled more British quota films overall but fewer at the top end of the range. British renters offered 115 long films: these included six treble quota and twenty double quota pictures. General Film Distributors was now the major British distributor and was responsible for most of the higher-end British films not backed by American companies. It released films by independent British producers for which it usually advanced 60–70 per cent of the budget and also handled the remaining Gainsborough films not released by MGM. The ledger includes eighteen features and two featurettes released by GFD at a total cost of a little over £820,000. These included three films – the Jack Buchanan vehicle *Break the News* (£104,540), Josef Somlo's *The Mikado* (£95,358) and Gabriel Pascal's *Pygmalion* (£57,537) – which met the criteria for treble quota. However, the average cost of GFD's treble quota films (£85,812) was significantly lower than the average of films in the same category from Fox (£149,812), MGM (£151,782) or United Artists (£138,588). GFD was unusual among the major renters for handling a preponderance of double quota pictures: Gainsborough's *Alf's Button Afloat* (£48,461), *Convict 99* (£34,944), *Crackerjack* (£42,080), *The Frozen Limits* (£42,111), *Hey! Hey! USA* (£43,055), *Old Bones of the River* (£40,094) and *Strange Boarders* (£45,767), J. G. and R. B. Wainwright's *Kate Plus Ten* (£40,236), G&S Films' *On the Night of the Fire* (£44,297) and Vogue Films' *Kicking the Moon Around* (£49,287) were all within the statutory criteria for double quota.

The Associated British Picture Corporation handled the largest quantity of British films with twenty-five features (and three featurettes). However, these included only three treble quota and one double quota feature. ABPC's high-cost films – *Jamaica Inn* (£128,331), *St Martin's Lane* (£107,271) and *Vessel of Wrath* (£69,640) – were produced by the Mayflower Pictures Corporation, set up in 1937 by actor Charles Laughton and German émigré producer Erich Pommer and which operated as an independent unit at Elstree with its films distributed in the United Kingdom by ABPC. Paramount acquired the films for world distribution and was able to claim them towards its quota under the reciprocity clause of the Cinematograph Films Act.[40] ABPC's one double quota picture was Jack Buchanan's *The Gang's All Here* (£56,828): Board of Trade records indicate that it started out as an independent production by Buchanan at Elstree who sold it as a package to ABPC when he ran into financial difficulties.[41] The average cost of ABPC's single quota pictures was £19,194 with a range between £13,320 (*Black Limelight*) and £25,606 (*Hold My Hand*): these are all within the range which the Bank of England saw as likely to recover their costs in the home market.[42]

ABPC also controlled the former British Instructional Films studio at Welwyn: this operated as a production facility for some of its parent company's lower-cost films and others from independent producers. Pathé Films acted as distributor for most of these. It has five feature films in the Bank of England ledger including four produced by Welwyn Films – *Night Alone* (£11,576), *Save a Little Sunshine* (£11,649), *Me and My Pal* (£12,080) and *Dead Men Are Dangerous* (£8,607) – and one by John Argyle: the horror picture *Dark Eyes of London* (£11,609). These films were all towards the bottom of the cost range for single quota. The case of *Dark Eyes of London* indicates how fine the margins could be for calculating quota eligibility: the Board of Trade undertook an audit and concluded that it was (just) eligible for renters' quota as the statutory cost exceeded the minimum threshold by £239.[43]

This left the group of smaller British producer-distributors, which the *Financial Times* suggested 'assume a national importance far beyond their size'. The three largest of these – Associated British Film Distributors, British Lion Film Distributors and Butcher's Film Service – collectively handled thirty-five British films. Associated British Film Distributors was the distribution arm of Associated Talking Pictures, owner of Ealing Studios. Basil Dean had been forced out of ATP early in 1938: he was replaced as director of production by Michael Balcon who had recently resigned as head of MGM's British unit. (Balcon's contract with MGM prevented him from accepting employment at another studio for two years: therefore his first films at Ealing were independent productions under the banner of COPAD – Co-operative Association of Producers and Distributors – which was a joint enterprise between ATP and Pinebrook Films.)[44] The Bank of England ledger includes eleven features produced by ATP or COPAD: *Penny Paradise* (£17,948), *It's in the Air* (£37,029), *The Gaunt Stranger* (£12,767), *The Ware Case* (£34,734), *Let's Be Famous* (£14,826), *Trouble Brewing* (£38,362), *The Four Just Men* (£34,659), *There Ain't No Justice* (£14,364), *Young Man's Fancy* (£34,217), *Cheer Boys Cheer* (£16,755) and *Come On George!* (£38,302). *Penny Paradise* and *It's in the Air* were the last two films produced by Basil Dean. The average cost of ATP's films (£26,724) was higher than ABPC, with six at double quota: *The Ware Case*, *The Four Just Men*, *Young Man's Fancy* and the three George Formby vehicles *It's in the Air*, *Trouble Brewing* and *Come On George!* ABFD also released a few Irish and Australian comedies below the threshold for renters' quota.[45]

The British Lion Film Corporation had increased its capital to £750,000 in 1935 and entered into a distribution agreement with the American corporation Republic Pictures.[46] Its distribution arm released eleven British quota films in 1938–9: these included four from its own production unit at Beaconsfield – *Around the Town* (£12,854), *I've Got a Horse* (£22,703), *Home from Home* (£19,661) and *All at Sea* (17,985) – at comparable costs to ABPC. These included three vehicles for Yorkshire comedian Sandy Powell and one for Vic Oliver (*Around the Town*), all produced at a cost that should have meant a profit from the home market. The rest of British Lion's roster were from other producers, including two double quota features: Tom Walls' *Old Iron* (£34,869) and William Rowland's *Mad About Money* (£34,869). The latter had been completed in 1937: it may be that it was held back in anticipation of the new Cinematograph Films Act in order to claim double quota. British Lion earned £108,116 from film distribution in 1939 and recorded a profit of £85,891.[47]

Anglo-American Film Distributors and Grand National Films were both new renters established following the Cinematograph Films Act. They dealt mostly in lower-cost films. Anglo-American Film Distributors, established in September 1938, offered seven films: these included two features produced by British National Films – *Old Mother Riley Joins Up* (£13,075) and *What Would You Do, Chum?* (£12,406) – and four featurettes under the threshold for renters' quota.[48] Grand National Films was an independent American renter that occasionally backed British films. It has five films in the ledger including four features: two Edgar Wallace adaptations by Jack Raymond Productions – *The Mind of Mr Reeder* (£15,650) and *The Missing People* (£12,506) – and two other crime subjects: *I Met a Murderer* (Gamma Films: £17,387) and *I Killed the Count* (Grafton Films: £15,650). Grand National's most important film is not included in the Bank of England ledger as it was not released until December 1939: *The Stars Look Down* – a northern social problem drama directed by Carol Reed and starring Michael Redgrave and Margaret Lockwood – was produced by Grafton Films at a cost reported in the press as £100,000.[49] However, the period following the Cinematograph Films Act was a difficult time for some independent renters. BIED (British Independent Exhibitors' Distributors) – a franchise of around 300 independent exhibitors set up in 1937 in an attempt to secure access to better-quality British films – was liquidated in October 1938.[50] It has three films in the ledger, but only one of them – *Stepping Toes* (£12,987) produced by John Baxter and John Barter – was eligible for renters' quota.

A particularly revealing feature of the Bank of England data is the persistence of low-cost British films under the threshold for renters' quota. The ledger includes thirty-eight long films (22 per cent of the total) below a statutory cost of £7,500. Butcher's Film Service was the main producer-distributor in this cost range: it produced ten features of which eight were under the quota threshold. The average statutory cost of Butcher's films was only £5,078. Anecdotal evidence that low-brow comedies with a regional flavour – the sort of films that passed unnoticed by West End critics – found favour with provincial audiences was offered by Alexander King, who owned the Caledonian cinema circuit in Scotland:

> I really was surprised to find that *Mountains of Mourne* and *Little Dolly Daydream* had not received Renter's quota. I can assure you some of these pictures are more valuable in Scottish working-class cinemas than some of the British supers. I had a picture last year which I understood the total cost was less than £15,000 and it took more money than most of the British pictures I showed and it also beat some of the American super cinemas.[51]

The genre of low-budget parochial comedy remains an unexplored area of British cinema: the fact that British renters were willing to offer such films despite their not counting towards quota would suggest there was a market for these films. For example, *Little Dolly Daydream* (1938) – a vehicle for child star Binkie Stuart, produced by John Argyle – was reported to be Butcher's most popular booking of the year.[52] Other films in this category included British National's *Lassie from Lancashire* (£13,070), the Mancunian Film Corporation's *Calling All Crooks* (£13,520) and John Argyle's *My Irish Molly* (£12,286).

It can therefore be seen that there were three main effects of the Cinematograph Films Act of 1938: an overall reduction in the number of films produced, an overall increase in production costs, and an increase in American investment in the British production sector. There had been a complete reversal of the situation that had pertained in the early 1930s insofar as the American renters were now responsible for most of the higher-cost films. The few 'quickies' that remained were now the preserve of smaller British distributors: the 1938 Act did not entirely remove the low-cost film, but the cheapest features were now eligible only for exhibitors' quota. At the end of the 1930s the British production sector was in a much healthier state than it had been only a year or two before: the quality of British films was deemed to have improved, and more films were registering at the box office. In turn, the greater stability of the industry persuaded investors that the conditions that had brought about the crisis of 1937 had been overcome. However, it was to be a short window of optimism. The gathering war clouds across Europe – presaged in films such as *The Lady Vanishes* and *Q-Planes* – were about to plunge British cinema into yet another existential crisis.

Notes

1. 'Finance and Faith', *The Era*, 30 March 1939, p. 1.
2. 'First Year of the Films Act', *The Economist*, 15 April 1939, p. 126.
3. 'Finance and Faith', p. 1.

4. *First Report of the Cinematograph Films Council relating to the year ending 31 March, 1939*, Cmd. 160 (18 July 1939), p. 18 (42).
5. 'Associated British Picture Corporation, Limited', *The Economist*, 12 August 1939, p. 334.
6. *First Report of the Cinematograph Films Council*, p. 16 (38).
7. 'British Films Under the 1938 Act: III', *The Financial Times*, 28 June 1939, p. 6.
8. Bank of England Archive (BEA) EC 4/248: Robert E. Dorton to H. A. Siepmann, 25 September 1939.
9. 'Film Chiefs are City's Outcasts', *Daily Mail*, 14 April 1939, p. 17.
10. 'Finance and Faith', p.1.
11. BEA SMT 2/42: 'British Features' Ledger 1 April 1938 to 30 November 1939. See Llewella Chapman, '"The highest salary ever paid to a human being": Creating a Database of Film Costs from the Bank of England Archive', *Journal of British Cinema and Television*, 19: 4 (2022), pp. 470–94.
12. A handwritten addendum to the main ledger includes estimated total costs for each film. The Bank of England estimated the total cost as 50 per cent more than the statutory cost. This very probably underestimates the total cost. The Board of Trade had worked on the assumption that the total cost was usually around twice the statutory cost in drafting the Cinematograph Films Bill. The total cost figures cited in this chapter are from the Bank of England ledger, but the actual costs were very likely higher.
13. BEA EC 4/248: 'Films: Note on Suggested Policy', 25 October 1939.
14. Ibid.: Dorton to G. F. Bolton, 4 October 1939.
15. Rachael Low, *The History of the British Film 1929–1939: Film Making in 1930s Britain* (London: George Allen & Unwin, 1985), p. 50.
16. Mark Glancy, 'Hollywood and Britain: MGM and the British "Quota" Legislation', in Jeffrey Richards (ed.), *The Unknown 1930s: An Alternative History of the British Cinema, 1929–1939* (London: I. B. Tauris, 1998), pp. 57–72.
17. 'Bob Rubin Stays On in London', *Variety*, 30 June 1937, p. 3.
18. Michael Balcon, *Michael Balcon Presents . . . A Lifetime of Films* (London: Hutchinson, 1969), p. 102.
19. The average cost of MGM's films in the late 1930s was US$777,000: this was around £172,600. See H. Mark Glancy, 'MGM Film Grosses, 1924–1948: The Eddie Mannix Ledger', *Historical Journal of Film, Radio and Television*, 12: 2 (1992), pp. 127–43.
20. The National Archives (TNA) BT 64/103: R. Fennelly to R. Somervell, 23 April 1938.
21. Maureen O'Sullivan was an MGM contract artiste – best known for her role as Jane in the Tarzan films opposite Johnny Weissmuller – whose film career had been entirely in Hollywood but who was able to be included as British on account of her Irish nationality.
22. Ibid.: MGM: *A Yank at Oxford*: Form C (Statement of British Labour Costs) Submitted to Board of Trade.
23. Roy Moseley (ed.), *Evergreen: Victor Saville in His Own Words* (Carbondale: Southern Illinois University Press, 2000), pp. 103–4.
24. 'Films Which Won the Box Office Stakes Last Year', *Kinematograph Weekly*, 12 January 1939, p. 61; 'Britain's Year of Triumph', *Kinematograph Weekly*, 11 January 1940, p. E1.
25. 'Films Act Has Failed', *The Daily Telegraph*, 2 January 1939, p. 6.
26. 'Anglo-American Film Agreement', *The Times*, 11 July 1938, p. 12.
27. Glancy, 'Hollywood and Britain', p. 66.

28. TNA BT 64/102: Minute by 'R. A.', 26 November 1937.
29. '20th-Fox British Plans', *Kinematograph Weekly*, 4 August 1939, p. 3.
30. Chapman, '"The highest salary ever paid to a human being"', p. 483.
31. Jeffrey Richards, *The Age of the Dream Palace: Cinema and Society in Britain, 1930–1939* (London: Routledge & Kegan Paul, 1984), p. 186.
32. 'Gainsborough Deal with 20th Century-Fox', *Kinematograph Weekly*, 22 December 1938, p. 17.
33. 'UA's New York Post for Silverstone', *Kinematograph Weekly*, 28 April 1938, p. 3.
34. 'David Rose Arrives to Supervise Para's British Production', *Kinematograph Weekly*, 23 June 1938, p. 27.
35. 'Pinewood Makes History', *Kinematograph Weekly*, 24 February 1938, p. 35.
36. British Film Producers' Association Executive Council Minute Books 1937–1940: Film Production Employers' Federation: Minutes of the Sixth Meeting, 9 June 1938 (in author's possession).
37. The costs for *Q-Planes* and *The Spy in Black* are not included in the Bank of England ledger but are documented in the Prudential Group Archive Box 2358: Harefield Productions Limited, 31 August 1940.
38. RKO had already produced two 'Saint' films in Hollywood and would produce another three there before returning to Britain for *The Saint's Vacation* (1941) and *The Saint Meets the Tiger* (1943).
39. Steve Chibnall, 'Hollywood on Thames: The British Productions of Warner Bros.–First National, 1931–1945', *Historical Journal of Film, Radio and Television*, 39: 4 (2019), p. 701.
40. 'Paramount World Release', *Kinematograph Weekly*, 9 March 1939, p. 3.
41. TNA BT 64/111: Robert Clark to Board of Trade, 12 May 1939.
42. The cost data for one ABPC film (*The Outsider*) is missing from the ledger: the average is calculated from the seventeen films for which costs are listed.
43. TNA BT 64/49: The 'Form C' for *Dark Eyes of London* revealed that salary payments (excluding Bela Lugosi) amounted to £7,739, of which £6,309 (81.5 per cent) was paid to British subjects.
44. 'Balcon to Make Twelve Subjects for A.D.F.D.', *Kinematograph Weekly*, 12 January 1939, p. 131.
45. These were *Blarney* (£9,672), an Irish film produced by Harry O'Donovan, and *The Rudd Family Goes to Town* (£11,356), one of a series of films starring comedian Bert Bailey produced in Australia by Cinesound Productions.
46. Low, *The History of the British Film 1929–1939*, p. 257.
47. 'British Lion Gross Profit £85,891', *Kinematograph Weekly*, 19 October 1939, p. 5.
48. The featurettes were *Consider Your Verdict* (£3.014) and *Trunk Crime* (£4,316) by Charter Film Productions (John and Roy Boulting) and *Two Days to Live* (£1,310) and *Trouble for Two* (£1,250) by Venture Films (Alfred Tennyson d'Eyncourt).
49. 'Grand National's British Production Programme', *Kinematograph Weekly*, 30 March 1939, p. 5.
50. 'Failure of £200,000 B.I.E.D. Company', *Kinematograph Weekly*, 27 October 1938, p. 3.
51. TNA BT 64/92: Alexander King to W. H. L. Patterson, 25 June 1938.
52. *Kinematograph Weekly*, 31 March 1938, p. 11.

CHAPTER 11

The Film Bank

The Second World War is now so widely regarded as a 'golden age' for British cinema that it is easy to overlook how precarious the future of the film industry seemed in late 1939.[1] The war had an immediate impact on the industry as one of the first acts of the government following the declaration of war on Germany on 3 September was to close all cinemas – and other places of public entertainment including theatres, music halls and sports venues – until further notice. This was a precautionary measure insofar as it had been widely expected that the outbreak of war would be marked by air raids against British cities in which densely packed public spaces would be potential death traps.[2] When the air raids did not immediately happen, however, discontent with the closure was quick to emerge within the cinema trade. Exhibitors were soon lobbying vociferously for the reopening of cinemas. The first wartime editorial of *Kine Weekly* advanced two arguments: that the closure was detrimental to public sobriety, as the only places left for people to congregate were public houses; and, somewhat more plausibly, that the cinema would be needed more than ever to provide entertainment and escapism. To this end it suggested that it was the trade's duty 'to present in pleasant, harmless form a relief from the very ugly world in which we are living to-day. Can one think of a safer anodyne to the disturbed public mind that the screen play?'[3]

In fact, the closure of cinemas was always intended as a temporary measure until the danger of air raids could be properly assessed: cinemas outside urban areas were allowed to reopen on 11 September, and from 15 September those in urban areas outside the West End of London could open until 10 p.m. From 4 October cinemas in the West End were allowed to stay open in the evenings, initially on a rota basis, and from 4 November all cinemas were able to stay open until 11 p.m.[4] They were to remain open throughout the war, even at the height of the Blitz. In one respect the Second World War certainly was a golden age: cinema attendances in Britain increased from 1,027 million in 1940 to 1,585 million in 1945.[5] The Wartime Social Survey of 1943 found that 70 per cent of adults attended the cinema on an occasional basis and that a third of the population were regular cinema-goers who attended at least once a week.[6] There were various reasons for the increased popularity of the cinema during the war: cinema-going was a cheap form of amusement and was particularly suited to the needs of a transient wartime population and mobile workforce. And cinema also benefited from the scarcity of consumer goods due to wartime austerity.

The most pressing concern for British producers at the outbreak of war was the continuation of the supply of production finance. As an editorial in *Kine Weekly* highlighted:

> Not since the 1924–26 studio slump has the British film been confronted with the disagreeable prospect of temporary extinction, and to prophesy the state of home production a year from now would be as hazardous as any other wartime prediction. Only the optimism of craziness foresees a revival in the worthwhile sense, and the task of keeping up a supply of product may necessitate a complete revolution in our methods of promotion and finance.[7]

The production sector was still recovering from the financial crisis of 1937 when the war broke out. It was feared that the extant problems of raising finance would be exacerbated by the uncertainty of war. For one thing the war would disrupt trade, and therefore the overseas markets on which the higher-cost British films were dependent to return a profit. And for another the threat of catastrophic risk – such as the abandonment of films due to damage to studios caused by enemy action – was significantly increased. The film industry was initially excluded from the schedule of businesses covered by War Indemnity Insurance – the government-backed scheme to provide cover against losses sustained as a consequence of war.[8] This was the context in which the idea of a state-backed film bank – first mooted during the crisis of 1937 but not progressed due to opposition from the Bank of England – gained traction early on in the war.

The producers most affected by the uncertainty over film finance early on in the war were the larger independent units operating outside the orbit of either the major combines or the American companies. The issue was highlighted shortly after the outbreak of war by Gabriel Pascal's *Major Barbara*. This film – Pascal's follow-up to his successful adaptation of George Bernard Shaw's *Pygmalion* – had been about to start shooting at Denham Studios in October 1939. General Film Distributors had agreed to advance £125,000 for the film, but following the outbreak of war they got cold feet and cancelled a contract 'verbally agreed but not actually signed'. United Artists – which had been increasing its presence in the British industry in the late 1930s – came forward with an offer to distribute *Major Barbara* 'on exceptionally favourable terms', offering the producer 70 per cent of receipts. Pascal therefore urgently needed a lender who would provide the cash finance for the film secured against the distributor's guarantee. Nicholas Davenport, a director of Pascal Film Productions, explained the problem to the Treasury:

> [It] is necessary to discount immediately the United Artists guarantee to pay $200,000 or the sterling equivalent on delivery of the negative in New York. There is unfortunately no financial organisation in existence to meet such discounting. At one time Lloyds [*sic* – Lloyd's] Underwriters used to guarantee the performance of the film contract, which enabled the Joint Stock Banks to advance money against an approved distributor's contract, but on account of losses incurred

through guaranteed performance of film contracts by unproved producers, Lloyds Underwriters no longer undertake this risk . . . With the protection of the Lloyds Producer's Indemnity Policy, distribution contracts have been discounted in private finance houses, but this channel has no doubt been closed by the outbreak of war. Unless, therefore, the Government assumes the war risk for film production, it is difficult to see how any financial facilities can be provided to British Producers.[9]

The Bank of England intervened to enable the National Provincial Bank to discount United Artists' guarantee: the Bank's approval was needed as the guarantee was made in dollars and the transaction was therefore subject to wartime currency controls.[10]

The case of *Major Barbara* threw into sharp relief the problem of interruption to the supply of production finance occasioned by the outbreak of war. It was following the 'rescue' of *Major Barbara*, which in the event had not involved any provision of public money, that the idea of a film bank was revived. In October 1939 a Treasury official wrote to the Bank of England: 'I shall be grateful for your reaction as regards setting up an organisation for financing British film production. In the long run, from the exchange point of view, it seems to me very desirable to do something to foster British film production in order that British films may replace American ones.' The Treasury's interest was to promote the production of more British films in order to reduce American imports and therefore dollar remittances: to this extent it argued that 'it would pay the Treasury better to lose money on financing British Films than to continue to spend dollars on renting American ones'.[11] The Board of Trade was also favourably disposed towards the idea in order to ensure stability in the provision of film finance. Rupert Somervell, the Permanent Under-Secretary of State with responsibility for film matters, explained that a particular concern was 'that a considerable proportion of the finance for existing film production is being provided by private individuals and may at any moment cease to be available through the death of the patron concerned or his unwillingness to continue his support'.[12] The individuals concerned were J. Arthur Rank, Lady Yule and Stephen Courtauld: the former was the major shareholder in the General Cinema Finance Corporation, the main provider of finance for independent producers, while the latter two bankrolled British National Films and Ealing Studios.

The main stumbling block to setting up an official film finance organisation remained the Bank of England. The Bank was no keener on the idea now than it had been three years earlier. As Deputy Governor Cameron Cobbold explained:

> The Governor is so alive to the increase through the war in the risk of this normally very speculative and little understood business that he does not see any present prospect of being able to raise finance in the City for a film bank, nor would he wish for his part to sponsor such an undertaking. Indeed he is unable to escape the conclusion that in these times no money can be found for British production in general without a guarantee or some form of subsidy – in addition to the quota – from HMG but, our contact with the industry having ceased upon conclusion of

the Enquiry to which I have made reference above, we no longer have that intimate knowledge which we should require for advising as to the best means by which financial assistance for the industry could be supplied.[13]

An internal Bank memorandum confirmed 'that what might be called the "catastrophic risk" – which could normally be insured against – had been so increased by the war that it was impossible to-day to organise centralised finance on a commercial basis with all that implied'.[14]

However, the issue would not go away. In November 1939 the Board of Trade asked the Cinematograph Films Council to 'examine the new measures necessary for placing British film production on an independent basis'. A sub-committee of the Council chaired by Sir Frederick Whyte, including representatives of the trade (Arthur Jarratt, Richard Norton) and unions (George Elvin) as well as economist Professor Arnold Plant (London School of Economics) and 'financial adviser' Albert Palache (Schroders merchant bank), conducted the review with considerable expediency. Initially the sub-committee seems to have envisaged a film bank subscribed by private capital. Norton, the managing director of D&P Studios, tried to argue that the film industry was a special case: 'It was necessary to convince the City that the ordinary rules for financing business projects did not apply in the case of film production. It was, for instance, impossible to provide any tangible security.'[15] However, Plant and Palache were sceptical that the City would want to be involved unless there was some form of official guarantee. At the end of January 1940 the sub-committee recommended 'that a Film Finance Corporation must be formed, and, from information at our disposal, it appears that this can only be undertaken by the Government, which will have to furnish the necessary permanent capital'.[16] The Council argued that stable finance was needed in order to produce enough British films to satisfy the quota:

> With the outbreak of war a prospective shortage of feature films at once made itself felt. It was due in part to doubts whether or not the Cinematograph Films Act of 1938 would be continued. Production plans were postponed and a subsequent announcement that the Act was to continue in force at least until 31 March 1940 has not entirely dissipated the doubts which retarded production. This growing feeling of uncertainty accentuated the already existing long-period problem created by the gradual drying up of finance for independent British production . . . These factors together have resulted in a definite, actual and prospective, shortage of British feature films.[17]

The Council suggested that 600 films of 'acceptable quality' a year 'should be considered a healthy supply of feature films' for exhibitors: a quarter of those films needed to be British in order to meet the quota. With American companies expected to produce thirty-five British features in 1940, this left around 115 films that would need to be financed with British capital.

The Films Council recommended setting up a Film Finance Corporation with a capital of £2.7 million of which two thirds would be subscribed by the Treasury and one third from commercial loans. Its role would be 'to provide finance on reasonable terms to the *British* Film Industry insofar as it cannot procure this itself on more favourable terms'. It was suggested that the corporation would lend up to 70 per cent of the production cost of films: it would aim to support sixty films in its first year, eighty films in its second and 100 films in its third. The Council recognised that past abuses in the industry needed to be stamped out: it accepted that 'due regard should be paid to the elimination of unnecessary intermediaries, extravagant internal charges, excessive distribution costs, and such other items which all together have inflated the true production cost of films made in this country'. The report nevertheless concluded that 'the national importance of upholding British production and creating a British Film Industry which will ultimately improve its credit so as to function independently offers ample justification for proceeding at once with this project'.[18]

The newly formed British Film Producers' Association expressed qualified support for the formation of the Film Finance Corporation. It cautioned 'that if such a Corporation is to be of the real benefit to British production that is obviously intended, its activities and scope should not be too closely restricted or confined by predetermined regulations' – an early indication that producers were concerned about the conditions that might be attached to the provision of finance – and recommended that as well as offering loans the Film Finance Corporation should provide 'substantial and adequate guarantees of completion': this was the facility for the provision of additional funds where films ran over budget during production. The BFPA also highlighted the different models of film finance for production units attached to a distributor and independent producers without such a link:

> Different producers will doubtless prefer different methods of financial assistance in accordance with the contemplated conditions of production and distribution, and it is obvious that a method which might be suitable and acceptable to a producer having definite channels of distribution and/or exploitation would be quite unsuitable in the case of an independent producer having no such established connections.[19]

The BFPA executive committee itself was split over this question (no doubt reflecting the presence of both types of producers in the Association): following lengthy discussion the memorandum included a suggestion 'that the Corporation should investigate the desirability of itself controlling the distribution of such pictures both at home and abroad'.

Following the Films Council's report, the Bank of England was asked once again '[to] examine the present state of the British Film Industry and to ascertain what steps and finance are required to put it onto a satisfactory basis and what support from HMG would be necessary to that end'.[20] The Bank could no longer evade the question: Montagu Norman agreed on the understanding that 'every precaution will be taken . . . to avoid this task becoming known to the Public and particularly to the Trade'.[21] A Bank of England representative was at pains to impress upon the Board of the Trade 'that the catastrophic risk was such that private finance could not undertake the business without a Government guarantee . . . Mr Skinner suggested that some guarantee might be evolved whereby films produced with the support of a new finance corporation should have some guaranteed market'.[22] The reference to a 'guaranteed market' was probably linked to an idea that had been mooted for a mandatory major circuit release for all British quota pictures. Somervell explained 'that if we want to see more and better British films made – and you may take it for granted that that is the Government's attitude – more finance is required since the existing sources are, we are told, strictly limited and are being fully used at the present time'.[23]

There followed several months of discussion between the Bank of England, the Treasury, the Board of Trade and the Cinematograph Films Council. There were various factors at play. The Bank of England was evidently still not keen on the scheme. At a meeting in April 1940 its representatives said that

> their examination of the problem had led them to the view that there was no lack of money for the production of films suitable as regards cost for this market alone and they asked whether the Government's main wish was to develop the industry in such a way as to produce films suitable for the American market and so put the film industry in a position to bargain for reciprocity with the Americans'.[24]

The Board of Trade suggested that the government might be able to match the Bank of England or private investors on a fifty-fifty basis in the provision of capital. However, the Bank was adamant that any capital issue should be underwritten by a Treasury guarantee. Montagu Norman's desire that the initiative should not become public knowledge was soon frustrated. *The Financial Times* reported that the trade was expecting the formation of a film credit bank based in the City with its capital raised under a Treasury guarantee. It extended a cautious welcome to the initiative: 'Such a plan, if sanctioned, would go a long way to eliminating the unsatisfactory methods adopted in financing film production in 1935 and 1936, and which led to the collapse of the boom in 1937.'[25] The source of the report is not clear: it may be speculated that it was leaked to the press in order to force the hand of the reluctant Governor to lend his support to the proposal.

In May 1940 Norman personally signed off on a plan for a Film Finance Corporation that was to be set up on a 'temporary and experimental' basis for five years. It was an ambitious plan that proposed to raise capital of £2,750,000 from a combination of loans raised in the City, share capital subscribed by the film industry, and a government guarantee. It proposed that £1 million would be raised from the City by offering five-year debenture stock at 4 per cent, £250,000 to be raised from the issue of ordinary shares, and £250,000 to be paid up from anticipated profits. The Treasury would provide £1 million as a guarantee against losses and an additional £250,000 as a reserve fund. The government's guarantee would allow the Film Finance Corporation to borrow at a low interest rate: its loans to producers would be repaid from box-office receipts. Any profits made by the corporation after payment of debenture interest would be divided between shareholders (25 per cent) and the reserve fund (75 per cent). Norman added that 'even I would accept a scheme on these lines if it could be put through to-day. I dare say the scheme will seem as satisfactory at a later date but the prospects of them putting it through are quite uncertain – due to war as *force majeure* or markets or politics or goodness knows what.'[26]

The urgency suggested in Norman's memorandum was due to the fact that the date (7 May 1940) coincided with the opening of the two-day 'Norway debate' in the House of Commons that would lead to the resignation of Prime Minister Neville Chamberlain and his replacement by Winston Churchill. The German invasion of France and the Low Countries on 10 May then pushed the film bank off the government's immediate priorities. Chancellor of the Exchequer Sir Kingsley Wood 'agreed that as soon as the crisis had passed – as to which Sir Andrew [Duncan] shall be the judge – to proceed on basis of a Statutory Film Corporation'.[27] (Sir Andrew Duncan was a director of Imperial Chemical Industries: he had been elected as a 'National' [non-party aligned] MP for the City of London in a by-election in January 1940 and had subsequently been appointed President of the Board of Trade.) A report in *The Financial Times* suggested another reason for the delay: 'The recent illness of a leading City personality has delayed the announcement of the Government's plan for the future of the film industry. Bound up with the proposals is a plan to set up a credit bank or corporation to finance British production, and it is this aspect of the scheme which requires consultation with City interests.'[28]

The film bank proposal was in abeyance for several months. Ironically it was *Major Barbara* which again brought the initiative back into play in August 1940. Pascal's film had exceeded its budget, and he was running out of money. He approached the Board of Trade to seek assistance in finding another £25,000 to complete it: otherwise, he said it would be necessary to 'ask United Artists . . . to take over the film and complete it in America'. The Treasury felt there was 'a prima facie case for thinking that the possibility of finding further money from non-Government sources to complete the film ought to be considered . . . Presumably the idea of starting a Film Finance Corporation has not advanced far enough to make it possible to arrange temporary financing on the basis that the liability will be taken over by the Film Finance Corporation when it is constituted.'[29] Sir Andrew Duncan was keen that the production should remain in Britain but at the same time he was determined not to be bounced into making a hasty policy decision in order to bail out one film: 'If this film is taken to America for completion, the consequences might be to bring about the formation of a Film Bank under political pressure. And this is not the way Sir Andrew wishes to work.'[30] In the event the National Provincial Bank came forward again to furnish the completion money. However, an internal Bank of England note suggests that they were still not keen on the idea of investing in the industry: 'NPD has agreed to £50,000 for completion "Major B." That answers ARD. But too much money is as bad almost as too little.'[31]

Duncan tasked the Cinematograph Films Council with bringing forward proposals for a Film Finance Corporation. The plan that emerged was based on the Bank of England's model from May: the main differences were that it was now to have a life of seven years rather than five and the debenture stock would be offered at 3.5 per cent rather than 4 per cent.[32] Duncan welcomed the plan but now suggested that the establishment of the corporation should be accompanied by the creation of a statutory regulatory body for the film industry. This was no doubt to appease the Bank of England, whose support for the film bank was conditional upon the imposition of safeguards to protect investors:

> I accept the necessity for an organisation that will provide, with proper safeguards, a stable basis for the finance of the industry but I do not think that the proposal goes far enough. The industry has a bad history, it lacks co-ordination, and there is little or no recognition by any of those engaged in it of the common interests either of the individual sections or of the industry as a whole . . . I believe, therefore, that it is vital to set up an independent Films Commission, somewhat on the lines recommended by the Moyne Committee. This recommendation was not accepted at the time by any section of the industry and it was consequently not included in the present Act, but times have changed and I am convinced that to-day it would be generally recognised as a wise and statesmanlike step.[33]

Duncan wanted to move ahead quickly with a White Paper: 'These consultations have taken a considerable time and there is a not unreasonable feeling of impatience on the part of the industry to know in broad outline the Government's intentions with regard to it.'

For Duncan the purpose of the Films Commission was 'to make the film industry a more cohesive and so a more economic and self-supporting whole. He hopes it may become – to its own and the national advantage – one industry instead of three.'[34] He envisaged a small group of between three and five permanent members appointed by the Board of Trade and independent of the industry but with an advisory group representing the different trade interests: it would be empowered to institute a register of 'approved' producers, collect statistics including details of film costs and revenues, and even to amend the quota including the introduction of a quality test if that were deemed desirable. In short, it was a plan to regulate the film industry without resorting to nationalisation. It is no surprise that the idea of a body with such far-reaching powers did not go down well with the trade. Arthur Jarratt told a meeting of the Cinematograph Films Council 'that he felt it was quite possible that if this Commission was the only means by which the industry could get money they might prefer to do without the money'.[35] Alexander King, chairman of Caledonian Associated Cinemas, the largest independent cinema circuit in Scotland, 'is definitely of the opinion that he is against handing over the control or regulation of our Industry to an independent Commission, in order to raise money for British production, although definitely he is most anxious that a Film Bank should be created'.[36] And D. E. Griffiths of the Kinematograph Renters' Society considered that the Films Commission was too much of an imposition: 'That financial aid is needed and desired by film producers is beyond question, but not at the cost of essential freedom of action. To proffer aid with such a condition attached falls little short of an affront to the industry.'[37]

It was now nearly a year since the Cinematograph Films Council had been asked to put forward recommendations for a Film Finance Corporation. The Council noted the reasons why the initiative had stalled but impressed that 'we feel bound to express our regret at the delay which has intervened since the presentation of our report. We have been told that nothing is as harmful to an industry as "threatened help"; and we feel that such a period of suspense cannot but be damaging to the welfare of the film industry as a whole.'[38] Sir Frederick Whyte recommended to Oliver Lyttelton, who replaced Sir Andrew Duncan as President of the Board of Trade when the latter became Minister of Supply in October 1940, that in view of the 'divergent views' within different sections of the trade, 'you should at once lay our proposals before the whole industry and seek their views on them'.[39] An accompanying paper summed up the problem as it stood:

> It was clear there was a considerable difference of opinion among the trade representatives about the desirability of a Films Commission of any kind. The producers' representatives were inclined to favour some kind of co-ordinating body. The representative of the British renters was non-committal; the American renters were frankly hostile; the exhibitors' representative seemed personally to be not unsympathetic but was doubtful about the reaction of his colleagues.[40]

Lyttelton agreed that the proposals should be discussed with the trade associations. Somervell explained: 'The object of the meeting will be to give the President a chance to explain what is in his mind to those sections of the industry who may be won over to the plan. The discussion would, of course, be conducted in the strictest confidence.'[41]

Even before Lyttelton was able to meet the trade, however, there is evidence that enthusiasm for the film bank was waning. By the winter of 1940–1 the industrial and economic contexts had changed significantly since the previous summer. For one thing it was increasingly apparent that the premise on which the film bank had been based – that secure finance was needed to support around 150 British features a year – was no longer realistic. The Cinematograph Films Council highlighted the changing conditions of production in the industry: 'The limited studio space and film production man-power which now remain available for producing British feature films are unlikely to suffice for an output of more than about 75 feature films a year . . . Indeed it is by no means certain that even this output can be obtained under existing conditions.'[42] The contraction of the production sector – brought about by the requisitoning of studios and the conscription of studio technicians into the services – meant that all the capital envisioned for the film bank might not be needed. In December 1940 Lyttelton told Montagu Norman that 'present circumstances make it difficult to expand film production and it might be thought that it was out of place to revive the idea at the present time'.[43] An earlier (unsent) draft of the letter had said:

> It looks as if the industry cannot in present circumstances hope for any expansion of their activities (which was, you will remember, the object of the additional

finance for which we were asking you) and must on the contrary expect a diminished output. In the circumstances we do not contemplate much, if any, call at present on finance made available through a Film Finance Corporation of the kind contemplated, but I should wish the legislation introduced to set up the Films Board or Commission, to provide for the Finance Corporation to be available, or brought into being as soon as it is needed.[44]

In the event, Lyttelton persisted with the film bank for the time being but downscaled its ambition: 'In view of the reduced opportunities for production at present I think that a fund of half a million pounds, subscribed mainly by the City but with some participation by the industry itself, is about the maximum at which we should aim for a start.'[5]

The Bank of England was evidently cooling on the idea. Montagu Norman, always a reluctant convert to the film bank, now took the opportunity to distance himself from it: 'So far as I am concerned, the taking of powers to set up a film credit organisation could not imply any promise that I should be able to organise capital or credit through the City for such an organisation at an unknown date and in unknown circumstances.'[46] Norman reiterated this position at a meeting with Rupert Somervell on 20 January 1941: 'The Governor said . . . he did not see how it would be possible for him to get people to commit themselves now to raising capital six months later in connection with a Bill that had not yet been drafted, much less passed by Parliament.'[47] A follow-up note by Somervell indicates that the Bank saw the establishment of the Films Commission as a necessary condition for the Film Finance Corporation: 'It is clear from the note of my interview at the Bank of England that we shall make no progress with the Films Bank unless we can produce the names of the Commissioners . . . Mr Skinner of the Bank of England thinks that none of the Commissioners ought to have had any connection with the trade.'[48]

For Oliver Lyttelton the issue now was whether he could sell the Films Commission to the trade. Lyttelton met representatives of producers, exhibitors and unions on 5 February 1941: the distributors were not invited. Sir Frederick Whyte, Simon Rowson and Winston Churchill's Principal Private Secretary Charles Peat MP were also present. Lyttelton explained that the film bank and the regulatory body were both part of the same package: 'The Films Board or Commission and the Films Bank hang together as part of the same plan, although independent in the sense that the Commission will not run the Bank. The Bank and Commission will, however, work in close contact and there may be some definite link, e.g. one Commissioner may be on the Board of the Bank.'[49] The official record stated that 'the producers welcomed the idea of the Commission as providing a central guiding and liaison body. The exhibitors reserved judgement: they welcomed any step which would enable more films to be produced, but doubted the efficiency of the Commission in this respect.'[50]

However, the reports of the meeting in the trade press told a different story. The Kinematograph Renters' Society (which had not been invited) declared that it was 'unreservedly opposed' to the Films Commission and passed a motion that it 'regrets the Board of Trade has departed from the usual practice of inviting suggestions from the trade when framing new legislation'.[51] An editorial in the *Daily Film Renter* suggested that 'Capt. Lyttelton would have done himself far more good if he had taken the industry into his confidence at an earlier stage, instead of more or less working out a plan and then casually putting it before only three sections of the trade almost as if he had expected them to approve it out of hand – and without even troubling to invite the distributors'.[52] *Kine Weekly* reported that the Cinematograph Exhibitors' Association also opposed the proposal.[53] Lyttelton, for his part, was furious that the content of the meeting had been reported in the trade press (he had asked the trade representatives to consult their associations but had not expected the discussions to be published) and regarded this as an attempt to force his hand: 'It is apparently quite impossible to have private consultations with this industry. There have been serious leakages in the Trade Press and it is desirable that I should make an announcement, giving an outline of the scheme and stating my intention to enter into immediate discussion with the different sections of the industry as to the various points of detail to be included in it.'[54]

However, the real damage from the leaks was that, contrary to the official record, the producers – those who stood to benefit from the film bank – were mostly opposed to the commission. Michael Balcon of Ealing Studios was the only one who seems to have been in favour: 'As a producer, knowing the wartime problems besetting British producers, I state most emphatically that unless a special Government department with strong powers is set up immediately to deal with these problems, British production is sunk.'[55] But, otherwise, Arthur Jarratt's prediction that the producers would prefer to go without the money if a condition of accepting it was further regulation, was proved correct. Maurice Ostrer of Gainsborough Pictures (who, like Balcon, had attended the meeting at the Board of Trade) and George Parish of British National were opposed to the scheme: 'We do not want a case of history repeating itself . . . The real solution is for producers to get out of their heads that they are a race apart. They must understand that like any other business men it is their responsibility to make their business pay and not go crying for help.'[56] Ostrer was even more outspoken in a comment quoted by the *Sunday Express*: 'Why should we go, cap in hand, for instructions on how to conduct the British film industry? No-one wants this commission and no-one wants the money.' The author of the article, film journalist Ernest Betts, highlighted the absurdity of the situation as it had developed: 'The astonishing situation of the Board of Trade offering £500,000 to the British film industry, and having the offer turned down flat, is the latest official muddle designed to advance the cause of British films.'[57]

The trade's near-unanimous opposition to the Films Commission had to all intents and purposes killed off the Film Finance Corporation. Lyttelton met representatives of the Bank of England and the City in May 1941 where 'the general conclusion was that there was neither need nor case at present in the film trade for the financial facilities that would be provided under the Film Bank proposal, in view of the limited capacity, manpower, etc, available now for the production of films'.[58] However, this was still not quite the end of the road for the Films Commission. Lyttelton appointed a small committee chaired by Sir Nigel Campbell of Schroders merchant bank 'to review the whole problem of film finance'.[59] Campbell's committee reported in September 1941 to Sir Andrew Duncan, who had returned to the Board of Trade, advising against proceeding with the film bank:

> We are strongly of opinion that in the present state of affairs – the standard of commercial morality prevalent throughout the industry, the absence of any corporative objective of cooperative spirit, the inability to produce a reasonably continuous supply of box-office worthy films – any attempt to put the industry on its feet by placing at its disposal increased financial facilities is doomed to failure ... We are therefore unable to recommend the setting up of a Film Bank, or any scheme for promoting the production of British films which would involve Government finance or guarantee.[60]

It was an excoriating verdict on the practices and professionalism of the film industry. It was therefore also no surprise that Campbell also recommended proceeding with the Films Commission, suggesting that it should comprise one commissioner and two assistant commissioners with far-ranging regulatory powers.

The Films Commission was kept alive for another year. In June 1942 a joint memorandum by Chancellor of the Exchequer Sir Kingsley Wood and another new President of the Board of Trade, Hugh Dalton, was put to the Lord President's committee of the War Cabinet recommending 'that a Films Commission should be established as soon as possible'.[61] The committee wanted more detail about its functions 'and as to the type of persons whom it was proposed should be appointed as members'.[62] However, by this time there is evidence that the Board of Trade was cooling on the idea. A draft constitution for the Films Commission suggested that 'the film industry (except on the production side) is among the most flourishing in the country (and incidentally among the least affected by the war): it can be assumed that, in these circumstances, to finance the Commission with public money would create an undesirable precedent for other industries which at some future date it may be thought desirable to regulate by similar methods'.[63] As late as October 1942 Rupert Somervell 'still believed this [the Films Commission] to be the right policy as a means of ensuring continuity of personal contact with the industry and of consideration of the policy required by them to carry the industry through the remainder of the war to ensure its successful recovery after the war'.[64] In February 1943, however, another joint memorandum from the Exchequer and Board of Trade stated that 'we have ... become increasingly doubtful as to the wisdom and necessity of our original proposal' and that 'the strongest arguments for setting up a Films Commission have lost much of their significance and urgency, while the difficulties in the way are greater than we at first supposed'. It amplified:

> [There] have been developments within the film industry which point to the emergence of strong groups under the control of business interests which seem likely

to operate according to the normal standards of commercial efficiency and honesty, which have not so far been conspicuous in the British film industry... The argument in favour of allowing the industry, if it can, to work out its own salvation without Governmental intervention is very strong when it comes to bargaining with the American film industry, since a Films Commission appointed by the British Government would find itself in a most difficult position in view of the talks on post-war commercial policy in which the two Governments will be engaged before long.[6]

It also mentioned 'the great difficulty of finding... as many as three first-class men who could be spared from more urgent war-time occupations' to act as commissioners.

The reference to 'strong groups under the control of business interests which seem likely to operate according to the normal standards of commercial efficiency and honesty' undoubtedly meant the J. Arthur Rank group, which by 1942 was responsible for around a quarter of all British commercial film production. Rank controlled over half the available studio space in Britain – including the largest studio that remained open to commercial producers (Denham) – and General Film Distributors, which was the major sponsor of British independent producers. It was estimated that since 1936 GFD 'have contributed to or provided the finance for British films costing in the aggregate more than £3,800,000'.[66] In effect Rank had become the banker of the British film industry: the Rank group supported through direct financing or distribution guarantees eight films in 1942 and twelve in 1943. The Bank of England felt that the General Cinema Finance Corporation – the parent company of General Film Distributors – 'is a good company and a good influence in the industry and merits support'.[67]

The contraction of the British production sector during the war had the effect of concentrating it in the hands of fewer production units. The four leading British producers by the middle of the war were the Rank group, Associated British Picture Corporation, Ealing Studios and British National Films. Collectively these four groups accounted for around half of all British feature films during the war with the remainder provided by American renters and smaller British producer-distributors who operated mostly in the lower-budget range. The Board of Trade records include a selective ledger of estimated costs for sixty-four British first features produced between 1941 and 1943: the average budget was £56,004. However, there were fewer exceptionally high-cost films than before the war. Only five films in the ledger were budgeted over £100,000: *The Demi-Paradise* (£185,176), *The Life and Death of Colonel Blimp* (£163,502), *The First of the Few* (£141,626), *The Flemish Farm* (£115,971) and *Flying Fortress* (£102,848). The first four of those films were all British-financed and were made by independent producers associated with the Rank group: British Aviation Pictures (*The First of the Few*), Two Cities Films (*The Demi-Paradise, The Flemish Farm*), and Michael Powell and Emeric Pressburger (*The Life and Death of Colonel Blimp*). *Flying Fortress* was produced by an American company (Warner Bros.).[68]

At the same time the combination of production economies and increasing cinema attendances during the war had created the conditions in which film production had become a more profitable undertaking than it had been during the 1930s. In 1944 Rank told the Board of Trade that 'it is possible at present for a British picture costing in the region of £100,000 to £150,000 to make a profit'.[69] The main British production groups budgeted their films at a level where they had a good chance of returning a profit. The Board of Trade ledger includes ten films by Gainsborough Pictures at an average cost of £68,194: *Dear Octopus* (£88,282), *The Man in Grey* (£84,675), *We Dive at Dawn* (£77,203), *Millions Like Us* (£70,927), *Uncensored* (£69,146), *Miss London Ltd* (£66,126), *King Arthur Was a Gentleman* (£63,198), *It's That Man Again* (£62,146), *Alibi* (£52,675) and *Back Room Boy* (£47,744). Ealing Studios produced eleven pictures at a lower average cost (£57,019) but mostly in a similar budget range: *Undercover* (£84,881), *The Bells Go Down* (£74,945), *The Foreman Went to France* (£69,604), *Ships With Wings* (£67,177), *Nine Men* (£60,486), *My Learned Friend* (£58,935), *The Black Sheep of Whitehall* (£48,446), *Turned Out Nice Again* (£50,941), *The Goose Steps Out* (£50,781), *The Ghost of St Michael's* (£43,518) and *The Big Blockade* (£17,496). British National Films was the most economical of the main British producers with ten films at an average cost of £25,460: *Let the People Sing* (£44,972), *This England* (£42,740), *The Common Touch* (£31,064), *Love on the Dole* (£28,825), *Penn of Pennsylvania* (£25,388), *Salute John Citizen* (£24,960), *Old Mother Riley's Circus* (£21,777), *Old Mother Riley Cleans Up* (£18,175), *Sabotage at Sea* (£9,950) and *Seventh Survivor* (£6,749). There are no films for the Associated British Picture Corporation in the ledger.

The initiative to set up an official film bank therefore came to nothing in the end: it was killed off by a combination of trade resistance to the terms on which finance would be offered and a changing industrial and economic context in which the need for a Film Finance Corporation was no longer as urgent as it had seemed a few years earlier. An improving outlook for British films by the middle of the war meant that at the end of 1942 the *Kine Year Book* could declare:

> No longer does the production chief concern himself on the subject of finance. For the first time in history, money is not one of his anxieties; there always seems to be enough available for any picture that has a practical basis. When it comes to studio space the supply is so much less than the demand that rents have soared beyond all reason; man-power is a painful problem; good stories want finding; but the lack of money, which has in the past ruined many promising ventures, is no longer a worry.[70]

NOTES

1. There is an extensive historical literature on British wartime cinema: key texts include Anthony Aldgate and Jeffrey Richards, *Britain Can Take It: The British Cinema in the Second World War* (Oxford: Basil Blackwell, 1986); Philip M. Taylor (ed.), *Britain and the Cinema in the Second World War* (London: Macmillan, 1987); and James Chapman, *The British at War: Cinema, State and Propaganda, 1939–1945* (London: I. B. Tauris, 1998).

2. Such an event had been imagined on film. Alexander Korda's *Things to Come* (1936) had predicted the outbreak of a European war in 1940. It features a harrowing sequence of an air raid against the city of 'Everytown' including a shot where a cinema receives a direct hit and explodes.
3. 'Reopen the Kinemas', *Kinematograph Weekly*, 7 September 1939, p. 2.
4. Mass-Observation Archive File Report 24: 'The Cinema in the First Three Months of the War', January 1940, pp. 11–12.
5. H. E. Browning and A. A. Sorrell, 'Cinema and Cinemagoing in Great Britain', *Journal of the Royal Statistical Society*, 117: 2 (1954), p. 134.
6. 'The Cinema Audience: An Inquiry made by the Wartime Social Survey for the Ministry of Information by Louis Moss and Kathleen Box' was published as an appendix in J. P. Mayer, *British Cinemas and their Audiences: Sociological Studies* (London: Dennis Dobson, 1948), pp. 251–75.
7. 'That Pecuniary Paralysis of British Films', *Kinematograph Weekly*, 21 December 1939, p. 18.
8. It was not until two years into the war that the Board of Trade agreed to a plan put forward by the Film Producers' Association whereby the amount spent on a film excluding the cost of developing story and script would be insured in fortnightly instalments until completion of the negative. 'Scheme for Insurance of British Production', *Kinematograph Weekly*, 4 September 1941, p. 3.
9. Bank of England Archive (BEA) EC 4/248: Nicholas Davenport to Secretary to the Treasury, 23 October 1939.
10. Ibid.: 'W. L.' to Deputy Governor (Cameron Cobbold), 1 November 1939.
11. BEA G14/233: T. K. Bewley to Cobbold, 24 October 1939.
12. The National Archives (TNA) BT 64/58: R. G. Somervell to E. H. D. Skinner, 1 March 1940.
13. BEA G14/233: Cobbold to Bewley, 5 December 1939.
14. Ibid.: Memorandum by E. H. D. Skinner, 27 December 1939.
15. TNA 64/4504: Cinematograph Films Council: Minutes of the Meeting of the Special Committee held at the Board of Trade on 5 December 1939.
16. Ibid.: Cinematograph Films Council: Report of the Sub-committee Appointed to Consider the Financing of British Film Production, 27 January 1940.
17. Ibid.
18. Ibid.
19. British Film Production Association Executive Council Minute Book 1938–40: Memorandum for Information of the Board of Trade and the Films Council, 15 February 1940.
20. BEA G14/233: 'British Films', 5 February 1940.
21. Ibid.: Montagu Norman to Sir William Brown, 19 February 1940.
22. TNA BT 64/58: Sir William Brown to R. G. Somervell, 9 February 1940.
23. Ibid.: Somervell to Skinner, 1 March 1940.
24. Ibid.: Note of Meeting between E. H. D. Skinner and Sir William Brown, 12 April 1940.
25. 'Financing of Films', *The Financial Times*, 23 April 1940, p. 3.
26. BEA G14/233: 'Film Finance Corporation', 7 May 1940, initialled 'M. N.'
27. Ibid.: 'Films', 27 May 1940.
28. 'Financing of Films: Credit Bank Delay', *The Financial Times*, 6 May 1940, p. 2.

29. BEA SMT 2/31: Wood (Treasury) to Cobbold, 13 August 1940.
30. Ibid.: E. H. D. Skinner to Cobbold, 21 August 1940.
31. Ibid.: Handwritten note by 'M St P', dated 26 August 1940.
32. BT 64/58: 'Film Finance Corporation' (no date).
33. Ibid.: 'Proposals for Legislation on Films' (no date).
34. Ibid.: Note dated 19 September 1940 (unsigned).
35. Ibid.: Report of a Meeting of the Finance Committee of the Cinematograph Films Council, 13 August 1940.
36. Ibid.: Note headed 'Dictated by Mr Alex King of Glasgow', 3 October 1940.
37. Ibid.: D. E. Griffiths to Sir Frederick Whyte, 1 October 1940.
38. Ibid.: Second Report of the Cinematograph Films Commission (unpublished draft).
39. TNA BT 64/58: Sir Frederick Whyte to Oliver Lyttelton, 26 October 1940.
40. Ibid.: 'Films Commission and Film Finance', October 1940.
41. TNA BT 64/61: Somervell to 'A. G.', 6 December 1940.
42. TNA BT 64/117: Cinematograph Films Council: Resources Now Available to United Kingdom Producers for Production of Long and Short Films.
43. TNA BT 64/61: Oliver Lyttelton to Montagu Norman, 11 December 1940.
44. Ibid.: Draft of Letter from Lyttelton to Norman (no date).
45. Ibid.: 'Proposals for the Film Industry' (no date).
46. Ibid.: Norman to Lyttelton, 18 December 1940.
47. Ibid.: Note of a Meeting between Montagu Norman, E. H. D. Skinner and Rupert Somervell, 20 January 1941.
48. Ibid.: Note by Rupert Somervell, 22 January 1941.
49. Ibid.: 'Present Position' (no date).
50. Ibid.: Minutes of a Meeting held at the Board of Trade, 5 February 1941.
51. 'General Council Rejects Films Commission Plans', *Daily Film Renter*, 13 February 1941, p. 1.
52. 'Wardour Street Gossip', *Daily Film Renter*, 13 February 1941, p. 2.
53. 'Secret CEA Discussion on Films Commission', *Kinematograph Weekly*, 20 February 1941, p. 9.
54. TNA BT 64/61: 'Proposals for the Film Industry', draft paper for the Home Policy Committee (no date).
55. 'Production is Sunk Without Commission', *Daily Film Renter*, 17 February 1941, p. 1.
56. 'Major Producers Turn Down Films Commission Flat', *Daily Film Renter*, 20 February 1941, p. 1.
57. 'Film Chiefs Say: We Can Find Our Own Money', *Sunday Express*, 23 February 1941, p. 4.
58. TNA BT 64/95: Nowell to Monier Williams, 23 May 1941.
59. Ibid.: Somervell to Monier Williams, 18 June 1941.
60. Ibid.: 'Report of Committee on Film Policy' (no date).
61. TNA CAB 71/9: War Cabinet: Lord President's Committee LP (42) 41, 'Proposals for the Film Industry', 24 June 1942.
62. TNA CAB 71/7: War Cabinet: Lord President's Committee: Minutes of the Meeting of 10 July 1942.
63. TNA BT 64/95: Draft Memorandum: Constitution and Function of Proposed Films Commission, 29 July 1942.
64. Ibid.: Minute by R. G. Somervell, 10 October 1942.

65. TNA CAB 71/12: War Cabinet: Lord President's Committee LP (43), 32, 'A Films Commission', 20 February 1943.
66. BEA SMT 2/31: Note – 'General Cinema Finance Corporation', 28 April 1941.
67. BEA EC 4/249: Skinner to Cobbold, 23 January 1941.
68. TNA BT 64/130: Estimated Costs of Production of British Feature Films, c. March 1943. Several films are listed under different titles from the film as released: *Undercover* is included under its working title *Chetnik* (this changed when the British government switched its support from the Chetniks to Tito's partisans); *Nine Men* is listed as *They Came in Khaki*; *Uncensored* is listed as *We Shall Rise Again*; and *The Life and Death of Colonel Blimp* is included under its original title *The Life and Death of Sugar Candy*.
69. TNA BT 64/95: J. Arthur Rank to Hugh Dalton, 'The Future of the British Film Production Industry', 1 July 1944.
70. S. G. Rayment, 'A Year of Struggle', *Kinematograph Year Book 1942* (London: Kinematograph Publications, 1942), p. 9.

CHAPTER 12

Remittances and Quotas

The Second World War saw a significant increase in cinema-going in Britain: annual cinema attendances increased from 1,027 million in 1940 to 1,585 million in 1945.[1] *Kine Weekly*'s annual surveys of the British box office suggested that American films by and large maintained their grip on the imagination of British cinema-goers: *Rebecca* was the 'biggest winner' in 1940 followed by *Mrs Miniver* in 1942, *Random Harvest* in 1943 and *For Whom the Bell Tolls* in 1944. *49th Parallel* was the only British film to top the annual box office, in 1941, although British films including *Pimpernel Smith*, *The First of the Few*, *One of Our Aircraft is Missing*, *In Which We Serve*, *The Life and Death of Colonel Blimp*, *The Man in Grey*, *This Happy Breed* and *Fanny by Gaslight* were placed among the 'runners up'.[2] The upturn in cinema admissions – and consequently in box-office receipts – meant that the exhibition sector enjoyed something of a boom period during the war. The Exchequer reaped the rewards: the amount raised by the cinema industry in Entertainment Duty – the level of which was raised three times during the war – increased from £5.6 million in 1940 to £41.4 million in 1945.[3]

Yet the income generated by the cinema industry also presented significant problems for the British government. For the Treasury the most pressing matter at the outbreak of the war was the balance of payments. The war would place severe pressure on Britain's foreign currency reserves: therefore, it was imperative to reduce the amount of foreign currency – most particularly US dollars – taken out of the country. This included the receipts earned from the distribution of American films – which accounted for a majority of box-office revenues in the United Kingdom. The Finance Regulations clauses of the Emergency Powers (Defence) Act of 1939 gave the Treasury authority to take any measures necessary to protect gold and foreign currency reserves: it delegated day-to-day administration to the Bank of England's Exchange Control Commission.[4] This affected the film industry in several ways. For example, the Bank's authority was now required to approve the repayment of production loans made by American banks to British producers from UK box-office receipts. The manager of the London branch of the Bank of America wrote to the Bank of England shortly after the outbreak of war:

> Films are an important item in the export trade of this country, and would be even more important but for the reluctance of the English banks to support the industry. Our loans in England follow the same general policy of our bank in California

in that we loan against the completed picture after it has been appraised and estimates received from the distributors of the world-wide receipts. All receipts of the picture are assigned to us and are paid directly to us by the distributor. In the case of all countries outside Great Britain, a foreign currency asset is created which is converted into sterling and remitted to this country . . . However, I am afraid our Finance Committee will not approve any further picture loans here if we must also assume a capital risk, as our only profit is derived from the interest we charge on the loans.[5]

The Bank of America – which was the primary lender for major British producers including Alexander Korda and Herbert Wilcox – was concerned that the introduction of a fixed exchange rate during the war would affect the repayment of loans made in dollars prior to the outbreak of war. This might help to explain why Korda and Wilcox both relocated their production activities to the United States in 1940.[6]

The most immediate concern for the Treasury in relation to the film industry was dollar remittances: the revenues earned by US distributors from their films in the United Kingdom. There was no reliable data regarding the value of US film earnings in Britain. In 1936 Korda put total distributors' receipts at £10 million, of which £8.5 million was remitted to the United States.[7] The Bank of England estimated that £9 million was remitted 'in a good year' from the British market and more from the rest of the Sterling Area.[8] American archives provide some evidence of the UK receipts of particular films. Mark Glancy's research into the exhibition of Hollywood films in wartime Britain includes UK rental receipts for three films produced by Walter Wanger: *Foreign Correspondent* (US$480,000), *Eagle Squadron* (US$585,828) and *Arabian Nights* (US$665,000).[9] *Kine Weekly* had *Foreign Correspondent* as one of the 'runners up' at the British box office in 1940. Glancy also provides the UK earnings for Twentieth Century-Fox during 1943–4: its most successful films in Britain were *Jane Eyre* (£300,000), *The Black Swan* (£275,000), *Coney Island* (£260,000), *Sweet Rosie O'Grady* (£250,000), *Hello, Frisco, Hello* (£240,000) and *Springtime in the Rockies* (£240,000).[10] *Kine* had Fox as the second most successful renter in 1943 with *The Black Swan* and *Hello, Frisco, Hello* among the 'runners up'; Fox also had the 'best output' in 1944 when *The Song of Bernadette*, *Jane Eyre* and *Sweet Rosie O'Grady* were all among the 'biggest winners'.[11] *Gone With the Wind* was by all accounts the most popular film shown in Britain during the war. It was released in London in April 1940 before going on general release in 1942: *Kine Weekly* created a one-off category for it in 1943 as 'Greatest Stayer of All Time'.[12] The Bank of England Archive records that *Gone With the Wind* 'earned £124,790 net during the year ended 29 July 1944'.[13] These figures suggest that the most successful films earned significant revenues – boosted by the wartime increase in cinema-going. Even films that were not ranked among the 'winners' and 'runners up' could earn over £100,000. The Bank of England Archive holds, somewhat arbitrarily, the UK distributors' receipts for six British quota films released by Columbia Pictures: *South American George* (£135,168), *Much Too Shy* (£140,919), *We'll Meet Again* (£89,519), *Get Cracking* (£139,043), *Rhythm Serenade* (£67,010) and *Bell-Bottom George* (£132,235).[14]

Various strategies were discussed as a means of reducing the 'dollar drain' to the United States. The idea of limiting American film imports was considered but dismissed: exhibitors needed a continuous supply of new films to meet demand. The figure of 600 new feature films a year came to be accepted as the minimum requirement for the exhibition sector: American films would likely comprise around three quarters of the total. In the event the policy adopted was to impose a limit on the amount of their film revenues that American distributors could withdraw from the United Kingdom. This would leave them holding 'blocked' or 'frozen' sterling balances that they would be allowed to spend in Britain. An early suggestion was that half the revenues of the American companies might be frozen: 'We might offer to guarantee during the whole period of the war to pay half in dollars providing the other half were expended in British film production. This would reduce our dollar purchases, and help us build up again our languishing film production industry – a most valuable propaganda agency.'[15]

The possibility that such a policy might prompt the American distributors to boycott Britain was considered but dismissed: '[The] probability was that even if a substantial portion of their takings were blocked in this country the American Companies would not in fact refuse, as a permanent policy, to send their films here. It costs them very little to send the films over and their takings are to a large extent pure gain.'[16] Britain was by some distance the biggest overseas market for the US film industry: most estimates suggested that Britain accounted for over 50 per cent of Hollywood's foreign revenues by the late 1930s.[17] A Bank of England memorandum suggested that 'there is a real possibility of achieving an arrangement, provided they [US companies] are also made to fear complete currency restriction. Without the British market, not an American film company could pay a dividend, even on its prior charges.'[18] For their part, the American companies were naturally concerned about proposals that would significantly reduce their earnings from the British market. The American ambassador Joseph Kennedy warned that 'any diminution in the revenue from the UK would constitute a crushing blow to the American industry and would have disastrous results not only upon the actual producing companies but upon real estate investment represented by cinemas throughout the US': he warned this would foster ill-feeling towards Great Britain in America.[19]

At the same time British producers were also concerned that the American companies would have so much blocked sterling that they would be able to squeeze out independent British producers by paying more for talent and driving up studio rental fees. *Kine*'s P. L. Mannock welcomed the presence of American-sponsored production units but cautioned that the best interests of the British industry would not be met if they concentrated solely on high-cost films: 'It is far more important to make ten films at £30,000 each than three at £100,000. Studio staffs can be kept going; more ideas find an outlet, and more talent of all kinds given scope, when a steady succession of subject is maintained.'[20] In contrast the Bank of England linked the production of higher-cost films by American producers in Britain to increasing the earnings of British films in the United States:

> The essence of the proposal would be that the Americans should not only provide more and better films in this country, but definitely produce them with an eye to the American market and have the full resources of the American film distributing system to give their British-made films the same market status as their corresponding American-made films. This proposal would be tied into the scheme by linking the amount for which we would provide $ with the $ earned by British-made films in the USA...
>
> One trade scheme proposes that in place of the 30 or so films costing about £25,000 each which American interests made here last year to comply with the Act (i.e. an expenditure of £750,000 in all), they should spend the same amount on 7 or 8 films costing about £100,000. The sponsor of this scheme thinks that these 7 or 8 films, properly designed and handled, could earn the equivalent of £3,000,000 in America.[21]

The identity of the trade 'sponsor' is undisclosed, but in any event the proposal did not take into account that (according to the Bank of England's own records) American companies had spent around £3 million on British production over the previous two years and that the average cost of American-sponsored films in 1938–9 was already around £80,000.

A temporary one-year agreement, known as the 'Embassy Agreement', was negotiated by Chancellor of the Exchequer John Simon and Joseph Kennedy and signed in November 1939: the American companies would be able to remit a maximum of US$17.5 million of their UK earnings (approximately £4.3 million). This was around half of their total UK earnings per year averaged over the last two years. The agreement applied to seven American companies: Universal (whose films were distributed in Britain by General Film Distributors) was not included. The blocked sterling balances of the American companies could be invested in film production, studios, acquisition of film rights or purchase of foreign distribution rights in British films.[22] The Embassy Agreement was followed by a revision of the quota requirement for American distributors, whereby they could opt either to continue with the footage quota (including double and treble quota credits) under the conditions of the Cinematograph Films Act of 1938 or to adopt a new monetary quota whereby they agreed to a minimum expenditure on British films regardless of their total footage. In August 1940 the Board of Trade estimated that the American companies (excluding Universal) would produce around twenty or twenty-one films under the new quota arrangements. It also suggested that wartime conditions would bring about a reduction in production expenditure: 'We also think that at the present time it would probably be difficult to spend more than £70,000 or £80,000 on a picture... I doubt if they will be able to spend as much as £1,000,000 on buying British films.'[23]

In the short term the American companies maintained their existing quota production strategies. MGM's *Busman's Honeymoon* (1940), for example, was reported to cost around £100,000, in line with its pre-war British films. *The Economist* observed: 'For their part, American producers still regard this country as their most valuable second market. It is now the only area in Europe where the films can obtain a showing, and hence, despite the temporary difficulties of payment, it seems a market of great value to American producers.'[24] However, the Bank of England came to regard the agreement as unsatisfactory:

> The old Film Agreement was itself a misrepresentation of the suggestions which we put forward last year. In effect we suggested that the American companies should be encouraged to increase the film industry of the UK and in particular to foster its exports. It was suggested that the additional proceeds coming from such new exports should be a vehicle for transmitting some of the blocked balances which would accrue to the companies. What the Film Agreement did was to eliminate virtually the whole of the dollar proceeds of the British film industry by giving the American distributors the right to pay in blocked sterling for all films acquired by them.[25]

The issue here was reciprocity (or rather the lack of it): the provision of the 1938 Act that American distributors could gain additional quota credit by purchasing the overseas rights of British quota films could now be met from their blocked sterling.

From the summer of 1940 negotiations were underway for a new agreement to replace the Embassy Agreement when it expired on 31 October. The British were adamant from the start that the amount of remittable revenue would need to be significantly reduced; they also expected (correctly) that the Americans would resist any reduction in their remittable revenue and would probably argue either for a higher threshold for remittances or a complete lifting of the restriction. A Miss Kilroy at the Board of Trade remarked that 'the American Ambassador is a hard bargainer and has indicated that he will oppose strongly any appreciable alteration in the present arrangements'.[26] The Treasury set out its position in August 1940:

> We must, I think, go for a drastic reduction in the amount of dollar remittances. We have every ground for doing so since the situation is entirely different from what it was last autumn. In the first place our dollar requirements have been magnified out of all recognition by the turn of the war. In the second place the Companies were warned, when the last agreement was negotiated, that they could not expect anything as good again; and that we only agreed to their being allowed to remit half their sterling earnings because of the initial difficulties and disturbances of their trade caused by the introduction of a scheme of control at short notice.[27]

The Treasury proposed to limit total remittances at no more than US$7 million as 'our final offer and we might, therefore, begin negotiations at $5 million'. Rupert Somervell, the civil servant at the Board of Trade in overall charge of film policy, replied: 'I have no doubt that the moment anything on these lines is shown to the

Americans we should have a loud outcry about the difficulties of making films in this country at the present time: indeed, [Fay] Allport has already started preparing the ground with me for this.'[28]

The British side felt that their position had been strengthened since the outbreak of war as the German occupation of most of continental Europe had closed off those markets: this further increased the importance of the British market. Another factor was that most of the American majors were orienting their production strategies towards fewer but bigger films that might expect to break even in the domestic North American market but would rely on overseas revenues for most of their profits. Miss Kilroy summed up the position:

> [It] seems clear that the proposal which I have recommended would be rejected out of hand by the Companies, and that they would have the active support of Mr Kennedy. The Americans have two weapons against us: (a) a natural reluctance on our part to disoblige or offend the Americans, or any important section of them at this time; (b) the fact that the British film producing industry cannot supply the needs of the home market . . . On the other side the very argument which the Americans will advance for keeping up the level of dollar remittances – viz that Hollywood is on the rocks because it has lost the rest of the European market – weakens the strength of their threat to cut down their exports to *this market*.[29]

Again, the possibility of the American trade interests retaliating with a full boycott of Britain was considered but dismissed. The view was that the Americans would not jeopardise their dominant market position for the sake of a temporary limitation on remittances.

In the event, the second Anglo-American Film Exchange Agreement covering the period from 1 November 1940 to 31 October 1941 was a compromise: the revised limit on remittances for the eight major renters (now including Universal) was set at US$12.9 million. This was more than the British had initially proposed but less than the Americans had wanted. The agreement allowed the Americans to withdraw up to three quarters of their remittable revenues in the first six months.[30] The Bank of England calculated that the total withdrawn by the major US companies in those six months was US$9,466,394 (73 per cent of the total allowed for the year).[31] On balance the new agreement was more favourable for the British as it meant a greater saving in dollars. However, it also meant that American companies had more blocked sterling that they would look to invest in British production. Among the American-backed British films during this period were *The Prime Minister* (Warner Bros., 1941), *Dangerous Moonlight* (RKO, 1941) and *Kipps* (Twentieth Century-Fox, 1941). This was a cause of concern for the Treasury, whose film policy representative E. A. Rowe-Dutton cautioned 'that I did not want to see American capital securing the equity of the post-war British film industry . . . This may not be our business, but I should feel that we had done the country but little service by creating another Hollywood in England and I believe we ought to make a great fight to secure the use of American money without allowing American control to come into it.'[32]

Another factor that influenced the Board of Trade in holding out for increasing the limit on remittances was that by 1940 it was apparent that the volume of British films would be significantly reduced: fewer British films meant that proportionately more of the total box-office revenues were earned by American films. From 108 British long quota films registered in the quota year 1939–40, the total fell to sixty-five in the quota year 1940–1 and the Cinematograph Films Council estimated that this would fall further to around fifty in 1941–2.[33] The reasons for the decline in production were the recruitment of industry technicians into the services and the requisitioning of studios. Film studios – especially the larger studios outside Greater London – were converted to wartime use: Sound City (Shepperton) was taken over by the Ministry of Aircraft Production, Elstree Studios was used as a storage depot by the War Office and Pinewood Studios became the temporary home of the Royal Mint (several stages were kept in use for making propaganda films by the Crown Film Unit).[34] The studios that remained in use – including Ealing, Highbury, Riverside, Shepherd's Bush and Teddington – tended to be smaller facilities with less capacity. Denham was the only large studio that remained open to commercial production. When the Ministry of Aircraft Production wanted to requisition Denham too, Richard Norton, the managing director of D&P Studios, wrote a pleading letter to Lord Beaverbrook explaining that 'there is now only one properly equipped studio left in England, and that is Denham, where good quality pictures have been shot and are continuing to be shot to provide some contribution towards our exports'.[35]

In the late 1930s the British film production sector had a surplus of studio capacity; by 1941 it was experiencing an acute shortage. This put great pressure on the available resources. The Board of Trade warned that the conscription of studio technicians meant that 'it may well become necessary to close one or more studios, and any such step would raise urgently the question of ensuring that studio space is used with the maximum of economy for the production of important films in some order of priority'.[36] A proposal was mooted to institute a form of centralised production control: that there would be a Controller General of Film Production who would be responsible for allotting films to studios and adjusting manpower between different productions as required, and a Controller of Feature Films who would prioritise films deemed to be of particular value to the war effort.[37] In the event, however, the proposal was not acted upon. For one thing, the most likely candidates for these posts were studio managers whom the existing production units could scarcely afford to lose. And for another, the Board of Trade had at the time instituted its own internal efficiency drive to cut down on activities 'not absolutely essential' to the war effort. As one official noted in April 1941: 'A drastic revision of our films policy should make a useful contribution to the cutting down of administrative work as well as releasing a certain amount of man (and woman) power. The film industry has so far done very well out of the war and made little sacrifice towards winning it.'[38] The Board of Trade accepted that British film production would be carried out at a lesser level for the foreseeable future. For Simon Rowson: 'It appears incontrovertibly clear to me that a nucleus industry must be maintained now at all hazards if we are to have a post-war industry of any importance. And such a nucleus industry would be sufficient if we could be assured a production at the rate of not less than 50 pictures – a large proportion being major pictures – a year.'[39]

The diminishing supply of British films inevitably brought the operation of the quota under scrutiny. The Board of Trade had initially resisted calls for a reduction of the quota or even the suspension of the Cinematograph Films Act: it maintained that 'the ideal method of meeting the exhibitors' difficulties would be not to reduce the quota but to improve the supply of British films'.[40] It also suggested that lifting restrictive trade practices including bars and fixed-term bookings would help exhibitors. However, the continuing decline in the number of British films obliged the Board of Trade to reconsider. In December 1941 it introduced a statutory instrument to amend the operation of the quota: renters' quota was reduced to 20 per cent for features and 15 per cent for shorts and exhibitors' quota was reduced to 15 per cent for features and 12.5 per cent for shorts, with effect from 1 April 1942 for a period of three years. It argued that the measure 'has become necessary because of war conditions. A good many studios have been taken over, a certain amount of labour has been drafted away, and, last but by no means least, the Government are making considerable demands on the cinema industry for the production of technical and instructional films which do not affect the quota at all.'[41] Following a low of forty-five long films in the quota year 1941–2, there was an upturn the following year when sixty-two films were registered.

The Board of Trade considered alternatives to the blocked sterling arrangement. One suggestion was to impose a limit on the import of American films. However, there were two arguments against this idea. One was that British producers were not in a position to increase their own output in order to make up the shortfall. The other was that reducing imports might disadvantage British films as it would mean the Americans would send only their best films:

> There is some danger however that such a policy might react very unfavourably against British pictures, which will now find themselves confronted with the competition of American pictures of higher average entertainment quality even more than before . . . It will take many years of successful pictures like *Pimpernel Smith*, *Night Train to Munich*, *Love on the Dole*, *Major Barbara* and *The Prime Minister*, and the George Formby and Gracie Fields series to offset the opinion that British pictures cannot expect to be as popular as American ones.[42]

Rowson suggested instead the introduction of single-feature programmes that would have the effect of rationing the supply of American films. However, this idea was also problematic as it would involve adjustment to the quota legislation. In particular, the independent exhibitors who had limited access to the best films (whether British or American) and depended upon double features would be disadvantaged by compulsory single-picture programmes.[43]

The Bank of England was responsible for monitoring the blocked sterling arrangement, but soon became highly jaundiced about its operation: 'We continue to have a lot of trouble about film sterling and the more the sterling balance increases the more trouble we shall have . . . [American companies] will always be devising ingenious ways of getting out which will eventually be impossible to resist.'[44] RKO Radio Pictures was one of the companies that tested the boundaries of the agreement. The production of *The Saint's Vacation* (1941) prompted the Board of Trade to caution 'that we must not allow these American Companies to inflate their labour costs by finding ingenious ways of including payments which ought really to be excluded': it suspected that RKO had inflated some salaries for double quota, although in the event the application was accepted.[45] The American companies, for their part, were keen to play up their investment in British production. Max Milder, the managing director of Warner Bros.' British studio, wrote to the Board of Trade:

> As part of our policy, we are spending large sums on making high class British films so that they can be distributed, not only in this country, but in America and throughout the World. Thus, *The Prime Minister*, made last year with John Gielgud and Diana Wynyard, cost over £64,000, and is guaranteed a wide distribution throughout the World. Our latest film, *Atlantic Ferry* – just completed – based on the history of the Cunard line – has cost over £95,000. Since the outbreak of War, and even before, it has been one of the primary objects of Warner Bros., both in England and America, to make films with a propaganda value. I believe no individual firm, and certainly no other Film Company, has done as much as Warner Bros., both in England and America, in support of the War effort of this country and in furtherance of Anglo-American friendship and co-operation.[46]

The context for this letter was Warner's bid to buy a 25 per cent stake in the Associated British Picture Corporation following the death of its founder John Maxwell.

The exchange agreement was renewed for 1941–2, when an improved dollar situation allowed the Treasury to set total remittances at a higher level of US$20 million. The operation of the agreement was also relaxed. In 1942 RKO was allowed, exceptionally, to remit more dollars than allowed for under the agreement due to its financial difficulties. Lord Halifax, the British ambassador to the United States, petitioned the Foreign Office 'that RKO were in [a] serious financial situation which might even lead to bankruptcy and had approached United States Treasury for their good offices with a view to obtaining release of their blocked sterling'.[47] The Bank of England warned 'that this may be followed by similar requests. I understand that there are at least three other producing groups in America in a rather difficult position and as soon as their banks know of the RKO decision they will probably press for similar treatment to be accorded to these companies.'[48] It came as no surprise that the RKO decision prompted similar petitions from other companies:

> We were prepared to help out the RKO Company, provided that this did not give rise to claims by the other Companies. We are now told that we are about to receive

a communication from the American Embassy applying for the transfer of the blocked sterling holdings of the Film Companies as a whole. We propose in the meantime to take no further action as regards the application of the RKO and to inform Sir F. Phillips accordingly.[49]

However, the Bank of England was sceptical of the claims of economic hardship made by the Americans: another memo suggested that 'the Film Companies' accounts . . . are quite easily cooked and an impending bankruptcy argument could, I believe, be produced by a number of companies.'[50]

The Bank had good reason for its scepticism as most US film companies were making substantial profits in the early 1940s. The combined profits of the 'big eight' Hollywood studios – MGM, Paramount, Twentieth Century-Fox, Warner Bros., RKO, Universal, Columbia and United Artists – increased from around US$20 million in 1940 to US$35 million in 1941 and nearly US$50 million in 1942.[51] Their profits were driven by an increase in cinema attendances in the United States. However, in the case of RKO there possibly was a case for exceptional treatment. RKO, the smallest of the vertically integrated corporations, had a history of fiscal instability, and had only emerged from receivership in 1940. In 1941 it recorded a modest net profit of US$588,692, increasing to US$736,240 in 1942: these profits came from exhibition, but it sustained a loss on production and was servicing a debt of US$1.6 million.[52] In 1940–1 RKO had remitted US$1,040,000 from the United Kingdom: this was nearly twice the company's total profit for 1941, indicating how important its British revenues were.[53] Rowson was more sympathetic to the American companies than the Bank of England:

> On the American side it is of the most urgent importance that the funds which are lying frozen to the credit of American film companies shall become quickly available to them again. These funds already amount to about £10 million . . . In effect these frozen credits are acting as reductions of the working capital upon which they rely for the making of further pictures now. The further accumulations in the near future must be a cause of genuine commercial anxiety to them. They should be, and must be, ready to welcome any solution which would relieve or remove those anxieties.[54]

Rowson estimated the cost of a normal 'first-class American feature' at around US$500,000: twenty films of the same grade in Britain would entail expenditure of £2.5 million.

The blocked sterling arrangement was always regarded as a stop-gap measure rather than as a long-term policy. According to Bank of England Governor Montagu Norman: 'We have always disliked blocked sterling in principle and only accepted the procedure because of our difficult exchange position at the time. In particular we have disliked blocking current earnings which only means deferring a liability.'[55] George Bolton, a member of the Bank's executive board, also sought to distance the Bank from the policy: 'Our policy has always been to persuade the Treasury that it was futile to try and force the American Companies to invest their sterling funds for the purpose of building up the British Film Industry . . . The improvement in our dollar position and Washington lobbying have caused this policy to be abandoned but I should tell you confidentially that the Treasury are looking into the possibilities of increasing taxation on film earnings.'[56]

The Anglo-American Film Exchange Agreement expired on 31 October 1942. The Treasury approved the transfer of the outstanding sterling balances of seven of the American companies amounting to £10,174,316. it did not approve the transfer for Columbia Pictures due to 'considerable doubt on the validity of the figure submitted by the Company'.[57] At the same time the Board of Trade proposed an amendment to renters' quota 'so as to relieve the major American film companies of quota obligations which under present circumstances they cannot fill'.[58] This allowed American renters who had adopted the monetary quota to fulfil their quota by producing or acquiring just one British long film a year provided that the rest of their quota liability was spent on the purchase of US distribution rights of British films. This further relaxation of the quota was occasioned by an investigation, which found that three of the six American companies that had adopted the monetary quota alternative (United Artists and Universal were the two that stuck with footage-based quota) were in default for the quota year 1942–3: MGM, Paramount and RKO had all defaulted. Warner Bros. and Columbia both spent marginally more than required, and Twentieth Century-Fox significantly more (£88,778): this was due to one high-cost British film, *The Young Mr Pitt* (1942), which was reported to have cost around £250,000.[59] A minute by Hugh Gaitskell, a senior civil servant at the Board of Trade, in April 1943 attests to the political contexts at play: '[Somervell] had taken the view that it was desirable, for psychological reasons, that the Americans should not be given complete freedom . . . I repeated to them Mr Somervell's argument that a cat and mouse policy made the Americans far better behaved.'[60]

The Treasury's aim with the blocked sterling agreement had been to save dollars: it was prepared to abandon the policy when changing economic and fiscal contexts mandated it. From the Treasury's perspective the policy had been a success:

> Blocked sterling balances have been of great value to the production side of the industry here and have been responsible for raising substantially the standard of the films now being produced compared with pre-war. This has been made possible by the fact that the Americans have an incentive to buy the American rights of British films and to give them proper showing in the USA.[61]

However, the Board of Trade's primary concern was to support the production of British films: in this respect blocked sterling had not brought about the increase in American investment in the British production sector that had initially been hoped. Simon Rowson had recognised in 1940 'that unless the American Companies are induced to spend much larger sums than the minimum they are compelled to spend under the Act or the alternative quota, there would remain a very large fund which they would want to remit . . . As at present advised, I can see no way of forcing an outlay by the American Companies of £3 to £4 million; and it might be much less.'[62] Rowson's estimate that the total would be 'much less' is borne out by the statistics released by the Board of Trade at the end of the war, which put American expenditure at only £900,000 in 1940–1, the first quota year following the introduction of the blocked sterling agreement, and at £1.2 million for each of the following three years, suggesting that in the end blocked sterling made little difference to overall levels of American investment in British production.[63]

Finally, by the later years of the war, there were encouraging signs that British films were starting to find a more secure foothold in the American market. The improvement in quality that contemporaries identified in British films saw the emergence of a greater awareness of British product in the United States, especially in cinephile cities such as New York and Chicago. While never consistently successful, in the way that American films were in Britain, some British films did exceptionally good business. Noël Coward's patriotic naval drama *In Which We Serve* (1942) was the first British 'blockbuster' in the United States, returning a distributor's gross of US$1.8 million.[64] The high point for British films in America came in 1946, when the US trade paper *Variety* estimated that twenty British films earned a total of US$8.5 million.[65] In September 1946, *Variety* reported:

> British pictures, after long years of minor financial takes, are now getting into the big American money class. Cash potentialities of the Anglo films aside from such exceptions as Coward's *In Which We Serve* and the Hitchcock sleeper *The Lady Vanishes*, were frittered away in the art houses and smaller circuits because of Yank exhibitor indifference. The films with improved production values and exploitation buildings are becoming a part of exhibitor booking plans.[66]

Among the British films returning North American rentals over US$1 million were *Henry V*, *The Seventh Veil* and *The Wicked Lady*, while *Caesar and Cleopatra* was expected to top US$2 million.[67] Sarah Street's research into the distribution of British films in the United States suggests that the figures quoted by *Variety* may have been exaggerated, but nevertheless finds that archival records indicate substantial rentals for *In Which We Serve* (US$1,516,069), *Henry V* (US$1,254,788) and *Caesar and Cleopatra* (US$1,363,371).[68] The success of these films went some way at least towards redressing the inequalities in film trade between Britain and America that had occasioned the imposition of dollar remittances in the first place. Most of the successful British films in the United States were prestige productions by the Rank Organisation: Rank's rise to power and the contexts of his challenge to Hollywood is considered in the last chapter.

Notes

1. H. E. Browning and A. A. Sorrell, 'Cinema and Cinemagoing in Great Britain', *Journal of the Royal Statistical Society*, 117: 2 (1954), p. 134.
2. James Chapman, '"The Billings verdict": *Kine Weekly* and the British Box Office, 1936–62', *Journal of British Cinema and Television*, 20: 2 (2023), pp. 200–38.

3. Political and Economic Planning, *The British Film Industry: A Report on its History and Present Organisation, with Special Reference to the Economic Problems of British Feature Film Production* (London: Political and Economic Planning, 1952), p. 125.
4. 'The UK Exchange Control: A Short History', *Bank of England Quarterly Review 1967*, 3 (1967), p. 2.
5. Bank of England Archive (BEA) EC 4/248: Robert E. Dorton to G. F. Bolton, 4 October 1939.
6. Korda finished *The Thief of Bagdad* (1940) in America and then produced *That Hamilton Woman* (1941) and *Jungle Book* (1942) in Hollywood, while Wilcox produced a trio of musicals in Hollywood: *Irene* (1940), *No, No, Nanette* (1940) and *Sonny* (1941).
7. BEA SMT 2/31: 'Memorandum on the Film Quota Act' by Alexander Korda, 18 February 1936.
8. BEA EC 4/248: 'Memorandum' (undated but c. October/November 1939).
9. H. Mark Glancy, *When Hollywood Loved Britain: The Hollywood 'British' Film, 1939–45* (Manchester: Manchester University Press, 1999), p. 32.
10. Ibid., p. 27.
11. Chapman, '"The Billings verdict"', p. 209.
12. 'The 1943 box office results', *Kinematograph Weekly*, 13 January 1944, p. 51.
13. BEA EC 4/252: 'Films' – Memorandum by C. R. P. Hamilton, 28 December 1944.
14. Ibid.
15. BEA EC 4/248: 'Films: Notes on Suggested Policy', 25 October 1939.
16. Ibid.: T. M. Smedley to C. F. Cobbold, 19 October 1939.
17. Glancy, *When Hollywood Loved Britain*, p. 26.
18. BEA EC 4/248: 'American Films' (undated but c. November 1939).
19. Quoted in Margaret Dickinson and Sarah Street, *Cinema and State: The Film Industry and the British Government 1927–84* (London: British Film Institute, 1985), pp. 121–2.
20. 'Strange Paradox of British Film Production', *Kinematograph Weekly*, 11 January 1940, p. 2.
21. BEA EC 4/248: 'Films: Note on Suggested Policy', by 'L. T. K', 25 November 1939.
22. BEA EC 4/249: 'Unremittable Sterling Funds of Film Companies'.
23. The National Archives (TNA) BT 64/61: R. G. Somervell to W. Rendell, 7 August 1940.
24. 'Movies for the Millions', *The Economist*, 27 July 1940, p. 115.
25. BEA EC 2/249: E. A. Skinner to Siepmann, 27 December 1940.
26. TNA BT 64/61: Minute by A. Kilroy, 25 September 1940.
27. Ibid.: Woods to Somervell, 13 August 1940.
28. Ibid.: Somervell to Woods, 21 August 1940.
29. Ibid.: Note by Miss Kilroy, 9 September 1940.
30. 'US Film Companies' UK Revenues', *The Financial Times*, 11 January 1941, p. 1.
31. BEA EC 4/250: Film Companies' Remittances to USA to 30 April 1941. The amounts remitted per company were: Columbia (US$716,450), MGM (US$2,211,094), Paramount (US$1,145,000), RKO (US$1,040,000), Twentieth Century-Fox (US$1,351,000 including US$25,000 for British Movietonews), United Artists (US$824,891), Universal (US$1,050,960) and Warner Bros. (US$1,127,000).
32. BEA EC 4/249: E. W. Rowe-Dutton to C. F. Cobbold, 9 January 1941.
33. TNA BT 64/117: Cinematograph Films Council: Resources Now Available to United Kingdom Producers for the Production of Long and Short Films (no date).

34. Sarah Street, 'Requisitioning Film Studios in Wartime Britain', *Historical Journal of Film, Radio and Television*, 43: 1 (2023), pp. 65–89.
35. TNA BT 64/61: Richard Norton to Lord Beaverbrook, 15 October 1940.
36. TNA BT 64/117: EAC to White, 31 July 1941.
37. Ibid.: Simon Rowson, 'Control of Studios for Film Production during the War', 28 July 1941.
38. TNA BT 64/61: Hughes to Monier Williams, 29 April 1941.
39. Ibid.: Simon Rowson to Monier Williams, 6 May 1941.
40. 'Board of Trade Refuses to Reduce Exhibitors' Quota', *Kinematograph Weekly*, 27 March 1941, p. 3.
41. *Parliamentary Debates: House of Commons*, vol. 376, 16 December 1941, col. 1909.
42. TNA BT 64/117: Simon Rowson, 'A Long Term Policy for Films: The Blocked Sterling Situation', 11 August 1941.
43. 'Double Features Waste of Film Product', *Kinematograph Weekly*, 3 April 1941, p. 11.
44. BEA EC 4/250: C. F. Cobbold to Montagu Norman, 21 May 1941.
45. TNA BT 64/118: Minute of 17 April 1941.
46. BEA SMT 2/44: Extract from letter from Max Milder to the President of the Board of Trade, 12 June 1941.
47. BEA EC 4/251: Lord Halifax to Foreign Office, 11 June 1942.
48. Ibid.: G. L. F. Bolton to Cobbold, 16 June 1942.
49. Ibid.: S. D. Waley to Sir D. Hopkins, 4 July 1942.
50. Ibid.: Bolton to Cobbold, 24 July 1942.
51. Thomas Schatz, *Boom and Bust: American Cinema in the 1940s* (Berkeley: University of California Press, 1997), p. 131.
52. 'RKO's 1942 Net profit Increased to $736,240', *Variety*, 19 May 1943, p. 24.
53. BEA EC 4/250: Film Companies' Remittances to USA to 30 April 1941.
54. TNA BT 64/117: Rowson, 'A Long Term Policy for Films', 11 August 1941.
55. BEA EC 4/251: Montagu Norman to Armitage (Commonwealth Bank of Australia), 12 November 1942.
56. Ibid.: G. L. F. Bolton to Rasminsky, 4 November 1942.
57. Ibid.: W. Rendell to F. W. Allport, 31 October 1942. The sterling balances for the other seven companies were: MGM (£2,799,295), Paramount (£1,443,844), RKO (£378,231), Twentieth Century-Fox (£2,080,855), United Artists (£871,819), Universal (£1,296,936) and Warner Bros. (£1,303,286).
58. TNA BT 64/95: S. Fieldhouse to G. F. Peake, 16 September 1942.
59. Ibid.: Statement showing particulars of the quota position attained during the year 1942–3 by the American renters who adopted the alternative condition in relation to long films.
60. Ibid.: Minute by Hugh Gaitskell, 10 April 1943.
61. BEA EC 4/251: Treasury to Phillips, 22 July 1942.
62. TNA BT 64/61: Simon Rowson, 'The Problem of Film Remittances (1940–1)', 7 August 1940.
63. *Parliamentary Debates: House of Commons*, 5th Series, 6 December 1945, col. 2707.
64. 'War Films Draw Top Money', *Variety*, 15 March 1943, p. 28.
65. '$8,500,000 British B.O. in U.S.', *Variety*, 20 November 1946, p. 3.
66. 'British Pix Finally Click in U.S.', *Variety*, 11 September 1946, p. 3.

67. '"Cleo" Figures $2,250,000 For U.S. Market; "Henry" Bigger on Profits', *Variety*, 26 February 1947, p. 20.
68. Sarah Street, *Transatlantic Crossings: British Feature Films in the United States* (London: Continuum, 2002), p. 94.

CHAPTER 13

The Rank Empire

The emergence of J. Arthur Rank as the dominant presence in the British cinema industry was the most important structural and financial development of the late 1930s and early 1940s.[1] Rank, who had inherited his father's highly successful flour business, had become interested in film through the Religious Film Society of which he was the treasurer (Rank was a devout Methodist). His first venture into film finance came in 1934 when he sponsored a film called *The Mastership of Christ*. In the same year he was one of the founding directors of British National Films with producer John Corfield and philanthropists Lady Yule and John Courtauld.[2] British National's first film was the low-key regional drama *Turn of the Tide* (1935). The lacklustre handling of the film by Gaumont-British Distributors prompted Rank to invest in General Film Distributors in 1935: this was a new independent distributor that became a major sponsor of British production.[3] In 1936 Rank was the principal investor in the General Cinema Finance Corporation which was set up for the purpose of buying 90 per cent of the share capital of General Film Distributors.[4] He was also one of the investors in a consortium to build Pinewood Studios: this was a modern new studio complex built at Iver Heath outside London.[5] In June 1936 *World Film News* observed 'that J. Arthur Rank, millionaire flour-maker, staunch Methodist, and owner of the *Methodist Times*, is extending his interest in the British film industry . . . [This] forty-year-old money baron is gradually becoming a major power behind the scenes in the British film industry.'[6]

Like the British colonial empire of the nineteenth century, there are conflicting views on whether the growth of Rank's film empire was a matter of accident or design. Rank's own assessment that 'I was being led by God' might be taken with a grain or two of salt: there is no doubting the strength of his religious conviction, but he was also a shrewd and hard-headed businessman whose interest in the film industry was not a philanthropic undertaking. 'As one of the myths of the film business', suggest Dickinson and Street, 'it has a prosaic, British quality: the Methodist flour miller who sets out to co-opt the big screen in the service of God and, finding his goal frustrated by a conspiracy of renters and cinema owners, resolves the difficulty by buying out half the conspiracy.'[7] Lady Yule, whose partnership with Rank ended amicably in 1937, later confided that his ambitions had been there from the start: 'He had, she said, far too ambitious schemes for her. She said that he was out to beat Hollywood and might easily burn his fingers.'[8] However, other accounts have tended to cast Rank as an accidental monopolist rather than an intentional empire-builder. For Rachael Low: 'Rank's progress in the industry in the thirties was not so much a deliberate attempt to take it by storm as a step by step response to changing events, drawing him further and further along the road to power.'[9] It is perhaps most accurate to see Rank's rise to prominence as part planned and part opportunistic. He held his nerve when other investors were deterred during the financing crisis of 1937 and took the opportunity to further expand his interests by acquiring Denham Studios from the debt-ridden Korda in 1938 and Amalgamated Studios at Borehamwood in 1939. It is widely speculated that his acquisition of Amalgamated Studios was in order to prevent it coming under the control of John Maxwell: Rank – who now owned three of the largest and newest studios in Britain – had an excess of production capacity. Amalgamated Studios was not used for film-making but was leased to the government for storage.[10]

Rank's position in the industry was consolidated between late 1940 and early 1942 when a sequence of largely unrelated events brought about changes in ownership and control of each of the three largest film concerns in Britain – Associated British Picture Corporation, Gaumont-British Picture Corporation and Odeon Theatres – that had fundamental and far-reaching consequences for the political economy of the British cinema industry. The first was the death of John Maxwell on 2 October 1940. Maxwell was the chairman, managing director and largest shareholder in ABPC. The obituary notices duly paid tribute to Maxwell as the 'financial genius' who built Associated British into a major production group and owner of the largest cinema cicuit in the country.[11] (The Bank of England's Ernest Skinner put it rather differently: 'The ABPC position was built up as a strong one under Maxwell, who was a disagreeable but competent old man who had enough sense, after burning his fingers, to get out of the production end of the business except in so far as necessary to satisfy his quota.'[12]) Maxwell's shares, worth £2 million, passed to his widow Catherine. Mrs Maxwell's solicitor Robert Clark approached the Bank of England to enquire whether the Film Finance Corporation (still under consideration at the time) would consider purchasing some or all of her shares. This was dressed up in the rhetoric of film patriotism ('Mrs Maxwell is anxious that her husband's shares should be used to further his vision of promoting a well-balanced and thriving British film industry'), but such a sale was outside the purpose of the proposed film bank. That left Rank or the American company Warner Bros. as possible buyers. In July 1941 it was reported that Warner Bros. had offered £900,000 for half of Mrs Maxwell's shares which would give it a 25 per cent stake in the company.[13] Mrs Maxwell 'regards the Warner participation as improving the Company's prospect and values'.[14] The Board of Trade approved the sale when Mrs Maxwell agreed to accept its nominee as chairman (Sir Ralph Wedgwood). Max Milder, managing director of Warner's British subsidiary, became joint managing director of Associated British with Eric Lightfoot, while E. G. Fletcher and Mrs Maxwell's son-in-law Philip Warter also joined the board.

Maxwell had been the driving force behind ABPC, but following his death there was a sense that the corporation lost direction. It continued to record profits, though these were largely on the back of its exhibition interests. In 1941, for example, it reported a trading profit of £1,427,257, but for the second year did not pay a dividend to ordinary shareholders.[15] However, ABPC's production activity was significantly curtailed during the war: it produced only five films in 1941, four in 1942 and three in 1943. This was due in large measure to the requisitioning of Elstree Studios, which left Associated British focusing its production activity at the smaller Welwyn Studios which were not equipped for larger-scale films. Indeed, the Board of Trade felt by the middle of the war that 'ABPC are at present producing little more than rubbish and cannot be regarded as a serious producing company'.[16] The corporation was also weakened by internal power struggles. In 1943 Simon Rowson reported that Mrs Maxwell was 'particularly incensed at the appointment of [Arthur] Jarratt, the displacement of [William] Moffat, and the pressure which Milder is constantly exerting for the booking of Warner pictures to the circuit at what Moffat considered onerous terms. She is also incensed with Mr Allen and Mr Warter, who are on the board as her nominees, not consulting her on major developments of this kind.'[17] A. G. Allen, for his part, felt that Mrs Maxwell was 'attempting to interfere in "certain essential matters of control". She and her family still tended to think of the concern as "Daddy's Company". The late John Maxwell had been a most dominating personality. All his assets were in ABPC and he had left considerable debts as well as having to meet heavy death duties.'[18]

The decline of Associated British coincided with the acquisition of its long-term rival the Gaumont-British Picture Corporation by the Rank group. By this time GBPC was an ailing giant: it had never really recovered from the failure of its attempt to get into the American market in the mid-1930s. Its production activity now focused on its Gainsborough Pictures subsidiary. By 1941 the Ostrers were ready to sell their interest. In October 1941 it was announced that General Film Distributors had acquired the Ostrers' shares in the holding company the Metropolis and Bradford Trust for a cash sum reported to be between £700,000 and £900,000.[19] The timing was propitious. Associated British had held an option on the Ostrers' shares since 1936 but this expired after five years. It might have been a different case had John Maxwell not passed away, but the post-Maxwell ABPC was in no position to make another bid for Gaumont-British. C. M. Woolf – whom *Kine Weekly* described as the 'prime mover' in the deal – became managing director of Gaumont-British and J. Arthur Rank its chairman.[20] The Ostrers resigned their directorships, although Maurice Ostrer stayed on as head of production of Gainsborough Pictures until 1945.

The Economist observed that Rank's acquisition of Gaumont-British

> definitely brings to a close a chapter in the financial evolution of the British film industry. On its completion, the two big vertical combines, which have come to own or control interests in film production, renting and exhibition (not to mention

restaurants, dance halls and real property), will have lost the Empire-builders who made them what they are – Associated British by the death of Mr John Maxwell and Gaumont-British by the 'abdication' of the brothers Ostrer.[21]

However, the acquisition represented more than just a changing of the guard. Rank already owned three of the largest studios in Britain as well as the major British distributor: the real benefit of the purchase for Rank was not the additional studio capacity (of which he already had more than he could use) but its chain of over 300 cinemas. There was some disquiet – not least among Gaumont-British shareholders – that Rank had acquired control of a corporation with an estimated value of £16 million for an investment of less than £1 million in a holding company. *Kine Weekly* reported that 'the shareholders who put up the bulk of the money . . . are entitled to know more than has been vouchsafed them'. It also speculated that the acquisition might be part of an empire-building strategy: 'There seems to be much more behind this development than appears on the surface . . . If Odeon is to come within the orbit of the Gaumont a big proportion of the British film Industry will be under one banner, and it is probable that the difficulties of the numerous smaller groups will be heightened.'[22]

The next (and final) stage in Rank's power grab did indeed involve Odeon Theatres. Odeon chairman Oscar Deutsch died on 5 December 1941: Rank – already a major shareholder and co-chairman of Odeon Theatres – was elected chairman in January 1942.[23] The Odeon chain numbered nearly 300 cinemas: most of these were new, large and well-appointed, and included key sites in the West End of London. If the acquisition of Gaumont-British had been opportunistic insofar as Rank moved in when ABPC's option expired and the Ostrers wanted to sell, the consolidation of his control of Odeon appears to have been a longer-term plan. Since first investing in Odeon Theatres in 1938, Rank had gradually increased his influence within the group. His place on the board was secured by the General Cinema Finance Corporation contributing to a capital restructuring of the Odeon group in 1939.[24] Rank then proceeded to consolidate his interest through three holding companies: Manorfield Investments (incorporated in August 1939 and controlled by Rank and his wife), Foy Investments (incorporated in April 1940 with Rank and Deutsch as the major shareholders) and Group Holdings (incorporated in December 1940: the original directors were Rank, Deutsch and two of Deutsch's business partners). Political and Economic Planning later averred that 'there seems to be no doubt that the reason for the various transactions among the holding companies at this period was basically a financial one. Mr Rank was called upon to increase his investment in the Odeon Group and in order to protect this investment some changes were made in the structure of control.'[25] For example, the Articles of Association were amended to allow the chairman of Group Holdings (Rank) a casting vote in the event of the directors being evenly split. Rank had therefore laid the groundwork for his takeover of Odeon Theatres before the death of Oscar Deutsch.

Rank's acquisition of Gaumont-British and Odeon had created the largest combined production-distribution-exhibition interest the British cinema industry had ever seen. The Rank group now owned or controlled five studios (Pinewood, Denham, Amalgamated, Shepherd's Bush and Islington), the biggest British distributor (General Film Distributors) and around 600 cinemas. Its subsidiaries included a newsreel (Gaumont-British News), a documentary production unit (GB Instructional) and cinema equipment manufacturer (British Optical and Precision Engineers). *The Economist* laid out the extent of Rank's influence not only across the whole industry but also within each sector:

> As a result of these transactions, Mr Rank gained control over the largest circuit of cinemas in the country – either by number, seating capacity or box office receipts – and over 60 per cent of the film industry's production capacity. He is the dominating personality in the industry both as a whole and in each of its sections separately. Though his financial control is not complete, he has established something which comes very close to an effective monopoly in the production capacity, and a powerful influence in the 'retail' end of an industry with a box office turnover of over £100,000,000, of which two-fifths are absorbed by the entertainments duty.[26]

Rupert Somervell of the Board of Trade felt that the consolidation of Rank's power was a mixed blessing: 'From this position Mr Rank is not only in a position largely to control film production in this country, but with his 600 theatres he has a potent argument to use in negotiation with the American companies. From this point of view the development is to be welcomed, but the danger of its becoming a monopoly must be kept in mind.'[27]

Some caveats need to be lodged about Rank's influence within the industry. One is that his expansion during the winter of 1941–2 had been so rapid that his empire was quite unwieldy in structure. The two cinema circuits operated more or less independently of each other: it was not until 1946 that booking policy for the Odeon and Gaumont cinemas was co-ordinated and not until the late 1950s that they were merged into one circuit. And there was no overall corporate management body until the formation of the J. Arthur Rank Organisation in 1946.[28] The main source of Rank's revenue was exhibition. Odeon Theatres recorded a pre-tax profit of £1.5 million in 1942: '[The] remarkable rise in profits was due solely to increased box office receipts – 55,000,000 more seats were sold than in 1940–41 – only partially offset by higher wages and prices for all commodities bought.'[29] Another issue was that Rank had been obliged to increase his borrowing quite significantly to complete his purchases. GCFC had raised a debenture loan from the National Provincial Bank for its purchase of the Metropolis and Bradford Trust shares. In October 1942 GCFC consolidated its control of Gaumont-British when it paid £450,000 for the 25 per cent of non-voting shares still held in the Metropolis and Bradford Trust by ABPC. Rank was stretched financially at this point: he might not have found it easy to undertake any further expansion.

The extent of Rank's influence over production is demonstrated by the fact that in 1942 the Rank group was responsible either directly or indirectly for around a third of the forty-five feature films produced in British studios in the course of the year. Gainsborough Pictures produced five features and GFD backed another ten, including major films by independent producers such as Paul Soskin (*The Day Will Dawn*), Marcel Hellman (*Secret Mission*) and Leslie Howard (*The First of the Few*).[30] Michael Powell and Emeric Pressburger, who had made two successful but modestly budgeted films for British National, joined Rank's Independent Producers group in 1942. Their first film for Rank (*The Life and Death of Colonel Blimp*) cost £208,909.[31] As Rank's biographer Alan Wood told it:

> Rank explained that he was resolved to keep British production going during the war, however much he had to pay for it. Powell and Pressburger explained that they were full of ideas for films, and that all they needed was someone to pay for them. Would Rank give them the money – not, as was usual, with strings attached and dictation from a distributor, but with full artistic freedom to make the kind of films they wanted? Rank said he would.[32]

The Board of Trade observed that General Film Distributors was 'the largest "wholesaler" of British films, distributing not only Mr Rank's own productions, but also those of other producers to whom he can offer preferential treatment by reason of his control of an extensive circuit of cinemas'.[33]

Rank also had a close relationship with Two Cities Films, an independent production unit set up by Italian émigré Filippo Del Giudice in 1937 which became a leading producer of high-end British films during the war. Following its success with the patriotic naval drama *In Which We Serve* (1942), which was released by British Lion when C. M. Woolf passed it up, Two Cities produced a sequence of films released by GFD including *The Gentle Sex* (1943), *The Demi-Paradise* (1943), *The Flemish Farm* (1943), *The Lamp Still Burns* (1943), *The Way Ahead* (1944) and *Henry V* (1944). Rank had no shareholding in Two Cities, which had a nominal capital of £27,000 held by Del Giudice, Sir John Keeling and Major Arthur Sassoon, but GFD had 'first choice' on Two Cities' films, which were shot at Denham. Del Giudice claimed that Two Cities 'have secured a contract . . . by which the cost of the film is guaranteed from the distribution of the film in the United Kingdom only, leaving them a free hand to negotiate the sale of their films for distribution in the USA, and all other parts of the world'.[34] However, the Bank of England noted that 'Rank seems to regard Two Cities as under his own wing. Newspaper chatter and gossip in film circles support this assumption . . . Guidice and Keeling contend, not without some foundation, that Two Cities are entirely independent of Rank and work with him only so far as suits their mutual interests.'[35]

There were mixed views about the growth of Rank's 'monopoly'. Some regarded him as a benevolent influence whose patronage was a force for good. In April 1941 the Bank of England expressed the view that 'GCFC were regarded as one of the surest and the best of the British concerns and I think it is safe to say that they are a good influence in the industry. Arthur Rank does really seem to have the interests of the industry at heart, otherwise he would not have risked so much money in it.'[36] A. W. Watkins, founder of the Association of Cine-Technicians, also thought Rank was a good influence:

> I have seen the arrival and departure in the film industry of all kinds of people, of all kinds of nationalities, whose contributions to the welfare of the business have been negligible, whereas, for perhaps the first time, we have at the head of affairs a person who is entirely English and intensely patriotic. I am convinced that Mr Rank's contribution is a perfectly unselfish one and that his one aim is to ensure that the films made in this country are given a square deal in all other countries throughout the world.[37]

And David Lean, another recruit to the Independent Producers group, wrote after the war: 'J. Arthur Rank is often spoken of as an all-embracing monopolist who must be watched lest he crush the creative talents of the British film industry. Let the facts speak for themselves, and I doubt if any group of film-makers in the world can claim as much freedom.'[38]

However, there was also significant opposition to Rank within the industry. This was an issue that united British and American interests. Sam Eckman Jr, the head of MGM's British distribution arm, wrote to the Board of Trade in June 1943 urging it to curb Rank's expansion: 'If the process continues unchecked a point will shortly be reached where, in my opinion, the entire British film industry will in effect be the long thick shadow of one man ... Such a development would be a misfortune at any time. At the present time, it would be a calamity.' Eckman argued that Rank's ownership of studios 'constitutes a virtual monopoly of production facilities – upon which all other sections of the industry must ultimately depend for their continued operation'.[39] It needs to be borne in mind that Eckman would no doubt have been concerned about the challenge that a powerful British combine would represent to Hollywood. However, Rank's most outspoken critic was Michael Balcon of Ealing Studios. Balcon used his seat on the Cinematograph Films Council to lobby the Board of Trade to launch an investigation into monopoly in the film industry. He wrote in his memoirs:

> [Reg] Baker and I were both pretty vocal on the tendencies towards monopoly, which became increasingly apparent. Although Associated British were also concerned, it must be admitted that our fire was mainly concentrated on Rank ... At the Films Council, aided and abetted by Miss Thelma Cazalet, MP (Mrs David Cazalet-Keir), and Sam Eckman, Jr, we conducted a campaign against Rank's activities which resulted in a committee being set up, presided over by Mr Albert Palache, a City financier, to report on 'tendencies to monopoly in the film industry'. Alan Wood, in his book *Mr Rank*, says: 'The resulting document was the most effective criticism of Rank's policies ever written.'[40]

The official records paint an even stronger picture of Balcon's antipathy towards Rank. Hugh Dalton, the President of the Board of Trade, met Baker and Ealing's principal shareholder Stephen Courtauld in May 1943 and recorded: 'They have an anti-Rank obsession. "The Octopus" they call him, and said his tentacles were rapidly spreading, especially in the last twelve months . . . They said that their Mr Balcon was very "hot up" about it and was regularly "bursting blood vessels."[41]

The concern over monopoly in the film industry reflected a wider debate around monopolies during the war. One of the consequences of the drive to eliminate inefficiency in wartime industry was the concentration of production. The film industry was one of those where the overall contraction of the production sector meant that existing powerful interests became even more dominant. *The Economist* summed up the pros and cons:

> Private monopolies are undesirable in principle; and in this particular industry they may be more harmful than in most . . . Not all the arguments are on one side. The curse of the cinema industry in this country has been its chaotic finance and it may be that to have a strong man, with large independent resources, in command is just what is needed to bring it to full health. It may be that Mr Rank's position is now so unassailable that he can protect the industry against the harmful effects of financial manoeuvring and concentrate on producing and showing the best available films. It may be that, having established a strong control at the top, he will encourage that decentralization of control, that originality, variety and experiment, which are essential in this industry. There is a sense in which it is only the monopolist who can afford to be an independent producer.[42]

The article suggested that, in preference to breaking up Rank's holdings, the best course would be to persuade Rank to 'consent to the appointment of a body of trustees for the public interest'. A Board of Trade memo records that Rank told Hugh Dalton 'that he now had two million pounds sunk in the film industry. It cost him a great deal of thought and trouble. He would be glad to get out at any time, if any English person can take over his interest. But he did not want to lose his money.'[43]

The Board of Trade devoted a good deal of attention to the question of monopoly in 1943. A review of the film industry was undertaken by Hugh Gaitskell, a former economics lecturer, now a temporary civil servant. In April 1943 Gaitskell wrote a memorandum that focused on the need for a competitive production sector and a sound financial base:

> We want three or four powerful concerns from production. These should not be ephemeral creations, but established companies who can conduct a long-term policy . . . There should also be room for independent producers who are temperamentally incapable of being tied with the larger companies. One method of providing for them would be the formation of a group of such producers, who would thus form a further production unit, and who might either, as a body, negotiate with distributors or form their own distribution organisation. It should not be impossible to devise some machinery by which these producers could obtain financial facilities. A small investment trust, for example, might be formed in the City for providing finance to the association, though, of course, each proposal would have to be carefully scrutinised and dealt with on its merits.[44]

Gaitskell suggested that three or four 'vertical combinations' should be sufficient to form the backbone of a healthy production sector. Rank and ABPC would be two of those: Gaitskell suggested that merging Ealing and British National would create 'a third strong producing company'. Alexander Korda – who had recently announced his intention to return to British production in association with MGM – might be the fourth.[45]

Gaitskell's memorandum was written as a starting point for analysing the problem rather than as a solution. Nevertheless, it seems to have influenced the subsequent policy direction in several key respects. Gaitskell was an economic liberal inclined to seek voluntary solutions and who saw state intervention as a last resort. To that end he suggested seeking assurances from Rank that he would not acquire further interests in the film industry without obtaining prior approval from the Board of Trade: 'We want him (a) not to go further along the monopoly road, (b) to get into his service people who know more about films. He has plenty of money, immense power, but now that C. M. Woolf is dead and Jarratt has left Gaumont-British there is a pretty serious shortage of showmen in his circle.'[46] Gaitskell's outlook was shared by Hugh Dalton: 'My aim has been to safeguard the public interest, in our customary British fashion, by sensible, voluntary arrangements between responsible people. If it should hereafter prove impossible to achieve this aim in this way, the Government would, no doubt, have to contemplate other procedures.'[47]

There followed a series of meetings between Dalton and the heads of the main production groups. The most important of these was Rank. Prior to the meeting there was some concern over the extent to which 'the President will find it possible to be frank and outspoken with Mr Rank' given that he had invested so much in the film industry.[48] At the time it was reported that Rank was looking to buy Sound City when the studio complex was returned to civilian use at the end of the war. Simon Rowson argued that if this purchase went ahead, 'the strangle hold of Mr Rank would become irresistible, and his domination would be impregnable'.[49] Sir Kingsley Wood, the Chancellor of the Exchequer, 'took the view that it would be impossible for the Government to allow Mr Rank a free run . . . He suggested that the best plan was for the President to see Mr Rank and ask him to give an undertaking not to extend his sphere of control any further without obtaining the consent of the Government.'[50] Dalton duly conveyed this message to Rank: 'I told him that we thought he was quite large enough. He said at once that that he saw no difficulty in giving such an undertaking.'[51] A formal confirmation followed from Rank 'that I have no desire to see anything in the nature of a monopoly in the film industry'.[52] He made a voluntary undertaking not to acquire more studios or cinemas without prior approval. Rank had been potentially the most difficult of the major interests: in the event he proved the most compliant.

The other meetings were less satisfactory. The suggestion of merging Ealing and British Lion did not progress very far. Following a meeting with Lady Yule and Charles Boot of British National, Dalton recorded that 'their scale of production is a limited one, and I am doubtful whether, with their present organisation, they could successfully compete with American entertainment films after the war'.[53] The Korda-MGM initiative seemed more promising: 'Metro-Goldwyn-Mayer were prepared to find all the capital from their sterling assets, but would welcome a British interest and, at my suggestion, Korda said they would act through a company with a majority British holding provided that such a holding would give financial control only and would not interfere with details of management.'[54] Not for the first time, however, Korda's ambition exceeded his ability to deliver. The tie-up with MGM resulted in just one film: *Perfect Strangers* (1945).

This left the Associated British Picture Corporation. ABPC was in a different position to Rank as it had a major presence in exhibition but had reduced its production output during the war. Dalton told Philip Warter 'that he saw no objection to ABPC expanding on the production side; indeed he would welcome it up to a certain point. But he could not view in quite the same way an increase in the number of cinemas they controlled, which was already very large.'[55] However, the main concern was that Mrs Maxwell might sell her shares either to Rank or to Warner Bros. Gaitskell was not keen on either party acquiring control of ABPC but concluded that Rank was the lesser of two evils. He was concerned that 'so long as there is any danger of Mrs Maxwell selling, it is always possible that, directly or indirectly, Mr Rank would somehow worm his way in'. 'On the other hand', he added, 'I should not be too pleased to see the hold of Warner Brothers increase. However well-intentioned Mr Milder himself may be, he is, in the last resort, under the orders of Mr [Jack] Warner, and it is by no means certain that Mr Warner's idea of good business would coincide with our ideas of what was good for the British film industry.'[56] In the event, a compromise was reached whereby Philip Warter gave an assurance on behalf of Mrs Maxwell and the trustees of her husband's will not to sell her interest without prior consultation with the Board of Trade.[57]

However, these voluntary agreements and undertakings were deemed unsatisfactory by the Cinematograph Films Council, whose report for 1943 suggested that 'a marked trend towards monopolistic control of the film industry became evident and it was clear that changes in the control of certain large companies would involve important issues of public policy'.[58] In late 1943 Dalton bowed to pressure and appointed a committee to investigate what were termed 'Tendencies to Monopoly in the Cinematograph Film Industry'.[59] The committee was chaired by Albert Palache of Schroder's merchant bank: its other members were Professor Arnold Plant (London School of Economics), Sir Walter Citrine (General Secretary of the Trades Union Congress) and historian Philip Guedalla. Palache and Plant had been members of the committee of the Cinematograph Films Council that recommended the establishment of a Film Finance Corporation in 1939. The committee took evidence from trade figures (including Rank and various producers) and delivered its report in July 1944. The report's preamble explained that it understood 'development of monopoly . . . to refer to tendencies which appear to threaten the future prospects of an independent and unfettered British film industry' and asserted that: 'The British public are vitally concerned that the British cinematograph industry should not be allowed to become either a mere reflection of a foreign atmosphere or a channel for disseminating the ideas and aspirations, no matter how worthy in themselves, of one or two dominating personalities in the industry.'[60]

The major recommendations of the Palache Report were that the Board of Trade's agreement should be required for any further cinema acquisitions by the vertically integrated combines, that the combines should consider independent trustees in order to block American control (*The Times* and *The Economist* had such arrangements), that the Board of Trade should have responsibility for allocating studio space, that independent exhibitors organised into collectives should receive equal treatment to the major circuits, that the Board of Trade should guarantee a proportion of screen time for independent productions, that blind booking should be banned, and that a British distribution organisation should be set up for the United States. The report also addressed the question of film finance ('The finance of feature film production should be placed on a healthier and more secure basis. The terms of distribution contracts should be adjusted to ensure that a reasonable share of the proceeds from exhibition find their way back to the producer') and proposed that a Film Finance Corporation should be established with authority to set up its own distribution organisation.[61]

Reactions to the Palache Report largely saw it as an attempt to impose a stricter degree of state control over the film industry. *Kine Weekly*, which usually set its face against regulation, felt that 'it foreshadows a control of the Industry more strict than hitherto when new film legislation becomes necessary, but that in many essential matters certain theories which have been expressed are not carried far enough to be a guide to practice'.[62] The *Daily Mirror* declared that the report 'is certainly a barrier in the way of millionaire film magnate J. Arthur Rank . . . The major effect of the report, if its recommendations were put into practice, would be to place the British film business firmly under Government control.'[63] However, *The Economist* thought that the report's recommendations were relatively modest:

> There is, of course, everything to be said for the elimination of undesirable monopolistic practices, if need be by legislation. Would-be producers must have access to studio space, to finance and to the screen. The ideal solution would be to restore effective competition at every stage from production to distribution – that is to prohibit horizontal combinations – as well as between the various stages, which would involve splitting up the two existing vertical combines. In practice, however, the restoration of perfect competition is hardly a practicable proposition. The Committee's own suggestions amount to a compromise. Horizontal combinations in restraint of trade are to be prohibited by legislation and the vertical combinations are to have their wings clipped.[64]

In the event very little of the report's recommendations made it into law. The Board of Trade showed no inclination to act on the report. Hugh Dalton invited responses from the trade associations and unions. In March 1945 he was still using this as a stalling tactic when asked about the matter in the House of Commons: 'So far, out of eight associations which, following the advice of the Films Council,

I have consulted, I have had replies from only three. It is not my intention to begin to form a view unless I have those communications.'[65] *The Economist* remarked that 'Mr Dalton's reply amounts to an invitation to those sections of the industry who might have an interest in the maintenance of the state of affairs disclosed in the Palache Report not to send in their replies or, at any rate, to postpone them indefinitely.'[66] The Board of Trade had no intention of getting involved in the allocation of studio space – this had been suggested in 1941 but had not progressed – and the Film Finance Corporation initiative had been abandoned several years earlier. The 'demobbing' of studios – it was planned that requisitioned studios would be returned to their civilian use as soon as the war was over – would free up space. (However, this process would take longer than expected: Pinewood did not reopen for commercial production until April 1946.) All of substance that was left from the report was to formalise the voluntary undertakings already entered into by Rank and ABPC not to expand their cinema holdings without prior agreement.

It also seems likely that the Board of Trade was reluctant to implement the full recommendations of the Palache Report because it had reasons for wanting to maintain the Rank Organisation at something like its present size. On the one hand Rank was a bullwark against further American encroachment into the British film industry. Hugh Gaitskell had observed in 1943 that 'only fairly large companies can produce big and important films and secure proper distribution arrangements for them, both at home and abroad. We cannot bargain with the American companies unless we have units to approach them in financial strength.'[67] And on the other hand Rank seemed to offer the best opportunity of securing a stronger foothold for British films in international markets – particularly in the United States – when the war was over. Towards the end of the war Rank was suggesting that the moment had come to step up British production to compete more effectively with the Americans:

> In the past, Hollywood has outdistanced this country in the quality, quantity and variety of films produced. British Producers have, however, made great advances in technique during the war and today make pictures equal to the best distributed elsewhere ... Once the studios have reverted to their pre-war facilities the disadvantage of having an insufficient number of films for export can, we believe, be overcome at an early date. No difficulties should be experienced in increasing production in order to ensure through some joint marketing arrangement a continuous flow of good films in sufficient volume to meet the needs of an adequate overseas distribution.[68]

Rank's international ambitions were not merely a form of film patriotism. He predicted (as it turned out correctly) that market conditions would change after the war: the wartime boom in cinema-going was unlikely to last and the home market alone would be insufficient to return a profit for anything but a modestly budgeted film. Rank was signalling his intent to step up production with a view to gaining a secure footing in the American market. He told the *Cine-Technician* in late 1943: 'It is all very well to talk of being able to make good pictures here without bothering about American or world markets, but in all honesty the continued existence of British film production depends on overseas trade. And to get that trade you must have power – the whole future of British films is bound up in the question of overseas trade.'[9]

Lady Yule's assessment that Rank 'was out to beat Hollywood' was lent credence by his production and distribution strategy in the mid-1940s. Early in 1944 he set up Eagle-Lion Film Distributors specifically for the purpose of releasing his films in the United States.[70] And he backed high-cost films, mostly by independent producers, that in production values and 'prestige' matched the best of Hollywood. Laurence Olivier's production of *Henry V* (1944) was a Technicolor epic that earned distrbutor's receipts of US$1,254,788 in North America and won a special Academy Award for its director-star.[71] The cost of *Henry V* was surpassed by Gabriel Pascal's *Caesar and Cleopatra* (1945) and the musical *London Town* (1946). These films became bywords for the sort of extravagance that had been absent from British cinema during the war years. *Caesar and Cleopatra* was budgeted at £550,000 and cost over twice that amount: the final cost is recorded as a staggering £1,371,494, making it by some distance the most expensive British film made to that time. The film overran its schedule (already a generous twenty-five weeks) by ten weeks and there were large overcosts on cast (£166,703), sets (£86,654), studio rent (£72,120), props (£25,180) and wardrobe (£26,115).[72] *Kine Weekly*'s studio correspondent P. L. Mannock averred that '*Caesar and Cleopatra*'s 80 shooting weeks [*sic*], attended by farcical extravagance, is something that never should have been allowed to go on for so long, and an example never, I hope, to be repeated.'[73] *Caesar and Cleopatra* is often written off as a box-office flop: in fact it earned distributor's receipts of US$1,363,371 in North America, but less than half of that was returned to Rank due to United Artists' share of the receipts and high promotional costs.[74] *London Town*, a vehicle for music hall comedian Sid Field, produced and directed by the American Wesley Ruggles, was budgeted at £432,887 and cost £821,973.[75]

Most of Rank's prestige pictures were produced by the Independent Producers group – Michael Powell and Emeric Pressburger (The Archers), David Lean, Anthony Havelock-Allan and Ronald Neame (Cineguild), and Frank Launder and Sidney Gilliat (Individual Pictures) – which enjoyed particularly privileged conditions. According to David Lean:

> We of Independent Producers can make any subject we wish, with as much money as we think that subject should have spent on it. We can cast whichever actors we choose, and we have no interference with the way the film is made. No one sees the films until they are finished, and no cuts are made without the consent of the director or producer, and what's more, not one of us is bound by any form of contract. We are there because we want to be there.[76]

The degree of fiscal and creative autonomy extended to Independent Producers in the mid-1940s was quite extraordinary. It seems likely that Rank (who never professed to having any understanding of film art) was inclined to be indulgent as a response to the concerns raised by the Palache Report that independent producers were compromised by their reliance upon him for financing and distribution. Evidence of the somewhat *laissez-faire* approach to budgeting can be found in a letter from Independent Producers' managing director George Archibald to production manager Tom White in respect of the production of *The Red Shoes* (1948):

> I imagine when you say that you will probably solve the "RED SHOES" casting problem, you also mean solving its costing problem . . . We have in some cases in the past been able to drift into making a highly expensive picture without there being any agreement with Arthur or with GFD as to its cost and have, to some extent, been justified in this because the expenditure was incurred before a production memorandum was submitted.[77]

For example Lean's *Great Expectations* (1946) and *Oliver Twist* (1948) and Powell and Pressburger's *A Matter of Life and Death* (1946), *Black Narcissus* (1947) and *The Red Shoes* (1948) were all estimated to cost around £275,000 with a maximum budget of £300,000: they all exceeded the maximum by over 20 per cent.[78] These films – and others including Laurence Olivier's *Hamlet* (1948) at a final cost of £572,500 – all cost significantly in exess of the level where they could expect to break even in the home market. As Powell observed in his memoirs: 'Emeric and I had made twelve films together, nearly all from original stories, and each one a little more ambitious than the last. Costs had mounted proportionately . . . Obviously, if we couldn't get the world market, then we were heading for disaster.'[79]

The disaster duly came. It took several years for Rank's ambitions to unravel, but the consequences became very apparent in 1949 when the Rank Organisation announced losses of £3,350,000 on film production and distribution.[80] However, it is unfair to blame Rank's problems entirely on his failure to break into the American market. Political and Economic Planning offered a more nuanced assessment of the 'prestige film experiment' in its report *The British Film Industry* published in 1952:

> To all appearances the 'prestige experiment' was a costly failure . . . They were certainly costly, but to say that the films 'flopped' is to over-simplify the issue. There is no doubt that they failed to achieve the main objective of capturing the mass American market, which was the only apparent one, but in creating a new market in the 'art theatres' and in attracting a new audience, the 'prestige' films did succeed to some measure in attaining the underlying object of the Rank production policy. It is important to distinguish between the short-term failure which was the occasion for much recrimination, and the ultimate benefit in the shape of a specific though limited American market which seems to have resulted from that failure.[81]

In fact some of Rank's most expensive films did exceptional business: the overseas receipts of *The Red Shoes* (£1,111,400) and *Hamlet* (£1,164,400) – most of which were earned in the United States – ensured that those films made a healthy profit.[82]

The problem for Rank was not the success or failure of single films but rather that his production programme as a whole was losing money. A schedule of production costs and distributors' receipts for thirty films produced by Rank between

1946 and 1949 reveals that only eight returned a profit when home and overseas receipts were combined: these were *Great Expectations* (+£21,200), *The Upturned Glass* (+£45,000), *Holiday Camp* (+£16,000), *Easy Money* (+£2,200), *Miranda* (+£5,600), *Oliver Twist* (+£8,900), *Portrait from Life* (+£4,100) and *The Blue Lagoon* (+£40,00). However, the profits per film were often very modest, and were wiped out by big losses on others including *The Hungry Hill* (-£201,200), *Blanche Fury* (-£135,000), *London Belongs To Me* (-£168,200), *The Passionate Friends* (-£127,400) and *Esther Waters* (-£305,706). A particular problem was that the middling-cost films that were still the bread and butter of Rank's output had become too expensive to return a profit at home but did not have the special exploitation value of high-end pictures such as *The Red Shoes* and the Shakespearean adaptations for the US market. Most of the films that Rank produced in the cost range between £125,000 and £250,000 were loss-makers: these included *Green for Danger* (-£26,200), *Take My Life* (-£84,900), *The Brothers* (-£55,200), *The End of the River* (-£78,000), *The Mark of Cain* (-£77,800), *Broken Journey* (-£63,900), *One Night With You* (-£173,000), *The Bad Lord Byron* (-£179,200), *The Weaker Sex* (-£69,400) and *The History of Mr Polly* (-£172,100).[83] The case of *Green for Danger* (1946) – a murder mystery produced by Frank Launder and Sidney Gilliat – exemplifies the problem. This film had been budgeted at £150,905 – the upper end of the range at which Rank estimated a film could recoup its cost from the home market – but ended up costing £202,400. It secured an above-average 2,820 cinema bookings in the United Kingdom, but its UK net distributor's receipts (£140,053) still left a deficit that was not compensated by overseas earnings.[84]

Rank would weather the crisis of the late 1940s by scaling back his production output and instituting economies. The Rank Organisation remained a major presence in the industry for the next two decades, but it never quite regained the pre-eminence it had experienced in the 1940s. In the event Rank's wings had been clipped, not by state intervention to dismantle his 'monopoly' but by his own over-expenditure on film production. Yet, as Geoffrey Macnab argues, Rank's tilt at the world market, while ultimately unsuccessful, was strategically well-conceived insofar as 'his attempt to carve British film a sizeable niche of the US market was more thorough, was better financed, and came closer to success than any attempts made on America by his predecessors or, indeed, successors'.[85]

Notes

1. The best history of the Rank Organisation is Geoffrey Macnab, *J. Arthur Rank and the British Film Industry* (London: Routledge, 1993). For a more contemporary, if somewhat hagiographical account, see Alan Wood, *Mr Rank: A Study of J. Arthur Rank and British Films* (London: Hodder & Stoughton, 1952).
2. British National Films was registered on 30 July 1934: its directors were Philip Ashworth, John Corfield, J. S. Courtauld , J. Arthur Rank and Lady Yule. Ashworth and Courtauld resigned after a few months. In 1935 British National increased its capital from £6,000 to £100,000 and Rank was elected chairman. The National Archives (TNA) BT 31/39574/290703: British National Films Ltd.

3. 'General Film Distributors Ltd Incorporated', *Kinematograph Weekly*, 10 October 1935, p. 38.
4. The General Cinema Finance Corporation was incorporated on 18 March 1936 with an authorised capital of £1,250,000: the directors were Lord Portal of Laverstoke, J. Arthur Rank, Paul Lindenberg and Leslie Farrow. Rank was the largest shareholder with 1,015,574 preferred shares at £1 each and 854,400 deferred shares at one shilling each. TNA BT 31/43485: General Cinema Finance Corporation.
5. 'Pinewood Challenge', *The Buckinghamshire Advertiser and Gazette*, 2 October 1936, p. 13.
6. 'Methodist Miller's Money Buys Hollywood Company for Britain', *World Film News*, 1: 3 (June 1936), p. 17.
7. Margaret Dickinson and Sarah Street, *Cinema and State: The Film Industry and the British Government 1927–84* (London: British Film Institute, 1985), p. 139.
8. *The Diaries of Robert Bruce Lockhart Volume II: 1939–1965*, ed. Kenneth Young (London: Macmillan, 1980), p. 454.
9. Rachael Low, *The History of the British Film 1929–1939: Film Making in 1930s Britain* (London: George Allen & Unwin, 1985), p. 216.
10. 'Mr J. A. Rank's Acquisition', *The Financial Times*, 13 February 1939, p. 5.
11. 'Maxwell as a Financial Genius', *Kinematograph Weekly*, 10 October 1940, p. 11.
12. Bank of England Archive (BEA) SMT 2/44: E. Skinner, 'Associated British Picture Corporation (ABPC)', 15 May 1944.
13. 'Warner Offer for ABPC Holding', *Kinematograph Weekly*, 10 July 1941, p. 17.
14. BEA SMT 2/44: Memorandum of an interview between the President of the Board of Trade and Mr Allen on 7 July 1941.
15. 'ABPC Again Withhold Ordinary Dividend', *Kinematograph Weekly*, 9 October 1941, p. 18.
16. TNA BT 64/4529: 'Mr Allen' (no date).
17. Ibid.: Simon Rowson to Hugh Gaitskell, 11 May 1943.
18. Ibid.: 'Mr Allen', Note of a Meeting with Hugh Dalton, 19 May 1943.
19. 'G-B Deal Completed', *Kinematograph Weekly*, 6 November 1941, p. 11.
20. 'C. M. Woolf's Bid for G-B Control', *Kinematograph Weekly*, 23 October 1941, p. 3.
21. 'British Film Finance', *The Economist*, 1 November 1941, p. 536.
22. 'Gaumont-British Control', *Kinematograph Weekly*, 6 November 1941, p. 3.
23. 'Odeon Theatres', *The Financial Times*, 12 January 1942, p. 2.
24. 'Odeon Plans for Control of Government', *The Financial Times*, 9 January 1939, p. 5.
25. Political and Economic Planning, *The British Film Industry: A Report on its History and Present Organisation, with Special Reference to the Economic Problems of British Feature Film Production* (London: Political and Economic Planning, 1952), pp. 86–7.
26. 'A Cinema Empire', *The Economist*, 3 July 1943, p. 6.
27. TNA BT 64/95: R. G. Somervell, 'Film Policy', 4 March 1942.
28. 'Davis has Key Rank Position', *Kinematograph Weekly*, 11 April 1946, p. 3.
29. 'Odeon Finance', *The Economist*, 17 October 1942, p. 491.
30. 'British Studios: 1942 Survey', *Kinematograph Weekly*, 14 January 1943, p. 94.
31. British Film Institute (BFI) TW Box 19: Independent Producers: Film Production Expenditure and Revenue Received from Commencement of Production to 29 September 1945.
32. Wood, *Mr Rank*, p. 153.
33. TNA BT 64/4529: Note – 'Mr Rank's Companies and Affiliations'.

34. Ibid.: Filippo Del Giudice to Morris L. Ernst, 30 November 1942.
35. BEA SMT 2/39: Skinner to Bolton, 16 January 1944.
36. BEA EC 4/248: E. D. H. Skinner to Bernard, 30 April 1941.
37. Ibid.: A. W. Watkins to Hugh Dalton, 15 June 1943.
38. David Lean, 'Brief Encounter', The Penguin Film Review, 4 (October 1947), p. 34.
39. TNA BT 64/4529: Sam Eckman Jr to E. Sutton, 3 June 1943.
40. Michael Balcon, Michael Balcon Presents . . . A Lifetime of Films (London: Hutchison, 1969), p. 152.
41. TNA BT 64/4529: 'Mr Stephen Courtauld and Major Baker', 21 May 1943.
42. 'A Cinema Empire', p. 5.
43. TNA BT 64/4529: 'Mr Rank', 18 May 1943.
44. Ibid.: Untitled Memorandum by Hugh Gaitskell, 13 April 1943.
45. 'MGM-Korda Film Merger', The Times, 10 March 1943, p. 4.
46. TNA BT 64/4529: Untitled Memorandum by Hugh Gaitskell, 13 April 1943.
47. Ibid.: 'Undertaking Given by Mr Warter Regarding Film Shares', 16 July 1943.
48. Ibid.: 'Notes for the President's Meeting with Mr Rank', 15 May 1943.
49. Ibid.: Simon Rowson to Hugh Gaitskell, 11 May 1943.
50. Ibid.: Minute of a Meeting between Hugh Gaitskell and Sir Kingsley Wood, 8 June 1943.
51. Ibid.: 'Note of a Conversation with Mr Rank' (no date).
52. Ibid.: J. Arthur Rank to Hugh Dalton, 30 June 1943. Rank nevertheless added a self-justifying caveat: 'I believe you appreciate that some degree of rationalisation was required if the British Industry is to be built on a sound basis, and given sufficient solidarity to compete in fields where powerful elements were already established.'
53. Ibid.: 'Lady Yule' (no date).
54. Ibid.: 'C. W.', 'Talk with Alexander Korda and Claud Serocold', 3 June 1943.
55. Ibid.: 'Note of Meeting with Mr Warter and Mr Fletcher', 7 September 1943.
56. Ibid.: Gaitskell to Liesching, 21 May 1943.
57. Ibid.: P. A. Warter to Dalton, 9 July 1943.
58. Fifth Report of the Cinematograph Films Council for the year ending 31 March, 1943 (London: HMSO, 1943), p. 4.
59. 'Film Trade Monopolies', Kinematograph Weekly, 5 June 1943, p. 2.
60. Tendencies to Monopoly in the Cinematograph Film Industry: Report of a Committee Appointed by the Cinematograph Films Council (London: HMSO, 1944), p. 6.
61. Ibid., pp. 14–15.
62. 'Trade Reactions to Monopoly Report', Kinematograph Weekly, 10 August 1944, p. 5.
63. 'Monopoly Report Shakes British Film Industry', Daily Mirror, 2 August 1944, p. 3.
64. 'Future of the Screen', The Economist, 12 August 1944, p. 18.
65. Parliamentary Debates: House of Commons, 5th Series, vol. 408, 6 March 1945, col. 1822.
66. 'Case of Procrastination', The Economist, 24 March 1945, p. 25.
67. TNA BT 64/4529: Memorandum by Hugh Gaitskell, 13 April 1943.
68. TNA BT 64/95: J. Arthur Rank to Hugh Dalton, 1 July 1944.
69. The Cine-Technician (November–December 1943), p. 124.
70. 'British Films for the World', Liverpool Daily Post, 19 February 1944, p. 2.
71. British Library Laurence Olivier Archive Films 3/1: General Film Distributors Royalty Statement, 30 August 1947, including certified cost of production of Henry V. The British Film Institute Reuben Library digitised microfiche for Henry V includes a

memo written for a screening of the film at the Sittingbourne Film Society in October 1965 which indicates a slightly higher cost (£475,708), although the source of this information is unstated.
72. BFI TW Box 20: *Caesar and Cleopatra*: Statement of Production Costs.
73. '"Caesar" – A Scandal', *Kinematograph Weekly*, 7 March 1946, p. 26A.
74. Sarah Street, *Transatlantic Crossings: British Feature Films in the United States* (London: Continuum, 2002), pp. 94, 106.
75. BFI TW Box 17: Ledger of Film Budgets and Estimated Costs for Independent Producers (*London Town* is included in the ledger despite not actually being under the Independent Producers banner).
76. Lean, '*Brief Encounter*', p. 35.
77. BFI TW Box 22: George Archibald to Tom White, 24 January1947.
78. *Great Expectations* cost £391,600 (30.5 per cent over the £300,000 maximum); *Oliver Twist* cost £371,500 (23.8 per cent over); *A Matter of Life and Death* cost £385,927 (28.6 per cent over), *Black Narcissus* cost £352,052 (17.4 per cent over); *The Red Shoes* cost £505,600 (68.5 per cent over).
79. Michael Powell, *A Life in Movies: An Autobiography* (London: Heinemann, 1986), p. 664.
80. 'Rank Tells the Story of His Losses', *Kinematograph Weekly*, 10 November 1949, p. 6.
81. Political and Economic Planning, *The British Film Industry*, pp. 97–8.
82. TNA BT 64/4490: J. Arthur Rank Organisation Ltd: Memorandum Regarding Information Required by the Board of Trade regarding Film Production and Distribution, Schedule VI.
83. Ibid.
84. BFI TW Box 13: *Green for Danger*: Production Cost and Receipts to 29/01/1949.
85. Macnab, *J. Arthur Rank and the British Film Industry*, p. 50.

Conclusion

Financing the British Film Industry has charted the trials and tribulations of British film finance and production over its first half century. During this time British cinema had developed from a cottage industry to a mature business enterprise. Yet throughout that period the domestic production sector remained chronically unstable: it was characterised by a recurring cycle of boom and bust that plunged it into a new crisis every decade or so. The headlines tended to focus on specific episodes that damaged the reputation of the industry and deterred investors: the mushroom companies launched on the exaggerated and unrealistic promises of share prospectuses, the proliferation of low-cost films that damaged the reputation of all British films, the extravagance on the part of producers such as Alexander Korda and Max Schach, and the ultimate failure by all British producers to compete on equal terms with Hollywood. However, the problems of the British cinema industry were not down to the box-office failure of individual films, the behaviour of particular producers or the bankruptcies of single companies. While characters like Korda and Schach brought colour and drama, they were symptoms of the industry's problems rather than the cause. The underlying weaknesses of the cinema industry in Britain were structural and endemic: the shortage of capital and the unprofitability of film production.

It has been suggested – not least by contemporary trade sources – that a major cause of the problems of the British cinema industry was that it was under-capitalised in comparison to its main competitor: the United States. This is correct to an extent but needs to be qualified. It is true that British investors were wary of the industry – with good reason, as the frequent cycles of boom and bust attest – and that the financial institutions of the City of London were initially reluctant to get involved in the new business. The antipathy of the Governor of the Bank of England towards the 'mucky people' in the film business was very likely also a factor here. It was not until the late 1920s that finance-capital took a significant stake in the British film industry with the entrance of banks and insurance companies whose capital supported a restructuring of the industry.

However, by the end of the Second World War the argument that the industry was under-capitalised becomes less convincing. In 1945 the Rank Organisation alone held fixed assets of £60 million in around 100 companies: the largest of these were the Gaumont-British Picture Corporation (with an authorised capital of £7,125,000) and Odeon Theatres (£6 million).[1] Rank was the only British corporation to operate on the same scale as the Hollywood majors: its capital assets were on a similar level to studios such as MGM and Warner Bros.[2] The Associated British Picture Corporation, the smaller of the two combines, nevertheless held fixed assets of around £24 million and had an issued capital of £9 million.[3]

The problem therefore was less the shortage of finance *per se* but rather the structure and nature of that finance. Much of the permanent capital in the cinema industry was invested in the exhibition sector: exhibition was the most profitable branch of the industry, especially during the 1930s and 1940s when cinema-going was 'the essential social habit of the age'.[4] However, after exhibitors had taken their share of box-office receipts, the lion's share of distributors' receipts was returned to American rather than British interests. This presented two problems: that much of the industry's revenues came from imported films, and that the bulk of the income generated by cinema exhibition did not feed back to British producers. The domestic production sector was always more precarious than exhibition as it was dependent upon loans: even the two combines borrowed cash for production, while independent producers were entirely dependent upon short-term finance. While the combines could depend upon their cinema chains to offset losses on production, the smaller production units and independents were more exposed to structural instability and interruptions to the supply of finance.

Furthermore, the structure of the market was weighted against British producers. Although John Sedgwick has shown that British films had a larger market share in the 1930s than had been assumed, the fact remains that the British market alone was insufficient to guarantee a return for anything but a modestly budgeted film.[5] Even when cinema-going was at its height during the Second World War, there was a cost ceiling above which British films become unprofitable. As J. Arthur Rank explained in a memorandum to the Board of Trade in 1944:

> The disadvantage of an inadequate financial margin arising from the smallness of the Home market, however, remains. The cost of making films in this country has risen greatly during the war. It is true that in spite of this, owing to the vast demand for entertainment, it is at present possible for a British picture costing in the region of £100,000 to £150,000 to make a profit. This state of affairs, however, is unlikely to continue and when peace comes most films costing up to these figures will be a risky speculation if they have to rely on the Home market alone.[6]

There were basically two strategies for British producers during this period. One – followed by Associated British, the British and Dominions Film Corporation, Associated Talking Pictures and the British Lion Film Corporation – was to produce lower-cost films that were not 'quickies' but were budgeted at a level at which they could reasonably expect to return a profit in the home market. However, the low return on investment, and in ATP's case the regular non-payment of dividends, did not have investors falling over themselves. The other strategy – exemplified with some success by Alexander Korda and Herbert Wilcox, with limited success by Gaumont-British and with abject failure by Max Schach and others – was to produce high-cost films that would depend on international markets to return a profit. This high-risk, high-reward strategy initially attracted speculative investors such as the Prudential Assurance Company, but when it became apparent that successes on the level of *The Private Life of Henry VIII* were the exception rather than the rule, the City soon came to regret its indulgence of such producers. The fallout of the financing crisis of 1937 and the film insurance scandal that unravelled in its wake deterred City investors from the film industry until the 1970s.

Curiously, perhaps, given the disruption to production activity, the one period when British films were profitable was during the Second World War. A combination of an expanding market, an economical approach to production and a reduction in the supply of British films meant that economic conditions shifted in favour of producers. The wartime contraction of the production sector meant that for once sufficient finance was available for British films. In 1942 the *Kinematograph Year Book Diary and Directory* observed that wartime conditions had created a leaner and more economical industry:

> Superior quality, even though the ultimate quantity might be reduced, has been generally the goal of our producers, and the improvement applies not, as in the past, to one or two outstanding and extravagantly budgeted films, but to a far wider circle of productions . . . The problem of feature production has been solved, not by skimping production, but rather by intelligent and accurate budgeting. This policy has been reflected not only in the splendid quality of war-time production but also in the fact that soundly-conceived schedules have found little difficulty in attracting the necessary finance, a rehabilitation of the financial prestige of British producers which enables the prospect of a healthy post-war industry to be regarded with certainty.[7]

However, this fortuitous combination of circumstances would not extend far beyond the end of the war: the combination of increasing costs and (after 1946) declining cinema attendances meant that by the end of the decade film production had become a largely unprofitable activity and the major producers were obliged to cut back on their programmes. Indeed, the economic contexts changed so rapidly after the war that in 1948 the new Labour government was obliged to set up the National Film Finance Corporation to support independent producers in raising their finance.

In the introduction, I noted the tension between culture and commerce, between art and industry, in which film-makers are cast as visionaries and finance providers as philistines interested only in the commercial bottom line. It is a narrative that continues to exert a strong hold on histories of British cinema. However, *Financing the British Film Industry* has shown that a flourishing British cinema – in the sense of films that were both popular with audiences and met the industry's criterion of quality – was possible only due to the entry of finance-capital into the industry. There were, inevitably, tensions, revealed by Alexander Korda's relationship with Prudential Assurance and the antipathy of the Bank of England towards an official film bank. At the same time, however, J. Arthur Rank's financing of Independent Producers indicates that there were moments (however brief) when capital and culture were working in harmony. In this sense the Second World War represents a golden age not only for British film-making but also for a commercially successful film industry. British cinema had never had it so good. It would never have it so good again.

Notes

1. Political and Economic Planning, *The British Film Industry: A Report on its History and Present Organisation, with Special Reference to the Economic Problems of British Feature Film Production* (London: Political and Economic Planning, 1952), pp. 133–5.
2. The net worth of the 'Big Five' in 1941 was approximately US$650 million: MGM and Warner Bros. were each worth around US$165 million, Twentieth Century-Fox US$130 million, Paramount US$110 million and RKO US$70 million. Thomas Schatz, *Boom and Bust: American Cinema in the 1940s* (Berkeley: University of California Press, 1997), p. 17.
3. Political and Economic Planning, *The British Film Industry*, pp. 141–2.
4. A. J. P. Taylor, *English History 1914–1945* (Oxford: Oxford University Press, 1965), p. 313.
5. John Sedgwick, *Popular Filmgoing in 1930s Britain: A Choice of Pleasures* (Exeter: University of Exeter Press, 2000), pp. 84–101.
6. The National Archives BT 64/95: J. Arthur Rank to Hugh Dalton, 'The Future of the British Film Industry', 1 July 1944.
7. A. L. Carter, 'Studio Work in 1941', *Kinematograph Year Book Diary and Directory 1942* (London: Kinematograph Publications, 1942), p. 278.

APPENDIX I

Statutory Costs of British Quota Films, 1 April 1932–31 March 1933

This appendix lists the statutory cost and length in feet of 158 films registered for renters' quota in 1932–3. The quota year ran from 1 April to 31 March. The statutory cost was the total paid to those employed in the production of the film: 75 per cent of this amount (excluding the salary of the director and one actor or actress) had to be paid to British subjects in order to be eligible for quota. The Board of Trade reckoned the statutory cost to be between 50–60 per cent of the total cost of production. The statutory cost per 100 feet is also included: £55 per 100 feet was equivalent to the 'pound-a-foot' total cost that was the unofficial yardstick of a 'quota quickie'.

Source: The National Archives BT64/97: Particulars of British Films Acquired by Renters during Quota Year 1932–3.

Renter (production co.)	Statutory cost	Length	Cost/ 100 ft
Ace Films			
Little Waitress (Delta Films)	£604	4,365 ft	£7
Associated Producing and Distributing Company			
When London Sleeps (Twickenham Studios)	£4,041	7,025 ft	£57
British Lion Film Distributors			
The Flying Squad (British Lion Film Corporation)	£7,912	7,140 ft	£111
Sally Bishop (British Lion Film Corporation)	£11,261	7,348 ft	£154
Where is This Lady? (Amalgamated Films)	£11,427	7,249 ft	£158
Butchers' Film Service			
Heroes of the Mine (Delta Films)	£371	4,375 ft	£8
Watch Beverley (Sound City Films)	£1,811	7,146 ft	£25
Equity British Films			
Smiling Along (Argyle Film Productions)	£1,684	3,520 ft	£48
On Thin Ice (Hallmark Productions)	£222	5,650 ft	£4
A Marshland Tragedy (Gem)	£549	3,625 ft	£15

First National Film Distributors
Illegal (Warner Bros. British Productions)	£6,300	7,468 ft	£85
High Society (Warner Bros. British Productions)	£2,828	4,537 ft	£62
Lucky Ladies (Warner Bros. British Productions)	£3,537	6,734 ft	£53
Little Fella (Warner Bros. British Productions)	£1,808	4,017 ft	£45
River House Ghost (Warner Bros. British Productions)	£2,255	4,788 ft	£49
Don't Be a Dummy (Warner Bros. British Productions)	£2,332	4,531 ft	£51
Mr Quincy of Monte Carlo (Warner Bros. British Productions)	£2,230	4,856 ft	£46
The Melody Maker (Warner Bros. British Productions)	£2,086	5,098 ft	£41

Fox Film Corporation
Double Dealing (Real Art Productions)	£2,848	4,378 ft	£66
Flat No. 9 (V. Deuchar)	£1,547	4,456 ft	£35
A Safe Proposition (Real Art Productions)	£2,776	4,191 ft	£66
After Dark (Fox British Productions)	£2,676	4,104 ft	£65
Holiday Lovers (H. D. Cohen)	£1,917	4,390 ft	£44
Hundred to One (Twickenham Studios)	£1,872	4,018 ft	£46
A Taxi to Paradise (George Smith)	£1,300	4,042 ft	£32
Yes, Madam (British Lion Film Corporation)	£1,858	4,110 ft	£45
To Brighton with Gladys (George King)	£2,127	4,051 ft	£53
Forging Ahead (H. D. Cohen)	£1,790	4,349 ft	£41
I'm an Explosive (George Smith)	£1,386	4,458 ft	£31

Gaumont Company
Rome Express (Gaumont-British)	£24,414	8,484 ft	£279
After the Ball (Gaumont-British)	£16,796	6,389 ft	£266
King of the Ritz (British Lion)	£12,828	7,395 ft	£175
With Cobham to Kivu (Gaumont-British)	£1,002	6,023 ft	£16

Ideal Films
The Faithful Heart (Gainsborough)	£13,246	7,504 ft	£126
Wedding Rehearsal (London Film Productions)	£13,766	7,595 ft	£183
Marry Me (Gainsborough)	£15,407	7,800 ft	£197
There Goes the Bride (Gainsborough)	£14,505	7,184 ft	£204
The Man from Toronto (Gainsborough)	£16,416	6,921 ft	£237
The Good Companions (Gaumont-British)	£32,406	10,146 ft	£326

International Productions
Hiking with Mademoiselle (International)	£987	3,659 ft	£27

Appendix I

MGM

A Tight Corner (Real Art Productions)	£2,885	4,409 ft	£65
Diamond Cut Diamond (Cinema House)	£19,884	6,385 ft	£315
Reunion (Sound City Films)	£1,092	5,476 ft	£20
Born Lucky (Westminster Films)	£3,284	7,005 ft	£46
She Was Only a Village Maiden (Sound City Films)	£1,367	5,487 ft	£25
The Wishbone (Sound City Films)	£2,689	7,100 ft	£27
Side Street (Sound City Films)	£1,175	4,243 ft	£27
The Golden Cage (Sound City Films)	£2,701	5,600 ft	£48

Paramount Film Service

Lily Christine (Paramount British Productions)	£18,910	7,452 ft	£255
Down Our Street (Paramount British Productions)	£5,891	6,795 ft	£87
Insult (Paramount British Productions)	£7,486	7,162 ft	£105
Money Means Nothing (B&D Film Corporation)	£5,167	6,569 ft	£82
Men of Tomorrow (London Film Productions)	£9,662	8,000 ft	£120
That Night in London (B&D Film Corporation)	£9,267	7,009 ft	£118
The Barton Mystery (B&D Film Corporation)	£4,392	6,974 ft	£63
Discord (B&D Film Corporation)	£4,892	7,235 ft	£67
Strange Evidence (London Film Productions)	£8,356	6,484 ft	£130
One Precious Year (B&D Film Corporation)	£5,274	6,894 ft	£77
Counsel's Opinion (London Film Productions)	£9,140	6,806 ft	£134
The Crime at Blossoms (B&D Film Corporation)	£4,769	6,921 ft	£69

Pathé

Tin Gods (British International Pictures)	£6,767	4,661 ft	£147
Bad Companions (British International Pictures)	£2,175	3,917 ft	£55
Mr Bill the Conqueror (British International Pictures)	£10,331	7,855 ft	£132
The Bachelor's Baby (British International Pictures)	£5,060	5,138 ft	£99
Strip, Strip, Hooray (British International Pictures)	£3,306	3,235 ft	£103
Verdict of the Sea (Regina Film Productions)	£7,605	5,793 ft	£133
Pyjamas Preferred (British International Pictures)	£3,376	4,708 ft	£73

Producers' Distributing Company

Here's George (Tom Arnold)	£2,358	5,793 ft	£41

RKO Radio Pictures

The Sign of Four (Associated Talking Pictures)	£12,742	6,097 ft	£187
The Impassive Footman (Associated Talking Pictures)	£8,928	6,233 ft	£144
Love on the Spot (Associated Talking Pictures)	£7,218	5,866 ft	£124
Looking on the Bright Side (Associated Talking Pictures)	£27,528	7,398 ft	£377

The Face at the Window (Real Art Productions)	£2,712	4,717 ft	£57
The World, the Flesh and the Devil (Real Art Productions)	£3,153	4,805 ft	£65
The Iron Stair (Real Art Productions)	£2,677	4,527 ft	£59
Called Back (Real Art Productions)	£2,752	4,527 ft	£61
The Medicine Man (Real Art Productions)	£2,728	4,704 ft	£58
Excess Baggage (Real Art Productions)	£3,538	5,358 ft	£66

Sterling Film Company

The First Mrs Fraser (Sterling Film Company)	£16,726	7,700 ft	£217
The Wonderful Story (Reginald Fogwell)	£2,261	6,456 ft	£35
Her First Affaire (St George's Productions)	£6,164	6,456 ft	£94

United Artists

His Lordship (Westminster Films)	£3,855	6.755 ft	£59
Men of Steel (Langham Productions)	£5,166	6,449 ft	£80
Puppets of Fate (Real Art Productions)	£5,748	6,541 ft	£88
Perfect Understanding (Gloria Swanson Productions)	£70,010	7,871 ft	£899
Daughters of Today (FWK Productions)	£5,432	6,694 ft	£83
The Shadow (Real Art Productions)	£5,702	6,752 ft	£85
Money for Speed (Hallmark Productions)	£2,724	6,639 ft	£41
Matinee Idol (Wyndham Productions)	£5,901	6,064 ft	£86
No Funny Business (John Stafford Productions)	£7,426	6,863 ft	£109

Universal

Betrayal (Reginald Fogwell)	£1,933	5,966 ft	£32
+ *Toll of Destiny* (Orient Productions)	£545	7,786 ft	£7
A 'Yell' of a Night (G. A. Minzensky)	£776	3,838 ft	£20
The Third Gun (British Sound Films)	£55	3,250 ft	£6
*Down on the Farm (Cinesound Productions)	£3,156	7,086 ft	£45
**His Royal Highness* (Efftree Productions)	£5,013	7,042 ft	£71
*Diggers (Efftree Productions)	£2,209	6,010 ft	£36
*The Haunted Barn (Efftree Productions)	£961	3,902 ft	£24
**Show Girl's Luck* (Australian Talkies)	£2,644	4,059 ft	£66
Spur of the Moment (Harwood Productions)	£1,122	3,815 ft	£29
**A Co-respondent's Course* (Efftree Productions)	£1,774	4,400 ft	£40
Double Bluff (British Pictorial)	£625	3,161 ft	£20
**A Sentimental Bloke* (Efftree Productions)	£5,264	7,786 ft	£70

W&F Film Service

White Face (Gainsborough)	£9,586	6,359 ft	£152
Jack's the Boy (Gaumont-British)	£18,214	8,004 ft	£227

Appendix I

The Mayor's Nest (B&D Film Corporation)	£8,895	6,684 ft	£134
Love on Wheels (Gainsborough)	£19,838	7,821 ft	£254
Thark (B&D Film Corporation)	£9,463	7,014 ft	£137
The Love Contract (B&D Film Corporation)	£19,574	7,233 ft	£140
The Lodger (Twickenham Studios)	£9,590	7,685 ft	£126
Leap Year (B&D Film Corporation)	£15,676	8,106 ft	£193
The Flag Lieutenant (B&D Film Corporation)	£7,696	7,748 ft	£92
Say It With Music (B&D Film Corporation)	£11,149	6,298 ft	£178
The Midshipmaid (Gaumont-British)	£21,521	7,532 ft	£286
It's a King (B&D Film Corporation)	£9,281	6,039 ft	£154
Yes, Mr Brown (B&D Film Corporation)	£23,943	7,852 ft	£306
The King's Cup (B&D Film Corporation)	£13,293	6,881 ft	£200
Just My Luck (B&D Film Corporation)	£12,293	6,931 ft	£192
Little Damozel (B&D Film Corporation)	£10,713	6,639 ft	£162
The Blarney Stone (B&D Film Corporation)	£15,476	7,218 ft	£214
Up for the Derby (B&D Film Corporation)	£10,897	6,287 ft	£172
Soldiers of the King (Gainsborough)	£20,574	7,271 ft	£285

Wardour Films

Josser Joins the Navy (British International Pictures)	£5,038	6,215 ft	£81
Brother Alfred (British International Pictures)	£8,532	6,633 ft	£129
Innocents of Chicago (British International Pictures)	£7,494	6,139 ft	£122
The Indiscretions of Eve (British International Pictures)	£9,093	5,702 ft	£159
Lucky Girl (British International Pictures)	£7,339	6,700 ft	£109
After Office Hours (British International Pictures)	£7,721	7,100 ft	£105
England Awake! (British International Pictures)	£1,163	3,208 ft	£36
Number Seventeen (British International Pictures)	£15,202	5,756 ft	£266
The Last Coupon (British International Pictures)	£8,136	7,533 ft	£108
Arms and the Man (British International Pictures)	£7,368	7,746 ft	£95
Josser on the Run (British International Pictures)	£6,557	6,868 ft	£96
The Fires of Fate (British International Pictures)	£14,617	6,650 ft	£221
Maid of the Mountain (British International Pictures)	£17,308	7,128 ft	£240
His Wife's Mother (British International Pictures)	£5,584	6,298 ft	£94
Josser in the Army (British International Pictures)	£7,492	7,200 ft	£104
Sleepless Nights (British International Pictures)	£11,472	6,560 ft	£176
Money Talks (British International Pictures)	£8,584	6,560 ft	£132
Let Me Explain, Dear (British International Pictures)	£7,307	7,000 ft	£104
Lord Camber's Ladies (British International Pictures)	£11,557	8,137 ft	£142
For the Love of Mike (British International Pictures)	£14,274	7,725 ft	£185
Letting in the Sunshine (British International Pictures)	£10,282	6,680 ft	£155
Their Night Out (British International Pictures)	£6,633	6,600 ft	£102
Old Spanish Customers (British International Pictures)	£7,150	6,215 ft	£115

Warner Bros. Film Distributors

The Silver Greyhound (Warner Bros. British Productions)	£2,696	3,866 ft	£70
The Blind Spot (Warner Bros. British Productions)	£7,693	6,796 ft	£114
Her Night Out (Warner Bros. British Productions)	£2,351	4,083 ft	£58
Naughty Cinderella (Warner Bros. British Productions)	£2,074	5,068 ft	£41
Little Miss Nobody (Warner Bros. British Productions)	£2,257	4,796 ft	£48
The Stolen Necklace (Warner Bros. British Productions)	£2,121	4,444 ft	£48
Out of the Past (Warner Bros. British Productions)	£2,051	4,642 ft	£44
Double Wedding (Warner Bros. British Productions)	£1,781	4,574 ft	£39
Going Straight (Warner Bros. British Productions)	£1,782	4,568 ft	£39
Too Many Wives (Warner Bros. British Productions)	£1,937	5,287 ft	£39
As Good as New (Warner Bros. British Productions)	£2,103	4,391 ft	£48
The Thirteenth Candle (Warner Bros. British Productions)	£2,331	6.172 ft	£38

WP Films

The Return of Raffles (Mansfield Markham)	£4,595	6,715 ft	£68

Notes:
* Australian film
+ Indian film

APPENDIX II

Schedule of Bank Loans to Film Producers and Repayments

This appendix includes details of bank advances to independent film producers in the mid-1930s and the amounts repaid. The table includes the film, the lending bank (including the number of loans in parenthesis), the total advanced for the film and the amount repaid. The amount of the loan does not necessarily equate to the full cost of the film. Where the full amounts of loans were not repaid from receipts, the insurance underwriters were liable for the loss.

Source: Aviva Group Archive CU 540/6: Film Financial Guarantee Policies: Schedule of Ultimate Losses on Loans.

Producer/Film	Lender	Loan	Repaid
Argyle British Productions			
Mutiny of the Elsinore (1937)	National Provincial Bank	£7,500	£7,500
Kathleen Mavourneen (1937)	National Provincial Bank	£9,500	£9,500
Atlantic Productions			
Thunder in the City (1937)	Lloyds Bank (5)	£58,570	£35,816
Beaumont Film Productions			
Toilers of the Sea (1939)	Westminster Bank (2)	£20,800	£38
British Unity Pictures			
The Girl in the Taxi (1937)	Midland Bank	£31,500	£31,500
British Artistic Films			
Gypsy Melody (1936)[1]	Barclays Bank	£17,500	£7,135
Buckingham Film Productions			
Jericho (1937)	District Bank	£50,000	£2,453
The Stars Look Down (unmade)	District Bank	£50,000	—
Accommodating loan	Chase National Bank	£14,000	—

Capitol Film Corporation

The Marriage of Corbal (1936)	Westminster Bank (2)	£60,000	£16,776
When Knights Were Bold (1936)	Westminster Bank (2)	£60,000	£27,218
Koenigsmark (1936)	Westminster Bank (2)	£60,000	£16,157
Love in Exile (1936)	Westminster Bank (2)	£60,000	£18,168
Public Nuisance No. 1 (1936)	Westminster Bank	£15,000	£15,000
Land Without Music (1936)	Westminster Bank	£45,000	£16,799
Southern Roses (1936)	Westminster Bank	£60,000	£15,794
Moscow Nights (1935)	Westminster Bank	£30,000	£397
Taras Bulba (unmade)	Westminster Bank	£30,000	—
For Valour (1937)	Westminster Bank	£30,000	£19,106
Passage des Princes (unmade)	Westminster Bank	£35,000	—
Jack Buchanan No. 2	Westminster Bank	£35,000	—
Walls-Lyn No. 2	Westminster Bank	£35,000	£229

Cecil Films

Public Nuisance No. 1 (1936)	Westminster Bank	£35,000	£25,137
Dishonour Bright (1936)	Westminster Bank	£35,000	£25,075
Lilac Domino (1937)	National Provincial Bank	£55,000	£312
Serpolette (unmade)	National Provincial Bank	£55,000	—
International Quartet (unmade)	Westminster Bank	£55,000	—
No Other Tiger (unmade)	Westminster Bank	£55,000	—
Provision Loan No. 6	Westminster Bank	£115,000	—
Lilac Domino FRI Loan	Westminster Bank	£12,000	—
Provision Loan No. 7	Westminster Bank	£30,000	—

City Film Corporation

Barnacle Bill (1935)	Westminster Bank	£3,500	£3,508
Joyride (1935)	Westminster Bank	£8,400	£8,000
Play Up the Band (1935)	Westminster Bank (3)	£17,950	£8,000
King of the Castle (1936)	Westminster Bank	£13,000	£6,989
The Improper Duchess (1936)	Westminster Bank	£20,000	£9,781
Tropical Trouble (1936)	Westminster Bank (3)	£27,500	£7,565
On Top of the World (1936)	Westminster Bank	£8,000	£3,744
You Must Get Married (1936)	Westminster Bank (3)	£43,000	£5,574
	District Bank	£13,750	—
Radio Lover (1936)	Westminster Bank (2)	£21,000	£9,681

John Clein Productions

The Mill on the Floss (1936)	Lloyds Bank	£22,000	—

Concordia Films
Robber Symphony (1936) | Midland Bank | £14,000 £14,000

Criterion Film Productions
The Amateur Gentleman (1936) | Westminster Bank (2) | £70,000 £52,158
Accused (1936) | Martins Bank | £69,000 £43,209
Crime Over London (1936) | Martins Bank | £69,000 £13,385
Jump for Glory (1937) | Martins Bank | £69,000 £27,792

De La Films British
Not Wanted on Voyage (1938) | Martins Bank (2) | £20,280 —

Embassy Pictures
Wanted (1937) | Westminster Bank | £15,000 £7,500
Merry Comes to Town (1937) | Westminster Bank | £15,000 £5,500
Riding High (1939) | Westminster Bank (2) | £15,000 —

Fortune Films
Big Fella (1937) | National Provincial Bank £32,000 £16,279

Franco-London Films
Guilty Melody (1936) | Chase National Bank (4) | £35,800 £29,672
Romance in Flanders (1937)[2] | Chase National Bank | £10,000 —
 | Martins Bank | £10,000 £645

Gaiety Films
Honeymoon for Three (1935) | Lloyds Bank | £22,500 £18,185

Garrick Film Company
Café Collette (1937) | Banque Belge | £22,000 £14,992

Grosvenor Sound Films
Hyde Park Corner (1935) | Westminster Bank | £20,000 £13,333
 Re: Sinclair Hill & Co. | Westminster Bank | £2,500 £2,500
The Cardinal (1936) | Westminster Bank | £20,000 £13,333
The Gay Adventure (1936) | Westminster Bank | £20,000 £13,333
Take a Chance (1937) | Westminster Bank | £30,000 £20,375
Midnight Menace (1937) | Westminster Bank | £30,000 £19,549
Command Performance (1937) | Westminster Bank | £30,000 £19,050

Hammer Film Productions
Mystery of the Marie Celeste (1935)	Barclays Bank	£24,000	£15,000
Song of Freedom (1936)	Barclays Bank	£30,000	£30,000
Sporting Love (1936)	Barclays Bank	£24,000	£15,466

Hope Bell Film Productions
Old Mother Riley (1937)	District Bank	£5,000	£5,000
Rose of Tralee (1937)	District Bank	£5,000	£5,000

Lawrence Huntingdon
Lieutenant Daring, RN (1935)	Westminster Bank	£3,500	£3,043
Full Speed Ahead (1936)	Westminster Bank	£5,000	£5,000

IFR Ltd
Calling the Tune (1936)	Barclays Bank	£25,000	£16,461
The House of the Spaniard (1936)	Barclays Bank (2)	£28,000	£18,000
Secret Lives (1938)	Barclays Bank	£25,000	£17,333
Brief Ecstasy (1937)	Barclays Bank	£25,000	£15,000
What a Man! (1939)	Barclays Bank	£25,000	£1,565

Incorporated Talking Pictures
Melody of My Heart (193)	District Bank	£4,000	£111

Independent Producers Studios
Skylarks (1936)	District Bank	£20,000	—
We Died Last Night (1936)	Royal Bank of Scotland	£11,000	£11,000

International Players Pictures
Runaway Ladies (1939)[3]	Midland Bank	£6,000	—

George King Productions
Sweeney Todd, the Demon Barber of Fleet Street (1936)	Westminster Bank	£4,000	£4,000
The Crimes of Stephen Hawke (1936)	Westminster Bank	£3,000	£3,000
'On 3 Films'	Westminster Bank	£8,000	£8,000

London and Continental
Dreams Come True (1936)	Westminster Bank	£22,500	£24

London Screenplays
Honeymoon Merrygoround (1936)[4]	Lloyds Bank (2)	£23.400	£23,400

Stanley Lupino Productions
Cheer Up (1936)   Lloyds Bank (2)   £31,100   £17,147

Mitchell Films
Cock o' the North (1935)   Westminster Bank   £4,500   £4,500

Mondover Film Productions
Little Miss Somebody (1937)[5]   District Bank   £3,500   £3,500
Annie Laurie (1936)   District Bank   £4,000   £4,000

New City Productions
Come Out of the Pantry (1935)   Westminster Bank   £36,666   £36,666

New Ideal Pictures
Her Last Affair (1935)   Westminster Bank   £15,000   £7,456
Can You Hear Me, Mother? (1935)   Westminster Bank   £15,000   £7,500
The Seat Burglars (1937)   Westminster Bank   £4,000   £500
[Undisclosed]   Westminster Bank   £3,000   £1,072

Oxford Films
My Partner, Mr Davis (1936)   Banque Belge (2)   £27,000   £21,000

Producers' Distributing Corporation
Loan No. 1   Westminster Bank   £20,000   £18,701
Loan No. 2   Westminster Bank   £20,000   £18,003

Radius Films
No Monkey Business (1935)   Westminster Bank   £25,000   £25,000

St George's Pictures
The Deputy Drummer (1935)   National Provincial Bank £6,150   £802
Trust the Navy (1935)   National Provincial Bank £6,750   £1,626
Hot News (1936)   National Provincial Bank £7,000   £1,709
Who's Your Father? (1935)   National Provincial Bank £5,000   £1,868

Soskin Productions
Two's Company (1936)   Westminster Bank (2)   £22,500   £10,118

John Stafford Productions
Admirals All (1935)   Westminster Bank   £20,000   £20,000
The Crouching Beast (193)   Westminster Bank   £20,000   £20,000

Beloved Imposter (1936)	Westminster Bank	£20,000	£20,000
Ball at Savoy (1936)	Westminster Bank	£20,000	£20,000
The Avenging Hand (1936)	Westminster Bank	£20,000	£20,000

Premier Stafford Productions

Wings Over Africa (1936)	Westminster Bank	£20,000	£20,000
Second Bureau (1936)	Westminster Bank	£20,000	£20,000
Wake Up Famous (1937)	Westminster Bank	£20,000	£20,000
The Wife of General Ling (1937)	Westminster Bank	£20,000	£20,000
The Return of a Stranger (1937)	Westminster Bank	£20,000	£20,000

Standard International Pictures

Make-Up (1937)	Lloyds Bank	£18,000	£18,000

Toeplitz Productions

Beloved Vagabond (1936)	Midland Bank (2)	£90,000	£55,157
She Took the Low Road[6]	Midland Bank	£50,000	£23,000

Trafalgar Film Productions

Pagliacci (1936)	Westminster Bank	£78,000	£13,900
Dreaming Lips (1937)	Westminster Bank	£78,000	£34,686
Love from a Stranger (1937)	Westminster Bank	£78,000	£41,667
Mademoiselle Docteur (1937)	Westminster Bank	£78,000	£5,118
Wheat (unmade)	Westminster Bank	£78,000	—
Little Lady of the Big House (unmade)	Westminster Bank	£78,000	—

Transatlantic Film

Ten-Minute Alibi (1935)	Westminster Bank	£11,000	£10,441

Transatlantic Talking Pictures

While Parents Sleep (1935)	Westminster Bank	£16,000	£6,088

Tudor Films

Everything in Life (1938)[7]	District Bank	£20,000	£12,784

UK Films

Man of Yesterday (1936)	National Provincial Bank	£13,000	£6,600
Hearts of Humanity (1936)	National Provincial Bank	£13,000	£400
Song of the Road (1937)	National Provincial Bank	£13,000	£1,144
Talking Feet (1937)	National Provincial Bank	£13,000	£9.290
'On 3 Films'	National Provincial Bank	£10,000	£10,000

United Plays
The Witch[8]   Westminster Bank   £50,000   £50,000

J. G. and R. B. Wainwright
Wolf's Clothing (1936)   National Provincial Bank   £5,000   £5,000
The Crimson Circle (1936)   National Provincial Bank   £5,000   £5,000
The Secret of Stamboul (1936)[9] National Provincial Bank (2) £8,000   £8,000
School for Husbands (1937)   National Provincial Bank   £8,000   £601
Kate Plus Ten (1938)   National Provincial Bank   £8,000   —

Herbert Wilcox Productions
Limelight (1936)   Westminster Bank   £55,000   £55,000
Fame (1936)   Westminster Bank   £55,000   £31,270
The Three Maxims (1936)   Westminster Bank   £55,000   £44,499
Millions (1936)   Westminster Bank   £55,000   £31,525
This'll Make You Whistle (1936) Westminster Bank   £55,000   £55,000
London Melody (1937)   Westminster Bank   £55,000   £30,000

T. A. Welsh Productions
Shipmates o' Mine (1936)   Barclays Bank   £5,000   £3,500

Wyndham Films
It Happened in Paris (1935)   Westminster Bank (3)   £19,000   —
                                  Chase National Bank (2)   £4,500   —

Total bank advances   £4,127,146

Repaid from receipts   £1,820,931
Repaid by underwriters   £1,444,941

Estimated ultimate net loss   £1,996,450

Notes

1. *Gypsy Melody* is listed in the ledger under the title *Juanita*.
2. *Romance in Flanders* is listed under the title *Widow's Island*.
3. *Runaway Ladies* was a British remake of a French film entitled *Le Voyage Imprévu* and is included in the ledger under that title.
4. *Honeymoon Merrygoround* is listed under the title *Olympic Honeymoon*.
5. *Little Miss Somebody* is listed under the title *Corduroy Diplomat*.
6. I have not been able to find a film of this title or an alternative film from Toeplitz Productions.
7. *Everything in Life* is listed under the title *Because of Love*.
8. I have not been able to find a film of this title.
9. *The Secret of Stamboul* is listed under the title *The Eunuch of Stamboul*.

APPENDIX III

Statutory Costs of British 'Long' Quota Films, 1 April 1938–30 November 1939

This appendix presents the costs of 171 British 'long' films (over 3,000 feet) registered by renters in the 18 months following the introduction of the Cinematograph Films Act of 1938. It includes the film, producer and statutory cost. The Bank of England reckoned the total production cost to be 50 per cent more than the statutory cost: e.g. a film with a statutory cost of £20,000 would indicate an estimated total cost of £30,000. This calculation is probably on the low side: the Board of Trade reckoned the total cost to be twice the statutory cost in drafting the 1938 Act. Quota eligibility was based on the statutory cost: £7,500 for single quota, £22,500 for double quota and £37,500 for treble quota. Films with a statutory cost below £7,500 were not eligible for renters' quota but could be included in exhibitors' quota.

Source: Bank of England Archive SMT 2/42: British Features 01.04.1938 to 30.11.1939.

Film (distributor/producer)	Length	Stat. cost	Quota
Anglo-American Film Distributors			
Consider Your Verdict (Charter Films)	3400 ft	£1,547	Exhibitors
Old Mother Riley Joins Up (British National)	6563 ft	£8,052	Single
Secret Journey (Anglo-American Film Corp)	6045 ft	£3,641	Exhibitors
Trunk Crime (Charter Films)	4600 ft	£2,156	Exhibitors
Two Days to Live (Venture Films)	4200 ft	£655	Exhibitors
Trouble for Two (Venture Films)	4014 ft	£626	Exhibitors
What Would You Do, Chum? (British National)	6753 ft	£8,271	Single
Associated British Film Distributors			
Blarney (O'D Productions)	5902 ft	£4,836	Exhibitors
Cheer, Boys, Cheer (Associated Talking Pictures)	7642 ft	£11,170	Single
Come on George! (Associated Talking Pictures)	7981 ft	£27,254	Double
The Four Just Men (Ealing)	7628 ft	£23,106	Double
The Gaunt Stranger (Northwood)	6631 ft	£8,511	Single
It's in the Air (Eltham)	7822 ft	£24,686	Double
Let's Be Famous (Associated Talking Pictures)	7316 ft	£9,884	Single

Mr Chedworth Steps Out (Cinesound)	7393 ft	£6,428	Exhibitors
Penny Paradise (Associated Talking Pictures)	6435 ft	£11,965	Single
The Rudd Family Goes to Town (Cinesound)	7040 ft	£5,678	Exhibitors
There Ain't No Justice (Ealing)	7262 ft	£9,576	Single
Trouble Brewing (Associated Talking Pictures)	7814 ft	£25,588	Double
The Ware Case (Associated Star Productions)	6823 ft	£23,156	Double
Young Man's Fancy (Ealing)	6965 ft	£22,811	Double

Associated British Picture Corporation

At the Villa Rose (ABPC)	6656 ft	£10,983	Single
Black Eyes (ABPC)	6419 ft	£14,097	Single
Black Limelight (ABPC)	6200 ft	£8,880	Single
Bonnie Scotland Calls You (ABPC)	3059 ft	£221	Exhibitors
Come Back to Erin (British National)	30124 ft	£699	Exhibitors
Dead Man's Shoes (ABPC)	6153 ft	£12,542	Single
The Gang's All Here (ABPC)	6877 ft	£28,414	Double
Hold My Hand (ABPC)	6709 ft	£	
Jamaica Inn (Mayflower Pictures)	9543 ft	£85,534	Treble
Jane Steps Out (ABPC)	6372 ft	£10,506	Single
Just William (ABPC)	6505 ft	£12,241	Single
Lassie from Lancashire (British National)	7364 ft	£2,309	Exhibitors
Luck of the Navy (ABFC)	6368 ft	£14,282	Single
Marigold (ABPC)	6666 ft	£11,441	Single
Meet Mr Penny (British National)	6335 ft	£9,356	Single
Murder in Soho (ABPC)	6346 ft	£11,851	Single
My Irish Molly (Argyle British Productions)	6300 ft	£6,145	Single
The Outsider (ABPC)	8220 ft	—	—
Poison Pen (ABPC)	7043 ft	£13,760	Single
Queer Cargo (ABPC)	5543 ft	£14,348	Single
St Martin's Lane (Mayflower Pictures)	7691 ft	£71,514	Exhibitors
Spies of the Air (British National)	6982 ft	£9,472	Single
Star of the Circus (ABPC)	6142 ft	£13,897	Single
The Terror (ABPC)	6594 ft	£10,951	Single
Vessel of Wrath (Mayflower Pictures)	8509 ft	£45,093	Treble
The Warning (British National)	3119 ft	£3,844	Exhibitors
Yellow Sands (ABPC)	6192 ft	£11,351	Single
Yes, Madam (ABPC)	6974 ft	£16,562	Single

BIED (British Independent Exhibitors' Distributors)

Scruffy (Vulcan)	5550 ft	£3,653	Exhibitors
Stepping Toes (John Baxter & John Barter)	7157 ft	£8,658	Single
You're the Doctor (New Georgian Productions)	7075 ft	£7,024	Exhibitors

British Lion Film Corporation

All at Sea (British Lion)	6563 ft	£11,090	Single
Around the Town (British Lion)	6115 ft	£8,569	Single
The Face at the Window (Pennant)	5911 ft	£4,998	Exhibitors
Home from Home (British Lion)	6593 ft	£13,701	Single
I've Got a Horse (British Lion)	6988 ft	£15,135	Single
Mad About Money (Morgan Productions)	6760 ft	£23,231	Double
No Parking (Herbert Wilcox Productions)	6390 ft	£15,135	Single
Old Iron (T. W. Productions)	7262 ft	£23,246	Double
The Return of the Frog (Imperator)	6831 ft	£17,139	Single
Riding High (Embassy)	6195 ft	£9,140	Single
What a Man (IFP)	6712 ft	£15,544	Single

British Screen Service

Hate in Paradise (Chesterfield Films)	5637 ft	£8,133	Single
Down Our Alley (British Screen Service)	5075 ft	£2,913	Exhibitors

Butcher's Film Service

Almost a Gentleman (Butcher's Film Service)	7043 ft	£5,456	Exhibitors
Anything to Declare (Butcher's Film Service)	6865 ft	£7,614	Single
The Girl Who Forgot (Butcher's Film Service)	6523 ft	£4,404	Exhibitors
Little Dolly Daydream (Butcher's Film Service)	6900 ft	£4,667	Exhibitors
Mountains o' Mourne (Butcher's Film Service)	7500 ft	£4,749	Exhibitors
Music Hall Parade (Butcher's Film Service)	7300 ft	£5,473	Exhibitors
Night Journey (Butcher's Film Service)	6900 ft	£6,846	Exhibitors
Old Mother Riley in Paris (Butcher's Film Service)	6379 ft	£5,177	Exhibitors
Old Mother Riley, MP (Butcher's Film Service)	6912 ft	£6,394	Exhibitors
Sword of Honour (Butcher's Film Service)	7570 ft	£7,592	Single

Columbia

Q-Planes (Harefield Productions)	7649 ft	—	
The Spy in Black (Harefield Productions)	7390 ft	—	
Ten Days in Paris (Irving Asher Productions)	7373 ft	£24,298	Double
Toilers of the Sea (Beaumont Film Productions)	7627 ft	£11,939	Single
Twenty-One Days (Denham Films)	6761 ft	£43,474	Treble

Equity British Films

Men Without Honour (Bernard Smith & Widgey Newman)	5225 ft	£420	Exhibitors

Exclusive Films

Runaway Ladies (International Player Productions)	4,423 ft	£3,800	Exhibitors
Two Minutes (GB International)	3574 ft	£1,433	Exhibitors

Fidelity Films

The Landlady (Charter Films)	3200 ft	£360	Exhibitors

First National Film Distributors

Confidential Lady (WBFN Productions)	6708 ft	6693 ft	Single
Dangerous Medicine (WBFN Productions)	6450 ft	£10,319	Single
The Good Old Days (WBFN Productions)	7129 ft	£26,349	Double
Many Tanks, Mr Atkins (WBFN Productions)	6145 ft	£10,576	Single
Thank Evans (WBFN Productions)	7015 ft	£12,289	Single
They Drive By Night (WBFN Productions)	7536 ft	£11,658	Single
Too Dangerous to Live (WBFN Productions)	6693 ft	£11,116	Single

General Film Distributors

Alf's Button Afloat (Gainsborough)	8062 ft	£32,307	Double
The Arsenal Stadium Mystery (G&S Films)	7775 ft	£18,694	Single
Break the News (Jack Buchanan Productions)	7037 ft	£69,516	Treble
Breakers Ahead (GB Instructional)	3318 ft	£1,002	Exhibitors
Convict 99 (Gainsborough)	7874 ft	£23,296	Double
Crackerjack (Gainsborough)	7134 ft	£28,053	Double
Follow Your Star (Belgrave Films)	7198 ft	£20,447	Single
The Frozen Limits (Gainsborough)	7587 ft	£28,074	Double
Full Speed Ahead (Trading Corp for Education)	3283 ft	£3,895	Exhibitors
Hey! Hey! USA (Gainsborough)	8189 ft	£28,703	Double
Kate Plus Ten (J. G. & R. B. Wainwright)	7250 ft	£26,837	Double
Kicking the Moon Around (Vogue Films)	7038 ft	£32,858	Double
Lightning Conductor (Pinebrook)	7131 ft	£11,448	Single
The Mikado (G&S Films)	8932 ft (LV) 8154 ft (SV)	£63,572	Treble
Old Bones of the River (Gainsborough)	8110 ft	£26,729	Double
On the Night of the Fire (G&S Films)	7981 ft	£29,531	Double
Pygmalion (Pascal Film Productions)	8609 ft	£38,358	Treble
A Spot of Bother (Pinebrook)	6348 ft	£11,650	Single
Strange Boarders (Gainsborough)	7038 ft	£30,511	Double
A Window in London (G&S Films)	6862 ft	£21,145	Single

Grand National Pictures

Discoveries (Grand National Pictures)	6.100 ft	£5,319	Exhibitors

I Killed the Count (Grafton Films)	8,024 ft	£10,784	Single
I Met a Murderer (Gamma Films)	7,089 ft	£11,591	Single
The Mind of Mr Reader (Jack Raymond Productions)	6,817 ft	£10,433	Single
The Missing People (Jack Raymond Productions)	6,322 ft	£8,337	Single

Liberty Films

Too Many Husbands (Liberty Films)	5352 ft	£1,071	Exhibitors

Mancunian Films

Calling All Crooks (Mancunian Films)	7763 ft	£6,760	Exhibitors

MGM

Ask a Policeman (Gainsborough Pictures)	7498 ft	£23,353	Double
The Citadel (MGM British Productions)	9970 ft	£90,157	Treble
Climbing High (Gainsborough Pictures)	7096 ft	£39,018	Treble
Goodbye, Mr Chips (MGM British Productions)	10,227 ft	£101,491	Treble
The Lady Vanishes (Gainsborough Pictures)	8650 ft	£39,492	Treble
The Lambeth Walk (Pinebrook Films)	7521 ft	£22,932	Double
A Yank at Oxford (MGM British Productions)	8471 ft	£111,913	Treble

Paramount

French Without Tears (Two Cities Films)	7757 ft	£29,411	Double
This Man is News (Pinebrook Films)	6947 ft	£7,871	Single
This Man in Paris (Pinebrook Films)	7745 ft	£13,324	Single
A Royal Divorce (Imperator Productions)	7623 ft	£37,506	Treble
The Silent Battle (Pinebrook Films)	6356 ft	£13,088	Single
A Stolen Life (Orion Productions)	8253 ft	£47,482	Treble

Pathé

Dark Eyes of London (John Argyle)	6853 ft	£7,739	Single
Dead Men Are Dangerous (Welwyn Studios)	6162 ft	£5,738	Exhibitors
Me and My Pal (Welwyn Studios)	6,626 ft	£8,053	Single
Night Alone (Welwyn Studios)	6865 ft	£7,717	Single
Pathé Parade of 1939 (Pathé)	3543 ft	£433	Exhibitors
Save a Little Sunshine (Welwyn Studios)	6798 ft	£7,766	Single

RKO Radio Pictures

Blind Folly (George Smith Productions)	7022 ft	£7,659	Single
Flying 55 (Admiral Film Company)	6439 ft	£8,127	Single

His Lordship Goes to Paris (George Smith Productions)	7254 ft	£7,612	Single
His Lordship Regrets (George Smith Productions)	7066 ft	£7,612	Single
Meet Maxwell Archer (RKO British Productions)	6655 ft	£7,813	Single
The Saint in London (RKO British Productions)	6749 ft	£14,932	Single
Shadowed Eyes (George Smith Productions)	6190 ft	£8,529	Single
Sixty Glorious Years (Imperator)	8,575 ft	£83,008	Treble
Weddings are Wonderful (George Smith Productions)	7583 ft	£7,583	Single

Tech

The Londoners (Realist Film Unit)	3,300 ft	£1,528	Exhibitors

Twentieth Century-Fox

A Girl Must Live (Gainsborough Pictures)	8349 ft	£27,281	Double
Inspector Hornleigh (Twentieth Century Prods)	7648 ft	£25,378	Double
Inspector Hornleigh on Holiday	7872 ft	£23,625	Double
Keep Smiling (Twentieth Century Productions)	8278 ft	£94,813	Treble
Shipyard Sally (Twentieth Century Productions)	7153 ft	£91,095	Treble
So This is London (Twentieth Century Prods)	7454 ft	£31,561	Double
We're Going to Be Rich (Fox British Productions)	7208 ft	£112,905	Treble
Where's That Fire? (Twentieth Century Prods)	6605 ft	£24,223	Double

Warner Bros. Film Distributors

Everything Happens to Me (WBFN Productions)	7453 ft	£20,706	Single
A Gentleman's Gentleman (WBFN Productions)	6338 ft	£12,911	Single
His Brother's Keeper (WBFN Productions)	6333 ft	£7,906	Single
Hoots Mon (WBFN Productions)	6966 ft	£8,204	Single
The Midas Touch (WBFN Productions)	6174 ft	£8,019	Single
Murder Will Out (WBFN Productions)	5926 ft	£8,048	Single
The Nursemaid That Disappeared (WBFN Productions)	8013 ft	£10,865	Single
The Return of Carol Deane (WBFN Productions)	6845 ft	£12,257	Single

United Artists

The Challenge (Denham Films)	7946 ft	£25,280	Double
The Drum (London Film Productions)	8726 ft	£73,563	Treble
The Four Feathers (London Film Productions)	10,381 ft	£96,619	Treble
An Englishman's Home (Aldwych Productions)	6900 ft	£27,839	Double
The Lion Has Wings (Alexander Korda)	6287 ft	£14,874	Single
Over the Moon (Denham Films)	7,112 ft	£106,992	Treble
Prison Without Bars (London Film Productions)	6993 ft	£26,135	Double

Unity Films

Beyond Our Horizon (G. H. W. Productions)	3851 ft	£1,391	Exhibitors

Viking Films

Take Off That Hat (Viking Films)	6984 ft (LV) 6984 ft (LV)	£5,378	Exhibitors

Notes:

* The ledger does not include cost information for *Q Planes* or *The Spy in Black*: the Prudential Archive (Box 2358) includes total costs of £67,503 for *Q Planes* and £46,862 for *The Spy in Black*.

+ No cost details are provided for *The Outsider*.

Bibliography

PRIMARY SOURCES

Archives

Aviva Group Archive, Norwich:
Commercial Union and British General Insurance archives.

Bank of England Archive, London:
SMT: Securities Management Trust, including papers relating to production costs of British films (1938–9) and the establishment of a film bank (1937–41).
EC: Exchange Control Commission, including papers relating to the Anglo-American Film Agreements of 1940 and 1942.

Barclays Group Archives, Manchester:
Barclays Bank: Advance registers, 1935–9.
Martins Bank: Standing Committee minutes, 1935–9.

British Film Institute Special Collections Unit, London:
Michael and Aileen Balcon Collection (MEB).
London Film Productions Collection (LFP).
Tom White Collection (TW).

Media History Digital Library, University of Wisconsin – Madison:
United Artists Corporate Minutes, 1930s.

The National Archives, Kew, London:
BT: Board of Trade Manufactures Department, papers and correspondence relating to the British film industry including quota legislation and the proposed film bank.
CAB: Cabinet Office minutes and papers, including papers on the Cinematograph Films Bill of 1927 and the proposed Films Commission.
INF: Ministry of Information, including production records and receipts of official films.
T: Treasury records, including papers and correspondence relating to the Anglo-American Film Agreements and the proposed film bank.

Prudential Group Archive, London:
Boxes 2352–2358: Financial records relating to London Film Productions, Denham Studios and Alexander Korda Film Productions.

Other sources:
British Film Producers' Association Executive Council Minute Books 1937–1940 (in author's possession).

Parliamentary proceedings (Hansard)

Parliamentary Debates: House of Commons, 5th Series (1909–81).
Parliamentary Debates: House of Lords, 5th Series (1909–81).

Official reports

Cinematograph Films Act, 1927: Report of the Committee appointed by the Board of Trade, Cmd. 5320 (November 1936).
First Report of the Cinematograph Films Council relating to the year ending 31 March, 1939, Cmd. 160 (18 July 1939).
Fifth Report of the Cinematograph Films Council for the year ending 31 March, 1943 (London: HMSO, 1943).
Minutes of Evidence Taken Before the Departmental Committee on Cinematograph Films together with Appendices and Index (London: HMSO, 1936).
Proposals for Legislation on Cinematograph Films, Cmd. 5529 (July 1937).
Tendencies to Monopoly in the Cinematograph Film Industry: Report of a Committee Appointed by the Cinematograph Films Council (London: HMSO, 1944).

Independent reports

The British Film Industry: A Report on its History and Present Organisation, with Special Reference to the Economic Problems of British Feature Film Production (London: Political and Economic Planning, 1952).
The Cinema: Its Present Position and Future Possibilities. Being the Report of and Chief Evidence Taken by the Cinema Commission of Enquiry instituted by the National Council of Morals (London: Williamson and Norgate, 1917).
Klingender, F. D., and Stuart Legg, *Money Behind the Screen: A Report Prepared on Behalf of the Film Council* (London: Lawrence and Wishart, 1937).

Newspapers and periodicals

The Bystander; Daily Chronicle; Daily Express; Daily Herald; Daily Mail; The Daily Telegraph; The Economist; Evening News; The Fife Free Press; The Financial News; The Financial Times; Los Angeles Times; Pall Mall Gazette; Reynolds's Illustrated News; The Scotsman; Sunday Dispatch; Sunday Express; Sunday Pictorial; The Times; Western Mail; The Yorkshire Post.

Film journals and trade papers

The Bioscope; The Cinema News and Property Gazette; Cinema Quarterly; Daily Film Renter; Documentary News Letter; The Era; Film Weekly; Kinematograph Weekly; Picturegoer Weekly; Sight & Sound; The Stage; Variety; World Film News.

Yearbooks

Kinematograph Year Book Diary and Directory (London: Kinematograph Publications, 1914–45).

Autobiographies and diaries

Balcon, Michael, *Michael Balcon Presents ... A Lifetime of Films* (London: Hutchinson, 1969).
Box, Sydney, *The Lion That Lost Its Way and Other Cautionary Tales of the Show Business Jungle*, ed. Andrew Spicer (Lanham, MA: Scarecrow Press, 2005).

Brunel, Adrian, *Nice Work: The Story of Thirty Years in British Film Production* (London: Forbes Roberston, 1949).
Dean, Basil, *Mind's Eye* (London: Hutchinson, 1973).
The Diaries of Robert Bruce Lockhart Volume I: 1915–1938, ed. Kenneth Young (London: Macmillan, 1973).
The Diaries of Robert Bruce Lockhart Volume II: 1939–1965, ed. Kenneth Young (London: Macmillan, 1980).
Hepworth, Cecil, *Came the Dawn: Memories of a Film Pioneer* (London: Phoenix House, 1951)
Korda, Michael, *Charmed Lives: A Family Romance* (London: Allen Lane, 1979).
Mycroft, Walter, *The Time of My Life: The Memoirs of a British Film Producer*, ed. Vincent Porter (Lanham, MD: Scarecrow Press, 2006).
Pascal, Valerie, *The Disciple and His Devil* (London: Michael Joseph, 1971).
Pearson, George, *Flashback* (London: George Allen & Unwin, 1957).
Powell, Michael, *A Life in Movies: An Autobiography* (London: William Heinemann, 1986).
Talbot, Frederick A., *Motion Pictures: How They Are Made and Worked* (London: William Heinemann, 1912), p. 114.
Wilcox, Herbert, *Twenty-Five Thousand Sunsets: The Autobiography of Herbert Wilcox* (New York: A. S. Barnes, 1969).

Secondary sources

Books and monographs

Aldgate, Anthony, and Jeffrey Richards, *Britain Can Take It: The British Cinema in the Second World War* (Oxford: Basil Blackwell, 1986).
Allen, Robert C., and Douglas Gomery, *Film History: Theory and Practice* (New York: McGraw-Hill, 1985).
Armes, Roy, *A Critical History of the British Cinema* (London: Secker & Warburg, 1978).
Balio, Tino, *United Artists: The Company Built by the Stars* (Madison: University of Wisconsin Press, 1976).
Barnes, John, *The Beginnings of the Cinema in England* (Newton Abbot: David & Charles, 1976).
Barnes, John, *Pioneers of the British Film: The Beginnings of the Cinema in England 1894–1901, Volume 3: 1898: The Rise of the Photoplay* (London: Bishopsgate Press, 1983).
Barnes, John, *The Rise of the Cinema in Great Britain: The Beginnings of the Cinema in England 1894–1901. Volume 2: Jubilee Year 1897* (London: Bishopsgate Press, 1983).
Barnes, John, *The Beginnings of the Cinema in England 1894–1901. Volume Four: Filming the Boer War 1899* (London: Bishopsgate Press, 1992).
Bernard, R. W., *A Century of Service: The Story of the Prudential 1848–1948* (London: Prudential Assurance, 1948).
Betts, Ernest, *The Film Business: A History of British Cinema 1896–1972* (London: George Allen & Unwin, 1973).
Botting, Josephine, *Adrian Brunel and British Cinema of the 1920s: The Artist versus the Moneybags* (Edinburgh: Edinburgh University Press, 2023).
Brown, Richard, and Barry Anthony, *A Victorian Film Enterprise: The History of the British Mutoscope and Biograph Company, 1897–1915* (Trowbridge: Flicks Books, 1999).
Brown, Simon, *Cecil Hepworth and the Rise of the British Film Industry 1899– 1911* (Exeter: University of Exeter Press, 2016).
Burrows, Jon, *The British Cinema Boom, 1909–1914: A Commercial History* (London: Palgrave Macmillan, 2017).
Chanan, Michael, *The Dream That Kicks: The Prehistory and Early Years of Cinema in Britain* (London: Routledge & Kegan Paul, 1980).

Chapman, James, *The British at War: Cinema, State and Propaganda, 1939–1945* (London: I. B. Tauris, 1998).
Chibnall, Steve, *Quota Quickies: The Birth of the British 'B' Film* (London: British Film Institute/Palgrave Macmillan, 2007).
Christie, Ian, *Robert Paul and the Origins of British Cinema* (Chicago, IL: University of Chicago Press, 2019).
Cook, Pam (ed.), *Gainsborough Pictures* (London: Cassell, 1997).
Curran, James, and Vincent Porter (eds), *British Cinema History* (London: Weidenfeld and Nicolson, 1983).
Daunton, Martin, *Wealth and Welfare: An Economic and Social History of Britain 1851–1951* (Oxford: Oxford University Press, 2007).
Davy, Charles (ed.), *Footnotes to the Film* (London: Lovat Dickson, 1937).
Dickinson, Margaret, and Sarah Street, *Cinema and State: The Film Industry and the British Government 1927–84* (London: British Film Institute, 1985).
Drazin, Charles, *Korda: Britain's Only Movie Mogul* (London: Sidgwick & Jackson, 2002).
Gilbert, Martin, *Prophet of Truth: Winston S. Churchill 1922–1939* (London: William Heinemann, 1976).
Glancy, H. Mark, *When Hollywood Loved Britain: The Hollywood 'British' Film, 1939–45* (Manchester: Manchester University Press, 1999).
Gledhill, Christine, *Reframing British Cinema 1918–1928: Between Restraint and Passion* (London: British Film Institute, 2003).
Gray, Frank, *The Brighton School and the Birth of British Film* (Cham, Switzerland: Palgrave Macmillan, 2019).
Hammond, Michael, *The Big Show: British Cinema Culture in the Great War 1914–1918* (Exeter: University of Exeter Press, 2006).
Hardy, Forsyth (ed.), *Grierson on the Movies* (London: Collins, 1946).
Hennessy, Elizabeth, *A Domestic History of the Bank of England* (Cambridge: Cambridge University Press, 2012).
Higson, Andrew, *Waving the Flag: Constructing a National Cinema in Britain* (Oxford: Clarendon Press, 1995).
Higson, Andrew (ed.), *Young and Innocent? The Cinema in Britain 1896–1930* (Exeter: University of Exeter Press, 2002).
Higson, Andrew, and Richard Maltby (eds), *'Film Europe' and 'Film America': Cinema, Commerce and Cultural Exchange 1920–1939* (Exeter: University of Exeter Press, 1999).
Koszarski, Richard, *An Evening's Entertainment: The Age of the Silent Feature Picture, 1915–1928* (Berkeley: University of California Press, 1990).
Kulik, Karol, *Alexander Korda: The Man Who Could Work Miracles* (London: W. H. Allen, 1975).
Lindgren, Ernest, *The Art of the Film: An Introduction to Film Appreciation* (London: George Allen & Unwin, 1948).
Low, Rachael, *The History of the British Film 1906–1914* (London: George Allen & Unwin, 1949).
Low, Rachael, *The History of the British Film 1914–1918* (London: George Allen & Unwin, 1950).
Low, Rachael, *The History of the British Film 1918–1929* (London: George Allen & Unwin, 1971).
Low, Rachael, *The History of the British Film 1929–1939: Film Making in 1930s Britain* (London: George Allen & Unwin, 1985).
Low, Rachael, and Roger Manvell, *The History of the British Film 1896–1906* (London: George Allen & Unwin, 1948).
McKernan, Luke, *Charles Urban: Pioneering the Non-Fiction Film in Britain and America, 1897–1925* (Exeter: University of Exeter Press, 2013).
Macnab, Geoffrey, *J. Arthur Rank and the British Film Industry* (London: Routledge, 1993).
Manvell, Roger, *Film* (Harmondsworth: Penguin, 1946 [1944]).
Mayer, J. P., *British Cinemas and their Audiences: Sociological Studies* (London: Dennis Dobson, 1948).

Moseley, Roy (ed.), *Evergreen: Victor Saville in His Own Words* (Carbondale: Southern Illinois University Press, 2000).
Murphy, Robert (ed.), *The British Cinema Book* (London: British Film Institute, 1997).
Napper, Lawrence, *British Cinema and Middlebrow Culture in the Interwar Years* (Exeter: University of Exeter Press, 2009).
Oakley, C. A., *Where We Came In: Seventy Years of the British Film Industry* (London: George Allen & Unwin, 1964).
Perry, George, *The Great British Picture Show* (London: Pavilion Books, 1985).
Porter, Laraine, 'The Talkies Come to Britain: British silent cinema and the transition to sound, 1928–30', in I. Q. Hunter, Laraine Porter and Justin Smith (eds), *The Routledge Companion to British Cinema History* (London: Routledge, 2017), pp. 87–98.
Reeves, Nicholas, *Official British Film Propaganda During the First World War* (London: Croom Helm, 1986).
Richards, Jeffrey, *The Age of the Dream Palace: Cinema and Society in Britain, 1930–1939* (London: Routledge & Kegan Paul, 1984).
Richards, Jeffrey (ed.), *The Unknown 1930s: An Alternative History of the British Cinema 1929–1939* (London: I. B. Tauris, 1998).
Robson, E. W. and M. M., *The Film Answers Back: An Historical Appreciation of the Cinema* (London: John Lane/The Bodley Head, 1939).
Rotha, Paul, with Richard Griffith, *The Film Till Now: A Survey of World Cinema* (London: Spring Books, 1967 [1930]).
Schatz, Thomas, *Boom and Bust: American Cinema in the 1940s* (Berkeley: University of California Press, 1997).
Sedgwick, John, *Popular Filmgoing in 1930s Britain: A Choice of Pleasures* (Exeter: University of Exeter Press, 2000).
Street, Sarah, *Transatlantic Crossings: British Feature Films in the United States* (London: Continuum, 2002).
Taylor, A. J. P., *English History 1914–1945* (Oxford: Oxford University Press, 1965).
Taylor, Philip M. (ed.), *Britain and the Cinema in the Second World War* (London: Methuen, 1987).
Thompson, Kristin, *Exporting Entertainment: America in the World Film Market 1907–1934* (London: British Film Institute, 1985).
Threadgall, Derek, *Shepperton Studios: An Independent View* (London: British Film Institute, 1994).
Truffaut, François, with Helen G. Scott, *Hitchcock* (London: Paladin, 1986 [1968]).
Turvey, Gerry, *The B&C Kinematograph Company and British Cinema: Early Twentieth-Century Spectacle and Melodrama* (Exeter: University of Exeter Press, 2021).
Walker, Greg, *The Private Life of Henry VIII: A British Film Guide* (London: I. B. Tauris, 2003).
Warren, Low, *The Film Game* (London: T. Werner Laurie, 1937).
Wood, Alan, *Mr Rank: A Study of J. Arthur Rank and British Films* (London: Hodder & Stoughton, 1952).
Wood, Linda (ed.), *British Films 1927–1939* (London: BFI Library Services, 1986).

Articles and book chapters

Asquith, Anthony, 'The Tenth Muse Climbs Parnassus', *The Penguin Film Review*, 1 (August 1946), pp. 10–26.
Badsey, Stephen, '*Battle of the Somme*: British war-propaganda', *Historical Journal of Film, Radio and Television*, 3: 2 (1983), pp. 99–115.
Barr, Charles, 'Introduction: Amnesia and schizophrenia', in Charles Barr (ed.), *All Our Yesterdays: 90 Years of British Cinema* (London: British Film Institute, 1986), pp. 1–30.
Bottomore, Stephen, 'From the Factory Gate to "Home Talent" Drama: An international overview of local films in the silent era', in Vanessa Toulmin, Simon Popple and Patrick Russell (eds),

The Lost World of Mitchell and Kenyon: Edwardian Britain on Film (London: British Film Institute, 2004), p. 36.

Browning, H. E., and A. A. Sorrell, 'Cinema and Cinemagoing in Great Britain', *Journal of the Royal Statistical Society*, 117: 2 (1954), pp. 133–65.

Burrows, Jon, and Richard Brown, 'Financing the Edwardian Cinema Boom, 1909–1914', *Historical Journal of Film, Radio and Television*, 30: 1 (2010), pp. 1–20.

Burton, Alan, and Julian Petley, 'Introduction', *Journal of Popular British Cinema*, 1 (1998), pp. 2–5.

Chapman, James, '"The Billings Verdict": *Kine Weekly* and the British box office, 1936–62', *Journal of British Cinema and Television*, 20: 2 (2023), pp. 200–38.

Chapman, James, 'Hitchcock's *Number Seventeen* (1932) and the British Film Quota', *Historical Journal of Film, Radio and Television*, 43: 4 (2023), pp. 1183–91.

Chapman, James, 'British Quota Production and Film Costs in the Early 1930s', *Journal of British Cinema and Television*, 21: 2 (2024), pp. 153–92.

Chapman, Llewella, '"The highest salary ever paid to a human being": Creating a database of film costs from the Bank of England Archive', *Journal of British Cinema and Television*, 19: 4 (2022), pp. 470–94.

Chibnall, Steve, 'Hollywood-on-Thames: The British productions of Warner Bros.–First National, 1931–1945', *Historical Journal of Film, Radio and Television*, 39: 4 (2019), pp. 687–724.

Collinson, Naomi, 'The Legacy of Max Schach', *Film History*, 15: 3 (2003), pp. 376–89.

Garside, W. R., 'Party Politics, Political Economy and British Protectionism, 1919–1932', *History*, 269 (1998), pp. 46–65.

Glancy, H. Mark, 'MGM Film Grosses, 1924–1948: The Eddie Mannix ledger', *Historical Journal of Film, Radio and Television*, 12: 2 (1992), pp. 127–43.

Gough-Yates, Kevin, 'Jews and Exiles in British Cinema', *The Leo Baeck Institute Year Book*, 37: 1 (1992), pp. 517–41.

Gruner, Olly, '"Good Business, Good Policy, Good Patriotism": The British film weeks of 1924', *Historical Journal of Film, Radio and Television*, 32: 1 (2013), pp. 41–56.

Miskell, Peter, 'Seduced by the Silver Screen: Film addicts, critics and cinema regulation in Britain in the 1930s and 1940s', *Business History*, 47: 3 (2005), pp. 433–48.

Morris, Nathalie, 'An Eminent British Series: *The Adventures of Sherlock Holmes* and the Stoll Film Company, 1921–23', *Journal of British Cinema and Television*, 4: 1 (2007), pp. 18–36.

Ramsden, J. A., 'Baldwin and Film', in Nicholas Pronay and D. W. Spring (eds), *Propaganda, Politics and Film, 1918–45* (London: Macmillan, 1982), pp. 126–43.

Richards, Jeffrey, and Jeffrey Hulbert, 'Censorship in Action: The case of *Lawrence of Arabia*', *Journal of Contemporary History*, 19: 1 (1984), pp. 154–67.

Rowson, Simon, 'A Statistical Survey of the Cinema Industry in Great Britain in 1934', *Journal of the Royal Statistical Society*, 99: 1 (1936), pp. 67–119.

Sedgwick, John, 'The Market for Feature Films in Britain in 1934: A viable national cinema', *Historical Journal of Film, Radio and Television*, 14: 1 (1994), pp. 15–36.

Sedgwick, John, 'Michael Balcon's Close Encounter with the American Market, 1934–1936', *Historical Journal of Film, Radio and Television*, 16: 3 (1996), pp. 333–48.

Sedgwick, John, 'The British Film Industry's Production Sector Difficulties in the Late 1930s', *Historical Journal of Film, Radio and Television*, 17: 1 (1997), pp. 49–66.

Street, Sarah, 'Alexander Korda, Prudential Assurance and British Film Finance in the 1930s', *Historical Journal of Film, Radio and Television*, 6: 2 (1986), pp. 161–79.

Street, Sarah, 'The Prudential Group Archive: Alexander Korda, London Film Productions and Denham Studios', *Journal of British Cinema and Television*, 19: 4 (2022), pp. 447–69.

Street, Sarah, 'Requisitioning Film Studios in Wartime Britain', *Historical Journal of Film, Radio and Television*, 43: 1 (2023), pp. 65–89.

Index

ABC *see* Associated British Cinemas
Abdul the Damned, 110
ABPC *see* Associated British Picture Corporation
Accused, 109
Acres, Birt, 8
ACT *see* Association of Cine Technicians
Action for Slander, 94
Aldgate Trustees, 109–10, 113, 115–16, 129, 131
Aldwych Films, 164
Alexander Korda Film Productions, 97–9
Alf's Button, 63
Alf's Button Afloat, 165
Alibi, 184
Allen, A. G., 205
Allen, Robert C., 1
Alliance Film Corporation, 37, 38
Allport, Fay, 151, 153, 193
Amalgamated Cinematograph Theatres, 16
Amalgamated Studios, 204
Amazing Quest of Mr Bliss, The, 109
American Mutoscope and Biograph Company, 12
Anglo-American Film Distributors, 167
Anglo-American Film Exchange Agreement, 191–8
Anthony, Barry, 10, 11, 12
Antony and Cleopatra, 19
Arabian Nights, 189
Archibald, George, 216
Argyle, John, 166, 168
Armes, Roy, 10
Arnold, Tom, 79
Arsenal Stadium Mystery, The, 97
Asher, Irving, 82, 97, 164
Ashfield, Lord, 43
Ask a Policeman, 162
Asquith, Anthony, 2–3
Associated British Cinemas, 57, 60
Associated British Film Distributors, 66, 129, 166–7

Associated British Picture Corporation, 58, 104, 107, 130–1, 144, 157, 166, 183–4, 196, 204–5, 212, 222; *see also* British International Pictures
Associated Provincial Picture Houses, 16, 26
Associated Talking Pictures, 66, 73, 82, 108, 131, 166, 222; *see also* Ealing Studios
Association of Cine Technicians, 73–4, 143–4, 150, 154, 164, 209
Atkinson, G. A., 116–17, 152
Atlanta Film Syndicate, 38
Atlantic, 58
Atlantic Ferry, 196
Atlantic Film Productions, 93, 103, 107
Austin, L. St John, 110
Aviva Group Archive, 5

Back Room Boy, 184
Baker, F. W., 129
Baker, Reginald, 39, 66, 129, 209
Balcon, Michael, 4, 5, 6, 33, 60–1, 63, 73, 161–2, 166, 181, 209–10
Baldwin, Stanley, 36, 40
Ball, (Sir) Joseph, 131
Bank of America, 64, 94, 98, 158, 188–9
Bank of England, 1, 5, 105, 108, 114, 124–37, 147, 158–9, 172–80, 188–92, 195–6, 208–9, 223
Bankers Trust (New York), 98–9
Banks, Monty, 163
Banque Belge, 108
Barclays Bank, 108, 109, 114
Barker Motion Photography, 30
Barker, Will, 19
Barnes, John, 9, 12
Barr, Charles, 13
Barrymore, Lionel, 162
Barton Mystery, The, 78, 81
Bass, William, 16
Battle of the Ancre and the Advance of the Tanks, 32
Battle of the Somme, 31–2

Battle of Waterloo, The, 19, 31
Baxter, Beverley, 111
Baxter, John, 167
Bayliss-Smith, Stanley, 105, 109, 116
Beaconsfield Studios, 65, 167
Beaumont Film Productions, 115
Beaverbrook, Lord, 41, 194
BECTU Oral History Project, 74
Bell-Bottom George, 189
Bells Go Down, The, 184
Berger, Ludwig, 98
Bergner, Elisabeth, 112
Bergner-Czinner Productions, 105
Bethune, (Sir) Edward, 55
Betts, Ernest, 9, 105, 181
Big Blockade, The, 184
Billings, R. H. ('Josh'), 162
Bioscope, The, 6, 8, 15, 27, 28, 47–8, 52, 82
Birth of a Nation, The, 28
Bishopsgate Nominees, 63
Black Narcissus, 216
Black Sheep of Whitehall, The, 184
Black Swan, The, 189
Black, Edward, 64
Blackmail, 58, 65
Blanche Fury, 217
Blattner Film Corporation, 53
Blarney, 158
Blighty, 74
Blind Polly, 165
Blind Spot, The, 82
Bloomfield, Albert Henry, 31
Blue Lagoon, The, 217
Board of Trade, 1, 5, 10, 24, 27, 40–1, 44, 56, 62, 71, 75–6, 115, 128, 140–52, 163, 172–84, 191–8, 205, 209–14
Boot, Charles, 211
Bottomore, Stephen, 12
Box, Sydney, 6
Break the News, 165
Brent, Romney, 163
British Actors' Film Company, 30
British and Colonial Kinematograph Company, 18, 30, 31
British and Continental Films, 105
British and Dominions Film Corporation, 53, 65–6, 78, 80–1, 131, 146, 222
British and Foreign Films, 37, 53
British Artistic Films, 114
British Associated Cinematograph Films, 53
British Aviation Pictures, 183

British Cine Alliance, 93, 105
British Exhibitors Films, 54
British Film Institute, 5, 142
British Film Producers' Association, 175
'British Film Weeks', 40
British Filmcraft Productions, 52, 55
British General Insurance Company, 5, 108, 109, 110
British Independent Exhibitors' Distributors, 167
British Instructional Films, 166
British International Pictures, 5, 6, 52, 57–9, 65, 77, 110; *see also* Associated British Picture Corporation
British Kinematograph Society, 1
British Lion Film Corporation, 52, 65, 78, 83, 129, 131, 167, 208, 222
British Movietonews, 56, 141
British Mutoscope and Biograph Company, 11–12
British National Film League, 39
British National Films, 86, 105, 108, 128, 167, 173, 181, 183–4, 203, 208, 211–12
British National Pictures, 57
British Oak Insurance Company, 118
British Screen Productions, 53, 55
British Sound Film Productions, 75
British Talking Pictures, 55
Broadwest Film Company, 30
Broken Blossoms, 114
Bromhead, Alfred, 39, 59, 61
Bromhead, Reginald, 59, 61
Brown, Richard, 10, 11, 12
Brown, Simon, 10, 13
Brunel, Adrian, 6, 74, 79, 153–4
Buchanan, Jack, 165, 166
Buckingham Film Productions, 105, 111–12
Bunbury, Evelyn, 128, 131, 134–5
Burlington Films, 52
Burrows, Jon, 2, 15, 17, 18
Busman's Honeymoon, 192
Butcher's Film Service, 30, 39, 78–80, 129, 168
Butt, (Sir) Alfred, 46
Bystander, The, 111

Caesar and Cleopatra, 4, 199, 215
Caledonian Associated Cinemas, 168, 178
Cameron, A. C., 142
Campbell, (Sir) Nigel, 135, 182
Capitol Film Corporation, 5, 108, 111, 119, 130
Capitol Film Productions, 93, 105, 110

Cardinal, The, 115
Carnival, 38
Catherine the Great, 88, 91–2
Cavalcade Film Corporation, 105
Cecil Films, 111, 130
Challenge, The, 94, 164
Chamberlain, Neville, 128, 131, 153, 177
Chanan, Michael, 10
Chaplin, Charles, 94–5
Charles Urban Trading Company, 12, 18, 30
Chase National Bank (New York), 108, 112
Chibnall, Steve, 2
Christie, Ian, 10
Chu Chin Chow, 63
Churchill, Winston, 40, 46–7, 93, 177
Cinema Commission of Enquiry (1917), 14, 18, 24–5, 26
Cinema News and Property Gazette, The, 6
Cinema Quarterly, 113
Cinematograph Company, 11
Cinematograph Act (1909), 15
Cinematograph Exhibitors' Association, 20, 42, 143–4, 148–9, 150, 152–3, 181
Cinematograph Films Act (1927), 2, 5, 24, 36, 38, 44–9, 52, 56, 65, 71, 73, 75, 83, 104, 126, 140
Cinematograph Films Act (1938), 5, 116, 138, 151–4, 157–61, 166, 168, 174, 191, 195
Cinematograph Films Advisory Committee, 1, 140–2, 151
Cinematograph Films Council, 137, 151, 157–8, 174–8, 180, 194, 209, 212
Cinematograph Finance Corporation, 16–17
Cinesound Productions, 83
Citadel, The, 157, 160–2
Citrine, (Sir) Walter, 212
City Film Corporation, 108, 113
Clark, Robert, 204
Clarke, (Sir) Basil, 55
Climbing High, 162
Close-Up, 54
Clue of the New Pin, The, 65
Clydesdale Bank, 59, 89
Cobbold, Cameron, 173–4
Cohen, Harvey, 82
Collinson, Naomi, 104
Columbia Pictures, 97, 164, 189, 197–8
Coming of Christopher Columbus, The, 19
Commercial Bank of Scotland, 57, 59
Commercial Union, 5, 108, 117
Common Touch, The, 184

Companies Act (1907), 15
Coney Island, 189
Convict 99, 165
Conquest of the Air, 93
Constant Nymph, The, 74
Conway, Jack, 161
Co-operative Association of Producers and Distributors, 166
Corfield, John, 128–9, 203
Counsel's Opinion, 87
Courtauld, John, 203
Courtauld, Stephen, 66, 173, 209–10
Cowan, Lawrence, 29
Coward, Noël, 199
C. T. Bowring & Co., 89
Crackerjack, 165
Craig, (Sir) Ernest Gordon, 56, 73, 141
Crazy Gang, 64
Cricklewood Studios, 79
Crime at Blossoms, The, 81
Crime Over London, 109
Cripps, (Sir) Stafford, 118
Criterion Film Productions, 105, 107, 108–9, 115
Crocker, W. A., 116
Cronin, A. J., 162
Crown Film Unit, 194
Crump, Percy, 89, 96
Crump, William A., 115
Cunliffe-Lister, (Sir) Philip, 24, 40, 42–6
Czinner, Paul, 105, 164

D&P Films, 97–8, 174, 194
Daily Bioscope (London), 14
Daily Chronicle, 47
Daily Express, 41, 71, 109, 111
Daily Film Renter, 181
Daily Herald, 47
Daily Mail, 47, 48, 61
Daily Mirror, 213
Daily Telegraph, 114
Dalton, Hugh, 182, 209–13
Dangerous Moonlight, 193
Dark Eyes of London, 166
Dark Journey, 94
Daughter of the Gods, A, 28
Davenport, Nicholas, 172–3
Day, Harry, 46, 47
Dean, Basil, 66, 73, 166
Dear Octopus, 184
Del Giudice, Filippo, 208

Delta Films, 80
Demi-Paradise, The, 183, 208
Denham Picture Houses, 60
Denham Productions, 94
Denham Securities, 89, 94, 134
Denham Studios, 89, 93–4, 96–7, 161, 172, 183, 194, 204, 208
Dent, Arthur, 57
Deutsch, Oscar, 206
Deutsche–Russiche Film Alliance, 55
Diamond Cut Diamond, 81
Dickinson, Margaret, 1–2, 49, 203
Dickson, W. K. L., 12
Dictator, The, 66, 110
Dietrich, Marlene, 95
Diggers, 83
Discord, 78, 81
Dishonour Bright, 111, 115
District Bank, 57, 108, 112
Divorce of Lady X, The, 88, 96
Dixey, A. C. N., 86
Dixon, Campbell, 114
Donat, Robert, 95
Down on the Farm, 83
Down Our Street, 81
Doyle, (Sir) Arhur Conan, 37
Dreaming Lips, 111–12, 115
Dreyer, Carl, 55
Drum, The, 88, 96, 98, 164
Duncan, (Sir) Andrew, 177–9, 182
Dundee Courier, 40
Dusty Ermine, 114
Dupont, E. A., 58

Eagle-Lion Film Distributors, 215
Eagle Squadron, 189
Ealing Studios, 5, 66, 80, 82, 166, 173, 181, 183–4, 209–10; *see also* Associated Talking Pictures
Easy Money, 217
Eckman, Sam, 81, 145, 209
Economist, The, 5–6, 52, 53, 56, 60, 63, 48–9, 113, 147, 150, 192, 205–6, 210, 211, 213, 214
Edison, Thomas, 8, 9, 12
Edwards, George, 18
Efftree Productions, 83
Electric Theatres, 16–17, 26
Elephant Boy, 88, 94
Eliza Comes to Stay, 114
Ellis, Frank, 109
Elstree Studios, 54, 57, 77, 81, 166, 194, 205

Elvin, George, 174
'Embassy Agreement', 191–2; *see also* Anglo-American Film Exchange Agreement
Emergency Powers (Defence) Act (1939), 188
Engel, Samuel G., 163
Englishman's Home, An, 164
Entertainment Duty, 32, 58, 188
Equitable Life Assurance Company, 124
Equity British Films, 76
Era, The, 30, 79, 116, 144, 157
Erich Pommer Productions, 105, 107
Escape, 66
Esther Waters, 217
Evening News, 104
Evergreen, 63
Exchange Control Commission, 5, 188

Fairbanks Jr, Douglas, 108
Fairbanks Sr, Douglas, 94
Famous Players-Lasky Corporation, 26, 39
Fanny by Gaslight, 2, 188
Farewell Again, 94
Farrow, Leslie, 131
Federation of British Industries, 41, 143
Fellner, Herman, 111
Fennelly, R. D., 143, 149, 152–3
Field, Sid, 215
Fields, Gracie, 66, 82, 163
film bank, 135–7, 171–84
Film Booking Office, 39
Film Company of Great Britain, 27
'Film Council', 131
Film Finance Corporation, 174–82, 204, 212–13; *see also* film bank
Films Commission, 148–50, 178–83
Financial Times, The, 5–6, 11, 13–14, 16, 17, 18, 38, 48, 58, 59, 90, 116, 154, 158, 166, 176, 177
Fire Over England, 94
First National Film Distributors, 80, 82, 165
First National-Pathé, 57
First of the Few, The, 183, 188
First World War, 24–33
Flag Lieutenant, The, 78
Flaherty, Robert, 95
Flemish Farm, The, 183, 208
Fletcher, E. G., 204
Flying Fifty-Five, 165
Flying Fortress, 183
Flying Squad, The, 78
For Whom the Bell Tolls, 188

Foreign Correspondent, 189
Foreman Went to France, The, 184
49th Parallel, 188
Four Feathers, The, 88, 97, 99, 158, 160, 164
Fox, William, 61
Fox Film Corporation, 26, 39, 61, 64, 82, 146; *see also* Twentieth Century-Fox
Foy Investments, 206
Frece, (Sir) Walter de, 38
French Without Tears, 164
Friese-Greene, William, 8
Frozen Limits, The, 165
Fuller, W. R., 150

G&S Films, 97, 165
Gainsborough Pictures, 5, 53, 54–5, 59, 60–1, 74, 77, 162, 163–4, 181, 184, 205, 208
Gaitskell, Hugh, 198, 210–12, 214
Galsworthy, John, 66
Gang's All Here, The, 166
Garrett-Klement Productions, 105, 107–8
Garrett, Robert, 109
Gaumont-British Picture Corporation, 5, 52, 59–64, 77, 107, 125, 129–31, 146, 161, 221, 205–6
Gaumont Film Company, 12, 13, 30, 59, 39
Gay Adventure, The, 115
General Cinema Finance Corporation, 129, 131, 203, 206, 207
General Electric Company, 65
General Film Distributors, 97, 107–8, 111, 112, 115, 129–31, 165, 172, 191, 203, 205, 208
General Film Renting Company, 37, 39
General Strike, 36
General Theatres Corporation, 60
Gentle Sex, The, 208
George V, King, 93
German Retreat and the Battle of Arras, The, 32
Gerrard Industries, 90
Get Cracking, 189
Ghost Goes West, The, 88, 91–2
Ghost of St Michael's, The, 184
Gilliat, Sidney, 215
Girl from Maxim's, The, 87
Girl Must Live, A, 164
Glancy, Mark, 189
Glanvill, Enthoven & Co., 109–10, 118–19
Gledhill, Christine, 39
Godal, Edward, 36
Golden Cage, The, 78
Goldsmith, Francis, 124

Goldwyn, Sam, 94
Gomery, Douglas, 1
Gone With the Wind, 189
Good Companions, The, 75
Goodbye, Mr Chips, 160–2
Goose Steps Out, The, 184
Gordon, Leon, 162
Gough-Yates, Kevin, 86
Grafton Films, 108, 111, 167
Grafton, Nicholas, 55
Graham, J. C., 81, 145
Graham, William, 141
Grand National Films, 167
Graves, Robert, 93
Gray, Frank, 10
Great Expectations, 216, 217
Great Game, The, 63
Green for Danger, 217
Grierson, John, 2, 4, 143
Griffith, D. W., 28
Griffith, Corinne, 81
Griffiths, D. E., 145, 178
Grossmith, George, 87
Grosvenor Sound Films, 105, 115
Group Holdings, 206
Grune, Karl, 110
Guedalla, Philip, 212
Guthrie, (Sir) Connop, 89, 90, 94, 97, 125, 146
Gwenn, Edmund, 162
Gypsy Melody, 114

Hagen, Julius, 78, 114, 161
Haggar, William, 8, 10
Hakim, Eric, 81
Halifax, Lord, 152, 196
Hallmark Productions, 76, 80
Hamilton, (Sir) Horace, 142
Hamlet, 216
Hammond, Michael, 28
Harefield Productions, 97
Havelock-Allan, Anthony, 74, 215
Hay, Will, 64
Hello, Frisco, Hello, 189
Hellman, Marcel, 105, 208
Henry V, 4, 199, 208, 215
Henry VIII, 19
Here's George, 79
Heroes of the Mine, 80
Hepworth, Cecil, 6, 8, 10, 11, 18, 19, 25, 29, 32–3
Hepworth Manufacturing Company, 12, 18, 30

Hepworth Picture Plays, 33
Hey! Hey! USA, 165
High Treason, 63
Higson, Andrew, 39
Hiking with Mademoiselle, 80
Hillman, George, 90
Hirst, (Sir) Hugo, 65
His Lordship Goes to Paris, 165
His Lordship Regrets, 165
His Royal Highness, 83
Hitchcock, Alfred, 5, 58, 77
Hobson, Valerie, 97
Holden, (Sir) Henry Cassie, 106
Holiday Camp, 217
Holmes, Joseph Stanley, 142
Howard, Leslie, 208
Hughes, Harry, 113
Humphreys, Basil, 113
Hungry Hill, The, 217
Hutchinson, William, 38
Hyde Park Corner, 115

I, Claudius, 92, 93
Ideal Films, 1, 28, 30, 59, 78
Illegal, 82
Impassive Footman, The, 82
Imperial Chemical Industries, 65, 177
Imperial Conference (1926), 44
Imperial Pictures, 19, 31, 39
Imperial Studios (Elstree), 65
Improper Duchess, The, 113
In the Soup, 114
In Which We Serve, 188, 199, 208
Ince, Ralph, 165
Independent Producers, 208–10, 215–16, 223
Inseperables, The, 55
Inspector Hornleigh, 164
Inspector Hornleigh on Holiday, 164
Insult, 81
International Productions, 80
International Quartet, 111
International Talking Picture Productions, 55–6
Intolerance, 28
Islington Studios, 54, 77, 163–4
It is for England, 29
It's That Man Again, 184

J. Arthur Rank Organisation *see* Rank Organisation
Jack Raymond Productions, 167
Jackson, Jerome, 74, 165

Jamaica Inn, 160, 166
Jane Eyre, 189
Jarratt, Arthur, 73, 174, 178, 181, 205
Jazz Singer, The, 54
Jericho, 111–12, 116
John Clein Productions, 114
John Stafford Productions, 80
Joint Trade Committee (1926), 43
Joint Trade Committee (1937), 149
Jones, Griffith, 162
Journey's End, 61, 63
Juan Jose, 55
Juggernaut, 114
Jungle Book, The, 99
Jupp, R. T., 16
Jury, (Sir) William, 19, 31

Kane, Robert, 163
Kate Plus Ten, 165
Keeling, (Sir) John, 208
Keep Smiling, 160, 163
Kennedy, Joseph, 152, 190–1
Kicking the Moon Around, 165
Kilroy, A., 192–3
Kinematograph & Lantern Weekly, The, 16, 19, 26; see also *Kinematograph Weekly*
Kinematograph Manufacturers' Association, 20, 30
Kinematograph Renters' Society, 1, 20, 42, 143–5, 150, 178, 180–1
Kinematograph Weekly, 6, 41, 43, 48, 55, 61, 64, 73, 79, 80, 83, 96, 106, 107, 109, 112, 116, 141, 148, 162, 171, 181, 188, 189, 205, 206, 213, 215; see also *Kinematograph & Lantern Weekly*
Kinematograph Year Book, 19, 24, 26, 27, 32, 37, 38, 40, 52, 184, 223
King Arthur Was a Gentleman, 184
King John, 12
King of the Castle, 113
King of the Ritz, 78
King, Alexander, 168, 178
King, George, 161
Kinnoch-Clarke, (Sir) Klement, 59
Kipps, 193
Klement, Otto, 105, 109
Klingender, F. D., 106–7
Knight Without Armour, 88, 94–5
Korda, Alexander, 5, 66, 86–100, 104, 126, 146, 154, 158, 164, 189, 204, 211, 212, 221–3
Korda, Michael, 87, 89–90, 98

Korda, Zoltan, 95, 98
Kossack, 115–16

Lady Hamilton see That Hamilton Woman
Lady Vanishes, The, 157, 162, 168
Lamp Still Burns, The, 208
Lanchester, Elsa, 87
Land Without Music, 111, 115
Lapworth, Charles, 55
Last Days of Pompeii, The, 19
Laughton, Charles, 87, 93, 166
Launder, Frank, 215
Law Debenture Corporation, 59
Lawrence of Arabia, 92, 93
Lean, David, 100, 209–10, 215
Lee, Lord (Lord Lee of Fareham), 61
Legg, Stuart, 106–7
Leicester Square Theatre (London), 88
Leigh, Vivien, 162
Let the People Sing, 184
Lever, E. H., 92, 96, 97, 114, 127–8, 131, 134–5
Life and Death of Colonel Blimp, The, 183, 188
Life of Charles Peace, The, 10
Lightfoot, Eric, 204
Lilac Domino, 111, 116
Lily Christine, 81
Lindenberg, Paul, 129–31
Lindgren, Ernest, 3
Lion Has Wings, The, 98, 164
Little Dolly Daydream, 168
Little Lady at the Big House, 111
Lloyd's of London, 116–17, 172
Lloyds Bank, 38, 66, 89, 108, 114, 131, 134
Lockhart, Robert Bruce, 105
Lockwood, Margaret, 167
Lodger, The, 78
London and Continental Pictures, 115
London and General Electric Theatres Company, 18
London Assurance Company, 109
London Belongs To Me, 217
London Film Company, 26, 28
London Film Productions, 5, 66, 78, 81, 86–97, 99, 104, 125, 131, 134, 146, 164
London Independent Trading Company, 39
London Screen Plays, 115
London Town, 215
Look Up and Laugh, 66
Looking on the Bright Side, 66, 82
Lord Byron Cinema (Paris), 88

Los Angeles Times, 26
Loudon, Norman, 78–9, 116
Love from a Stranger, 111–12, 115
Love in Exile, 111
Love on the Dole, 184
Love on the Spot, 82
Low, Rachael, 1, 8–9, 24, 28, 30, 32, 37, 49, 74, 76, 86, 119, 204
Lukas, Paul, 163
Lyttelton, Oliver, 179–81

MacDonald, James Ramsay, 45–6
Macnab, Geoffrey, 217
Mademoiselle Docteur, 111–12, 115–16
Magic Box, The, 8
Maid of the Mountains, 77
Major Barbara, 172–3, 177
Malins, Geoffrey, 31
Mallon, J. J., 142
Man in Grey, The, 184, 188
Man in the Mirror, The, 114
Man Who Could Work Miracles, The, 88, 91
Mancunian Film Corporation, 168
Mander, Geoffrey, 73, 141
Mannock, P. L., 55, 73, 141, 190, 215
Manorfield Investments, 206
Manvell, Roger, 3, 8
Manxman, The, 28
Marble Arch Pavilion, 59
Marriage of Corbal, The, 111
Marriot, R. B., 157
Marsh, Hubert T., 65
Martins Bank, 108–9, 115
Matter of Life and Death, A, 4, 216
Matthews, A. E., 38
Maurier, Gerald du, 38
Maxwell, Catherine, 204–5
Maxwell, John, 57–9, 64, 66, 104–5, 144–5, 157, 196, 204
Mayflower Pictures Corporation, 166
McCann, (Sir) Harry, 65
McDowell, J. B., 31
McKenna Duties, 40–1
McKenna, (Sir) Reginald, 27, 32
McKernan, Luke, 10, 12
Media History Digital Library, 5
Meet Maxwell Archer, 165
Men Are Not Gods, 91
Men of Tomorrow, 87
Menjou, Adolphe, 81
Metcalfe, C. P., 142

Metro-Goldwyn-Mayer, 78, 81, 83, 126–7, 145, 161, 192, 197, 212, 222
Metropolis and Bradford Trust, 61–4, 205, 207
MGM *see* Metro-Goldwyn-Mayer
Midland Bank, 56, 63, 89–90, 106, 108
Mikado, The, 165
Milder, Max, 196, 204–5
Mill on the Floss, The, 114
Millar, Adelqui, 55
Millions Like Us, 184
Mind of Mr Reeder, The, 167
Ministry of Information (1918), 24–5
Ministry of Information (1939–46), 163
Miranda, 217
'Miss Annabella', 163
Miss London Ltd, 184
Mrs Miniver, 188
Mitchell and Kenyon, 12–13
Moffat, William, 205
Money Behind the Screen (book), 106–7, 131
Money for Speed, 80
Montgomery, H. B., 25–6
Morgan, Sidney, 29
Moscow Nights, 91
Motion Picture Patents Company, 9, 13
Motion Picture Producers and Distributors of America, 38, 150–1
Mountains of Mourne, 168
Moyne Committee, 73, 105, 126–7
Moyne, Lord (Lord Moyne of Bury St Edmunds), 142
MPPDA *see* Motion Picture Producers and Distributors of America
Much Too Shy, 189
Munro, Gordon, 128, 131
My Irish Molly, 168
My Learned Friend, 184
Mycroft, Walter, 6, 111

Nakhimoff, Edward, 80
National Archives, 10
National Council of Public Morals, 14, 24
National Film Finance Corporation, 223
National Film Library, 2
National Government, 58
National Provincial Bank, 63, 108, 111, 173, 177, 207
National Provincial Distributors, 114
Neame, Ronald, 215
Neel, Louis, 110
Nell Gwyn, 66

New Era National Pictures, 53, 55
New World Pictures, 93, 163
Newman, Widgey, 80
Newton, Lord, 41
Nine Men, 184
No Funny Business, 80
No Other Tiger, 111
Norman, Montagu, 114, 124, 127–8, 134–5, 137–8, 175–7, 179–80, 197
Norton, Richard, 174, 194
Number Seventeen, 5, 77–8
Nurse Edith Cavell, 158

O'Sullivan, Maureen, 162
Oakley, Charles, 9
Oberon, Merle, 93
Odeon Theatres, 206–7, 221
Old Bones of the River, 165
Old Mother Riley Cleans Up, 184
Old Mother Riley Joins Up, 167
Old Mother Riley's Circus, 184
Oliver Twist, 217
Oliver, Vic, 167
Olivier, Laurence, 215, 216
Oman, (Sir) Charles, 46
On the Night of the Fire, 97, 165
On Thin Ice, 76
One of Our Aircraft is Missing, 188
Ormiston, Tom, 42
Ostrer, Isidore, 60, 62, 63, 64, 66, 125, 205
Ostrer, Mark, 60, 66, 125, 205
Ostrer, Maurice, 60, 61, 125, 163, 181, 205
Over the Moon, 96, 158, 160, 164
Oxford Films, 115

Pagliacci, 111–12, 115
Palache Report, 213
Palache, Albert, 174, 213
Pall Mall Gazette, 29
Pall Mall Productions, 105
Paradise for Two, 94
Paramount Pictures, 26, 74, 80–1, 83, 145, 164, 197–8
Parish, George, 181
Pascal, Gabriel, 165, 172–3, 177, 215
Passion of Joan of Arc, The, 55
Passionate Friends, The, 217
Pathé Cinematograph Company, 12, 39
Pathé Films, 166
Paul, Robert, 8, 11
Peacock, (Sir) Edward, 127, 138

Pearson, George, 79
Peat, Charles, 180
Peg of Old Drury, 66
Pendennis Picture Corporation, 93
Penn of Pennsylvania, 184
Perceval, Hugh, 74
Perfect Strangers, 212
Perfect Understanding, 66, 75, 80
Perry, George, 86
Pickford, Mary, 94–5
Picturegoer, 87
Pimpernel Smith, 188
Pinebrook Films, 164
Pinewood Studios, 66, 97, 112, 129, 194, 203, 214
Pioneer Pictures, 90
Plant, Arnold, 174, 212
Plume, Eleanor, 143
Pogson, Norman, 55
Political and Economic Planning, 106, 206, 216
Pommer, Erich, 93, 94, 105, 166
Portal, Lord (Lord Portal of Laverstoke), 124–5, 129–31
Portrait from Life, 217
Powell, Michael, 4, 6, 74, 98, 183, 208, 215, 216
Powell, Sandy, 167
Premier Productions 26
Pressburger, Emeric, 4, 183, 208, 215
Prime Minister, The, 193, 196
Prince and the Pauper, The, 87
Prison Without Bars, 96, 165
Private Life of Don Juan, The, 88, 91–2
Private Life of Helen of Troy, The, 87
Private Life of Henry VIII, The, 86–8, 90–2, 93, 98, 99, 104, 107, 223
Procter, Henry, 106, 110, 111
Producers' Distributing Company, 79
Provincial Cinematograph Theatres, 16, 26, 41, 60
Prudential Assurance Company, 63, 86, 89–97, 114, 125, 127, 134, 137, 146, 223
Prudential Group Archive, 5
Public Nuisance No. 1, 111
Pygmalion, 2, 157, 165

Q-Planes, 97, 164, 168
Quo Vadis?, 19
Quota Act *see* Cinematograph Films Act (1927); Cinematograph Films Act (1938)
'quota quickies', 5, 49, 65, 73–5, 79–80, 83, 140–2, 152

Radio City Music Hall (New York), 88
Radio Corporation of America, 54
Ramsden, John, 36
Random Harvest, 188
Rank, J. Arthur, 4, 131, 157, 173, 214–15, 222–3; *see also* Rank Organisation
Rank Organisation, 4, 183, 199, 207, 214, 221, 217
Ray, Satyajit, 2
Rayart Film Productions, 55
Rayment, S. G., 39, 48, 52
RCA *see* Radio Corporation of America
Real Art Productions, 78, 81, 82
Rebecca, 188
Red Shoes, The, 216, 217
Redgrave, Michael, 167
Reed, Carol, 167
Reeves, Nicholas, 31
Remar, J. R., 62
Rembrandt, 88, 91, 93
Renaissance Films, 27
Republic Pictures, 167
Rescued by Rover, 10, 13
Return of the Scarlet Pimpernel, The, 96
Reynolds's Illustrated News, 39, 117
Rhythm Serenade, 189
Richards, Jeffrey, 73
Ringer, The, 65
RKO Radio Pictures, 77, 78, 81–2, 83, 165, 196, 197–8
Robeson, Paul, 112
Robson, E. W. and M. M., 3–4
Rome Express, 63
Rookery Nook, 63
Rose, David, 164
Rotha, Paul, 2, 143
Rothschilds (merchant bank), 137
Rowe-Dutton, E. A., 193
Rowland, William, 167
Rowson, Simon, 1, 38, 72, 75, 77, 126–7, 130, 143, 145–6, 180, 194, 197–9, 205, 211
Royal Bank of Scotland, 59, 63
Royal Divorce, A, 164
Ruggles, Wesley, 215
Runciman, Walter, 46, 149

St George and the Dragon, 55
St Martin's Lane, 166
Saint in London, The, 165
Saint's Vacation, The, 196
Sally Bishop, 78

Sally in Our Alley, 66
Sanders of the River, 88, 91–2, 98
Sassoon, Arthur, 208
Saville, Victor, 93, 94, 107, 162
Savoy Cinemas, 57
Scarlet Pimpernel, The, 88, 90, 91, 92, 99
Schach, Max, 5, 86, 104–6, 110–12, 115–16, 119, 221, 222
Schenck, Joseph M., 64
Schroders (merchant bank), 182, 212
Schuster, Harold D., 163
Scottish Cinema and Variety Theatres, 57
Second Mrs Tanqueray, The, 28
Second World War, 6, 79, 100, 171–84, 188–99, 223
Secret Mission, 184
Securities Management Trust, 5, 124–5, 128
Security National Bank (Los Angeles), 99
Sedgwick, John, 2, 74, 76, 92, 222
Selig Polyscope Company, 19
Sentimental Bloke, A, 83
Serocold, Claud, 125
Seventh Veil, The, 199
Shaftesbury Avenue Pavilion, 59
Shaw, George Bernard, 172
Sheffield Photo Company, 12
Shepherd's Bush Studios, 63, 77
Shepperton Studios *see* Sound City Studios
Ships With Wings, 184
Shipyard Sally, 160, 163
Sign of Four, The, 82
Silent Battle, The, 164
Simon, (Sir) John, 191
Sing As We Go, 66
Singing Fools, The, 54
Singleton, Mr Justice, 118
Sixty Glorious Years, 157–8, 160, 165
Sixty Years a Queen, 19
Skinner, Ernest, 128, 135, 138, 176, 204
Smith, G. A., 8, 12
Smith, George, 74, 82
Smith, Herbert, 65
Smith, S. W., 65, 129
So This is London, 164
Somerset House, 17
Somervell, Rupert, 173, 179–80, 182, 192–3, 207
Somlo, Josef, 165
Sound City Studios, 78–9, 81, 131, 194, 211
South American George, 189
South Riding, 94

Southern Roses, 115
Speers, (Sir) Edward, 64
Springtime in the Rockies, 189
Spy in Black, The, 97, 164
Spy of Napoleon, 114
Squeaker, The, 94, 96
Staake Filmwerke, 55
Standard Feature Film Company, 30
Standard Film Company, 60
Stanley, Oliver, 149, 151, 153
Stars Look Down, The, 167
Sternberg, Josef Von, 93
Stolen Life, A, 164
Stoll Picture Productions, 37, 39
Stoll, (Sir) Oswald, 47
Storm in a Teacup, 94
Strange Boarders, 165
Strange Evidence, 87
Street, Sarah, 1–2, 49, 86, 199, 203
Stuart, Binkie, 168
Sunday Dispatch, 113
Sunday Express, 105
Sunday Pictorial, 47
Sutro, John, 89
Sutro, Leopold, 89
Swanson, Gloria, 66, 75, 80
Sweet Rosie O'Grady, 189
Switzerland & General (insurance company), 118

Tauber, Richard, 112
Taylor, Robert, 161
Technicolor Corporation, 90
Teddington Studios, 82, 165
Ten Days in Paris, 164
Tennyson, Charles, 41
That Hamilton Woman, 99
That Night in London, 87
Thief of Bagdad, The, 98–9
Things to Come, 88, 91–2, 185n
Third Gun, The, 75
Thirteenth Candle, The, 82
39 Steps, The, 63
This England, 184
This Happy Breed, 188
This Man in Paris, 164
This Man is News, 164
Thompson, Kristin, 28
Thorpe, J. A., 57
Three Musketeers, The, 19
Times, The, 27, 31, 43, 48

Tivoli Cinema, 60
Toeplitz, Giuseppe, 87
Toeplitz, Ludovico, 66, 87, 105–6
Toeplitz Productions, 105–6, 110
Toll of Destiny, 83
Topical Committee for Films, 31–2
Tower Film Productions, 105
Trafalgar Film Productions, 93, 105, 107, 111
Treasury, 98, 172–7, 188–92, 198
Tree, Herbert Beerbohm, 12, 19
Tritton, Herbert, 124
Tropical Trouble, 113
Turned Out Nice Again, 184
Turvey, Gerry, 31
Twentieth Century-Fox, 125, 159, 162–3, 189, 197–8; *see also* Fox Film Corporation; Twentieth Century Productions
Twentieth Century Productions, 163–4
Twenty-One Days, 164
Twickenham Film Studios, 54, 78, 92, 114, 127
Two Cities Films, 164, 183, 208

UFA *see* Universum Film Aktiengesellschaft
Uncensored, 184
Undercover, 184
Union Cinemas, 55
Union Insurance Society of Canton, 118
United Artists, 5, 66, 75, 78, 80, 83, 87–9, 94–5, 97, 107, 111, 115–16, 137, 146, 160, 164, 172–3, 177, 197–8, 215
United Electric Theatres 17, 26
United Picture Theatres, 62
Universal Pictures, 75, 82–3, 131, 191, 193, 197–8
Universum Film Aktiengesellschaft, 41, 110
Upturned Glass, The, 217
Urban, Charles, 12

Variety, 161, 199
Veidt, Conrad, 97
vertical integration 26, 52, 56, 59
Vessel of Wrath, 166
Victor Saville Productions, 105
Vidor, King, 162
Vogue Films, 165

W&F Film Service, 59, 78
Wagg, Alfred, 125
Wainwright, J. G. and R. B., 108, 165
Wallace, Edgar, 65, 167
Walls, Tom, 167

Walton Studios, 54
Wanger, Walter, 189
War Office, 31
War Office Official Topical Budget, 32
Wardour Films, 30, 39, 57, 77, 83
Warner Bros., 77, 82, 145, 165, 183, 196, 197, 204
Warner, Jack, 212
Warter, Philip, 204–5, 212
Wartime Social Survey, 171
Warwick Trading Company, 12, 13, 18, 19
Watkins, Arthur, 209
Watkins, Leopold, 109
Watson, W. J., 18
Way Ahead, The, 208
Way to the Stars, The, 2
We Dive at Dawn, 184
We'll Meet Again, 189
We're Going To Be Rich, 159, 160, 163
Wedding Rehearsal, 87
Wedgwood, Josiah, 48
Wells, (Sir) Richard, 40
Welwyn Studios, 166, 205
Wembley Studios, 74, 162–3
Westminster Bank, 104, 108, 110, 111, 114, 116, 118–19
Westminster Films, 81
Western Electric, 54
Wheat, 111
Whelan, Tim, 98
When Knights Were Bold, 111
Where's That Fire?, 164
White, Tom, 216
Whitehall Films, 52
Whyte, (Sir) Frederick, 174, 179–80
Wicked Lady, The, 199
Wilcox, Herbert, 6, 107, 124, 158, 165, 189, 222
Willey, F. Vernon, 41
Williams, J. D., 56
Williams, Tom, 152
Williamson, James, 8, 18
Wills, (Sir) Ernest, 59
Wilson, (Sir) Arnold, 143
Wilson, (Sir) Horace, 128, 137
Window in London, A, 97
Wings of the Morning, 163
Woman Alone, A, 109
Wood, Alan, 208
Wood, (Sir) Kingsley, 177, 182, 211
Wood, Linda, 79
Wood, Sam, 162

Woolf, C. M., 54, 59, 61, 66, 107–8, 129–30, 205, 208
Woolfe, Harry Bruce, 143
World Film News, 87–8, 131, 148, 203
World Studio Centre, 56, 141
Wilcox, Herbert, 33, 65–6, 108

Yank at Oxford, A, 160–2

Yarrow, (Sir) Harold, 59
Yes, Mrs Brown, 78
Yorke, Philip, 18
You Must Get Married, 113
Young Mr Pitt, The, 198
Yule, Lady Henrietta, 86, 173, 203, 211

Zanuck, Darryl F., 163